Autonomous Minds

Autonomous Minds

How Agentic AI Predicts and Learns to Enable Productivity and Empowerment

FRANCISCO JAVIER CAMPOS ZABALA

WILEY

For general information on our other products and services or for technical support, please contact our Customer Care Department within the United States at (800) 762-2974, outside the United States at (317) 572-3993 or fax (317) 572-4002.

Wiley also publishes its books in a variety of electronic formats. Some content that appears in print may not be available in electronic formats. For more information about Wiley products, visit our website at www.wiley.com.

Library of Congress Cataloging-in-Publication Data Applied for:

Paper ISBN: 9781394350100
ePDF ISBN: 9781394350124
ePub ISBN: 9781394350117
oBook ISBN: 9781394352562

Cover Design: Wiley
Cover Image: © Anna Pavlova/Getty Images

Set in 10/12 STIX Two Text by Lumina Datamatics
Printed and bound by CPI Group (UK) Ltd, Croydon, CR0 4YY

C9781394350100_040925

To my wife Sarah, whose unwavering support made this journey possible, and to our children, James, Sofia, Harry, and Lily—may this work inspire your own creative paths as you grow and shape tomorrow's world.

Contents

Acknowledgments

In a world where AI systems increasingly demonstrate "autonomous minds," Newton's timeless insight takes on new meaning: "If I have seen further it is by standing on the shoulders of giants." As we enter an era where machine and human intelligence converge, this metaphor transforms from mere observation to active collaboration.

My professional journey from the structured environments of Accenture and WPP to the agile innovation of scale-up AdTech at Fenestra has provided a unique vantage point from which to observe this technological revolution. This path, complemented by my work with the Cambridge AI Safety Hub, has taught me that true innovation thrives at the intersection of enterprise scale and entrepreneurial experimentation.

We stand at a watershed moment where AI capabilities are advancing at breathtaking speed. The systems emerging today demonstrate capabilities that were once the realm of science fiction, promising unprecedented possibilities while demanding thoughtful governance. This book represents an attempt to navigate this critical juncture with both excitement and responsibility.

I am profoundly grateful to the visionary leaders who have generously shared their insights and experiences for this project. In no particular order, I extend my deepest thanks to Sonia Casado Suarez, Chief Transformation and AI Officer at Dentsu Spain; Vilmos Lorincz, Managing Director at Lloyds Bank; Marco Vernocchi, Global Chief Data Officer at Ernst & Young; Gary Heffernan, investor, dealmaker, and former Accenture senior executive; Steve Thomas, Senior Managing Director at Experian; Jose Maria Sanabria, former regional and country CEO at Big 6 Media agencies; Matthew Graham-Hyde, former Global CIO Insights and Certified Executive Coach; Alvaro de Nicolas, CEO de DNA Ventures; and Edward Young and Jason Brown, University of Cambridge, Department of Computer Science and Technology. Their willingness to explore the frontiers of what's possible while remaining grounded in practical reality has enriched this book immeasurably.

To my publisher, editorial team, and all those who have supported the creation of this work—your patience, insight, and dedication have been essential to transforming complex ideas into clear, actionable guidance. This book represents not just my voice, but the collective wisdom of a remarkable community that continues to shape the frontier of intelligent technologies.

To my family, dogs, and team: thank you for enduring my late-night debates about all things AI and my constant exploration of agentic futures. Your patience and support form the bedrock of this work.

As we navigate the emergence of systems with increasingly independent capabilities, I remain optimistic that by working together—humans and AI in concert—we can orchestrate a future of unprecedented possibility. May we wield these "autonomous minds" not just with curiosity but with care. The next movement of humanity's symphony is ours to compose.

Introduction

YOUR GUIDE TO THE AI AGENT REVOLUTION

Imagine a world where your most tedious tasks vanish, where creative collaboration reaches new heights, and where complex problem-solving becomes exponentially more efficient. This isn't a futuristic fantasy taken from a science fiction book; it's the unfolding reality of the AI agent revolution. You've probably already glimpsed its potential—a smart assistant that proactively manages your day, software that anticipates your needs before you even articulate them, or even teams of autonomous systems coordinating complex operations with seamless precision. These are not just incremental improvements on existing technology; they represent a fundamental shift in how we interact with and leverage artificial intelligence. This book serves as your essential guide to understanding this profound revolution, not just as a passive observer on the sidelines but as a knowledgeable and informed participant fully prepared to navigate and actively shape its future course.

From AI Winter to Agentic Spring: A Personal Journey

My fascination with machines and autonomy began long before I encountered the complexities of AI. As a child, I was captivated by the Japanese anime series Mazinger Z—a show that, depending on where you grew up, might sound obscure, but for me, it was a portal to imagining a future where humans and machines collaborated as equals. Premiering in 1972, Mazinger Z introduced the revolutionary concept of a human-piloted giant robot, controlled from a cockpit embedded in its head. Koji Kabuto, the hot-blooded teenage protagonist, fought mechanical beasts and other colossal robots created by the villainous Dr. Hell. To my young mind, **Mazinger Z** wasn't just a weapon; it was an extension of human will—a metaphor for how technology could amplify our agency. The series' blend of mechanical ingenuity and moral stakes—where heroes faced loss and sacrifice—taught me that machines could be both awe-inspiring and deeply human.

This early obsession with robotic autonomy took a more tangible form when, in my early teens, I acquired a **Sinclair ZX Spectrum** (see Figure 1). The Spectrum, with its rubber keys and 48KB of RAM, became my first canvas for exploring programmed "agency." I devoured books like *Spectrum Machine Language for the Absolute Beginner*, learning to write simple code that made the machine perform tasks—from solving math problems to crude text-based games. The thrill of commanding the computer to execute my instructions felt like a miniature version of piloting Mazinger Z: I was no longer just a spectator but a creator, shaping outcomes through logic and creativity. This hands-on experience ignited my passion for automation—the idea that machines could act for us, not just because of us.

FIGURE 1   Sinclair Spectrum ZX[1]

Bill Bertram / Wikimedia commons / CC BY SA 2.5

---

[1] By Bill Bertram—Own work, CC BY-SA 2.5

By the time I entered university to study robotics, these childhood and adolescent influences had crystallized into a career path. Yet the field I encountered in the mid-1990s was far from the dynamic, agentic future I'd imagined. The **"AI winter"** was a sobering reality: progress was fragmented, systems were brittle (very!), and the grand visions of autonomous machines felt perpetually out of reach. Early neural networks and expert systems were like Mazinger Z's Mechanical Beasts—powerful in isolation but lacking the cohesion to form a true "symphony" of intelligence. My work during this period often felt like reassembling the scattered limbs of those childhood robots: incremental advances in sensor calibration, motor control, and rule-based logic, but no unifying conductor.

Looking back, the parallels between my journey and the evolution of AI are striking. Just as Koji Kabuto's battles required both raw power and strategic ingenuity, modern agentic systems demand a fusion of specialized tools (machine learning, symbolic reasoning) and holistic design. The ZX Spectrum taught me that even limited machines could achieve remarkable things with the right instructions—a lesson that resonates today as we layer autonomy atop narrow AI. My childhood fascination with giant robots, once dismissed as fantasy, now feels prophetic: we are inching closer to a world where machines act not just as tools but as partners, their "symphonic" potential finally within reach.

As I said, my own journey in artificial intelligence began in the mid-1990s, during what the field dubbed an **"AI winter."** Fresh from completing my robotics degree, I entered a landscape where earlier enthusiasm had frozen over, promised breakthroughs remained distant, and existing AI systems showed stark limitations. Those early years taught me that progress in AI rarely follows a straight line. Like a scientist tracking glacial movement, I witnessed the field's slow advances, its periods of apparent stillness, and those rare moments when the ice suddenly shifted, revealing new possibilities beneath. AI remained largely compartmentalized—a collection of extremely specialized tools excelling at specific tasks but lacking broader understanding or autonomy. The analogy of an orchestra comes to mind: we had incredibly talented individual musicians, each mastering their instrument, but the creation of truly symphonic experiences still required constant direction and a meticulously written score.

However, the last decade has been unlike any other. The pace of progress has not just accelerated; it feels exponential. In 2022, after contributing to the **Bank of England and Financial Conduct Authority's AI Public-Private Forum (AIPP)**, I recognized a significant gap between the theoretical capabilities of AI and its practical implementation in most enterprises. This observation led me to write *Grow Your Business with AI*,[2]

---

[2] https://www.amazon.co.uk/Grow-Your-Business-Principles-Intelligence/dp/1484296680

focusing on bridging that divide with the tools and techniques available at the time. But then came 2023, and with it, a seismic shift. The arrival of large language models (LLMs) with capabilities parallel to GPT-4 fundamentally altered the landscape. For the first time, I experienced AI that could not just process information but understand context, reason with a degree of sophistication, and, crucially, act autonomously when embedded within an agent architecture. It was like witnessing those individual musicians suddenly gain the ability to not only play their parts flawlessly but also understand the entire composition, anticipate the conductor's intentions, and even improvise with remarkable creativity.

The Genesis of This Book: Bridging the Understanding Gap

This profound shift is the very reason I felt compelled to write this book. The **"AI winter"** taught me patience, the rise of machine learning taught me its power, but the emergence of agentic AI ignited a new sense of urgency. I saw a familiar pattern emerging: a groundbreaking technology with the potential to reshape our world yet surrounded by both breathless hype and understandable confusion. Many perceive the next leap in AI as hinging on achieving artificial general intelligence (AGI)—a hypothetical point where machines possess human-level intelligence across all domains. While the pursuit of AGI is a fascinating endeavor, this book argues that a revolution is already underway, driven by AI agents, and it doesn't require reaching some distant, undefined future of AGI to have a transformative impact.

The critical gap in understanding that I personally observed wasn't merely a technical divide between cutting-edge AI technology and its effective integration into mainstream business operations; it was a much broader societal gap between the genuinely breathtaking transformative potential of practical agentic AI systems and the general public's overall comprehension, awareness, and informed understanding of this rapidly evolving field. I witnessed firsthand in my own research and applied projects how these newly emergent AI systems, when thoughtfully designed and strategically implemented as intelligent agents with defined goals and autonomous decision-making capabilities, could effectively tackle increasingly complex, open-ended tasks and dynamic real-world challenges with a level of adaptability, proactive reasoning, and independent action that was simply unimaginable with previous generations of traditional AI systems. This transformative shift is fundamentally not about simply replacing human workers across industries with automated robots or sentient machines; it is far more constructively about strategically augmenting and expanding core human capabilities, nurturing powerful new paradigms of synergistic partnerships and collaborative workflows between human professionals and increasingly intelligent machines, and ultimately empowering both individual professionals and large-scale organizations to achieve significantly more, innovate faster, and create greater value than ever before in the history of human endeavor.

Furthermore, recognizing the immense power of these emerging technologies, I've also joined a group of dedicated researchers at the **Cambridge AI Safety Hub**.[3] Our work focuses on developing practical tools and frameworks to ensure the safe and beneficial development of AI agents. As I will elaborate on in Chapter 9, the alignment of these powerful systems with human values is a critical area of focus, and our research aims to contribute to a future where AI agents are both intelligent and responsible.

Why This Book Matters

"But wait," you might be thinking, "isn't this just another book about AGI and the singularity?" The answer is a definitive and emphatic no. This book takes a different approach. We don't need AGI to experience profound changes in how we work and live. The revolution is already happening through AI agents—focused, specialized systems that can perceive, decide, and act within specific domains.

Deep Dive: What Makes AI Agents Different?

AI agents have the following capabilities over traditional AI systems:

- Goal-oriented behavior
- Autonomous decision-making
- Ability to learn and adapt
- Environmental awareness

Beyond the Hype: Understanding Agentic AI from First Principles

To truly grasp the significance of the AI agent revolution, we need to move beyond surface-level descriptions and dig into the fundamental principles that underpin it. This book adopts a first-principles approach, breaking down complex concepts into their core components. Just as understanding

---

[3] https://www.cambridgeaisafety.org

the individual instruments and the principles of harmony is essential to appreciating the complexity and beauty of an orchestra, understanding the fundamental elements of intelligence and agency is crucial to understanding AI agents. We will explore what constitutes intelligence in a machine, what it means for an AI to possess agency, and how these elements combine to create systems capable of independent thought and action.

Throughout this exploration, we will return to our orchestra analogy, using it as a metaphor to illuminate the evolving capabilities of AI. From individual instruments representing specialized AI tools to sections of the orchestra embodying more complex, goal-oriented systems, and ultimately to the fully agentic orchestra capable of dynamically adapting and creating novel performances, this analogy will provide a relatable framework for understanding the increasing sophistication of AI. We believe that by grounding our understanding in these fundamental principles, we can move beyond the hype and develop a clear-eyed perspective on the true potential and the practical implications of agentic AI.

The AI agent revolution is not a distant possibility; it is happening now. It is a wave of innovation that promises to reshape our work, our lives, and our future in profound ways. This book is your guide, providing you with the knowledge, insights, and frameworks to not only understand this revolution but also to actively participate in shaping its direction.

Why Now?

The timing of this book is crucial. We're at an inflection point where AI agents are mature enough to be practical but still early enough that understanding their fundamentals can give you a significant advantage. Whether you're a business leader, professional, or simply someone interested in the future of technology, the insights in this book will help you prepare for and thrive in the age of AI agents.

HOW TO USE THIS BOOK

Think of this book as your personal GPS for navigating the rapidly evolving landscape of AI agents. Just as a GPS offers multiple routes to your destination depending on your priorities—fastest time, shortest distance, avoiding tolls—this book is designed to be flexible, allowing you to chart your own course through the material based on your specific interests and needs. Whether you're a business leader seeking to understand the strategic implications of agentic AI, a technology enthusiast eager to delve into the underlying principles, or a knowledge worker looking to adapt to the changing demands of the future, this section will guide you on how to best utilize the resources within these pages.

This section is designed to help you navigate *Autonomous Minds* in the way that best serves your needs and interests. Whether you're a business executive looking to understand AI agents' impact on your industry, a professional seeking to future-proof your career, or simply someone fascinated by the future of technology, we've structured this book to provide multiple pathways through its content.

Core Reading Paths

We've organized this book into three distinct parts, each serving a specific purpose:

- **Part I: Foundations of the Agent Revolution** provides the essential building blocks for understanding AI agents. If you're new to the concept of agentic AI, start here.
- **Part II: The Transforming World** explores practical applications and immediate impacts across various domains.
- **Part III: Navigating the Future** focuses on long-term implications and personal preparation strategies.

Recommended Reading Approaches

While the book is structured to provide a comprehensive understanding of AI agents, progressing from foundational concepts to real-world applications and future implications, we recognize that your journey may not be strictly linear. For those seeking a complete understanding, reading the book sequentially, from the introduction to the concluding chapters, will provide a robust and cohesive framework. Part I, "Foundations of the Agent Revolution," lays the groundwork by defining agentic AI from first principles, exploring its core components, and tracing its evolution from traditional AI. This part is crucial for building a solid understanding of the fundamental concepts that underpin the agent revolution. Think of it as understanding the instruments and basic musical theory before appreciating a complex symphony.

However, if you have specific areas of interest, feel free to navigate directly to the relevant sections. For instance:

For Business Leaders:
- Begin with Chapter 1 for context.
- Focus on Chapters 5 and 6 for economic and enterprise impacts.
- Conclude with Chapter 10's action planning.

For Technology Professionals:
- Start with Chapters 2 and 3 for technical depth.
- Pay special attention to the "Deep Dive" boxes throughout.
- Focus on Chapter 7's career development strategies.

For General Interest Readers:
- Follow the chapters sequentially.
- Use the "Why This Matters" sections to connect concepts to daily life.
- Focus on the case studies that resonate with your interests.

Special Features

Throughout the book, you'll encounter several recurring elements designed to enhance your understanding:
- **Deep Dive Boxes:** Technical details for those wanting to explore concepts further
- **Expert Insights:** Direct quotes and perspectives from leading researchers and practitioners
- **Key Takeaways:** Essential points summarized at the end of each chapter

Making It Practical

To maximize your learning:
- Keep a notebook for insights and questions.
- Visit our companion website for updated resources and examples.
- Join our online community to discuss concepts with other readers.
- Use the end-of-chapter exercises to apply concepts to your context.

Remember, this book is designed to grow with you. As you progress through your AI journey, you may find yourself returning to earlier chapters with new perspectives and questions.

Quick-Start Guide

1. Read the chapter summaries.
2. Choose your reading path.
3. Focus on relevant case studies.
4. Engage with online resources.

The journey ahead is exciting and transformative. Whether you're reading cover-to-cover or focusing on specific sections, we're here to guide you through the AI agent revolution. Let's begin.

As we move forward, let's meet the team of experts who contributed to making this book a comprehensive guide to the future of AI agents.

THE AI AGENT TEAM BEHIND THIS BOOK

While my name is on the cover and of course I have to thank all the human collaborators and contributors, it's also crucial to acknowledge the extensive background work undertaken by a dedicated team of AI agents. Think of me as the conductor of an orchestra, shaping the symphony but relying heavily on the instrumentalists to provide the foundational music. These agents didn't write the book in my stead, but they acted as invaluable partners, significantly enhancing the depth, breadth, and accuracy of the final product. Their work accelerated the process, but the thinking—the connective tissue binding these ideas—remained fundamentally human.

The Symphony of Minds: My Journey with AI Collaborators

As I sit here reflecting on the creation of this book, I'm struck by the remarkable journey that brought these pages to life.

Picture, if you will, a virtual writing studio where 10 distinct AI personalities gathered around my digital desk, each bringing their unique strengths to our shared mission (see Figure 2). Here's my remarkable team; I chose their names carefully to reflect their roles and capabilities:

Alexandria (Research Assistant): Named after the ancient library, reflecting her vast knowledge gathering abilities

Ada (Data Scientist): Named after Ada Lovelace, bringing mathematical rigor and predictive modeling

Marco (First Principles Architect): Named after Marco Polo, exploring new territories through foundational thinking

Scheherazade (Narrative Harmonizer): Named after the legendary storyteller, weaving complex ideas into engaging narratives

Gabriel (Writing Assistant): Named after Gabriel García Márquez, crafting flowing prose and maintaining narrative consistency (one of my favorite books is *Hundred Years of Solitude*)

Eleanor (Senior Editor): Named after Eleanor Roosevelt, showing diplomatic skill in balancing different perspectives

Sofia (Language Enhancement Specialist): Named after Sofia Kovalevskaya, bringing mathematical precision to language

Atlas (Graphic Designer): Named after the titan who carried the world, bearing the weight of visual communication

Terra (Publishing Assistant): Named after Mother Earth, grounding our work in practical, technical reality

Minerva (Quality Assurance): Named after the goddess of wisdom, ensuring accuracy and maintaining standards

These agents operated less as independent thinkers and more as cognitive amplifiers—specialized tools that could retrieve information, surface patterns, or prototype ideas at digital speeds. When discussing neural memory architectures, Marco might generate foundational schematics while Alexandria cross-referenced neuroscience papers, but the interpretive leap connecting these to agentic systems remained my own.

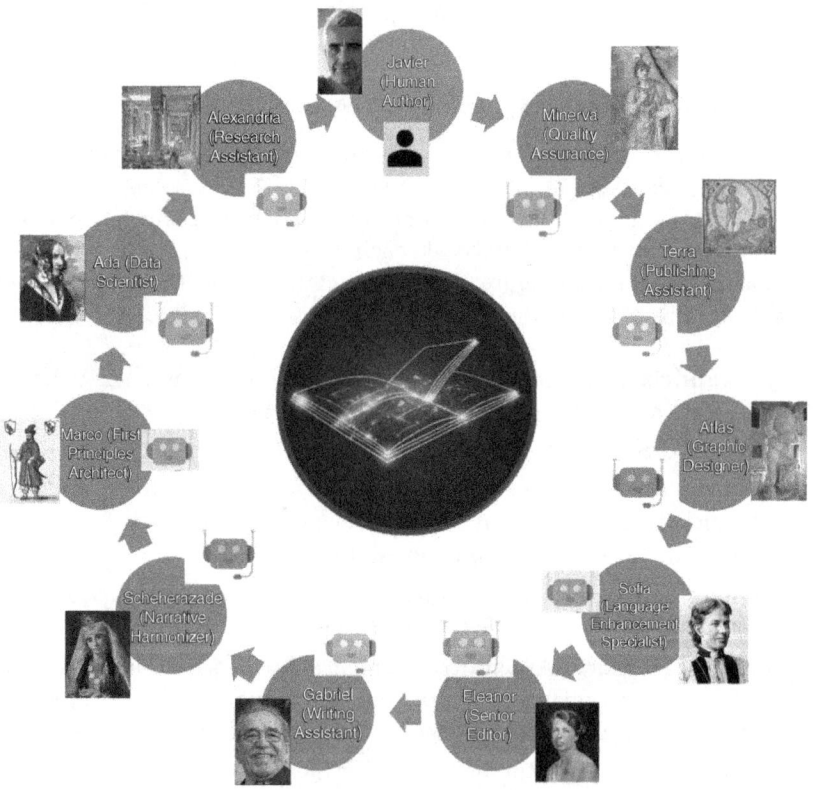

FIGURE 2   The author and his awesome agentic AI team

Generated with AI using DALL·E - OpenAI

Technical Foundations

The collaboration was powered by four powerful key agentic-based frameworks:

AutoGen Orchestration: Microsoft's multi-agent framework enabled dynamic workflows where agents could chain tasks (e.g., Alexandria feeding research to Ada for statistical modeling, then passing results to Scheherazade for narrative framing). Custom reward functions prioritized depth over speed, favoring iterative refinement.

Stanford University STORM System[4]: Integrated for dynamic knowledge mapping, this tool created living concept networks that evolved with each chapter. When writing about AI ethics, STORM visualized how related concepts (bias mitigation, constitutional AI) intersected across disciplines.

Google DeepMind's NotebookLM[5]: Adapted for real-time collaboration, this environment allowed hybrid workflows and citation research—I might draft a paragraph on neuromorphic computing while agents concurrently populated a sidebar with relevant chip architectures or energy-efficiency metrics.

OpenAI's Deep Research agents[6]: These agents ensured chapters reflected state-of-the-art advancements, scouring arXiv (home of key research papers), industry whitepapers, and policy drafts to maintain relevance in a fast-moving field.

This collaboration wasn't without its challenges. Early attempts required careful refinement of communication and workflow patterns. Yet these very challenges provided valuable insights into human-AI collaboration that enriched our understanding of agentic AI systems. Additionally, when agents proposed conflicting interpretations of AI safety research, I became the arbiter, weighing evidence through an experiential lens no algorithm could replicate.

This hybrid approach transformed the writing process. What once required weeks of solitary research became a dialogue—I'd pose questions to the agent team before dawn, review their synthesized findings by breakfast, and spend afternoons refining insights into narrative.

---

[4] https://storm.genie.stanford.edu/

[5] https://notebooklm.google.com/

[6] https://openai.com/index/introducing-deep-research/

The book you hold is more than just a collection of chapters about AI—it's a testament to the potential of human-AI collaboration. Every page represents a harmony between human insight and artificial intelligence, between creativity and computation, between art and algorithm. As we stand on the brink of an AI-augmented future, this process has shown me that the most exciting possibilities lie not in AI replacing human effort but in the magic that happens when both work together in concert.

The chapters that follow will build upon this foundation, exploring how AI agents are transforming our world and how we can harness their potential while navigating the challenges ahead.

Foundations of the Agent Revolution

CHAPTER 1

The AI Revolution 2.0

"The future is already here—it's just not evenly distributed."

—William Gibson

A VERY PERSONAL JOURNEY

It was a quiet Tuesday afternoon in 2023 when I witnessed something that made me question everything I thought I knew about artificial intelligence. I had been working with AI systems for decades, but this was different. An AI agent, when tasked with a complex operation by another agent, independently searched for, downloaded, and successfully installed a missing library—all without human intervention. I sat there, coffee growing cold in my hand, watching as these digital entities collaborated with a level of autonomy that felt almost organic. This moment, seemingly small, was as profound as other transformative moments in my journey with technology.

But let me step back. My journey with transformative technologies began long before this moment, and each step along the way has been a reminder that the future often arrives quietly, in unexpected breakthroughs that initially seem modest but prove revolutionary. These moments, while unexpected, are not random; they are the result of the persistent efforts of many talented individuals, building on previous breakthroughs and insights.

In 1999, I was part of a team working on what seemed like an impossible dream: streaming high-quality video over consumer cable networks. Today, when we casually stream 4K content on our phones, it's hard to convey the excitement we felt when we first achieved what would later become the foundation for services like Netflix. I remember the skepticism from industry veterans: "The bandwidth requirements are impossible," they

TABLE 1.1 Streaming Technologies Progress: 1999 vs. 2024

Feature	VoD Cable Network 1999	Netflix (2024)
Bandwidth	1.5–2 Mbps	25 Mbps (4K streaming)
Resolution	480p (640×480)	Up to 4K (3840×2160)
Video Codec	MPEG-2	H.265/HEVC, VP9, AV1
Hardware Speed	~500 MHz CPU	Multicore GHz CPUs, dedicated GPUs
Compression	~200:1	~1000:1 (for 4K)

said. "Consumers will never adapt to this." Yet here we are, in a world where streaming video is as natural as turning on a tap (see Table 1.1).

Another pivotal moment came when I first laid eyes on the PlayStation 2's architecture blueprints. As someone very familiar with traditional Intel and AMD designs, this was like discovering alien technology. The Emotion Engine, as Sony called it, represented a completely different approach to processing architecture. It wasn't just different; it was revolutionary in its ability to handle complex 3D calculations in real time, something that would later influence modern GPU design.

These experiences taught me an important lesson: *true technological revolutions don't just improve what exists—they fundamentally reshape what's possible.* But nothing prepared me for what I would witness in the realm of AI agents.

The moment I mentioned earlier—watching an AI agent independently solve its own operational needs—might seem simple compared to the dazzling demonstrations of large language models or image generation systems that make headlines. But its significance was profound. This wasn't just a program following prewritten instructions; it was demonstrating genuine problem-solving capability, much like a human would.

What makes this development particularly striking is the contrast with traditional AI systems and the evolution of how we interact with machines. In traditional software development, we programmed machines to follow explicit instructions—we told them exactly what rules to execute and how to execute them. Every possible scenario had to be anticipated and coded, which meant that when circumstances changed or new challenges arose, the software couldn't adapt on its own. It was rigid, bound by the exact parameters we defined, and any adjustment required us to manually rewrite the code.

Then came the first generation of AI, which marked a significant shift from this rigidity. Instead of specifying every rule, we began to define an *objective function*—a goal for the machine to achieve. The AI systems were designed to optimize this function, adjusting their behavior based on data inputs to meet the desired outcome. This adaptability was a massive improvement over traditional software, allowing machines to handle variability and learn from experience. However, crafting the right objective function was often complex and time-consuming. It required deep domain expertise to ensure the AI system would perform correctly and not exhibit unintended behaviors.

Now, with the advent of AI agents, we've taken another monumental leap forward. Rather than detailing specific rules or meticulously defining an objective function, we simply provide these agents with high-level goals. The agents are empowered to figure out the best way to achieve these goals on their own, utilizing advanced algorithms and vast amounts of data. They can make autonomous decisions, adapt to new information, and even navigate unforeseen challenges—all without the need for constant human intervention.

Throughout my career, I've worked with numerous AI implementations—pattern recognition systems, decision trees, neural networks—but they all operated within strictly defined parameters. They were sophisticated, yes, but ultimately limited by their initial programming and the specific objectives we set for them. The rise of AI agents represents a transformative shift: from machines that follow predefined instructions or optimize given functions to intelligent entities that understand and pursue goals in dynamic environments. This flexibility and autonomy were unimaginable in earlier systems, and it fundamentally changes the way we design, interact with, and leverage technology. The new generation of AI agents represents something fundamentally different. They exhibit what I call *adaptive autonomy*—the ability to not just process information but to actively engage with their environment, make decisions, and, most importantly, learn and adapt their behavior based on new situations.

This realization hit me with the same force as seeing that first video stream or the PS2 architecture. It wasn't just an incremental improvement; it was a paradigm shift. We're not just creating better tools; we're developing digital entities that can meaningfully interact with their environment and each other.

As I write this, I'm acutely aware that we're standing at the threshold of something extraordinary. The development of truly agentic AI isn't just another step in technological evolution—it's the beginning of a new chapter in human-machine interaction. The implications are both exciting and profound, touching everything from how we work and create to how we solve problems and make decisions.

In the sections that follow, we'll explore this new frontier in detail—understanding what makes AI agents different, how they're already impacting our world, and what their emergence means for our future. But first, it's imperative to understand how we got here, tracing the evolution from traditional AI to these new, more capable systems.

The journey continues to surprise and humble me. Each breakthrough reminds me that we're not just witnesses to technological progress—we're active participants in shaping a future that continues to exceed our imagination.

THE AI EVOLUTION: CONVERGENCE OF MULTIPLE FRONTIERS

In the summer of 1956, a group of brilliant minds gathered at Dartmouth College, united by an audacious dream: to create machines that could think. Their optimism was boundless, their vision revolutionary. They believed they could crack the code of human intelligence in a single summer. While their timeline proved naive, their ambitious vision planted the seeds for one of humanity's greatest technological adventures—a journey that would span decades and transform our world in ways they could scarcely have imagined. This journey, like the development of any great symphony, required many movements, each building on the foundations created by the previous ones.

The development of AI is best understood not as a solo journey but as an orchestra of innovations playing in harmony. Like tributaries flowing into a mighty river, various streams of technological progress—computing power, data availability, and algorithmic breakthroughs—have converged to create what we now recognize as modern AI. Each breakthrough, each setback, and each unexpected discovery has contributed to this remarkable evolution, demonstrating how the persistence of scientists, engineers, and innovators can transform bold dreams into practical realities.

- **The foundation years:** The historic Dartmouth Conference of 1956 marked the moment when AI emerged from the realm of science fiction into serious scientific pursuit. John McCarthy and Marvin Minsky, along with their colleagues, didn't just coin the term *artificial intelligence*—they laid out a vision that would inspire generations of researchers. Their original proposal captured both the ambition and the innocence of those early days. These early pioneers were like the composers who first conceived the grand ideas that would one day become magnificent symphonies; they established the fundamental concepts that would guide subsequent generations:

Dartmouth Conference Objective

"We propose that a 2-month, 10-man study of artificial intelligence be carried out during the summer of 1956 at Dartmouth College in Hanover, New Hampshire. The study is to proceed on the basis of the conjecture that every aspect of learning or any other feature of intelligence can in principle be so precisely described that a machine can be made to simulate it. An attempt will be made to find how to make machines use language, form abstractions and concepts, solve kinds of problems now reserved for humans, and improve themselves. We think that a significant advance can be made in one or more of these problems if a carefully selected group of scientists work on it together for a summer."

- **Seasons of innovation:** The AI cycle is like any great scientific endeavor. AI's journey has been marked by dramatic cycles of breakthrough and consolidation, triumph, and reassessment. These cycles, known in the field as *AI summers* and *AI winters*, tell a story not just of technological progress but of human persistence in the face of challenges. These cycles are like the different movements within a symphony, each with its own tempo, tone, and contribution to the whole.
- **The first summer (1956–1969):** This time blazed with the excitement of foundational discoveries in symbolic reasoning. Researchers created programs that could prove mathematical theorems and engage in basic conversation, sparking dreams of imminent human-like machines. But as the initial euphoria faded, the field entered its first winter (1970s), when the severe limitations of early systems became apparent. This first movement, while full of promise, reached its natural conclusion, leading to a period of reflection and readjustment, like the pause between movements in a grand symphony.
- **The second summer (1980s):** This season dawned with the promise of expert systems—programs that could capture human expertise in specific domains. For the first time, AI found practical commercial applications.
- **Second winter (late 1980s–1990s):** Once again winter followed as the limitations of purely rule-based approaches became clear. The second movement in the symphony of AI development, full of new ideas and commercial potential, also ultimately led to a need for recalibration and innovation.

The Convergence That Changed Everything

What makes our current era—often called the third summer—different from these earlier cycles is the unprecedented convergence of three critical factors that had been developing in parallel for decades. This convergence is like the moment when all the sections of an orchestra come together, creating a unified and powerful sound, demonstrating how the interplay of individual parts can create something greater than the sum of its parts.

First, *computational power* has grown exponentially, following a journey from room-sized ENIAC computers to today's quantum computing experiments. Modern GPUs and specialized AI chips have particularly accelerated deep learning capabilities, enabling calculations that would have taken years in the past to be completed in hours or minutes. This exponential increase in computing power is like the improvement in instrument manufacturing that allows each player in the orchestra to perform more accurately and efficiently, contributing to a higher quality of music.

Second, the *data revolution* has transformed the landscape of possibility. From the humble punch cards of the 1950s to today's vast data lakehouses, our ability to collect, store, and process information has expanded beyond the wildest dreams of AI's pioneers. This data revolution, with the transformation from limited structured data to vast amounts of unstructured data lakes, is like the discovery of new musical scores, each more complex than the last, providing the raw material for innovation and refinement. This progression tells its own story.

The early days saw AI limited by the scarcity of relevant data, often stored on punch cards. In the 1980s, the rise of relational databases improved the organization and accessibility of data. The emergence of Big Data in the 2000s presented new opportunities and challenges in handling vast amounts of information. Finally, in the 2020s, the integration of structured and unstructured data in data lakehouses provided a flexible and scalable framework for harnessing the full power of data.

Third, *algorithmic breakthroughs* have built upon each other like layers of a coral reef. While many fundamental algorithms—neural networks in the 1950s, backpropagation in the 1970s—were developed early, they required the convergence of modern computing power and vast datasets to reach their full potential. The recent success of deep learning perfectly illustrates this synergy: algorithms conceived decades ago have finally found their moment in the sun. These algorithmic breakthroughs are like the development of musical theory and compositional techniques, allowing composers and musicians to create increasingly sophisticated and nuanced pieces.

This current era is defined by the powerful interplay of computing power, data availability, and algorithmic advancements, an orchestra of technological forces working in harmony to produce unprecedented achievements in AI. This convergence of factors is what sets our current era apart and creates the perfect conditions for the emergence of agentic AI, followed potentially by artificial general intelligence (AGI) and even super intelligence.

Within the current AI summer, a revolutionary shift has emerged: the transition from passive AI systems to agentic AI. While traditional AI systems excel at specific tasks, agentic AI represents a fundamental evolution in artificial intelligence—systems that can autonomously plan, reason, and take action to achieve specified goals. This shift is like the evolution of a musical performance from a simple solo to the complex and dynamic interaction of a full orchestra, where each section contributes its unique abilities to achieve a unified musical expression.

The breakthrough moment came with the convergence of several key developments:

- Large language models (LLMs) providing sophisticated natural language understanding
- Reinforcement learning with human feedback (RLHF) enabling better alignment with human intentions
- Reasoning layer, innovated by models from OpenAI o1 and 3, and Chinese Deepseek in late 2024 and early 2025
- Advanced planning algorithms allowing for multistep reasoning
- Improved context awareness and memory systems

This shift became particularly visible in 2022–2025+ with the emergence of AI agents that could do the following:

- Navigate complex web interfaces independently
- Execute multistep tasks without constant human guidance
- Learn from their mistakes and adapt their strategies
- Collaborate with other AI agents to solve problems
- Maintain long-term memory and context awareness

The development of agentic AI marks a vital turning point in the current AI summer, moving us closer to systems that don't just respond to queries but actively work to achieve objectives. This represents a significant step toward the original vision of the Dartmouth Conference—machines that can truly simulate aspects of human intelligence and autonomous behavior. The development of these agentic systems can be compared to the formation of a complex orchestra, where each instrument has its own purpose and the sections work in concert to perform intricate musical scores. Figure 1.1 shows the evolution.

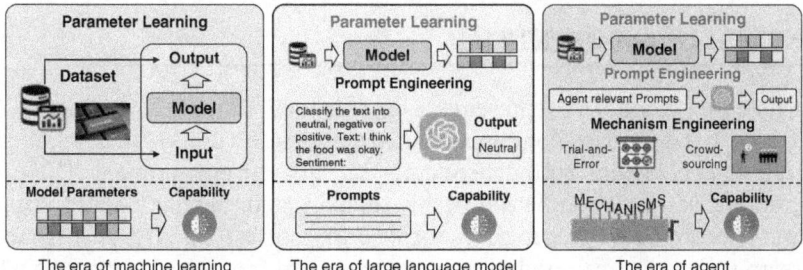

FIGURE 1.1 The three AI eras: ML, LLM, and now agentic
Wang et al., 2024 /https://arxiv.org/pdf/2308.11432, last accessed on 11 March 2025 / Springer Nature / CC BY 4.0

The Future Convergence

What makes the current moment particularly exciting is the imminent convergence of several breakthrough technologies:

- **Quantum computing + AI:** As quantum computers move from theory to practice, they promise to solve complex problems that classical computers find impossible, potentially revolutionizing areas like drug discovery and climate modeling.
- **Metaverse + AI:** The merger of artificial intelligence with virtual and augmented reality will create new forms of human-computer interaction, generating unprecedented amounts of behavioral data while enabling more natural and intuitive interfaces.
- **Biotechnology + AI:** The combination of AI with genetic engineering tools like CRISPR opens new frontiers in healthcare, potentially leading to personalized medicine and solutions for previously incurable diseases.

The next wave of AI evolution will likely be characterized by even greater convergence. We're moving from an era where AI systems operated in isolation to one where they work in concert with other breakthrough technologies. This convergence is creating a multiplicative effect, where the whole is greater than the sum of its parts. Just as a symphony is much more than the sum of its individual instrumental parts, the convergence of these technologies promises a more powerful and versatile future for AI.

The lesson from AI's history is clear: breakthrough moments occur when different technological streams converge. As we stand on the brink of several major technological leaps, the potential for transformation is greater than ever before. We must carefully consider what each instrument will bring to the ensemble and how the different parts will work together to create a harmonious whole.

UNDERSTANDING AGENTIC AI

At its core, agentic AI represents a fundamental shift from traditional AI systems that simply respond to inputs toward autonomous systems that can perceive, decide, and act independently within their environment. Think of traditional software and AI as a highly sophisticated calculator—it processes inputs according to predetermined rules. In contrast, an AI agent is more like an intern who can understand context, learn from experience, and take initiative when appropriate. The evolution from traditional AI to agentic AI is like the shift from a single instrument performing a simple melody to a complex orchestra performing a grand symphony.

Definition of Agentic AI

Agentic AI systems independently pursue goals and make decisions with minimal human oversight. Their key features include:

1. Autonomous adaptation to changing circumstances while pursuing objectives
2. Multistep planning with dynamic adjustments
3. Active environmental engagement beyond simple input-output responses
4. Breaking complex goals into manageable subtasks
5. Self-initiated learning to address knowledge gaps

Core Components of AI Agents

For an AI system to be truly agentic, it must possess several essential components that work in harmony. These components (profile, memory, planning, and action) form the foundation of any effective agent system, regardless of its specific implementation or domain. Let's examine these core modules that control different aspects of the agent's operation. Just as a symphony orchestra needs its diverse sections to create a cohesive sound, an AI agent relies on its core components to function effectively.

Imagine walking into a grand concert hall where an orchestra is about to perform. Each musician, each section, and the conductor all work together to create a magnificent piece of music. This is not unlike how an AI agent operates—a beautiful harmony of different components working in perfect synchronization.

Let me tell you about Sarah, an experienced orchestra conductor who recently attended an AI conference. As she watched demonstrations of various AI systems, she couldn't help but draw parallels between her orchestra and these fascinating digital autonomous minds.

"You see," she explained to her colleague, "just as my orchestra needs four essential sections to perform a symphony, an AI agent requires four core components to function effectively."

First, there's what we call the **Profile**, or perception, system, much like the conductor's ability to read the musical score and observe the musicians. It's the AI's way of understanding its world, gathering information, and knowing its role—just as each musician knows their instrument and part in the symphony. This is the foundation for how the agent engages with the world.

Then comes the **Memory** architecture, which Sarah compares to both the individual musicians' memory of the piece and the collective memory of the orchestra. "Some memories are like our quick notes during rehearsal," she says, "while others are like our deep understanding of Mozart's style built over years of performance." The AI, too, needs this dual memory system to operate effectively. These memories, both short term and long term, are essential for the AI to learn and adapt over time.

The **Decision-Making/Planning** framework reminds Sarah of her role as a conductor. "When I conduct," she explains, "I'm constantly making decisions about tempo, volume, and emphasis—just as an AI must make strategic decisions about its actions and goals." This component is like the conductor's brain, planning ahead while considering all possible outcomes and ensuring every decision serves the greater purpose of the performance. Without a robust planning component, the AI cannot move from data gathering to action.

Finally, there's the **Action** generation system, which Sarah likens to the actual playing of instruments. "It's one thing to know the music," she says, "but another entirely to transform that knowledge into beautiful sound." Similarly, an AI must convert its decisions into concrete actions, continuously adjusting and improving based on feedback—just as musicians adjust their playing based on what they hear. The action component is the way that the AI influences and modifies its environment.

But here's the real magic: just as an orchestra isn't simply four separate sections playing independently, these AI components must work together in perfect harmony. Each part influences and responds to the others, creating a seamless whole that's greater than the sum of its parts.

"In my orchestra," Sarah concludes, "if the strings section can't hear the woodwinds or if the percussion isn't in sync with my conducting, the entire performance falls apart. The same is true for AI—all components must be in perfect synchronization."

> **NOTE**
>
> In the following chapters, we'll dive deeper into each of these components, exploring their intricate workings and complex interactions. We'll examine specific technologies, algorithms, and implementations that make each component function effectively. For now, understanding this

harmonious relationship between the core components provides the foundation for our journey into the fascinating world of AI agents. We will also explore the potential challenges and risks inherent in these complex systems, and why it is imperative that we create them in a responsible way.

As Sarah's analogy shows us, creating an AI agent isn't just about assembling pieces—it's about orchestrating them into a cohesive, intelligent system capable of perceiving, remembering, deciding, and acting in meaningful ways. Just as every great orchestra must master both the individual sections and their integration, every effective AI agent must excel at both component-level operation and system-wide coordination (see Figure 1.2).

THE ORCHESTRA AND THE SOLO PERFORMER: UNDERSTANDING AI'S EVOLUTION

Sarah often tells her students about the difference between conducting a full orchestra and directing a solo performer. "A solo performer, while incredibly skilled, follows a more structured path—the notes are set, the tempo is

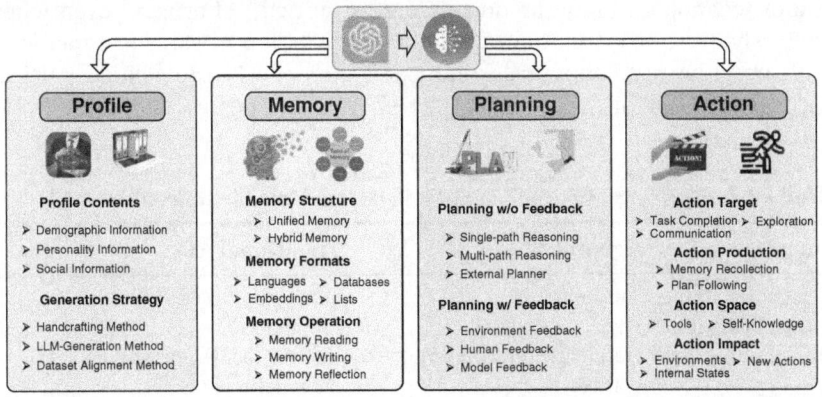

FIGURE 1.2   Agent modules
Wang et al., 2024 /https://arxiv.org/pdf/2308.11432/ Springer Nature / CC BY 4.0

largely predetermined, and variations are limited," she explains, gesturing to a framed photo of a pianist on her wall. "But an orchestra? That's a living, breathing entity that can adapt, evolve, and tackle incredibly complex pieces through the coordinated effort of many musicians."

This distinction perfectly mirrors the evolution from traditional AI to agentic AI systems. Traditional AI is like that talented solo performer—impressive within its specific repertoire but constrained by its predetermined programming. Agentic AI, on the other hand, resembles Sarah's orchestra—a dynamic, adaptable ensemble that can harmonize multiple tools and approaches, learn from each performance, and tackle complex symphonies that require coordinated decision-making across many sections. This evolution represents a major change in what is possible with AI.

As Sarah reviews next season's program, she pulls out a comparison sheet that helps new orchestra members understand the difference between solo and orchestral performances. "Let me show you something similar that highlights the key differences between traditional and agentic AI systems," she says, pointing to Table 1.2, which breaks down these distinctions across various aspects.

This comparison helps us understand not just what makes agentic AI different but why it represents such a significant leap forward in artificial intelligence—much like the leap from a solo recital to a full symphonic performance. This new capability opens up amazing opportunities, but we must also be aware of the potential risks.

Myths vs. Realities: Separating True Agents from Pretenders

The recent surge in AI popularity has led to a familiar pattern: the overhyping of technology. Many products are now labeled "AI-driven," even when they rely on simple techniques like linear regression or statistical methods. This trend has created a misleading perception of AI's capabilities, particularly in the realm of AI agents. While true AI agents possess decision-making

TABLE 1.2 Agentic AI vs. Traditional AI: Breaking Down the Differences

Aspect	Agentic AI	Traditional AI
Decision-making	Autonomous	Often rule-based
Adaptability	High	Limited
Task complexity	Handles multistep, complex tasks	Usually focused on specific, predefined tasks
Learning	Continuous, self-improving	Often static after initial training
Interaction	Can use multiple tools and data sources	Typically limited to predefined inputs

autonomy and advanced memory functions, many so-called "AI agents" are merely sophisticated document retrieval systems enhanced with some limited prompt engineering. This discrepancy between marketing claims and technological reality highlights the importance of critical thinking when evaluating AI products. As genuine AI advancements continue to emerge, it's essential to distinguish between genuine innovation and mere marketing hype. We must learn to critically assess the new tools that become available, so we can make informed decisions about when and how to use them.

There are a few common myths circulating within social networks and enterprises:

- **Myth:** "Any AI with a chat interface is an agent."
  - **Reality:** Many chatbots are simply response generators without true agency or goal-oriented behavior.
- **Myth:** "AI that can complete tasks automatically is an agent"
  - **Reality:** Automation alone doesn't constitute agency; true agents must be able to adapt and make decisions autonomously.

To truly understand and verify the presence of genuine agency in artificial intelligence systems, we must examine several critical capabilities and behavioral patterns. The verification process can be approached through two fundamental lenses: **system capabilities** and **demonstrated behaviors**. We must be rigorous in our assessment, because the future of our interaction with technology depends on the reliability and validity of these assessments.

When evaluating system capabilities, we must first assess whether the AI can modify its approach when presented with new information, showing genuine flexibility rather than rigid programming. This adaptability should be coupled with the ability to learn from both its successes and failures, incorporating these experiences into future decision-making processes. Furthermore, a truly agentic system must demonstrate the capability to operate autonomously over extended periods without constant human intervention or guidance. Perhaps most importantly, it should display competence in making decisions under conditions of uncertainty, mirroring the complex decision-making processes that characterize genuine agency. The capacity for self-improvement and autonomous action is what truly separates agentic AI from previous approaches.

Beyond these core capabilities, we must also look for specific behavioral indicators that signify true agency. The system should exhibit clear goal-oriented behavior, showing not just the ability to achieve predetermined objectives, but to pursue them with purpose and persistence. Effective resource management is another key indicator, as it reflects the system's ability to optimize its use of available resources in pursuit of its goals. The presence of strategic planning capabilities further supports the case for true agency, demonstrating the system's ability to think ahead and develop comprehensive approaches to achieving its objectives. Finally, adaptive learning behavior shows that the system can evolve and improve over time, incorporating new information and experiences into its decision-making framework. These are all indicators of a system that is capable of true agency, and we must hold them to this standard.

Together, these capabilities and behavioral patterns form a comprehensive framework for evaluating true agency in AI systems.

THE EVOLVING LANDSCAPE OF AGENTIC AI PLATFORMS

The landscape of agentic AI platforms is experiencing unprecedented rapid evolution. It's critical to acknowledge that by the time readers engage with this analysis, the platforms discussed may have evolved significantly or been superseded by new solutions. This inherent dynamism underscores the importance of analyzing these systems through first principles rather than their current feature sets. Rather than getting caught up in the latest features of a particular platform, we must focus on the underlying architecture and its adherence to core principles.

From personal experience in implementing agentic systems, I've found that platforms like AutoGen and Langraph provide robust foundations for development. However, this preference stems from their alignment with fundamental agent principles rather than specific features, which may change rapidly. Our focus is not on any specific brand or platform, but rather on the principles that enable effective system design.

A particularly critical consideration is the accelerating software lifecycle of AI platforms. What was once measured in years is now measured in months or even weeks. Organizations must factor this compressed evolution into their selection and implementation strategies, focusing on adaptability and fundamental capabilities rather than current feature sets. This accelerating evolution demands flexibility and adaptability in our approach.

Let's go back to Sarah, our orchestra conductor. She has found herself in an interesting situation when renovating her concert hall. "You know," she explained to the board of directors, "choosing an AI platform today is much like selecting instruments for an orchestra in a world where instrument makers are constantly innovating at an unprecedented pace."

She picked up her beloved violin, crafted in Cremona centuries ago. "Traditional instruments like this violin have evolved over hundreds of years to reach their current form. But imagine if violin makers were introducing revolutionary new models every few months. How would we choose? What would we standardize on?"

This is exactly the challenge organizations face with agentic AI platforms today. Just as an orchestra needs different sections—strings, woodwinds, brass, and percussion—the AI landscape offers different platforms, each with its own strengths.

Microsoft's Semantic Kernel has emerged as an *agentic platform*, offering enterprise-grade support for building AI agents and orchestrating multi-agent workflows. Its framework integrates with tools like planners, plugins, and connectors, enabling developers to embed autonomous decision-making and collaboration into applications. The platform is designed to align with business processes, leveraging Microsoft's ecosystem (e.g., Azure AI, Fabric, and SharePoint) for scalability and security.

Meanwhile, AutoGen, originally an open-source multi-agent framework from Microsoft Research, underwent a strategic split in late 2024. The community-driven branch, AG2, remains open-source for experimental use, while Microsoft rebranded its internal iteration to focus on tighter integration with Semantic Kernel and Azure AI services. This bifurcation allows developers to experiment with cutting-edge patterns in AG2 while transitioning to Semantic Kernel for production-grade deployments with institutional backing.

LangChain and its new companion Langraph are more like a versatile jazz ensemble—highly flexible, with the ability to improvise and adapt quickly to new situations. They offer a rich ecosystem of tools and approaches, though they might require more expertise to orchestrate effectively. Their flexibility is well suited for organizations looking for dynamic solutions.

CrewAI, the newest addition to our musical landscape, is like a chamber orchestra specialized in intimate performances. It excels in coordinated, focused tasks with clear role distribution among its performers. This is well suited for focused task driven solutions.

"But here's the essential point," Sarah emphasizes, tapping her conductor's baton thoughtfully. "In a world where instruments evolve so quickly, we shouldn't build our entire repertoire around any single manufacturer's instruments. Instead, we should focus on the fundamental principles of music-making."

This wisdom translates directly to agentic AI implementation. Rather than becoming overly dependent on any single platform, organizations should:

- Build modular architectures that can adapt to change
- Focus on the fundamental components (profile, memory, planning, and action) rather than specific platform features
- Ensure there is a clear and easy migration plan, specifically for Memory and Decision-Making/Planning components

- Maintain flexibility to incorporate new innovations as they emerge
- Consider hybrid approaches that leverage the strengths of different platforms

This approach acknowledges both the need for robust current solutions and the inevitability of rapid evolution in the field. Focusing on fundamentals while maintaining adaptability enables organizations to build sustainable agentic AI implementations in this dynamic landscape. This approach will ensure that your solutions will not become obsolete as the technology changes.

> **NOTE**
>
> In subsequent chapters, we'll dive deeper into each platform's specific capabilities, architectural patterns, and implementation considerations. We'll explore detailed use cases and practical implementation strategies for each of these platforms.

Understanding agentic AI platforms through their core components reveals that these systems are indeed in their early stages. Each platform has made different trade-offs and architectural decisions in implementing these fundamental components. The field's maturity will likely be marked by more sophisticated implementations of these core components, particularly in areas of memory persistence, dynamic planning, and multi-agent coordination. As we look ahead, we can expect a significant amount of innovation in these core areas.

REAL-WORLD IMPACT: THE AI REVOLUTION IN ACTION

As AI agents move from research labs into the real world, they're fundamentally transforming how industries operate and how value is created. Let's explore these changes through specific sectors, examining both current implementations and near-horizon possibilities. This exploration is like listening to different sections of an orchestra, each with its own distinct characteristics, but all contributing to the overall performance.

Before we deep dive into the specific industry applications, it's critical to understand that this overview represents a broad landscape of potential agentic AI solutions. In the subsequent chapters of this exploration, we will conduct deep-dive case studies into select, groundbreaking examples that showcase the transformative potential of agentic AI. The examples presented here are intended to provide a panoramic view of the emerging areas where researchers, technologists, and innovators are developing intelligent, autonomous systems capable of complex reasoning, adaptive decision-making, and proactive problem-solving. These snapshots offer a glimpse into the promising frontier of agentic AI, highlighting the industries and domains where these advanced systems are destined to create significant value and drive technological innovation.

While agentic AI is still an emerging technology, there are some examples of its application or development in various industries. Here are some instances across the sectors mentioned.

Healthcare

Agentic AI in healthcare is showing promising applications in patient care and medical operations:

- **Personalized treatment plans:** AI agents can analyze patient data, including genetic information, medical history, and lifestyle factors, to tailor treatment plans for individual patients. For example, in managing chronic conditions like diabetes, these systems can monitor blood sugar levels in real time and adjust medication dosages accordingly.
- **Remote patient monitoring:** AI-powered wearables can continuously monitor vital signs and alert healthcare providers to potential issues before they become serious. This enables early interventions and reduces hospital readmissions.
- **Care coordination:** AI agents gather data from electronic health records, care management platforms, and scheduling systems to streamline workflows. They can predict which high-risk patients need immediate intervention and automate collaboration across care teams, reducing preventable readmissions.

Financial Services

In the financial sector, agentic AI is being developed for various applications:

- **Fraud detection:** AI agents monitor transactions in real time, identifying and flagging suspicious activities that could indicate fraud. These systems can adapt their strategies based on new patterns of fraudulent behavior.

- **Portfolio management:** In trading and investment, agentic AI systems are being developed to analyze market trends, make split-second trading decisions, and dynamically adjust investment strategies based on real-time economic data and news events.[1]

Manufacturing

The manufacturing industry is exploring agentic AI for:

- **Supply chain optimization:** AI agents analyze data from various sources to streamline logistics, predict demand, and optimize inventory levels, ensuring timely delivery of goods. These systems can autonomously adjust supply chain strategies based on changing market conditions. This is an example of how AI can manage complexity in a way that is not possible with human intervention alone.

AdTech/Marketing

This is my current professional focus area, so there are quite a few places where agentic AI can improve the current business processes:

- **Dynamic ad optimization:** AI agents can analyze user behavior in real time, autonomously adjusting ad placements, content, and targeting strategies to maximize engagement and conversion rates.
- **Campaign planning:** AI agents can collaborate to extract from individual experts in the different areas such as media consumption, audience design, historical data, etc. This is like bringing different sections of an orchestra together to create a complex and compelling piece of music.

Telecommunications

In the telecommunications sector, agentic AI could be applied for:

- **Network optimization:** AI agents could autonomously monitor network traffic, predict congestion, and dynamically allocate resources to ensure optimal performance. These systems could learn from network patterns and proactively address potential issues. This demonstrates how agentic AI can proactively manage complex systems.

---

[1] https://www.forbes.com/sites/bernardmarr/2024/09/06/agentic-ai-the-next-big-breakthrough-thats-transforming-business-and-technology

It's important to note that many of these applications are still in development or early stages of implementation. The full potential of agentic AI is yet to be realized across these industries. As the technology matures, we can expect to see more concrete and widespread examples of agentic AI in action. We will continue to explore these advancements in subsequent chapters.

TIP: How to Achieve Success with Agentic AI

The most successful implementations of AI agents share three key characteristics:

1. Clear operational boundaries
2. Robust feedback mechanisms
3. Seamless human-AI collaboration protocols

As we move forward, the challenge isn't just technical implementation but designing systems that effectively balance autonomous operation with appropriate human oversight and intervention. This balance between human and AI involvement is fundamental for the successful integration of agentic AI.

This section demonstrates how AI agents are moving beyond theoretical possibilities to deliver benefits across industries. The next section will explore the future implications of these developments and what they mean for society at large.

FUTURE IMPLICATIONS

As we stand at the threshold of widespread AI agent adoption, the implications ripple across every facet of society. Let's explore these transformative changes while maintaining a balanced perspective on both opportunities and challenges. The future of AI is not predetermined; it is something we create through our choices.

As these systems continue to evolve, we're witnessing the emergence of a new kind of industrial ecosystem. AI agents are beginning to coordinate across traditional sector boundaries, creating a web of intelligence that spans supply chains, financial systems, and customer interactions. This is a shift from fragmented systems to a coordinated whole, much like the way an orchestra creates a unified sound.

Imagine a world where an unexpected surge in customer demand is instantly communicated across this network. Manufacturing schedules adjust, transportation logistics are optimized, inventory levels are rebalanced, and financial hedging strategies are updated—all in real time, with minimal human intervention. This level of responsiveness and coordination would not be possible without agentic AI.

This interconnected ecosystem of AI agents represents more than just an improvement in efficiency. It's a fundamental shift in how business operations are conducted and how value is created in the modern economy. This shift will require us to rethink how we organize our economies and societies.

As we enter a new era, the challenge isn't just technical implementation. It's about designing systems that effectively balance autonomous operation with appropriate human oversight and intervention. It's about creating a future where AI agents enhance human potential, rather than diminish it. This requires us to consider ethical implications, governance, and long-term impact.

The AI revolution is no longer a distant possibility—it's unfolding before our eyes, reshaping industries and redefining what's possible. As we move forward, we must approach this new frontier with a mix of excitement and thoughtful consideration, always keeping in mind the ultimate goal: to create a future where technology serves humanity, enhancing our capabilities and enriching our lives in ways we're only beginning to imagine. The responsibility is on us to create a future that benefits everyone.

The Dawn of Agentic AI: A Preview of Our Transforming World

As we stand on the brink of a new era in human-machine collaboration, agentic AI promises to revolutionize every aspect of our lives. This book will guide you through the multifaceted implications of this transformation, exploring how these intelligent agents will reshape our world.

In the workplace, AI agents are set to become our daily collaborators, transforming productivity and redefining professional roles. Picture a workplace where AI handles routine tasks while humans focus on creative and strategic decisions. The specifics of this evolution, including emerging job roles and economic implications, will be thoroughly examined in Chapter 4. We must prepare for the changes to the workplace that are coming.

Our personal lives won't remain untouched. AI agents will soon serve as digital companions in our daily decision-making, from health management to educational pursuits. The complex dynamics of these human-AI relationships, including critical questions about privacy and dependency, will be explored in depth in Chapters 5 and 7. We must prepare to navigate the complexities of human-AI interactions.

The societal impact of agentic AI spans multiple domains—healthcare, education, and social interaction. While these advances promise remarkable benefits, they also raise important ethical considerations. Chapters 4 and 7 will further explore these opportunities and challenges, providing a comprehensive analysis of their implications. These impacts will be far reaching, and we must prepare for both the opportunities and risks.

Legal frameworks and liability considerations represent another critical aspect of the agentic AI revolution. Who bears responsibility when AI decisions lead to unexpected outcomes? Chapter 9 will address these complex legal questions, examining proposed frameworks and potential solutions. We must develop legal systems that are appropriate for these new technologies.

The successful integration of AI agents into society demands careful attention to governance, education, and ethical guidelines. These critical elements of the integration process will be thoroughly discussed in Chapter 8, complete with practical recommendations and case studies. These are essential elements to ensure the responsible development of AI.

As we start the journey on this exploration of agentic AI, remember that each challenge and opportunity mentioned here will be examined in detail in the following chapters. Our journey through this book will equip you with the knowledge and insights needed to understand and prepare for this transformative technology. The next chapter will cover the practical strategies needed to navigate the complex landscape of agentic AI systems.

KEY TAKEAWAYS

As we reach the conclusion of this chapter, it is helpful to recap the key concepts we have explored in our journey through the AI Revolution 2.0. We've traced the evolution from traditional AI to agentic systems, examined how these autonomous agents are fundamentally reshaping industries, and contemplated their future implications. Through personal experiences and real-world examples, we've seen how AI agents represent not just an incremental improvement but a paradigm shift in human-machine interaction. The ability of these systems to perceive, decide, and act independently while learning from experience marks a historic turning point in technological evolution. As we stand at this threshold, understanding these developments isn't just academic—it's essential for anyone looking to navigate and thrive in an AI-enabled future. We must move from passive observers to active participants in the evolution of AI. Let's recap the key takeaways:

1. **The AI agent revolution is fundamentally different.**
   - KEY INSIGHTS:
     - AI agents represent a shift from rule-based systems to autonomous, goal-oriented entities.
     - They can perceive, decide, and act independently while learning from experience.

- DO:
  - Understand the distinct capabilities of agentic AI versus traditional AI.
  - Prepare for systems that can handle complex, multistep tasks autonomously.
- DON'T:
  - Confuse simple automation or chatbots with true AI agents.
  - Underestimate the transformative potential of this technology. It is more important than any other development we have seen so far in the field of AI.

2. Integration requires balanced implementation.
- KEY INSIGHTS:
  - Successful deployment depends on clear boundaries and robust feedback mechanisms.
  - Cross-industry applications are creating new value propositions.
- DO:
  - Establish clear operational parameters and oversight mechanisms.
  - Focus on human-AI collaboration rather than replacement. It is imperative that we approach this from a perspective of augmentation and not replacement.
- DON'T:
  - Rush implementation without proper governance frameworks.
  - Ignore the human factor in AI agent deployment. Ultimately, the goal is to improve the human condition

3. Future preparedness is critical.
- KEY INSIGHTS:
  - Widespread adoption will transform workplaces, personal lives, and society.
  - Legal and ethical frameworks must evolve alongside the technology.
- DO:
  - Invest in digital literacy and workforce adaptation.
  - Develop proactive governance and ethical guidelines.
- DON'T:
  - Wait for problems to arise before addressing regulatory needs.
  - Overlook the importance of maintaining human agency and values. The human element remains the most important part of this new future.

As we move forward into this new era of AI, it's imperative to remember that the future isn't something that just happens to us—it's something we actively shape. Let's embrace the transformative potential of AI agents while thoughtfully considering their implications, so we can ensure that this technology enhances human potential and contributes positively to society. The next chapter will dive into the practical strategies that are needed to successfully navigate the coming AI revolution, providing a concrete road map for implementation.

CHAPTER 2

Understanding Agentic AI

"As we build AI systems, we're building our future. Let's make it one we want to live in."

—Stuart Russell

DECONSTRUCTING INTELLIGENCE AND AGENCY

On a warm summer day in 1907, a young patent clerk sat at his desk in Bern, Switzerland, contemplating a profound puzzle. Albert Einstein wasn't satisfied with the existing theories of physics—something didn't add up.

He knew the established laws of motion and gravity, the clockwork precision of the Newtonian universe. Yet, anomalies persisted, tiny cracks in the edifice of classical physics. To reconcile these discrepancies, Einstein didn't just tinker with existing equations; he embarked on a journey of super-abstraction.

Through a remarkable feat of abstract thinking, he imagined himself riding alongside a beam of light. This simple yet powerful thought experiment would eventually lead him to revolutionize our understanding of the universe through his theory of relativity.

In his journey, he questioned the very nature of time and space, concepts considered immutable and absolute for centuries. To fit all the pieces together, to resolve the inconsistencies he observed, he conceived of a radical idea: time is not constant; it is relative, dependent on the observer's motion. This leap, unthinkable at the time, wasn't born from incremental improvements but from a fundamental re-evaluation of core assumptions. It was an act of profound intellectual agency, driven by the ability to construct an entirely new, higher-level understanding of the universe. This act of super-abstraction, of building new mental models from foundational principles, lies at the heart of intelligence, both human and artificial. As we go deep into the world of AI agents, we too must start with first principles, dissecting the fundamental building blocks of intelligence and agency to truly grasp the transformative power that lies ahead.

Einstein's journey illustrates a fundamental aspect of intelligence that we're only now beginning to understand and replicate in artificial systems: the ability to create higher-level abstractions from existing knowledge and use them to solve novel problems. This capacity for abstract thinking and problem-solving forms the cornerstone of what we consider intelligence, whether natural or artificial. See Figure 2.1.

Defining intelligence is a notoriously difficult task, a challenge that has occupied philosophers, psychologists, and computer scientists for decades. In fact, the topic is so complex and multifaceted that it could easily fill entire bookshelves. As Robert J. Sternberg noted, "Looked at in one way, everyone knows what intelligence is; looked at in another way, no one does." This lack of a universal consensus highlights the depth and breadth of this field

FIGURE 2.1   Albert Einstein's super-abstraction capabilities

Generated with AI using Google Gemini 2.5 Pro

of study. When prominent psychologists were asked to define intelligence, they all gave divergent answers (Sternberg & Detterman, 1986). Even within the more focused field of AI, researchers have proposed numerous definitions, often reflecting different perspectives on what constitutes "intelligent" behavior. One useful summary, proposed by Legg and Hutter in 2007 after reviewing more than 70 definitions, states that "Intelligence measures an agent's ability to achieve goals in a wide range of environments," which emphasizes both task-specific skills and the ability to adapt to new situations. This duality is a critical point of understanding and will be explored in the sections to come. This lack of consensus should not discourage us but rather motivate a deeper dive into the core components that, when assembled, result in the phenomenon we call intelligence.

A Practical Starting Point: AI vs. Traditional Software

To understand how AI differs from traditional software, let's consider a practical definition. According to the Bank of England and Financial Conduct Authority's AIPP document, *artificial intelligence* (AI) encompasses the study and creation of computer systems capable of executing tasks that previously demanded human intellect. AI is a vast field, with machine learning (ML) as an important subfield. Machine learning involves computer programs that can adapt models or identify patterns from data without explicit programming and with minimal to no human intervention. This is a significant departure from "rules-based algorithms," where human programmers explicitly dictate the decisions made under specific world states. Instead of being explicitly programmed, an ML algorithm will make decisions based on the patterns it identifies in the data it is given. This difference provides a good framework for thinking about AI as a system that learns and adapts rather than simply following pre-set instructions. This adaptability is one of the key markers of an intelligent system. See Figure 2.2.

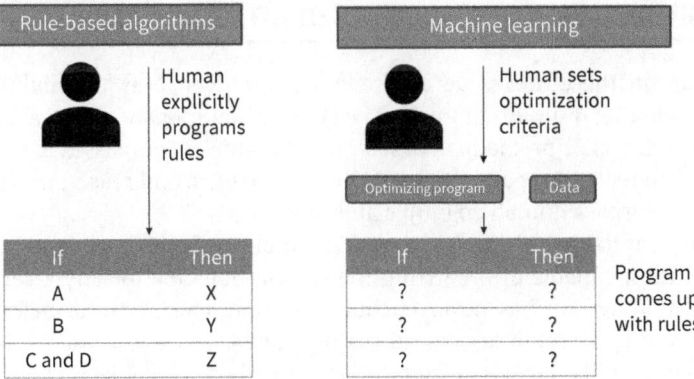

FIGURE 2.2   ML algorithms make decisions without being explicitly programmed

THE SPARK OF CREATIVITY IN AI

Intelligence, in its most profound form, is closely linked with creativity. Consider the recent breakthroughs in AI that exhibit different levels of creative behavior. There are three levels of AI creativity:

- **Interpolation:** This is the most basic level, where AI generates outputs by averaging or combining what it has seen. For example, generating a new image of a cat by combining millions of existing cat images. While the output is technically "new," it's mostly a recombination of existing patterns.
- **Extrapolation:** This is where AI moves beyond its training data to discover novel solutions and in this sense is more closely linked to the idea of "intelligence." This is visible in cutting-edge AI agents that show emergent behaviors like spontaneous reflection, self-correction, "a ha moments" where they pause and restart with new insight, and adaptive output length based on problem complexity. They can even mix languages to optimize problem-solving, showing a level of flexibility not seen in purely rule-based systems.
- **True innovation:** This highest level involves creating entirely new concepts or systems, like inventing the game of Go itself. Or discovering a completely new law of physics like Einstein did. This level remains a significant challenge, and we are not there yet. This is a goal that is still years in the future for AI.

This creativity framework demonstrates that intelligence is not just about recognizing patterns but also about creating new patterns, new solutions, and new ways of seeing the world.

REVISITING THE FIRST PRINCIPLES OF INTELLIGENCE

Building on these ideas, we can redefine intelligence as the ability of an agent (whether human, animal, or AI) to autonomously learn, adapt, and make decisions or predictions based on data. This encompasses the system's capacity to recognize patterns, identify relationships, and reason in ways that mimic or surpass human cognitive abilities.

At a fundamental level, the goal of intelligence is to develop a model or algorithm capable of predicting the correct outcome for any given input, even if that system has never encountered that specific input before. This is achieved by developing algorithms that can generalize from the patterns and relationships they learn from the training data. The objective is to create systems that can adapt and make accurate predictions or decisions in novel, unseen situations. This ability is what allows for the creation of more robust and versatile solutions that can handle a wide range of problems and adapt to new information or changing environments. This adaptability is fundamental for real-world applications, where the data is often dynamic, and the systems must be capable of adjusting to new circumstances and making informed decisions without constant human intervention.

It is important to keep in mind that at its fundamental level, we are trying to find the best model that, fitting whatever data we have seen so far (training dataset), will be able to predict the right outcome in new circumstances. This requires an ability to abstract and make new conclusions, which is the core concept of intelligence.

We can decompose this into its core components:

- **Pattern recognition:** The ability to identify meaningful structures in data, whether they are visual, auditory, or conceptual. This is the foundation upon which all other aspects of intelligence are built.
- **Knowledge acquisition:** The capacity to learn from experience, data, and external sources, building an internal model of the world. This involves not just memorizing information but also organizing it in a meaningful way.
- **Abstract reasoning:** Creating higher-level concepts, generalizations, and mental models from basic observations and acquired knowledge. This moves beyond concrete examples to form general rules and principles. This is where true creativity sparks, as described by the levels of creativity above, and builds upon the ability to extrapolate beyond the training data.
- **Adaptive behavior:** Modifying actions and strategies based on new information, changing conditions, and feedback from the environment. This is the capacity to adjust to changing circumstances and to learn from errors and successes.
- **Goal-directed action:** Working toward specific objectives and planning and executing actions that lead to desired outcomes. This requires understanding the context of a situation and anticipating the results of actions.

These core components are deeply interconnected, each influencing the others in a complex dance. They are the very building blocks of intelligent action.

The Power of Abstraction

The "super-abstraction" point, the capacity to create higher-level concepts and generalize across different situations, is precisely what humans and many animals exhibit to navigate our complex world. Our current most advanced AI models are still showing limited capabilities in this area, mostly excelling at extrapolation within their narrow task. This ability to generalize is not just about combining existing patterns (interpolation) but about seeing beyond the data to find underlying principles and create entirely new solutions (extrapolation), as also mentioned earlier with AI creativity levels. This links to a key debate in the field, summarized by the "On the Measure of Intelligence" paper, which discusses if intelligence is just a set of special-purpose skills or more of a general-purpose skill. Some researchers argue for task-specific modules while others highlight the "blank slate" approach that learns from experience. The reality is probably a mix of both, and our models are constantly being updated as we gain new information in the field. This ability to abstract and extrapolate can relate to the idea of fluid intelligence, introduced by Cattell in 1971, which refers to the capacity to think logically and solve novel problems independently of acquired knowledge, in contrast with crystallized intelligence (the knowledge from previous learning). This is where we see creativity and true intelligence.

Consider Einstein once more. He mastered the existing frameworks of physics—the data points, if you will. But his genius wasn't just in knowing these laws; it was in his ability to see beyond them, to recognize their limitations, and to construct an entirely new framework that encompassed and explained the existing observations in a more comprehensive way. His thought experiments, his ability to imagine scenarios and deduce their consequences, were acts of generating higher abstractions. This process of moving from specific instances to general principles, from data to understanding, is a trademark of intelligence, a principle that applies equally to human cognition and the aspirations of artificial intelligence. It's like a composer who, after mastering the rules of harmony, then innovates to create something entirely new.

Understanding AI Classifications

Building upon these first principles of intelligence, we can better understand the landscape of artificial intelligence, often described with a spectrum of terms reflecting different levels of capability. As we touched upon earlier, at the broadest level, AI simply refers to the ability of machines to perform tasks that typically require human intelligence. This is a vast domain. Within this domain lies narrow AI, also known as weak AI. These are AI systems designed and trained for specific tasks. Your email spam filter, recommendation algorithms, and even sophisticated image recognition software fall under this category. They excel within their defined parameters but lack the ability to generalize their intelligence to other domains.

Currently, much of the excitement revolves around advanced models capable of sophisticated language processing and generation. Terms like *narrow AGI* have emerged to describe these models, acknowledging their impressive capabilities within specific domains while implicitly recognizing their lack of true general intelligence. It's vital to understand that even these advanced "thinking" models, as impressive as they are, operate within the confines of their training data and specific architectures. They demonstrate sophisticated pattern recognition and complex statistical modeling, but they don't possess the generalized understanding or the capacity for abstract thought that characterizes genuine AGI.

The aspiration of many AI researchers is artificial general intelligence (AGI), sometimes called strong AI or human-level AI. An AGI would possess the ability to understand, learn, and apply knowledge across a wide range of tasks, much like a human being. It could theoretically learn any intellectual task a human can.

Finally, artificial superintelligence (ASI) represents a hypothetical future where AI surpasses human intelligence in all aspects. While AGI remains a significant research target, ASI is firmly in the realm of theoretical speculation. Understanding these distinctions is imperative for business leaders and professionals making decisions about AI implementation. Not every solution requires AGI—many practical applications can be achieved through well-designed narrow AI agents working in concert. This is like having a skilled section in an orchestra versus a full orchestra. Each has its purpose and its place, and understanding the limitations of each technology will be key for successful implementations and realistic expectations.

Why Does This Matter?

Understanding these classifications is critical because it helps manage expectations and focus resources on AI solutions that are achievable today. It also prevents us from falling into the trap of thinking we need to solve general AI for each small problem we encounter. It is important to understand that while the idea of an AGI or ASI is captivating, at the moment, most AI applications in use are based on narrow AI agents, and there is still a long way to go before the other applications reach maturity.

The First Principles of Agency

Now, let's shift our focus to the concept of agency. At its most fundamental, agency is the capacity to act and exert influence on an environment to achieve a goal. This simple definition has profound implications when applied to artificial intelligence. The key insight here is that complex, even seemingly intelligent behavior can emerge from the interaction of multiple agents, each with relatively simple individual goals, without requiring any single agent to possess AGI or superintelligence. Think of a flock of birds. Each individual bird follows relatively simple rules—stay close to its neighbors, avoid obstacles. Yet, the collective behavior of the flock is remarkably complex and coordinated, capable of intricate aerial maneuvers. Similarly, in the realm of AI, a system of multiple agents, each with its own defined objective and the ability to act within an environment, can achieve sophisticated outcomes through their interactions and coordinated efforts.

Agency in Action: Interacting with the World

This concept of agency marks a significant departure from many traditional AI systems. While reinforcement learning (RL) models, for instance, also interact with an environment and learn through trial and error to maximize a reward, their agency is typically constrained to achieving a single, predefined goal. An RL agent learning to play a game aims solely to win that game.

Furthermore, while large language models (LLMs) are trained using language modeling (LM) objectives—predicting the next word in a sequence—agency introduces the critical element of real-world interaction and the ability to effect change. An LLM can generate compelling text describing a course of action, but an AI agent can actually execute that action, interacting with its environment to achieve a desired outcome. Consider the difference between a smart home controlled by a central AI versus a smart home populated by AI agents. In the former, a central system dictates the actions of various devices. In the latter, individual agents within the home—a lighting agent, a temperature agent, a security agent—could independently assess their environment and take actions to optimize their specific goals, while also coordinating with each other for overall efficiency and comfort. This ability to act, to influence the environment, is the defining characteristic of agency and the key to unlocking the transformative potential of agentic AI.

The Distributed Intelligence Paradigm

One of the most exciting revelations in modern AI development is that human-like behavior can emerge from distributed systems of specialized agents without requiring true AGI. This insight has profound implications for how we approach AI development and implementation.

Why Does This Matter?

Understanding the first principles of agency helps us move beyond the limitations of thinking about AI solely in terms of isolated tasks or centralized control. It opens possibilities for creating AI systems that are more adaptable, resilient, and capable of tackling complex, real-world problems through collaboration and distributed intelligence.

In this section, we have laid the foundational groundwork for understanding agentic AI by deconstructing the core concepts of intelligence and agency from their first principles. We explored intelligence as the ability to learn and abstract, using Einstein's groundbreaking work as a prime example. We then navigated the spectrum of artificial intelligence, clarifying the distinctions between narrow AI, AGI, and superintelligence. Finally, we dive into the essence of agency, emphasizing its reliance on interaction and the ability to effect change and highlighting how complex behaviors can emerge from systems of multiple agents. This foundational understanding sets the stage for the next section, where we will explore the specific components that comprise these intelligent and acting entities we call AI agents.

As we move forward in our exploration of AI agents, we'll build upon these fundamental concepts to understand how modern AI systems are implementing these principles in practical applications. The next section will probe deeper into the core components that make AI agents work, examining the technical architecture that enables their functionality.

Core Components of AI Agents

Building on our orchestra metaphor from Chapter 1, let's dive deeper into the four essential components that make AI agents function. Just as each section of an orchestra contributes its unique voice to create a symphony, these components work together to create an intelligent, autonomous system. Understanding these components from a first-principles perspective and dissecting their essential functions will provide a solid foundation for navigating the exciting world of AI agents. See Figure 2.3.

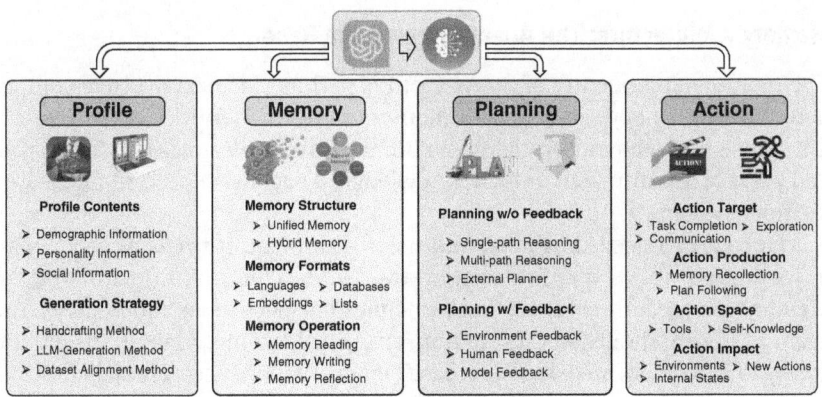

FIGURE 2.3 Agent modules

Springer Nature / https://arxiv.org/pdf/2308.11432 / CC BY 4.0

Perception/Profiling: The Agent's Sensory Input

At its most fundamental, an AI agent exists within an environment, and to act effectively within that environment, it must first be able to perceive it. This is the role of the Perception system. From a first-principles standpoint, this component is responsible for acquiring raw data from the environment and transforming it into a structured representation that the agent can understand. This is like how a musician reads a music score, taking raw symbols and translating them into musical meaning.

Think of our experienced conductor, Sarah, stepping onto the podium. Her perception system—her eyes and ears—immediately begins to gather information: the arrangement of the musicians, the instruments they hold, the ambient sounds of the hall, the expectant faces in the audience. She's constantly "profiling" the current state of affairs. Similarly, an AI agent utilizes various sensors to gather data. These sensors are the agent's interface with the world, translating physical phenomena into digital signals. A self-driving car uses cameras, lidar, and radar; a financial trading agent uses market data feeds; a software assistant uses information from your calendar and emails. However, raw data alone is insufficient. The perception system must then process this data, filtering out noise and extracting relevant features. This involves complex processes like image recognition, natural language processing, and data parsing. Just as Sarah interprets the notes on the musical score and understands the posture of her musicians, the AI agent transforms raw data into meaningful information about its current state and the state of its environment. This "profile" allows the agent to understand its capabilities, limitations, and the resources available to it.

Memory Architecture: The Agent's Knowledge Base

The memory architecture of an AI agent is perhaps its most decisive component, serving as both its working memory and long-term knowledge store. Like musicians who must remember both the immediate notes they're playing and years of accumulated musical knowledge, AI agents require sophisticated memory systems.

Once an AI agent has perceived its environment, it needs a mechanism to retain and utilize that information over time. This is the function of the Memory architecture. From a first-principles perspective, memory allows the agent to store and retrieve information, enabling learning, adaptation, and the ability to make informed decisions based on past experiences. Sarah likens this to the memory of her orchestra. "Some memories are like our quick notes during rehearsal," she explains, "reminders of specific cues or difficult passages. Others are like our deep understanding of a composer's style, built over years of performing their works." AI agents, too, require different types of memory.

Modern AI agents employ two primary types of memory:

- Short-term memory, or working memory, acts as a temporary buffer, holding information relevant to the agent's immediate tasks. It handles immediate tasks and current context. This is analogous to a musician focusing on the current measure of the score. It allows the agent to process information sequentially and keep track of ongoing interactions.
- Long-term memory, on the other hand, provides persistent storage for knowledge, learned patterns, and experiences accumulated over time. This could include learned facts, successful strategies, and even the outcomes of past failures. Different memory architectures, such as knowledge graphs or vector databases, are employed depending on the type of information being stored and the retrieval needs of the agent. The ability to effectively access and utilize information from its memory is critical for an agent to learn from experience and improve its performance over time.

REAL-WORLD EXAMPLE

Consider a personal assistant AI. Its short-term memory helps it remember the context of your current conversation, while its long-term memory stores your preferences, past requests, and important dates.

Decision-Making/Planning Framework: The Agent's Strategic Core

The Decision-Making/Planning framework is analogous to a conductor's interpretation of the music. It takes input from the profile and memory systems to plan and execute actions that align with the agent's goals.

With a perception of its environment and a memory of its past, the AI agent can then engage in decision-making. The Decision-Making/Planning framework is the core component responsible for evaluating information, setting goals, and formulating plans to achieve those goals.

From a first-principles perspective, this involves reasoning about the current state, considering available options, and predicting the potential outcomes of different actions. Sarah compares this to her role as the conductor. "When I conduct," she explains, "I'm constantly making decisions about tempo, dynamics, and phrasing, all in service of the composer's vision and the desired emotional impact of the music." The Decision-Making/Planning framework often employs algorithms that range from simple rule-based systems to complex optimization algorithms and sophisticated AI planning techniques. The agent's goals can be explicitly programmed or learned through interaction with the environment. The framework must weigh various factors, assess risks and rewards, and select a course of action that maximizes the likelihood of achieving the agent's objectives. This often involves breaking down complex goals into smaller, manageable sub-tasks and sequencing these tasks into a coherent plan. This is how a conductor breaks down a large musical piece into smaller parts.

Key components include:

- Goal representation
- Planning algorithms
- Risk assessment
- Resource optimization
- Learning mechanisms

Action Generation System: The Agent's Interface with the World

The final component transforms decisions into concrete actions. Like musicians translating sheet music into sound, this system converts abstract plans into specific outputs or actions.

The Action Generation system is responsible for translating the agent's decisions into concrete actions that affect its environment. From a first-principles perspective, this is the mechanism through which the agent exerts its agency and brings about change. Sarah likens this to the actual playing of the instruments. "It's one thing to understand the music and for me to decide on the interpretation," she says, "but the true magic happens when the musicians translate that understanding and those decisions into beautiful sound."

The Action Generation system is highly dependent on the agent's embodiment and the environment it operates in. For a robotic agent, this involves controlling motors, actuators, and other hardware components. For a software agent, it might involve sending commands to other software systems, displaying information to users, or manipulating data. The key here is the ability to take the output of the decision-making framework and transform it into actions that have a tangible effect on the world. This component often incorporates feedback loops, allowing the agent to sense the consequences of its actions and adjust its subsequent behavior, much like musicians listen to their own playing and that of others to refine their performance in real-time. This continuous feedback and adjustment loop allows for ever more impressive performances.

Why Does This Matter?

Without an effective Action Generation system, the agent's intelligence and planning capabilities would be purely theoretical. This component is the fundamental link between thought and action, enabling the agent to exert its influence and achieve its goals.

Conclusion

Just as a symphony is the result of the harmonious interplay of distinct musical sections, an AI agent's capabilities stem from the coordinated function of its core components. The Perception system provides the necessary sensory input, the Memory architecture stores and retrieves vital information, the Decision-Making/ Planning framework charts a strategic course, and the Action Generation system translates those decisions into tangible actions. Sarah's orchestra analogy beautifully illustrates this interconnectedness: "In my orchestra," she concludes, "if the strings section can't hear the woodwinds, or if the percussion isn't in sync with my conducting, the entire performance falls apart. The same is true for AI—all components must be in perfect synchronization."

This understanding of these fundamental building blocks from a first-principles perspective allows us to gain a deeper appreciation for the complexity and potential of AI agents. This understanding will be critical as we move forward to explore how these components contribute to the overall intelligence of agentic systems, the focus of our next section on the Agent Intelligence Pyramid.

The Symphony of Components

Just as an orchestra's excellence depends on the seamless integration of its sections, an AI agent's effectiveness relies on the harmonious interaction of its components. Each component must not only excel in its function but also communicate and coordinate with the others. See Figure 2.4.

Understanding these core components is essential for anyone working with or implementing AI agents. In the next section, we'll explore how these components combine to create different levels of agent intelligence, introducing the Agent Intelligence Pyramid.

THE AGENT INTELLIGENCE PYRAMID

Just as an orchestra builds complex symphonies from individual notes to intricate harmonies, AI agents exhibit intelligence across multiple levels of sophistication. Picture a conductor who must understand both the capabilities of individual musicians and how they combine to create something greater than the sum of their parts. This hierarchical nature of intelligence forms what we call the Agent Intelligence Pyramid—a framework that helps us understand how AI agents evolve from simple reactive systems to sophisticated collaborative entities.

Imagine the conductor of our AI orchestra, the agent, no longer simply following a fixed score, but now dynamically interpreting the music, anticipating the needs of the musicians, and even composing new melodies on the

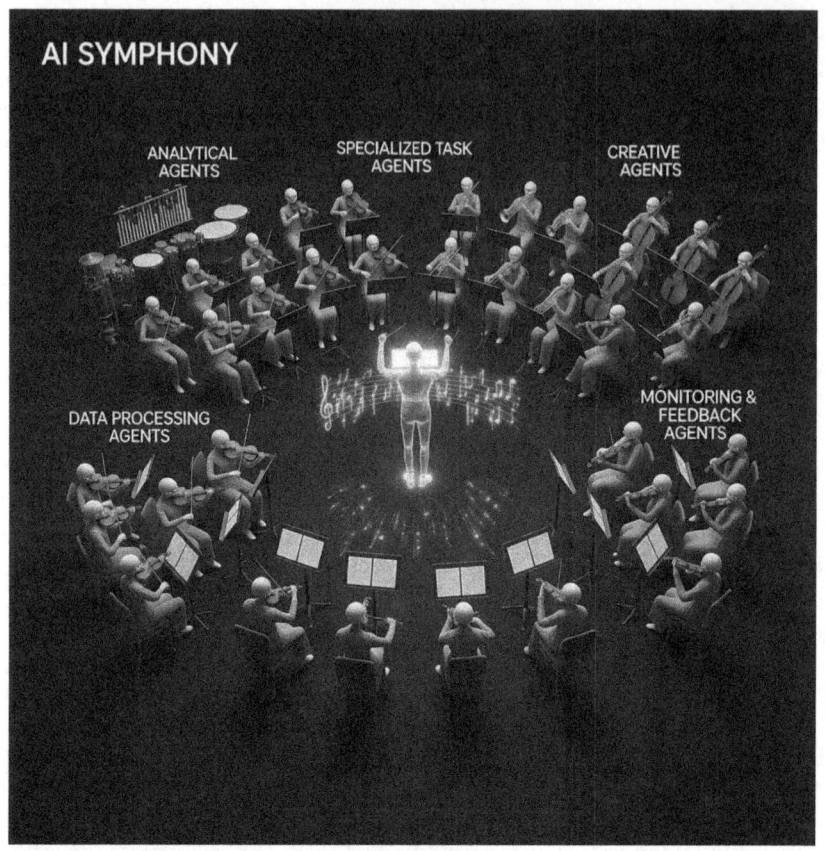

FIGURE 2.4 Orchestra analogy for agentic AI

Generated with AI using Google Gemini 2.5 Pro

fly. In the previous section, we explored the core components that constitute an AI agent—its ability to perceive, reason, and act within an environment. But just as there's a vast spectrum of talent among musicians, there exists a similar range in the capabilities of AI agents. Some agents are akin to novice players, adept at following instructions precisely but lacking in improvisation or deeper understanding. Others, however, are emerging as virtuosos, capable of complex decision-making, learning from experience, and even exhibiting a form of creativity. To understand this spectrum, we introduce the Agent Intelligence Pyramid, a framework for categorizing AI agents based on the sophistication of their cognitive abilities. This pyramid isn't about ranking agents in a competitive sense, but rather about providing a clear, first-principles understanding of the increasing levels of intelligence and autonomy we can expect from these systems. Understanding this hierarchy is vital for seizing the transformative potential of agentic AI and its implications for our work, lives, and future.

Level 1: Reactive Agents—The Foundational Layer

At the base of our Agent Intelligence Pyramid reside reactive agents. These are the simplest form of AI agents, operating on a "sense and react" principle. Think of a Roomba vacuum cleaner. It perceives its environment through sensors, detecting obstacles and dirt, and reacts with preprogrammed actions—turning away from a wall, changing direction upon encountering an object, or initiating a cleaning cycle when it detects debris. Reactive agents don't possess memory of past events, nor do they engage in planning or complex reasoning. Their actions are solely determined by the current state of their environment and a set of predefined rules. From a first-principles perspective, the intelligence of a reactive agent is largely embedded in its design. The engineers who create it anticipate the likely scenarios it will encounter and hard-code the appropriate responses. While effective for well-defined tasks in stable environments, reactive agents are brittle. Introduce an unforeseen element—a misplaced chair in the Roomba's path, for instance—and its programmed responses might prove inadequate or even counterproductive. Consider a thermostat, another example of a reactive agent. It senses the temperature and reacts by turning the heating or cooling system on or off to maintain a set point. It doesn't "understand" the concept of comfort or learn your preferred temperature over time; it simply follows its programmed instructions.

Why Does This Matter?

While seemingly rudimentary, reactive agents form the foundation of many automated systems we rely on daily. From simple chatbots providing canned responses to basic industrial control systems, their efficiency and predictability in structured environments are invaluable. Understanding their limitations, however, is key to appreciating the need for more sophisticated agent architectures.

Level 2: Deliberative Agents—Adding Planning and Goals

Moving up the pyramid, we encounter deliberative agents. These agents represent a significant step forward in complexity, as they incorporate internal representations of the world and the ability to plan and reason toward goals. Unlike their reactive counterparts, deliberative agents don't just react to immediate stimuli; they analyze their environment, consider potential future states, and choose actions that are likely to achieve their objectives. Imagine a chess-playing AI. It doesn't simply react to your moves; it evaluates numerous potential moves, considers their consequences several steps ahead, and selects the move that maximizes its chances of winning. This involves building an internal model of the chessboard, understanding the rules of the game, and employing search algorithms to explore the vast space of possible move sequences. From a first-principles perspective, the key addition here is the concept of a goal and the ability to perform search. The agent needs to define what it wants to achieve (e.g., checkmate the opponent) and then systematically explore different action sequences to find a path to that goal. This often involves techniques like minimax or Monte Carlo tree search. Consider a more mundane example: a route planning application like Google Maps. When you ask for directions, it doesn't just react to your current location. It consults a map database, considers traffic conditions, and calculates the optimal route to your destination based on your chosen criteria (e.g., shortest distance, fastest time). This involves a form of planning—a sequence of actions (turns, lane changes) designed to achieve the goal of reaching your destination efficiently.

Why Does This Matter?

Deliberative agents are key for tasks that require foresight and strategic thinking. From logistics and supply chain optimization to complex scheduling and resource allocation, their ability to plan and reason allows them to tackle problems that are beyond the capabilities of reactive systems. They bring a level of proactive decision-making that unlocks significant value.

REAL-WORLD EXAMPLE

Consider the evolution of warehouse automation. Early automated guided vehicles (AGVs) were essentially reactive agents, following predefined paths marked on the floor. Modern warehouse robots, however, are increasingly deliberative. Equipped with advanced sensors and planning algorithms, they can dynamically navigate complex environments, optimize routes to pick and place items, and even coordinate their actions with other robots to fulfil orders efficiently. This shift toward deliberative agency significantly increases flexibility and efficiency in warehouse operations.

Level 3: Learning Agents—Adapting and Improving

The next level of our pyramid is occupied by learning agents. These agents possess the remarkable ability to improve their performance over time through experience. They don't just follow preprogrammed rules or static plans; they learn from their successes and failures, adapting their behavior to become more effective in their environment. This adaptability is a hallmark of more advanced forms of intelligence. Think of a self-driving car. While it utilizes deliberative planning to navigate roads, its true power lies in its ability to learn from the vast amounts of data it collects—recognizing patterns in traffic flow, understanding pedestrian behavior, and adapting to unforeseen circumstances like road closures or inclement weather. From a first-principles perspective, learning agents incorporate mechanisms for updating their internal models and decision-making processes based on new information. This often involves machine learning algorithms like reinforcement learning, where the agent learns through trial and error, receiving rewards for desirable actions and penalties for undesirable ones. Consider a spam filter in your email inbox. Initially, it might make mistakes, flagging legitimate emails as spam or letting some spam slip through. However, as you mark emails as "spam" or "not spam," the filter learns from your feedback, refining its algorithms to better distinguish between wanted and unwanted messages. This continuous learning process allows it to adapt to evolving spam techniques and become increasingly accurate over time.

Why Does This Matter?

Learning agents are essential for tackling dynamic and unpredictable environments where preprogrammed solutions are insufficient. Their ability to adapt and improve makes them invaluable in fields like personalized medicine, fraud detection, and cybersecurity, where the landscape is constantly changing.

Level 4: Collaborative Agents—Mastering Cooperation

At the peak of our Agent Intelligence Pyramid, we find collaborative agents. These agents possess not only individual intelligence but also the ability to interact and cooperate effectively with other agents, both artificial and human, to achieve shared goals. This requires communication, coordination, and an understanding of other agents' intentions and capabilities. Imagine a team of robotic surgeons working together in an operating room. Each robot specializes in a specific task, and they need to coordinate their movements precisely to perform complex procedures. This involves sharing information about their progress, anticipating each other's actions, and adapting their plans in response to unforeseen complications. From a first-principles perspective, collaborative agents require mechanisms for communication, negotiation, and potentially even the ability to form and maintain shared mental models of the task and the capabilities of their collaborators. Consider a team of autonomous vehicles navigating a busy city. They need to communicate with each other to avoid collisions, optimize traffic flow, and adapt to changing road conditions. This involves sharing information about their location, speed, and intended maneuvers, as well as understanding the traffic rules and the expected behavior of other vehicles.

Why Does This Matter?

Collaborative agents are essential for tackling complex problems that require the combined skills and resources of multiple entities. From distributed scientific research and large-scale infrastructure management to collaborative manufacturing and disaster response, their ability to work together unlocks new possibilities and efficiencies.

REAL-WORLD EXAMPLE

The development of multi-agent systems is transforming logistics. Imagine a fleet of delivery drones coordinating their routes and schedules to ensure timely delivery of packages. These drones not only navigate independently but also communicate with each other to avoid congestion, optimize delivery paths based on real-time information, and even re-allocate tasks in case of drone malfunction or unforeseen delays. This collaborative approach significantly enhances the efficiency and resilience of delivery networks.

The Agent Intelligence Pyramid provides a valuable framework for understanding the diverse capabilities of AI agents and their potential evolution. From the simple reactivity of a thermostat to the sophisticated cooperation of collaborative agents at the peak, this model highlights the increasing levels of cognitive sophistication and autonomy we are witnessing in these systems. Understanding these levels is not merely an academic exercise; it's essential for businesses seeking to leverage the power of AI agents effectively, for policymakers grappling with the societal implications of this technology, and for individuals seeking to navigate a future increasingly shaped by intelligent machines. As we move forward, the distinctions between these levels will become increasingly important in determining the roles AI agents will play in our work, our lives, and our future. This framework will serve as a foundation as we dig deeper into the transition from traditional AI to the more dynamic and adaptable world of agentic systems in the next section.

FROM TRADITIONAL AI TO AGENTIC SYSTEMS

Imagine a seasoned call center agent, meticulously following a flowchart on their screen to address customer queries. Each step is predetermined, each answer scripted. This interaction, while seemingly intelligent, represents the essence of traditional AI—a system designed to execute specific tasks based on predefined rules or learned patterns, but lacking the autonomy to truly understand, adapt, and act independently. Now, picture a different scenario: a personal assistant AI, seamlessly managing your schedule, proactively booking flights based on your preferences and calendar availability, and even rescheduling meetings when conflicts arise, all without requiring explicit, step-by-step instructions. This shift, from reactive tools to proactive partners, embodies the evolution from traditional AI to the burgeoning world of agentic systems. This section will explore this transformative journey, tracing the key differences and highlighting the driving forces behind this paradigm shift.

The Evolution of Intelligence

The journey from traditional AI to agentic systems represents one of the most significant paradigms shifts in the field of artificial intelligence. Early AI systems were like that solo pianist, confined to rigid rules and predetermined responses. Rule-based systems of the 1980s could play their "piece" perfectly—whether it was diagnosing specific medical conditions or playing chess—but lacked the ability to adapt or learn from experience.

We explained the early stages of AI evolution in Chapter 1; we will focus now on the rise of agentic AI (2020 to now).

Figure 2.5 illustrates the growth trend in the field of LLM-based autonomous agents. The papers' authors present the cumulative number of papers published from January 2021 to August 2023. Different colors represent various agent categories. For example, a game agent aims to simulate a game player, while a tool agent mainly focuses on tool using. For each time period, a curated list of studies with diverse agent categories is provided.

The machine learning revolution of the 2000s introduced systems that could learn from data, much like a musician learning from practice. Yet these systems still operated within narrow domains. The deep learning breakthrough of the 2010s expanded these capabilities dramatically, enabling systems to recognize patterns and make decisions with unprecedented accuracy.

The LLM Catalyst

The recent explosion of interest and progress in agentic AI is largely fueled by advancements in large language models (LLMs). Models like GPT-4.5 and its

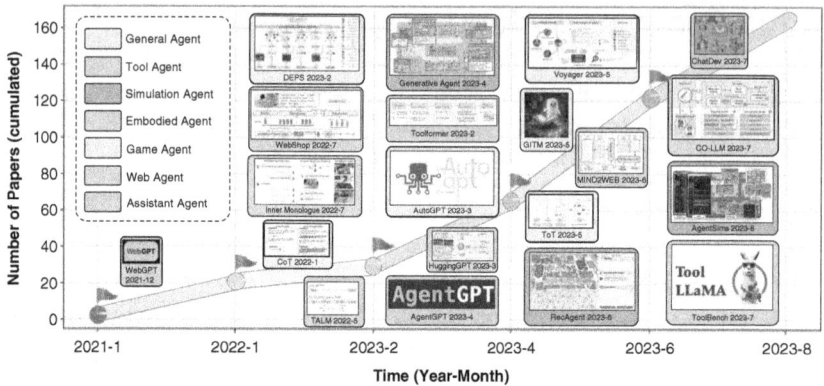

FIGURE 2.5   Recent evolution of agentic papers

Springer Nature / https://arxiv.org/abs/2308.11432 / last accessed March 19, 2025 / CC BY 4.0

successors have demonstrated an unprecedented ability to understand and generate human-quality text. This breakthrough has provided AI agents with a powerful tool for natural language understanding, communication, and reasoning, enabling them to interact with their environment and with humans in more sophisticated ways. LLMs provide the "cognitive fuel" for agents to understand complex instructions, break down goals into subtasks, and generate plans to achieve them. They allow agents to not just process information, but to comprehend its meaning and context in a way that was previously unattainable.

Consider how the Agent Intelligence Pyramid we discussed in the previous section maps onto this evolution. Reactive agents, at the base, represent early forms of AI. Deliberative and learning agents embody a transition toward greater autonomy, and collaborative agents showcase the potential for complex, goal-oriented interactions. Agentic AI is essentially the realization of the higher levels of that pyramid, powered by advancements like LLMs.

Dr. Dario Amodei, CEO of Anthropic, describes in his famous essay "Machines of Loving Grace" what he calls "Powerful AI"—the likely next evolution of today's large language models (LLMs). According to Amodei, these advanced systems might retain similarities to current LLMs but could feature different architectures, involve multiple interacting models, or employ new training methods. What would truly define this Powerful AI is its capabilities: it would surpass Nobel Prize–winning intellect across domains like biology, programming, mathematics, engineering, and writing—solving unsolved mathematical theorems, creating exceptional novels, and developing complex software from scratch.

These models became the common language through which different components of AI systems could communicate and coordinate, much like how musical notation enables orchestra members to play together. This breakthrough laid the groundwork for truly agentic systems.

The Rise of Agency

The transition to agentic systems represents a fundamental shift along each level of the Agent Intelligence Pyramid we explored earlier. At the base level, perception evolved from simple pattern recognition to contextual understanding. Decision-making transformed from predetermined rules to dynamic reasoning about goals and means. Action capability expanded from single-task execution to coordinated, multistep plans.

The emergence of agentic AI marks a significant departure from these traditional approaches. At its core, agentic AI is characterized by autonomy and goal orientation. As we discussed in the previous section, AI agents possess the ability to perceive their environment, reason about it, and act to achieve specific goals. This inherent drive toward a defined objective, coupled with the capacity to make independent decisions about how to reach it, distinguishes agentic systems from their predecessors. Instead of passively executing instructions or making predictions based on learned patterns, agentic AI actively seeks out information, formulates plans, and executes actions to achieve its designated aims. This is a proactive rather than a reactive stance.

Think back to our orchestra analogy. Traditional AI is like having individual musicians who are incredibly skilled but require a conductor for every piece. Agentic AI, in contrast, envisions each section of the orchestra, or even individual musicians, capable of understanding the overall goal of the performance and dynamically adjusting their playing, improvising, and collaborating with others to achieve a harmonious and impactful result, perhaps with a more strategic guidance from the conductor rather than a strict moment-to-moment direction. This is where we see real potential and flexibility.

Orchestrating Intelligence

Returning to our orchestra metaphor, modern agentic systems demonstrate what we might call *orchestrated intelligence*. Each component (agent) possesses specific capabilities, but their true power emerges from their ability to coordinate and collaborate. This mirrors how individual musicians in an orchestra create harmony through coordinated yet independent action. The whole is greater than the sum of its parts.

Why Does This Matter?

This transformation has profound implications for how we interact with AI systems. Traditional AI tools required explicit instructions and operated within strict boundaries. Agentic systems, in contrast, can understand our intentions, adapt to changing circumstances, and work collaboratively toward complex goals. For businesses and individuals alike, this means shifting from thinking about AI as a tool to thinking about it as a capable collaborator. The possibilities for use are greatly enhanced with this kind of system.

As we move forward, understanding this evolution helps us better prepare for the future of human-AI collaboration. The next section will explore expert perspectives on how this transformation is already reshaping various industries and what it means for our future work and lives.

REAL-WORLD EXAMPLE

Consider the development of AI-powered customer service agents. Early chatbots relied on preprogrammed scripts and keyword recognition, often leading to frustrating and impersonal interactions. Modern agentic AI systems, powered by LLMs, can understand the nuances of customer requests, access relevant information from various sources, and dynamically generate personalized responses, often resolving complex issues without human intervention. This represents a significant leap in capability, moving from reactive information retrieval to proactive problem-solving.

Key Differences and the Spectrum of Agency

To further clarify the distinction, let's examine some key differences between traditional AI and agentic systems:

- **Goal setting:** Traditional AI typically requires explicit goals and instructions from humans. Agentic AI can be given high-level goals and then independently formulate subgoals and plans to achieve them.
- **Autonomy:** Traditional AI operates within predefined parameters. Agentic AI possesses a greater degree of autonomy in decision-making and action selection.
- **Adaptability:** While machine learning models can adapt to new data, agentic AI can adapt its strategies and plans in real time based on environmental feedback.

- **Interaction:** Traditional AI often interacts in a limited, transactional manner. Agentic AI can engage in more complex, conversational, and collaborative interactions with both humans and other agents.

It's important to recognize that the transition from traditional AI to agentic systems is not a binary switch but rather a spectrum. We are witnessing a gradual evolution, with many current AI systems exhibiting characteristics of both approaches. A self-driving car, for example, uses traditional machine learning for object recognition but also employs agentic principles for navigation and decision-making in complex traffic scenarios.

Thinking again of our orchestral analogy, we can visualize this spectrum. At one end, we have solo musicians playing strictly from sheet music (traditional AI). Moving along the spectrum, we see musicians with more freedom to interpret and embellish the score (advanced ML). Further along, we have small ensembles collaborating and improvising within a defined structure (early agentic systems). And at the far end, we envision a full orchestra where individual sections and musicians possess a deep understanding of the composer's intent and can dynamically adapt their performance to create a truly breathtaking and novel experience (fully realized agentic AI). We are working toward that full and beautiful orchestral performance with our AI systems.

Why Does This Matter?

Understanding this spectrum allows us to appreciate the varying levels of sophistication and capability within the broader landscape of AI. It helps us to identify where agentic principles are already being applied and where their adoption could lead to significant advancements.

The journey from traditional AI to agentic systems represents a fundamental shift in how we conceive, design, and interact with artificial intelligence. While traditional AI has provided us with powerful tools for automation and analysis, the emergence of agentic AI, fueled by advancements in areas like LLMs, promises a future where AI systems can act as true partners, tackling complex problems with autonomy, adaptability, and a clear sense of purpose. Understanding this evolution, from the rule-based systems of the past to the goal-oriented agents of the present and future, is critical for navigating the transformative potential of this technology. This transition, built upon the foundations we established with the Agent Intelligence Pyramid, sets the stage for us to explore the practical implications and exciting possibilities that lie ahead as we explore expert insights on the nature of agency in the next section.

EXPERT INSIGHT: LEADING AI RESEARCHERS

Imagine sitting in on a late-night conversation between the architects of our future—the leading researchers pushing the boundaries of artificial intelligence. The air crackles with ideas as they debate the very nature of agency in machines, the ethical considerations, and the practical challenges of building truly intelligent agents. While we've explored the building blocks of agency and its evolutionary path, gaining insight from those at the cutting edge provides a critical perspective. This section brings those expert voices into our discussion, offering their unique viewpoints on the definition, development, and the future of agentic AI. Their insights, grounded in years of research and practical experimentation, provide a vital complement to our first-principles exploration, illuminating the path forward and highlighting the critical questions that remain. This is how we can really grasp the challenges ahead.

AI agency research is a rapidly evolving field, with researchers worldwide exploring how artificial intelligence can exhibit goal-directed behavior and operate autonomously.

Emergence of Agency

What does it truly mean for an AI to possess agency? While we've established a working definition rooted in the ability to perceive, reason, and act, the nuances of this concept are a subject of ongoing discussion within the research community. Breaking this down using first principles, we can see that researchers are grappling with how to imbue AI systems with genuine intentionality—the ability to form goals that are not simply preprogrammed but arise from an understanding of the environment and the agent's own capabilities. This also involves developing robust mechanisms for belief representation—allowing agents to build and maintain accurate models of the world and update those models based on new information. Furthermore, the action selection process is a key area of focus, moving beyond simple pattern matching to enable agents to make informed choices that align with their goals and beliefs. These are the key concepts that researchers are trying to understand.

The challenge lies in moving beyond systems that merely simulate agency to creating those that genuinely possess it. As a leading expert in robotics and embodied AI explains, "True agency isn't just about executing a sequence of commands. It's about the ability to adapt, to learn from mistakes, and to pursue goals even when faced with unexpected obstacles." This highlights the importance of endowing agents with the capacity for meta-cognition—the ability to think about their own thinking, to evaluate their performance, and to adjust their strategies accordingly. From a research perspective, this involves exploring novel architectures that allow for greater flexibility and adaptability, moving beyond traditional fixed algorithms to systems that can dynamically reconfigure themselves based on experience.

Researchers at leading organizations like OpenAI, Anthropic, and Google DeepMind are investigating how complex, goal-directed behaviors emerge from simpler components in AI systems. This phenomenon, often referred to as *emergent behavior*, highlights that agency is not directly programmed but arises from sophisticated learning algorithms interacting with dynamic environments. For instance, OpenAI's work on reinforcement learning demonstrates how agents can develop strategies to achieve objectives without explicit programming. This is a key step in truly autonomous behavior.

Architectural Approaches

Academic institutions such as Stanford University and UC Berkeley are focusing on the architectural design of AI systems. This includes studying how components like perception, planning, and execution can be structured to enable agentic behavior. The Stanford AI Index Report emphasizes the importance of modular architectures in creating scalable and adaptable AI systems.

Alignment and Safety

Fundamentally, the research community is deeply engaged with the question of AI safety and alignment. Ensuring that increasingly autonomous AI agents act in accordance with human values and intentions is paramount. This is a complex challenge, requiring research into methods for specifying and verifying agent goals, preventing unintended consequences, and building robust safeguards against misuse.

In fact, I am personally involved with the Cambridge AI Safety Hub in 2025, where we are working on a paper investigating the misalignment of AI agents. Our project focuses on how the behavior of LLMs can differ significantly when embedded within an agent architecture compared to their performance in standard dialogue-based settings. We hypothesize that current methods for aligning LLMs through techniques like Reinforcement Learning from Human Feedback (RLHF) may be insufficient to guarantee the safety of LLM agents in real-world scenarios where they have the opportunity to take independent actions. We are developing datasets of environments where LLM agents might perform misaligned actions to benchmark their behavior against their dialogue-based alignment.

Ensuring that AI systems align with human values is a critical area of research. Institutions like MIT and Cambridge University are at the forefront of this effort. For example, the Cambridge Centre for the Study of Existential Risk investigates how to ensure that AI systems behave reliably and ethically when deployed in real-world scenarios. This involves addressing challenges such as the "deployment gap," where AI systems may behave differently in controlled testing environments compared to real-world applications.

Current Areas of Investigation

The following are current areas of investigation:

Meta-Learning Meta-learning, or "learning to learn," is a key focus for researchers aiming to create adaptable AI agents. By enabling systems to generalize across tasks, meta-learning moves beyond task-specific models to more flexible solutions. McKinsey's 2024 report highlights how advancements in meta-learning are driving innovation in AI adaptability.

Multi-Agent Systems The coordination of multiple AI agents—both among themselves and with humans—is another prominent research area. Frameworks for cooperation are being developed to ensure effective collaboration, parallel to an orchestra where each musician (or agent) plays a role in harmony with others.

Transparency and Explainability Improving transparency in decision-making processes is vital for nurturing trust in AI systems. Researchers are working on techniques to make AI decisions more interpretable, ensuring that users understand the rationale behind an agent's actions.

Safety and Future Directions The safety of autonomous AI agents remains a top priority. Researchers are addressing challenges such as ensuring consistent behavior in unpredictable environments and mitigating risks associated with generative AI tools. According to McKinsey's 2024 survey, organizations are increasingly investing in safety measures as they integrate generative AI into their operations.

Promising Directions Looking ahead, researchers are focusing on:
- **Robust alignment techniques:** Developing methods to ensure that AI systems consistently act in accordance with human values
- **Enhanced cooperation protocols:** Creating frameworks for seamless human-AI collaboration
- **Ethical integration:** Embedding ethical considerations into the design of agent architectures
- **Improved risk mitigation:** Addressing challenges like data privacy, security, and bias in generative models

KEY TAKEAWAYS

This chapter provided a first-principles examination of intelligence and agency in AI systems, breaking down the fundamental components and capabilities that enable agentic behavior. We explored how AI is evolving from traditional narrow systems to more autonomous, goal-directed agents, enabled by advances in large language models and other technologies. Understanding this transition and the underlying architecture of AI agents is essential for organizations looking to harness their transformative potential while managing associated risks.

1. **Understand intelligence and agency from first principles.**
   - KEY INSIGHTS:
     - Intelligence fundamentally involves learning and generating higher abstractions.
     - Agency requires the ability to perceive, reason, and act autonomously toward goals.
     - Complex behavior can emerge from systems of specialized agents without requiring AGI.
   - DO:
     - Break down AI capabilities into fundamental components when evaluating solutions.
     - Consider both individual agent capabilities and potential emergent behaviors.
     - Focus on practical applications rather than chasing AGI.
   - DON'T:
     - Assume more complex solutions are always better.
     - Overlook the importance of proper goal specification.
     - Confuse sophisticated pattern matching with true understanding.

2. **We are moving toward agentic systems.**
   - KEY INSIGHTS:
     - LLMs have enabled a quantum leap in AI capabilities and potential for agency.
     - The transition from traditional AI to agentic systems is gradual and continuous.
     - Different levels of agency are appropriate for different applications.
   - DO:
     - Evaluate where agentic approaches can add most value.
     - Start with simple, well-defined use cases.
     - Build in safety and control mechanisms from the beginning.

- DON'T:
  - Rush to implement agentic systems without clear objectives.
  - Ignore the importance of human oversight and control.
  - Underestimate the complexity of deployment in real-world settings.

3. **You need to understand component architecture and intelligence hierarchy.**
   - KEY INSIGHTS:
     - AI agents require four core components: perception, memory, decision-making, and action generation.
     - Agent intelligence exists on a spectrum from reactive to collaborative.
     - System architecture significantly impacts capabilities and limitations.
   - DO:
     - Design systems with clear separation of components.
     - Consider the appropriate level of intelligence for each task.
     - Plan for integration and coordination between components.
   - DON'T:
     - Overlook the importance of robust memory architecture.
     - Assume components will naturally work together effectively.
     - Underestimate the complexity of multi-agent coordination.

As we move into the next chapter on practical applications of agentic AI, we'll explore how these fundamental principles translate into real-world implementations across different industries and use cases. Understanding the theoretical foundations laid out here will be central for making informed decisions about where and how to deploy these powerful new technologies.

CHAPTER 3

The Agent Architecture: How AI Thinks and Acts

"Building truly intelligent agents requires architectures that can seamlessly integrate perception, memory, planning, and action. It's about creating a cognitive symphony, not just isolated instruments."

—Yann LeCun[1]

COGNITIVE ARCHITECTURE OF AI AGENTS

Just as a symphony orchestra creates breathtaking music through the precise coordination of diverse instruments, an AI agent's architecture orchestrates multiple components to produce intelligent behavior. This chapter will take you behind the scenes of this technological symphony, revealing how each component contributes to the harmonious whole.

Imagine stepping into the conductor's shoes of a grand orchestra. Before you, not musicians with physical instruments, but intricate algorithms and vast datasets hum with potential energy. This is the essence of an agentic AI system, and you, as the orchestrator, are trying to understand how it produces the harmonious (or sometimes discordant) symphony of its actions. Just as a conductor understands the roles of each instrument section, the dynamics between them, and how the score dictates the overall performance, understanding the cognitive architecture of AI agents is crucial to grasping how these intelligent entities "think" and subsequently act in the world. We will explore the layers of these sophisticated systems, revealing the fundamental

---

[1] https://ai.meta.com/blog/yann-lecun-advances-in-ai-research/

building blocks that enable agentic AI to perceive, process, and, ultimately, perform. We won't just be looking at code and algorithms; we'll be exploring the very mechanisms that give rise to intelligent behavior in machines, offering a first-principles perspective accessible to anyone curious about the future of intelligence.

The rise of agentic AI represents a significant leap beyond traditional AI models. While classic AI often focused on narrow tasks like image recognition or language translation, agentic AI aims for something more parallel to autonomous, goal-directed behavior. Think of it this way: a traditional AI might be a brilliant individual musician, capable of playing incredibly complex solos. An AI agent, on the other hand, is closer to the entire orchestra, with the capacity to coordinate multiple "instruments" (internal components) to achieve a complex, multifaceted performance. Understanding the cognitive architecture—the underlying structure and organization of these internal components—is the key to unlocking the potential of this revolutionary technology.

At its heart, an AI agent's cognitive architecture consists of four essential components that work in concert. These components, much like the different sections of an orchestra, each play a vital role, and their seamless interaction is what creates the overall intelligence of the agent. These core components are:

- **Perception System:** Just as a conductor must clearly hear every instrument, an agent's perception system takes in and processes information from its environment. This includes understanding natural language, processing visual data, and interpreting other sensory inputs. Modern perception systems leverage deep neural networks and transformer architectures to convert raw inputs into meaningful representations, allowing the agent to "sense" the world around it.
- **Memory Systems:** Like a conductor drawing on years of musical knowledge, agents require both working memory (for immediate task context) and long-term memory (for accumulated knowledge and experiences). These memory systems allow agents to:
  - Maintain context during extended interactions, remembering past turns in a conversation or previous steps in a task.
  - Learn from past experiences, identifying patterns and improving performance based on what has happened before.
  - Build and update world models, creating an internal representation of their environment and how it works.
  - Store and retrieve relevant knowledge, accessing information needed for specific situations and decisions.

- **Reasoning Engine:** Similar to how a conductor must make real-time decisions about tempo, dynamics, and interpretation, an agent's reasoning engine:
  - Processes information using both rule-based and neural approaches, combining structured rules with flexible learning.
  - Makes inferences and draws conclusions, going beyond the surface level of information to understand deeper meanings and implications.
  - Evaluates options and makes decisions, choosing the best course of action from a range of possibilities.
  - Plans sequences of actions to achieve goals, strategizing and thinking ahead to reach desired outcomes.
- **Action Generation:** Just as a conductor's gestures guide the orchestra, an agent's action generation system converts decisions into concrete outputs, whether text responses, API calls, or physical actions in a robotic system.

Deep Dive: Memory Architectures

Modern agent memory systems often employ a hybrid approach:

- Transformer-based working memory (limited context window)
- Vector database long-term memory (unlimited storage)
- Retrieval mechanisms to surface relevant information
- Memory consolidation to extract and store key learnings

The Symphony of Intelligence

These components don't operate in isolation; they form an integrated system, a dynamic interplay where each part influences the others. It's in this intricate dance that the true intelligence of the agent emerges, much like the beauty of a symphony arises from the coordinated interaction of individual instruments.

- Perception feeds into both working memory and reasoning, for immediate processing, and the reasoning engine, to inform decision-making.
- Reasoning, the conductor of this internal orchestra, draws upon both short-term and long-term memory to make informed decisions, ensuring actions are both contextually relevant and knowledge driven.
- Actions, the performance itself, in turn influence future perceptions, changing the environment and providing new sensory input that updates the agent's memories.
- The entire system is designed to learn and adapt over time, constantly refining its processes and improving its performance through experience.

This tight integration enables increasingly sophisticated capabilities, allowing agentic AI to move beyond simple tasks and tackle complex challenges:

- **Multistep reasoning:** Agents can solve problems that require a sequence of logical steps, breaking down complex issues into smaller, manageable parts.
- **Learning from experience:** Agents can improve their performance over time by analyzing past actions and outcomes, adapting their strategies based on what they have learned.
- **Adapting to new situations:** Agents can handle novel scenarios and unexpected changes in their environment, demonstrating flexibility and resilience.
- **Maintaining coherent long-term interactions:** Agents can engage in extended conversations and tasks, remembering past interactions and maintaining context across long periods.

Why Does This Matter?

The cognitive architecture determines what kinds of tasks an agent can tackle and how effectively it approaches them. Understanding these building blocks is therefore central for:

- **Evaluating agent capabilities:** Assessing what an AI agent is truly capable of and identifying its strengths and weaknesses
- **Choosing the right architecture for specific use cases:** Selecting the most appropriate type of agent architecture for a particular application or problem
- **Anticipating limitations and failure modes:** Understanding where an agent might struggle or fail, allowing for proactive mitigation of potential issues
- **Planning future improvements:** Identifying areas for development and enhancement to push the boundaries of agentic AI capabilities

The Human Connection

While inspired by human cognition, agent architectures don't exactly mirror the human brain. Instead, they implement core cognitive functions in ways that leverage the strengths of modern AI. It's about creating systems that are *inspired* by human intelligence, not necessarily replicas of it. This approach emphasizes:

- **Massive parallel processing:** Harnessing the power of computers to perform many calculations simultaneously, far exceeding human capacity in certain areas.

- **Perfect recall when needed:** Utilizing digital memory to achieve flawless recall of stored information, a capability that surpasses human memory in terms of accuracy and detail.
- **Explicit reasoning steps:** Designing systems where the reasoning process is transparent and traceable, allowing for analysis and debugging in ways that are difficult with the human brain.
- **Modular, upgradeable components:** Building AI systems from interchangeable parts that can be updated and improved independently, facilitating rapid progress and customization.

This creates systems that can *complement* human intelligence rather than simply trying to replicate it. Understanding how these "autonomous minds" are constructed is important, as we can then better anticipate their capabilities, predict their limitations, and, ultimately, harness their power to transform our world for the better.

The Profiling Module: Defining the Agent's Identity

Every member of an orchestra has a specific role, defined by their instrument, their section within the orchestra, and even the individual conductor's interpretation of their part. Similarly, the journey of an AI agent from raw computational power to a focused, acting entity begins with a crucial first step: defining its identity. This is the function of the *profiling module*, the component responsible for shaping the agent's persona, its intended purpose, and its operational context. Think of it as setting the stage for the agent's performance, defining the character it will play in the symphony of intelligent systems.

The profiling module essentially injects context into the agent, moving it beyond a generic problem-solving tool into a specialized entity. This "context" can encompass a range of information, much like the detailed character sketches actors use to prepare for a role. At its most basic, profiling might involve assigning the agent a specific task or domain of expertise. For example, an agent might be profiled as a "customer service representative," equipped with the knowledge and communication protocols relevant to that role. More sophisticated profiling can dig into attributes akin to personality traits, defining how the agent approaches tasks—is it cautious and analytical, or bold and experimental? Just as an orchestra might have different sections with distinct characteristics (the powerful brass, the melodic strings), different profiles equip agents with varying operational styles.

Deep Dive: Methods of Agent Profiling

- **Handcrafting:** Explicitly programming the agent's role, goals, and constraints. This offers precise control but can be labor intensive.
- **LLM generation:** Leveraging the capabilities of large language models (LLMs) to automatically generate agent profiles based on a set of guiding principles or examples. This allows for creating a diverse population of agents more efficiently.
- **Dataset alignment:** Deriving agent profiles from real-world datasets, mirroring the attributes and behaviors of individuals within that data. This ensures the simulated agents reflect real-world characteristics.

Consider, for example, designing AI agents to simulate a bustling online marketplace. The profiling module would be instrumental in creating distinct agent types: buyers with different purchasing habits and preferences, sellers with varying inventory and pricing strategies, and even moderators responsible for maintaining order. Each agent's profile, carefully crafted or generated, dictates its initial motivations and how it interacts within the simulated environment. This meticulous profiling is essential for generating realistic and insightful simulations, allowing us to study complex economic behaviors in a controlled setting.

Why Does This Matter?

Because the initial profile profoundly influences all subsequent cognitive processes. An agent profiled as a meticulous financial analyst will approach data with a different lens than an agent profiled as a creative marketing strategist. The profiling module, therefore, is not merely a preliminary step; it's the foundational act of bestowing an identity upon the AI, shaping its perceptions, its priorities, and ultimately, its actions within the complex environment it inhabits.

The Memory Module: Learning from the Past

Just as musicians in an orchestra rely on their memory of the score, past performances, and rehearsals to deliver a cohesive performance, AI agents require a mechanism to store and retrieve information: a *memory module*. This component enables agents to learn from past experiences, adapt to changing circumstances, and maintain a sense of continuity in their interactions. Without memory, an agent would be perpetually starting anew, unable to leverage prior knowledge or build upon past successes (or learn from failures). It would be like an orchestra forgetting the music after each movement, forced to start from scratch every time.

The memory module is not a monolithic block but rather a sophisticated system with various components, each serving a distinct purpose. Think of it as the orchestra's library, containing not just the current score but also annotations from previous performances, recordings of past concerts, and even biographical information about the composers. At a fundamental level, the memory module stores the agent's experiences, which can include sensory inputs, actions taken, and the outcomes of those actions. This raw data forms the basis of the agent's personal history, the record of its interactions with the world.

Deep Dive: Structures of Agent Memory

- **Unified memory:** Similar to short-term human memory, this approach keeps recent and relevant information directly accessible, often within the context window of the AI model itself. This is efficient for immediate tasks but limited in capacity.
- **Hybrid memory:** Mimicking the human brain's short-term and long-term memory, this architecture combines a temporary buffer for immediate information with an external store for persistent knowledge. This allows agents to access vast amounts of historical data efficiently.
- **Memory formats:** Exploring into how information is stored, from natural language summaries to encoded embeddings in vector databases, each offering different strengths for retrieval and processing.

Consider an AI agent tasked with managing your daily schedule. Its memory module would store information about past appointments, your preferences for meeting times, and even notes on recurring tasks. This allows the agent to not only recall upcoming events but also to anticipate your needs and proactively suggest optimal scheduling solutions based on your historical patterns. For instance, if the memory module notes that you consistently reschedule early morning meetings, it might suggest later times for future appointments, learning from your past behavior to improve future scheduling.

The ability to selectively retrieve relevant information from memory is just as fundamental as the storage itself. This involves complex mechanisms for filtering and prioritizing information based on its recency, relevance to the current situation, and overall importance. Imagine the conductor quickly referencing a specific passage in the score based on the current movement and tempo—this is analogous to the agent efficiently accessing the most pertinent memories to inform its current actions, ensuring it uses the right information at the right time.

Why Does This Matter?

Because memory is the bedrock of learning and adaptation. It transforms an AI from a reactive machine into a proactive, learning entity. As we move toward more complex and long-lived AI agents, the sophistication and efficiency of their memory modules will be a key determinant of their overall intelligence and effectiveness.

The Planning Module: Charting a Course of Action

With an understanding of its identity and a repository of past experiences, the AI agent is now ready to look toward the future and devise strategies to achieve its goals. This is the domain of the *planning module*, the cognitive engine responsible for formulating sequences of actions, anticipating potential obstacles, and optimizing pathways to success. In our orchestra analogy, this is analogous to the conductor interpreting the score, anticipating the flow of the music, and planning the transitions between movements, ensuring a cohesive and impactful performance.

The planning module operates by taking the agent's current state, its defined goals (derived from its profile), and relevant information from its memory to generate a road map for action. This process often involves breaking down complex goals into smaller, more manageable subtasks, much like a conductor might rehearse individual sections of the orchestra before bringing them together for the full piece. The planning module also needs to consider the potential consequences of different actions, weighing the risks and rewards associated with each possible path, ensuring the chosen plan is both effective and safe.

Deep Dive: Approaches to Agent Planning

- **Planning without feedback:** Generating a complete plan up front, based on initial information and without anticipating dynamic changes in the environment. This is suitable for predictable scenarios.
- **Planning with feedback:** Iteratively refining plans based on real-time observations and feedback from the environment. This allows for greater adaptability and resilience in dynamic situations.

■ **Utilizing external planners:** Leveraging specialized AI systems or tools designed specifically for planning, which can offer more sophisticated algorithms and domain-specific knowledge.

Consider an AI agent tasked with managing a complex logistics network. Its planning module would need to consider factors like delivery deadlines, transportation costs, traffic conditions, and potential disruptions to calculate optimal delivery routes. This might involve complex optimization algorithms and simulations to predict the most efficient course of action. Should unexpected delays occur, a sophisticated planning module would be able to dynamically re-plan, adjusting routes and schedules to minimize disruption, ensuring deliveries are still made as efficiently as possible despite unforeseen challenges.

The planning module isn't just about executing a predetermined script; it's about adapting to unforeseen circumstances and making strategic decisions in real time. Just as a conductor might subtly adjust the tempo or dynamics based on the audience's reaction or the acoustics of the hall, an effective planning module allows the agent to be responsive and flexible in its approach, ensuring the best possible outcome even when faced with uncertainty.

Why Does This Matter?

Because the ability to plan effectively is a hallmark of intelligent behavior. It allows AI agents to move beyond simply reacting to their immediate environment and to actively shape their future.

The Action Module: Interacting with the World

Finally, the culmination of all the internal cognitive processes lies in the *action module*, the component responsible for translating the agent's plans and decisions into tangible actions within its environment. This is the moment the orchestra begins to play, the carefully crafted plans transforming into sound. The action module is the interface through which the AI agent interacts with the world, whether that world is a digital simulation, a physical environment, or a combination of both, making its presence known and its intentions manifest.

The action module's capabilities are defined by the set of actions the agent is capable of performing. This *action space* can range from simple commands in a software interface to complex physical manipulations in a robotic system. For an AI managing your smart home, the action space might include commands like "turn on the lights," "adjust the thermostat," or "play music." For a robotic agent in a warehouse, the action space would involve physical movements like grasping objects, navigating through aisles, and placing items on shelves. The nature of these actions dictates how the agent can influence and interact with its surroundings.

The execution of actions is not always straightforward. The action module needs to consider the current state of the environment and ensure that the intended action is feasible. Just as a musician needs to ensure their instrument is in tune and their fingers are positioned correctly, the action module needs to verify the preconditions for successful action execution. Furthermore, the action module needs to handle the consequences of its actions, observing the changes in the environment and feeding that information back into the memory module for future learning, creating a continuous cycle of action and feedback.

Why Does This Matter?

Ultimately, the impact of an AI agent is determined by its ability to act effectively in the world. All the sophisticated cognitive processing in the world is meaningless if it cannot be translated into meaningful actions that achieve the agent's goals. The action module, where the theoretical meets the practical, is where the agent's intelligence manifests itself in tangible results.

Conclusion

Understanding the cognitive architecture of AI agents, with its interconnected modules for profiling, memory, planning, and action, is essential for comprehending how these intelligent systems operate. Just as a deep understanding of an orchestra's instrumentation and the conductor's score allows us to appreciate the complexity and artistry of the music, exploring the internal workings of AI agents allows us to grasp their potential and the intricacies of their "thought" processes. While each module performs a distinct function, it is the intricate interplay and communication between them that ultimately gives rise to the emergent intelligence and goal-directed behavior that defines agentic AI. In the next section, we will go deeper into one of these crucial modules, exploring the diverse mechanisms that underpin the decision-making systems of AI agents, the very heart of their intelligent actions.

DECISION-MAKING SYSTEMS

Imagine a world-class orchestra preparing for a complex symphony. Each musician, an expert in their own right, understands their instrument and the nuances of the score. Yet, without a conductor to guide them, to make decisions about tempo, dynamics, and the entry of different sections, the result would be cacophony, not harmony. Similarly, within the intricate architecture of an AI agent, the decision-making system acts as the conductor, orchestrating the flow of information and determining the agent's actions in pursuit of its goals. This "conductor" within the AI, built upon sophisticated algorithms and logic, is what transforms raw data and potential actions into purposeful, intelligent behavior. Understanding these decision-making systems is crucial to grasping how AI agents navigate the world and achieve their objectives. It's the engine room where perception meets action, and where the agent's intelligence truly comes to life, driving its behavior in a meaningful direction.

The First Principles of Decision-Making in AI Agents

At its core, decision-making, whether by a human or an AI agent, boils down to a few fundamental components. Let's break this down using first principles, stripping away the complexity to reveal the essential steps:

First, there needs to be **input**. Just as a musician needs to see the musical score, an AI agent requires sensory data or information about its environment. This could be anything from the pixels in an image for a self-driving car to the text of an email for a virtual assistant. This input provides the raw material, the context upon which the decision will be based.

Next, there's a process of **evaluation**. The agent needs a way to assess the current situation and potential actions. This often involves comparing different options based on predefined criteria or learned preferences. Think of a chess-playing AI evaluating the potential moves and their resulting board states, weighing the pros and cons of each option.

Following evaluation comes **selection**. Based on the evaluation, the agent chooses a course of action. This is where the core logic and algorithms of the decision-making system come into play. Different agents might employ various strategies here, from simple rule-based systems to complex probabilistic models, each reflecting a different approach to making the final selection.

Finally, there's **output**, the action taken based on the decision. This could be a physical movement, a digital command, or a piece of generated text. The output changes the agent's environment, which then feeds back into the system as new input, creating a continuous cycle of perception, decision, and action, a dynamic loop that drives the agent's ongoing behavior.

In AI agents, these fundamental components are realized through various technical implementations. Many research papers highlight the rise of LLM-based agents. In these sophisticated systems, the LLM itself often forms the core of the decision-making process. It leverages its vast knowledge and reasoning capabilities, honed through exposure to massive amounts of text and code, to evaluate situations and generate appropriate actions, acting as a powerful and flexible decision-making engine.

Deep Dive: Neural Architecture of Decision-Making

Modern AI agents typically implement these components through:

- Transformer-based language models for knowledge processing
- Monte Carlo tree search for option exploration
- Neural simulation networks for outcome prediction
- Reinforcement learning for action selection optimization

Navigating the Choices: Architectures of Decision

The way an AI agent makes decisions is largely determined by its underlying architecture. Think of it as different schools of thought for our AI conductor, each with its own approach to orchestrating the musical performance of decision-making. Some common approaches include:

- **Rule-based systems:** These are the most straightforward, operating on a set of "if-then" rules explicitly programmed by developers. For instance, an email filtering agent might have a rule stating, "If the subject line contains 'Urgent' and the sender is unknown, then mark as potential spam." While easy to understand and implement for simple tasks, rule-based systems can become unwieldy and difficult to maintain as complexity grows, struggling to handle nuanced or unexpected situations.
- **Reinforcement learning (RL):** Here, the agent learns through trial and error, receiving rewards or penalties based on its actions. Imagine training an AI to play a video game. It explores different strategies, and when it achieves a high score, those actions are reinforced, making it more likely to repeat them in the future. RL is particularly effective in dynamic environments where the optimal strategy is not immediately obvious and where the agent needs to learn from its own interactions.
- **Probabilistic models:** These systems make decisions based on probabilities and statistical analysis. They weigh different possible outcomes and choose the action with the highest likelihood of achieving the desired

goal. Consider a weather forecasting AI; it analyzes vast amounts of atmospheric data and uses probabilistic models to predict future weather patterns, providing the most likely forecast based on available data.

- **LLM-driven decision-making:** As discussed in the paper "A Survey on Large Language Model based Autonomous Agents,"[2] the emergence of LLMs has introduced a powerful new paradigm for decision-making. These models, capable of understanding natural language and reasoning about complex situations, can make decisions based on contextual understanding and learned patterns. For example, an LLM-powered customer service chatbot can understand the nuances of a customer's query and make decisions about the best way to respond or resolve the issue.

The choice of architecture depends heavily on the specific task and the environment in which the agent operates. Often, hybrid approaches are employed, combining the strengths of different methods. For example, an autonomous robot might use RL for navigation but rely on rule-based systems for basic safety protocols.

The Interplay of Memory, Planning, and Decision-Making

Decision-making doesn't happen in isolation. It's deeply intertwined with the other key components of an AI agent's architecture, particularly its memory and planning mechanisms, concepts we touched upon in the previous section. These three systems work in a coordinated fashion, each informing and influencing the others.

- **Memory:** Provides the context and historical data that informs decisions. Just as a conductor remembers past performances and adapts their approach, an AI agent leverages its memory to understand the current situation considering past experiences. For an LLM-based agent, this memory can manifest as the **context window**, allowing it to consider previous turns in a conversation or relevant information retrieved from a knowledge base, providing the necessary background for informed decisions.
- **Planning:** Allows the agent to anticipate future outcomes and make decisions that align with its long-term goals. Like a conductor planning the pacing of an entire symphony, an AI agent might break down a complex task into smaller steps and make decisions at each stage to move

---

[2] https://arxiv.org/pdf/2308.11432

toward the overall objective. An AI agent tasked with writing a report, for instance, would plan the different sections, research relevant information, and then make decisions about the content and structure of each paragraph, ensuring each decision contributes to the plan.

The interaction between these three systems is dynamic and iterative. The agent uses its memory to understand the current state, its planning capabilities to consider future possibilities, and its decision-making system to choose the best course of action, constantly updating its memory and refining its plans based on the outcomes of its decisions. This continuous loop of interaction ensures that the agent's decision-making is informed, strategic, and adaptive.

Decision-Making in Action: Real-World Examples

To truly appreciate the role of decision-making systems, let's consider a few concrete examples:

- **Autonomous driving:** A self-driving car constantly makes decisions based on sensor data. Its decision-making system, a complex blend of probabilistic models and rule-based systems, processes information from cameras, lidar,[3] and radar to decide whether to accelerate, brake, turn, or maintain its current course. These decisions are made in real time, with potentially life-or-death consequences, highlighting the critical importance of robust and reliable decision-making.
- **Financial trading bots:** These AI agents analyze market data and make split-second decisions about buying and selling stocks. Their decision-making systems, often leveraging sophisticated statistical models and reinforcement learning, aim to maximize profits while minimizing risks, operating in a highly dynamic and competitive environment.
- **Personalized recommendation systems:** Platforms like Netflix and Spotify use AI agents to recommend movies and music. Their decision-making systems analyze user preferences, viewing history, and trending content to decide which items are most likely to be of interest to a particular user, shaping our entertainment experiences in subtle but significant ways.

---

[3] Light Detection and Ranging (LiDAR) measures distances by timing laser light as it reflects off objects.

- **Smart home assistants:** Virtual assistants like Siri, Alexa, and Google Assistant make decisions based on voice commands and sensor data. They might decide to turn on the lights, play music, or adjust the thermostat based on the user's request and the current state of the home environment, automating and personalizing our living spaces.

These examples highlight the diverse ways in which decision-making systems are implemented in AI agents and the significant impact they have on our daily lives, shaping everything from our transportation to our entertainment and our homes.

Why Does This Matter?

Understanding the decision-making systems of AI agents is no longer the sole domain of engineers and computer scientists. As AI agents become increasingly integrated into our work and lives, it's crucial for everyone to have a basic understanding of how these "minds" arrive at their conclusions. This understanding allows us to:

- **Build trust and transparency:** Understanding the principles and architectures behind AI decisions allows us to develop greater trust in these systems and better understand why they make the choices they do, moving beyond blind faith to informed confidence.
- **Identify potential biases and limitations:** Examining the decision-making process can reveal potential biases embedded in the data or algorithms, allowing for more equitable and ethical AI development, addressing potential issues before they become widespread.
- **Collaborate effectively with AI:** As we increasingly work alongside AI agents, understanding their decision-making logic will enable more effective collaboration and task delegation, allowing us to leverage their strengths and compensate for their weaknesses.
- **Shape the future of AI:** By engaging in informed discussions about the design and deployment of AI decision-making systems, we can collectively shape the future of this transformative technology, ensuring it aligns with our values and serves our collective needs.

Conclusion

The decision-making system is the beating heart of an AI agent, the mechanism that transforms perception into action. From simple rule-based logic to the sophisticated reasoning of LLMs, these systems are diverse and constantly evolving. Understanding their fundamental principles, architectural variations, and connections to memory and planning is essential for navigating the age of intelligent machines. As we move forward, the ability to design, evaluate, and understand these systems will be paramount. In the next section, we will probe deeper into another crucial aspect of agent architecture: the mechanisms that allow AI agents to remember, learn, and adapt over time, the very foundation of their ongoing development and improvement.

Memory and Learning Mechanisms

Just as a symphony orchestra builds its repertoire through countless hours of practice and retains complex musical scores in its collective memory, AI agents must develop sophisticated mechanisms for both storing information and learning from experience. These twin capabilities—memory and learning—form the cognitive foundation that enables agents to evolve beyond simple input-output machines into systems capable of accumulating knowledge and adapting their behaviors over time. Without the ability to recall previous notes and anticipate upcoming passages, the performance would descend into chaos. Similarly, for an AI agent to navigate the complexities of the real world, it needs more than just the ability to process information in the present moment. It needs mechanisms for storing past experiences—what we call *memory*—and for adapting its behavior based on those experiences, which is the essence of learning. These two intertwined capabilities form the bedrock of an agent's intelligence, allowing it to act consistently, improve over time, and handle novel situations with increasing proficiency. Without robust memory and learning, our AI agents would be perpetually stuck in the present, repeating past mistakes and unable to leverage the rich tapestry of their interactions with the world, limiting their potential to grow and evolve.

Memory: The Agent's Retrospective Repertoire

At its core, memory within an AI agent serves the same fundamental purpose as our own: to retain information for future use. However, the ways in which AI agents store and access this information can differ significantly from the intricate biological processes within our brains. From a first-principles perspective, memory in an AI agent can be broken down into two primary categories: short-term memory and long-term memory, each serving distinct but complementary roles.

Think of *short-term memory* as the conductor's immediate focus during a performance. It holds the current musical phrase, the tempo being set, and perhaps a reminder of an upcoming difficult passage. In an AI agent, short-term memory, often implemented as a limited context window or a working memory buffer, holds the most recent perceptions, actions, and intermediate results. For instance, an agent navigating a virtual environment might store the layout of the immediate surroundings, the last few actions it took (e.g., "moved forward," "turned left"), and the sensory feedback received (e.g., "obstacle detected"). This allows the agent to make decisions based on the immediate context, like avoiding an obstacle it just encountered. This can be thought of as "unified memory," where the immediate input within the LLM's context window acts as this short-term store, providing readily accessible information for immediate processing.

Long-term memory, on the other hand, is akin to the orchestra's extensive library of musical scores. It's the repository of all the pieces they've learned and can recall for future performances. In an AI agent, long-term memory is a more persistent storage mechanism for accumulating knowledge and experiences over time. This could take the form of a database, a vector store (a sophisticated way of organizing information based on its meaning), or even patterns embedded within the agent's own neural network. An AI customer service agent, for example, might store information about past customer interactions, common issues and their resolutions, and individual customer preferences in its long-term memory. This allows it to provide personalized and efficient support, even if it hasn't interacted with that specific customer recently. Combining short-term and long-term memory creates a "hybrid memory" system, allowing agents to draw on both immediate context and past experience, leveraging the strengths of both types of memory.

The effectiveness of an agent's memory isn't just about storage capacity; it's also about *retrieval*. Like a skilled librarian efficiently finding the right score, an AI agent needs efficient mechanisms to access relevant information from its memory. This often involves sophisticated search algorithms and indexing techniques that allow the agent to quickly locate the specific information needed for the task at hand. Imagine our orchestra suddenly needs to perform a specific type of waltz. Their long-term memory, the music library, needs a system—a catalog—to quickly locate the relevant scores. Similarly, an AI agent needs efficient retrieval mechanisms to access the knowledge relevant to its current situation, ensuring it can effectively utilize its stored information.

The format in which memory is stored also plays a crucial role. Information can be stored as raw text, as structured data in a database, or as abstract numerical representations called *embeddings*. Embeddings are particularly powerful because they capture the meaning and relationships between different pieces of information, allowing the agent to make more nuanced connections. For example, storing customer inquiries as embeddings allows the AI to recognize that two differently worded questions might actually be asking about the same underlying issue, enabling more intelligent and flexible information processing.

Deep Dive: Memory Implementation

Modern AI agents typically implement memory through:

- Transformer attention mechanisms for working memory
- Vector databases for episodic storage
- Knowledge graphs for semantic relationships
- Neural networks for memory integration

Why Does This Matter?

Effective memory is the foundation upon which an AI agent builds experience and consistency. Without it, the agent would be forced to relearn everything from scratch with each new interaction, making it inefficient and unreliable, constantly starting from zero. Robust memory allows agents to build upon past successes, avoid repeating mistakes, and develop a coherent and consistent behavior over time.

Learning: Refining the Agent's Performance

While memory provides the raw material of past experience, *learning* is the process by which an AI agent refines its behavior and improves its performance over time. Thinking in terms of first principles, learning in an AI agent involves adjusting its internal parameters or strategies based on feedback from the environment or new information it encounters. This is analogous to the orchestra rehearsing a difficult piece, adjusting their playing based on the conductor's feedback until they achieve a flawless rendition, constantly refining their performance through practice and guidance.

There are several key paradigms of learning employed by AI agents, each offering different ways for agents to acquire knowledge and improve their abilities:

- **Learning from experience (reinforcement learning):** Imagine a musician practicing a challenging solo, receiving feedback after each attempt—a missed note, a rushed tempo. Through repeated trials and adjustments based on this feedback, the musician gradually improves. Similarly, reinforcement learning (RL) equips agents with the ability to learn through trial and error within an environment. The agent takes actions, receives feedback in the form of rewards or penalties, and adjusts its strategy to maximize its cumulative reward. A classic example is an AI agent learning to play a video game. It tries different actions, receives points for positive outcomes (like scoring), and learns to favor actions that lead to higher scores. Many research papers highlight RL as a key contrast to LLM-based agents, emphasizing the latter's advantage in leveraging pre-existing knowledge. However, RL remains a powerful tool for specialized skill acquisition, particularly in dynamic and interactive environments.

- **Learning from data (supervised and unsupervised learning):** Consider a music student studying recordings of master performers. They analyze the nuances of their phrasing, timing, and tone, learning to emulate their excellence. Similarly, AI agents can learn from vast amounts of data. In *supervised learning*, the agent is provided with labeled data—examples of inputs and their corresponding desired outputs. For instance, an AI agent learning to classify different musical genres might be trained on a dataset of songs labeled with their genre. *Unsupervised learning*, on the other hand, involves the agent finding patterns and structures within unlabeled data. An AI agent might analyze a vast library of music to identify recurring melodic patterns or harmonic progressions without being explicitly told what to look for, discovering hidden structures and relationships within the data itself.
- **Learning through interaction:** Think of musicians in a chamber ensemble, constantly listening to and adjusting to each other's playing. They learn to anticipate each other's moves, creating a cohesive and dynamic performance. AI agents can also learn through interaction with other agents or with humans. This can involve *collaboration*, where agents work together to achieve a common goal, learning from each other's strengths and weaknesses. It can also involve learning from *feedback* provided by humans, correcting mistakes and refining behaviors based on expert guidance. It is important to highlight how human feedback can help align agents with human values, ensuring they operate in a way that is both effective and ethically sound.

Why Does This Matter?

Learning allows AI agents to adapt to new environments, improve their skills, and solve complex problems that would be impossible to tackle with pre-programmed instructions alone.

The Symphony of Memory and Learning: A Dynamic Duet

The true power of an intelligent agent emerges from the seamless interplay between memory and learning. These are not separate functions but rather two sides of the same coin, working in concert to shape the agent's behavior.

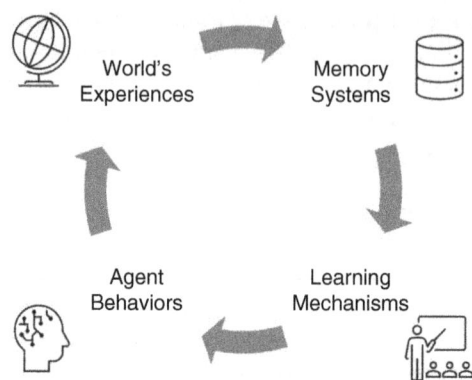

FIGURE 3.1 The circle of agentic information

Memory provides the raw material—the history of experiences—while learning is the process of analyzing and internalizing those experiences to guide future actions. This dynamic interaction is what allows agents to grow and evolve, becoming more intelligent and effective over time.

Think back to our orchestra analogy. The musicians' memory of past performances—what worked well, what didn't—informs their learning process during rehearsals. They don't just repeat the same mistakes; they use their memory to identify areas for improvement and adjust their playing accordingly, constantly refining their performance based on past experiences.

Consider an AI agent designed to manage your personal finances. Its memory stores your past spending habits, investment decisions, and financial goals. Its learning mechanisms analyze this data to identify patterns, predict future cash flow, and suggest optimized investment strategies. If a past investment performed poorly (stored in memory), the learning mechanism might adjust its future recommendations to avoid similar mistakes. As shown in Figure 3.1, this continuous feedback loop between memory and learning is what enables the agent to become increasingly effective and personalized over time.

Deep Dive: Embedding Vectors in Memory

One of the key technologies enabling sophisticated memory retrieval in AI agents is the use of embedding vectors. Imagine representing each musical note not just as a discrete entity but as a point in a multidimensional space, where the proximity of points reflects the harmonic relationship between notes. Similarly, embedding vectors transform words, phrases, or even entire experiences into numerical representations in a high-dimensional space. Information that is semantically similar (e.g., it has related meanings) will have embedding vectors that are close to each other in this space. This allows agents to perform "similarity searches" in their memory, retrieving information that is conceptually related to the current situation, even if the exact wording or context is different. This is far more powerful than simply searching for exact matches, enabling agents to understand and retrieve information based on meaning and context rather than just keywords.

Limitations and Challenges

While current memory and learning mechanisms represent significant advances, important limitations remain:

- **Catastrophic forgetting:** Agents can lose previously learned capabilities when acquiring new ones, struggling to retain old knowledge while learning new things.
- **Memory capacity:** Practical constraints on the amount of information can be stored and processed, limiting the long-term memory capabilities of agents.
- **Transfer learning:** Difficulty applying knowledge from one domain to another can make it challenging for agents to generalize learning across different tasks and environments.

Conclusion

Memory and learning are the dynamic duo that empower AI agents to move beyond simple task execution toward genuine intelligence. Memory provides the essential record of past experiences, while learning allows the agent to extract insights from that record and adapt its behavior for future success. As we continue to refine these mechanisms, our AI agents will become increasingly adept at navigating the complexities of the world, offering more personalized, efficient, and ultimately transformative solutions across a vast range of applications. Just as a great orchestra relies on the collective memory and learning of its musicians, the future of agentic AI depends on our ability to imbue these systems with the power to remember, learn, and evolve, constantly improving and adapting to new challenges and opportunities.

As we move forward to examine communication and collaboration capabilities in the next section, remember that these abilities build upon the foundation of memory and learning. An agent that can remember past interactions and learn from new information is far better equipped to communicate effectively and collaborate successfully with other agents and humans.

Communication and Collaboration Capabilities

Imagine an orchestra where each musician plays their instrument beautifully but cannot hear or coordinate with the others. The result would be chaos rather than harmony. The individual brilliance would be lost in a sea of uncoordinated sounds.

As another example, now imagine the intricate dance of a flock of birds, each seemingly acting independently yet moving in perfect synchronicity, avoiding obstacles and predators with an almost telepathic understanding. This elegant coordination isn't driven by a central conductor but emerges from the individual birds' ability to sense their environment and communicate subtle cues to their neighbors, a decentralized yet highly effective form of collaboration.

Similarly, for AI agents to work effectively in our increasingly connected world, they must master not just individual tasks but also the intricate dance of communication and collaboration—with both other agents and humans. Indeed, the true power of AI agents isn't just in their individual intelligence but in their capacity to communicate and collaborate, forming intelligent ecosystems that can tackle challenges far beyond the reach of a solitary system. This ability to connect and cooperate is a cornerstone of the agent architecture, enabling them to function effectively in complex, real-world scenarios, where tasks often require coordinated efforts and shared understanding.

At its heart, communication for AI agents mirrors the fundamental principles of communication we understand in the human world, albeit translated into the digital realm. Recall our foundational understanding of an AI agent from Chapter 2—a system with the ability to perceive, reason, and act. For agents to collaborate effectively, they need a mechanism to share their perceptions, their reasoning, and their intentions. Without this capacity for exchange, each agent would operate in isolation, a brilliant but ultimately limited entity. This section dives into the core components that enable AI agent communication and collaboration, revealing how these digital minds can orchestrate complex interactions, working together to achieve common objectives.

The Language of Agents: Sharing Information and Intentions

Consider our orchestral analogy from earlier chapters. While each instrument, representing an individual AI agent, possesses its unique capabilities, the true magic happens when they play together. But how does the trumpet know when to herald the arrival of the hero, or the violins when to weave a melancholic melody? They follow the score, a common language understood by all. Similarly, AI agents need a shared language and protocols to exchange information and coordinate their actions. This shared language is the foundation for any form of meaningful communication.

At the most fundamental level, agent communication involves the transmission of data. This data might represent a perceived change in the environment—"the temperature in sector 7 is rising"—or a reasoned conclusion—"based on current data, we predict a 90% chance of rain within the next hour." This information is often structured in specific formats, allowing agents to parse and interpret the meaning efficiently. Think of it like structured data tables that different software applications can understand and utilize. For instance, an agent monitoring traffic flow might communicate congestion levels using a standardized numerical scale, easily understood by other traffic management agents, facilitating coordinated responses to traffic issues.

However, effective communication goes beyond simply transmitting raw data. Agents also need to convey their *intentions*. Imagine an agent tasked with optimizing energy consumption in a building. It might need to communicate its plan to other agents responsible for lighting and HVAC systems: "I intend to reduce the thermostat setting by 2 degrees in the next 5 minutes to align with predicted lower occupancy." This sharing of intentions allows for proactive coordination and prevents conflicting actions. Without this clarity, the lighting agent might simultaneously be increasing illumination levels, counteracting the energy-saving efforts, highlighting the importance of intention sharing in collaborative contexts.

Deep Dive: Communication Protocols

"The seamless exchange of information between AI agents relies heavily on standardized communication protocols. These protocols define the rules and formats for data transmission, ensuring interoperability between different agent systems. Common examples include message queues, where agents can post and retrieve information asynchronously, and direct API calls, allowing for synchronous communication and immediate responses. The choice of protocol often depends on the specific needs of the application and the level of interaction required between agents."

Many research papers highlight the use of natural language processing (NLP) in facilitating communication, particularly with large language models (LLMs) acting as central controllers. This allows for more flexible and human-interpretable exchanges. Imagine agents collaborating on a research project. They could share insights and findings using natural language summaries, much like human researchers would discuss their work. This approach leverages the inherent understanding within LLMs to facilitate richer and more nuanced communication, making collaboration more intuitive and efficient.

Why Does This Matter?

Why this matters is clear: without the ability to communicate effectively, AI agents remain isolated entities, their potential severely limited. It's through the exchange of information and intentions that they can build a shared understanding of their environment and coordinate their actions to achieve complex goals. This communication infrastructure is the nervous system of any multi-agent system, enabling it to react intelligently and adapt to changing circumstances, functioning as a cohesive and coordinated whole.

Collaborative Problem Solving: Working Toward Shared Objectives

Communication is the foundation, but collaboration is the true manifestation of collective intelligence. Collaboration among AI agents involves working together toward a shared objective, leveraging the unique strengths and capabilities of each agent. This requires not just the ability to exchange information but also mechanisms for planning, coordinating, and resolving conflicts, ensuring agents can work together effectively and harmoniously.

Consider a team of robotic agents tasked with exploring a disaster zone to locate survivors. Each robot might be equipped with different sensors and capabilities—one with thermal imaging, another with advanced acoustic sensors, and a third with the ability to navigate difficult terrain. For this team to be effective, they need to collaborate. The robot with thermal imaging might detect a heat signature and communicate the location to the navigation robot, which can then navigate to the area. The acoustic sensor robot could listen for sounds of distress, further refining the search, demonstrating how diverse capabilities can be combined through collaboration for a more effective outcome.

This collaborative problem-solving often involves a degree of distributed decision-making. Instead of relying on a central command, each agent contributes to the overall strategy based on its local information and expertise. Think back to our orchestra: the conductor provides the overall vision and tempo, but the individual musicians interpret the score and make real-time adjustments to their playing based on what they hear from their colleagues.

Similarly, AI agents can adapt their actions based on the ongoing contributions of others, creating a dynamic and responsive collaborative system.

We explored in Chapter 2 the concept of a "planning module" within the agent architecture. In a collaborative setting, this planning extends beyond individual agents. Agents might need to negotiate and coordinate their individual plans to ensure they align with the overall mission. Imagine a team of autonomous vehicles coordinating their routes in a busy city. They need to communicate their intended paths to avoid collisions and optimize traffic flow. This requires a level of sophisticated planning and negotiation, ensuring each agent's individual actions contribute to the collective good, preventing conflicts and maximizing overall efficiency.

REAL-WORLD EXAMPLE

Consider a smart factory where robotic agents collaborate on the assembly line. One agent might be responsible for picking components, another for assembling them, and a third for quality control. They communicate the status of each stage of the process, ensuring a smooth and efficient workflow. If one agent encounters a problem—a missing component, for example—it can communicate this issue to the other agents, allowing them to adjust their actions accordingly and minimize downtime, demonstrating the practical benefits of collaborative agent systems in real-world applications.

Why Does This Matter?

Many of the most complex challenges we face in the real world require a coordinated effort. From managing complex supply chains to tackling climate change, no single AI agent, no matter how intelligent, can solve these problems alone. The ability for AI agents to collaborate effectively unlocks a new level of problem-solving potential, allowing us to tackle challenges that were previously insurmountable and opening new possibilities for addressing complex global issues.

Building Trust and Understanding: The Social Dynamics of Agent Teams

As AI agents become more sophisticated and their collaborations more intricate, the concept of "trust" within agent teams becomes increasingly important. Trust, in this context, isn't about emotional bonds but rather about an agent's ability to reliably predict the behavior and capabilities of its collaborators. An agent needs to trust that another agent will perform its assigned tasks competently and communicate accurate information, ensuring reliable and predictable collaboration.

Building this trust requires mechanisms for agents to assess each other's capabilities and track their performance over time. Imagine an agent learning that a particular collaborator consistently provides accurate sensor readings, while another is prone to errors. This agent will naturally place more weight on the information received from the reliable source. This dynamic can lead to the formation of specialized roles within agent teams, with certain agents becoming trusted experts in specific areas, leveraging individual strengths and promoting efficient division of labor.

Furthermore, understanding the "intentions" of other agents is crucial for effective collaboration. This goes beyond simply knowing what an agent is *doing* but understanding *why* it's doing it. Imagine two agents approaching the same resource. If they can understand each other's objectives—perhaps one needs the resource immediately for a critical task, while the other can wait—they can negotiate a solution that benefits the overall mission, resolving potential conflicts and optimizing resource allocation through mutual understanding.

As we saw in Chapter 2, the "profiling module" assigns roles and characteristics to agents. This profiling can contribute to establishing a baseline for understanding agent behavior and capabilities, fostering a degree of predictability that underpins trust. Just as understanding the personality and expertise of a human colleague helps build trust in a human team, understanding the profile of an AI agent can contribute to the same dynamic in an agent team, facilitating smoother and more reliable collaboration.

Expert Insight

Leading AI researchers emphasize the importance of transparency in AI agent communication to nurture trust. If agents can clearly explain their reasoning and intentions, it becomes easier for other agents (and humans) to understand and trust their actions. This echoes the principles of explainable AI (XAI), which aims to make the decision-making processes of AI systems more transparent and understandable, promoting trust and accountability.

Why Does This Matter?

Effective collaboration relies on mutual understanding and trust. Without these elements, agent teams can become inefficient and prone to conflict, obstructing their ability to achieve shared goals. As AI agents become more integrated into our lives and workplaces, understanding the social dynamics of these digital teams will be crucial for ensuring their effectiveness and fostering productive human-agent partnerships, building a future where humans and AI agents can work together seamlessly and effectively.

Conclusion: The Symphony of Collective Intelligence

The ability of AI agents to communicate and collaborate is far more than a mere technical feature; it's the key to unlocking their full potential. Like instruments in an orchestra, individual agents, when connected and coordinated, can create a symphony of intelligence, capable of tackling complex tasks and solving challenging problems. This section has explored the fundamental principles underlying this collaborative capability, from the basic exchange of information to the more nuanced aspects of trust and shared understanding.

As we move forward in the age of intelligent agents, the sophistication of their communication and collaboration abilities will only continue to grow. We can anticipate the development of more intuitive and efficient communication protocols, more robust mechanisms for building trust, and increasingly complex forms of collaborative problem-solving. Understanding these foundational elements is crucial for appreciating the transformative power of AI agents and preparing for a future where intelligent collaboration is the norm, not the exception. The ability for these digital minds to work together will be a defining characteristic of the next wave of technological advancement, shaping our work, our lives, and our future in profound ways, promising a new era of collaborative intelligence.

Future Watch: Next-Generation Architectures

Imagine stepping into the conductor's shoes, not of a traditional orchestra, but of a vast, interconnected network of AI agents. The instruments are no longer strings and horns, but sophisticated processing units, advanced memory systems, and intricate communication protocols. As we've explored in the preceding sections, the current agent architectures are already capable of remarkable feats. However, the symphony of tomorrow promises even greater complexity, adaptability, and ultimately, capability. Just as musical instruments have evolved over centuries, AI agent architectures are on the cusp of significant breakthroughs. This section offers a glimpse into the exciting future of how these intelligent entities will be designed, built, and interconnected, promising a new era of sophisticated AI interaction. We'll explore the emerging trends that are destined to redefine the very fabric of agentic intelligence, moving beyond the foundational structures we've established to foresee the truly revolutionary designs that lie ahead.

Modular Minds: The Rise of Composable Architectures

The current agent architectures, while powerful, often resemble monolithic structures—complex systems where components are tightly intertwined. Looking ahead, we anticipate a significant shift toward modular architectures. Think of this as moving from a single, grand piano capable of many sounds to an orchestra where each instrument, specialized for its role, contributes to the overall harmony. In a modular agent architecture, intelligence is built from distinct, self-contained modules, each responsible for a specific function. One module might handle perception, processing sensory input like visual data or natural language. Another could manage memory, storing and retrieving information efficiently. A separate module could be dedicated to planning and decision-making, while yet another focuses on communication and interaction with other agents or humans.

This approach offers several compelling advantages. First and foremost is increased flexibility and adaptability. Just as a conductor can swap out a damaged violin without disrupting the entire orchestra, a modular architecture allows for the easy replacement or upgrade of individual modules. If a new, more efficient algorithm for natural language processing emerges, it can be seamlessly integrated into the agent by replacing the existing language module. This "plug-and-play" capability significantly accelerates innovation and reduces the risk of system-wide failures, making it easier to keep agents up-to-date and improve their performance.

Secondly, modularity promotes specialization and optimization. Each module can be designed and trained for its specific task, allowing for the use of the most appropriate algorithms and data. Imagine a perception module specifically trained on vast datasets of images and videos, becoming an expert in visual understanding. This contrasts with a monolithic approach where a single, general-purpose system must handle all tasks, potentially leading to compromises in performance and efficiency. Specialization allows for focused development and optimization of each component.

Finally, modular architectures promote reusability and scalability. Well-defined modules can be reused across different agents and applications. A sophisticated planning module developed for a manufacturing robot could potentially be adapted for a personal assistant agent with minimal modifications. This reduces development time and cost and facilitates the creation of increasingly complex agent systems by combining proven components. As we move toward a world populated by diverse AI agents, the ability to easily construct and scale these intelligences will be paramount, driving efficiency and accelerating the deployment of agentic AI solutions.

Deep Dive: First Principles of Modularity

Applying first principles, we see that modularity is driven by the need to manage complexity and improve efficiency. Decomposing a complex system into smaller, independent units reduces the cognitive load required to understand and modify it. This aligns with fundamental principles of engineering and design, where breaking down problems into manageable parts is a core strategy for solving them effectively. Modularity simplifies development, maintenance, and scalability of complex systems, making them more robust and adaptable.

REAL-WORLD EXAMPLE

Consider the development of self-driving cars. Early attempts relied on tightly integrated systems. Now, companies are increasingly adopting a modular approach. They might have separate modules for sensor data processing (lidar, cameras, radar), path planning, vehicle control, and user interface. This modularity allows for specialized development teams to work concurrently and for easier integration of cutting-edge sensor technologies as they emerge, accelerating development and facilitating innovation in this complex field.

However, the shift to modularity isn't without its challenges. Effective communication and coordination between modules become critical. Just as an orchestra needs a skilled conductor to ensure the different sections play in harmony, a modular agent requires a robust communication framework to ensure seamless interaction between its components. Designing this framework, ensuring data flows efficiently and decisions are made collaboratively, is a key area of ongoing research. Furthermore, defining clear interfaces and responsibilities for each module is essential to prevent conflicts and ensure the overall system functions cohesively, requiring careful design and engineering of modular agent systems.

Deep Dive: The Foundations of Modularity Key Enabling Technologies

- **Neural routing networks:** Allowing for dynamic routing of information between different modules, enabling flexible and adaptive information flow within the agent.

- **Attention-based module selection:** Enabling the agent to dynamically select and activate relevant modules based on the current task and context, optimizing resource allocation and focusing computational power where it's most needed.
- **Dynamic neural architecture search:** Automating the process of designing and optimizing modular architectures, allowing for the discovery of novel and efficient modular designs tailored to specific tasks.
- **Meta-learning for architecture optimization:** Enabling agents to learn how to optimize their own modular architecture over time, adapting their structure and connections to improve performance and efficiency in changing environments.

Why Does This Matter?

The move toward modular architectures signifies a fundamental shift in how we build AI. It moves us away from treating intelligence as a black box and toward a more structured, engineerable approach. This will lead to more robust, adaptable, and ultimately, more capable AI agents that can be readily deployed across a wider range of applications, making AI more accessible, customizable, and impactful across diverse domains.

Dynamic and Adaptive Architectures: Intelligence That Evolves

Building upon the concept of modularity, the future of agent architectures will also embrace dynamic and adaptive capabilities. Imagine an orchestra that not only plays the notes on the page but can also improvise, learn new musical styles, and even reconfigure its instrumentation based on the environment or the audience's reaction. Similarly, dynamic agent architectures can adjust their internal structure and behavior in response to changing circumstances and new information, moving beyond fixed configurations to embrace flexibility and evolution.

Unlike static architectures with fixed configurations, dynamic architectures can reorganize their modules or adjust the connections between them on the fly. For example, an agent operating in a noisy environment might dynamically allocate more resources to its perception module to filter out irrelevant information. Conversely, in a situation requiring complex reasoning, it might prioritize its planning and decision-making modules. This adaptability allows agents to optimize their performance in diverse and unpredictable situations, moving beyond pre-programmed responses to truly intelligent adaptation, constantly adjusting to optimize performance.

Furthermore, adaptive architectures incorporate learning mechanisms that allow them to evolve over time. This goes beyond simply updating knowledge; it involves modifying the very structure of the agent based on its experiences. Imagine an agent initially designed for a specific task, like managing a warehouse inventory. Through its interactions and the data it collects, it might learn new patterns and relationships, leading it to develop new modules or refine existing ones, perhaps even acquiring the ability to optimize delivery routes or predict supply chain disruptions, expanding its capabilities and evolving beyond its initial design.

REAL-WORLD EXAMPLE

Consider a customer service chatbot. A dynamic architecture could allow the bot to identify when it's encountering a situation it can't handle. Instead of giving a generic answer, it could dynamically activate a module that connects it to a human agent, ensuring the customer gets the necessary support. An adaptive architecture could further learn from these interactions, improving its ability to handle similar complex queries in the future, potentially even creating new sub-modules to address specific recurring issues, continuously improving its ability to handle a wider range of customer needs.

The development of dynamic and adaptive architectures draws inspiration from the neuroplasticity of the human brain, its ability to reorganize itself by forming new neural connections throughout life. Mirroring this biological principle allows us to create AI agents that are more resilient, versatile, and capable of continuous improvement, mimicking the brain's remarkable ability to adapt and learn throughout life.

Why Does This Matter?

Dynamic and adaptive architectures are crucial for creating truly intelligent agents that can operate effectively in the real world. The world is complex and ever-changing, and AI agents must be able to adapt to these fluctuations. This ability to learn and evolve is key to unlocking the full potential of agentic AI, allowing them to tackle increasingly complex and nuanced tasks, and operate effectively in unpredictable real-world scenarios.

Bridging Two Worlds: Hybrid Symbolic-Neural Architectures

As we look toward the future, it's becoming increasingly clear that a single architectural approach may not be sufficient to address the diverse challenges and opportunities presented by AI agents. The most promising path forward lies in **hybrid architectures**, which combine the strengths of different approaches to create more powerful and versatile systems. Think of a symphony orchestra that occasionally incorporates electronic instruments or unconventional sound sources to create entirely new musical experiences, expanding its sonic palette and pushing creative boundaries.

Hybrid architectures might combine the structured clarity of symbolic AI with the learning prowess of connectionist models. For example, an agent might use a symbolic reasoning module for high-level planning and decision-making, while relying on neural networks for complex pattern recognition and sensory processing. This allows the agent to leverage the strengths of each approach, achieving a balance between explicit knowledge representation and the ability to learn from vast amounts of data, combining the best of both worlds.

Another form of hybrid architecture involves integrating reactive and deliberative components. A reactive component allows the agent to respond quickly and efficiently to immediate stimuli, like a reflex action. A deliberative component, on the other hand, enables the agent to engage in more complex planning and reasoning, considering long-term goals and potential consequences. A self-driving car, for instance, needs both reactive capabilities to make split-second decisions to avoid obstacles and deliberative capabilities to plan the optimal route to its destination, combining immediate responsiveness with long-term planning.

REAL-WORLD EXAMPLE

Imagine a financial trading agent. A hybrid architecture might use a reactive component to execute trades based on pre-defined rules and real-time market fluctuations. Simultaneously, a deliberative component could analyze broader economic trends and news events to identify potential investment opportunities or risks, adjusting the trading strategy accordingly, combining immediate tactical execution with strategic long-term planning.

Deep Dive: Neural-Symbolic Integration Technical Approaches

- **Differentiable logic programming:** Allowing for the integration of logical reasoning within neural networks, enabling agents to perform symbolic reasoning using gradient-based learning.

- **Neuro-symbolic program synthesis:** Enabling the automatic generation of symbolic programs from neural network representations, bridging the gap between neural learning and symbolic program execution.
- **Hybrid knowledge graphs:** Combining the structured knowledge representation of knowledge graphs with the learning capabilities of neural networks, creating rich and flexible knowledge bases that can be both reasoned over and learned from.
- **Symbolic rule extraction from neural networks:** Enabling the extraction of symbolic rules from trained neural networks, making the decision-making processes of neural networks more transparent and understandable, bridging the gap between black-box neural networks and interpretable symbolic rules.

Hybrid architectures can also involve combining different learning paradigms, such as reinforcement learning for acquiring skills through trial and error and supervised learning for leveraging labeled data. This allows agents to learn in a more comprehensive and efficient manner, drawing upon diverse sources of information and learning signals, maximizing learning efficiency and versatility.

Why Does This Matter?

Hybrid architectures represent a pragmatic approach to building the next generation of AI agents. Selectively combining the best features of different architectural styles allows us to create systems that are more robust, adaptable, and capable of tackling a wider range of complex tasks. This blending of approaches is likely to be a defining characteristic of future AI development, leading to more powerful and versatile AI systems.

Enhanced Memory and Reflection

Perhaps the most transformative architectural innovation is the development of more sophisticated memory and self-reflection capabilities. Next-generation agents will be able to learn from experience, refine their own cognitive processes, and develop increasingly sophisticated mental models, moving beyond simple information storage to deeper cognitive capabilities.

Key advances include:

- **Hierarchical memory systems:** Systems that combine episodic and semantic memory, allowing agents to store both specific experiences and general knowledge in a structured and interconnected way.

- **Meta-learning capabilities:** Enabling agents to learn how to learn more effectively, refining their learning strategies and adapting to new learning challenges.
- **Self-modification of cognitive architectures:** Allowing agents to modify their own internal architecture based on experience, adapting their structure and functionality to optimize performance over time.
- **Causal learning and model building:** Enabling agents to learn causal relationships and build more accurate and robust models of the world, going beyond correlation to understand cause and effect.

For businesses, these enhanced capabilities mean agents that can:

- **Continuously improve their performance** without explicit retraining, reducing the need for constant human intervention and improving long-term efficiency.
- **Develop deeper understanding of specific business contexts**, becoming more attuned to the nuances and complexities of particular industries and organizations.
- **Transfer learning** more effectively across tasks, applying knowledge gained in one area to new challenges in related domains, improving versatility and reducing the need for task-specific training from scratch.
- Provide **more transparent reasoning** about their decisions, enhancing trust and accountability and making it easier for humans to understand and collaborate with AI agents.

Conclusion

The future of AI agent architectures is one of increasing complexity, flexibility, and adaptability. We are moving beyond monolithic designs toward modular systems that can be easily upgraded and specialized. Dynamic architectures will allow agents to reconfigure themselves in response to changing circumstances, while adaptive architectures will enable continuous learning and evolution. Ultimately, hybrid architectures, combining the best aspects of different approaches, promise to deliver the most powerful and versatile AI agents. Just as the orchestra has evolved over centuries, incorporating new instruments and musical styles, so too will AI agent architectures continue to evolve, driven by the relentless pursuit of more intelligent and capable systems. This ongoing evolution promises a future where AI agents can seamlessly integrate into our lives, transforming our work, our leisure, and our understanding of intelligence itself. This sets the stage for the next part of our exploration, where we examine the real-world impact of these increasingly sophisticated minds, examining how these advancements are shaping our world.

KEY TAKEAWAYS

AI agent architecture represents the fundamental blueprint for creating intelligent systems capable of perceiving, reasoning, and acting in the world. Understanding these architectures is crucial for anyone working with or impacted by AI, as they determine both the capabilities and limitations of artificial intelligence systems, shaping what AI can and cannot do.

AI agents are sophisticated systems comprised of interconnected modules that enable them to perceive, reason, act, and learn. Understanding their cognitive architecture, including memory, planning, decision-making, and communication mechanisms, is crucial for appreciating their capabilities and potential impact. Future trends point toward more modular, adaptive, and hybrid architectures that will enhance their intelligence and versatility, shaping the future of AI development.

1. **Understanding the core components unlocks comprehension.**
   - KEY INSIGHTS:
     - AI agents are not monolithic black boxes but are built upon fundamental components that mirror cognitive processes.
     - The four key components—Perception, Memory, Reasoning, and Action—provide a framework for understanding any agent's capabilities.
     - Different memory systems (short-term and long-term) and learning paradigms (reinforcement, supervised, unsupervised) enable diverse forms of intelligence, allowing for specialization and adaptation to different tasks and environments.
   - DO:
     - When evaluating an AI agent, consider its capabilities within each of the core components, assessing its strengths and weaknesses in perception, memory, reasoning, and action.
     - Deconstruct complex agent behaviors by tracing the flow of information through its architecture, understanding how different components contribute to the overall behavior.
     - Explore the specific types of memory and learning mechanisms employed by a particular agent.
   - DON'T:
     - Assume all AI agents function in the same way; their architectures can vary significantly.
     - Overlook the importance of the interplay and communication between different architectural components.
     - Focus solely on the output of an agent without understanding the underlying processes.

2. Architecture shapes capability and potential.
- KEY INSIGHTS:
  - The design of an agent's architecture directly influences the types of tasks it can perform and how effectively it can perform them.
  - Modular architectures offer flexibility and adaptability, while hybrid architectures leverage the strengths of different approaches.
  - Dynamic and adaptive architectures enable agents to learn and evolve over time, increasing their resilience and versatility.
- DO:
  - Consider the architectural choices when selecting an AI agent for a specific application.
  - Recognize the trade-offs associated with different architectural approaches (e.g., rule-based vs. learning-based).
  - Stay informed about emerging architectural trends like modularity and hybrid systems.
- DON'T:
  - Expect a single architectural approach to be optimal for all tasks.
  - Underestimate the impact of architectural choices on an agent's long-term performance and adaptability.
  - Ignore the limitations imposed by the underlying architecture when evaluating an agent's capabilities.

3. Communication and collaboration are key to unleashing collective intelligence.
- KEY INSIGHTS:
  - Effective communication between AI agents, and between agents and humans, is crucial for coordinated action.
  - Shared communication protocols and the ability to convey intentions are essential for collaboration.
  - Trust and understanding within agent teams are critical for efficient and reliable collective problem-solving.
- DO:
  - Investigate the communication protocols and collaboration mechanisms employed by multi-agent systems.
  - Consider how agent profiles and shared understanding contribute to building trust within agent teams.
  - Recognize the importance of transparency in agent communication for nurturing trust and effective collaboration.
- DON'T:
  - Assume that simply connecting AI agents will automatically lead to effective collaboration.

- Overlook the challenges of ensuring interoperability and consistent communication between diverse agent systems.
- Neglect the social dynamics and the importance of trust when designing collaborative AI systems.

Understanding the intricate design and functionality of AI agent architectures provides a solid foundation for appreciating their current capabilities and anticipating their future evolution. As we move into the next chapter, we will shift our focus from the internal workings of these intelligent entities to their external interactions, exploring the diverse ways in which AI agents are being deployed and the transformative impact they are having across various industries and aspects of our lives. This transition will build upon the architectural foundations we've established in this chapter, demonstrating how these internal designs translate into real-world applications and impacts.

Remember, architecture is not just about technical design—it's about creating intelligent systems that can effectively interact with humans and their environment while continuously learning and improving. The choices we make in architectural design today will shape the capabilities and limitations of AI systems tomorrow, influencing the future trajectory of AI and its impact on society.

Two

The Transforming World

CHAPTER 4

The Five Domains of Change

"The illiterate of the twenty-first century will not be those who cannot read and write, but those who cannot learn, unlearn, and relearn."

—Alvin Toffler

Imagine the world awakening to a new symphony, one composed not of strings and horns, but of algorithms and intelligent agents. A quote attributed to a few authors, including Microsoft's founder, Bill Gates, expressed a recurrent theme about people's perception on how quickly technology can change reality "Most people overestimate what can be done in one year and underestimate what can be done in 10 years."

Indeed, when it comes to the agentic future, most people will have difficulty grasping the potential big changes ahead of us. We've explored the inner workings of these intelligent systems—their cognitive architectures, decision-making processes, and learning mechanisms. Now, it's time to turn our attention outward, to the world they are rapidly transforming.

In this chapter, we board on a journey through the five "domains of change," the key areas where agentic AI is set to reshape our world most dramatically. Think of these domains as the major movements in our AI symphony: home and personal life, work and career, education and learning, healthcare and well-being, and entertainment and leisure. Each domain represents a distinct area of human experience, yet all are interconnected, influenced, and transformed by the rising tide of intelligent agents.

This chapter is not about breathless pronouncements of utopian futures or dystopian nightmares. Instead, it's a grounded exploration of the tangible shifts already underway and the potential transformations on the horizon. We'll go deep into each domain, examining the first principles driving change, illustrating with concrete examples, and always maintaining a balanced perspective. We will acknowledge the immense opportunities agentic AI presents while also remaining clear-eyed about the challenges and risks that proactive planning and responsible development must address.

Just as understanding the score and instruments of an orchestra allows us to appreciate the complexity and artistry of music, understanding the domains of change will empower us to navigate the evolving landscape of agentic AI. This knowledge is not just for technologists or policymakers; it's for everyone who will live, work, learn, and play in a world increasingly shaped by these intelligent systems. Let's begin our exploration with the most personal and intimate domain: our homes and personal lives.

HOME AND PERSONAL LIFE REVOLUTION

Sarah walks into her kitchen after a long day at work. "Hey, Sarah, I've preheated the oven and ordered fresh groceries based on the meal plan we discussed this morning," her home AI agent announces. "I also rescheduled tomorrow's virtual doctor appointment since your quarterly review got moved up. Would you like me to start playing the new audiobook while you cook?"

This scenario isn't science fiction—it's a preview into how AI agents will transform our homes and personal lives within the next decade. While today's smart home devices and virtual assistants offer hints of this future, the emergence of agentic AI systems represents a fundamental shift in how technology will support and enhance our daily lives.

To understand this transformation, let's break it down to first principles. At its core, managing a home and personal life requires three fundamental capabilities: perception (understanding the environment and needs), planning (organizing and coordinating activities), and action (executing tasks and adapting to changes). Traditional smart home systems excel at perception through sensors but struggle with planning and adaptive action. AI agents, by contrast, combine all three capabilities through their cognitive architecture.

Deep Dive: The Agent Home Architecture

Modern AI agents use a layered architecture for home management:

- **Perception layer:** Processes input from sensors, cameras, and user communication
- **Cognitive layer:** Maintains home state model, plans activities, and makes decisions

- **Action layer:** Controls connected devices and systems, communicates with residents

This architecture enables fluid coordination across all home systems and activities.

For decades, we've interacted with AI in its more rudimentary forms—the voice assistant that plays your favorite song, the algorithm that recommends your next online purchase. These are valuable tools, but they operate on explicit commands, reactive rather than proactive. Now, a new kind of artificial intelligence is emerging: the AI agent. Unlike their predecessors, AI agents possess a degree of autonomy, capable of perceiving their environment, setting their own goals, and taking actions to achieve them. In essence, they are becoming intelligent digital assistants capable of understanding our needs, sometimes even before we articulate them ourselves.

To understand this shift, let's revisit the foundational elements that empower these agents. As we explored in Chapter 2, agentic AI isn't about a monolithic super-intelligence, but rather a carefully orchestrated system of interconnected components working toward a common objective. Think of it like this: intelligence isn't a singular entity but a capability arising from the interaction of perception, reasoning, memory, and action. An AI agent designed for your home life, for example, might use sensors (its perception) to understand the current state of your refrigerator's contents or your calendar's schedule. It then employs sophisticated reasoning algorithms to decide what actions to take, such as ordering groceries or suggesting optimal times for appointments. Critically, these agents learn and adapt, remembering your preferences and patterns (its memory) to refine their future actions. This closed-loop system of perception, reasoning, memory, and action is the core engine driving the AI agent revolution in our personal spaces.

Consider the mundane yet essential task of managing household supplies. Traditionally, this falls on us—noticing the shrinking supply of dish soap, adding it to a shopping list (mental or digital), and then physically acquiring it. An AI agent, however, can automate this entirely. Equipped with sensors in your pantry and connected to your preferred online retailers, it can monitor stock levels, predict when supplies will run low based on usage patterns, and autonomously place orders for replenishment. This isn't just about convenience; it's about freeing up mental bandwidth, allowing us to focus on more meaningful aspects of our lives.

This extends beyond mere logistical support. Imagine an AI agent acting as a personalized health and wellness companion. Continuously monitoring your sleep patterns, activity levels tracked by wearable devices, and even subtle vocal cues during conversations, allows your agent to proactively suggest adjustments to your routine. Feeling stressed? Your agent might suggest a guided meditation session or a walk in nature, understanding your past responses to such interventions. Noticing a persistent cough? It might remind you to schedule a check-up, having already cross-referenced your symptoms with publicly available health information and your personal medical history (with appropriate privacy safeguards, of course).

Shopping preferences can also be embedded into the agent; in terms of your favorite brands, attitude toward eco-friendly products and a long list. Incidentally, as we use more and more agentic capabilities to interact with the brands, the fundamentals of marketing will change: at some point, brands will have to worry how to convince your agent instead of the human, and this will force many interesting changes in the marketing industry.

Think back to our earlier analogy of the orchestra (Chapter 3). Just as a conductor orchestrates the various instruments to create a harmonious symphony, your personal AI agent can orchestrate the different smart devices and digital services in your home to create a seamless and supportive environment. Your smart lighting system adjusting its atmosphere based on your mood, your entertainment system queuing up your preferred genre for the evening, your thermostat optimizing energy consumption while maintaining your comfort—these are all individual instruments playing in concert, guided by the intelligent orchestration of your AI agent. It's not just about isolated smart devices; it's about intelligent coordination, creating a truly responsive and harmonious home ecosystem.

The implications for our daily routines are profound. Meal planning becomes less of a chore and more of a collaborative process, with your agent suggesting recipes based on your dietary needs and preferences, even considering the season and local availability of ingredients. Managing your personal finances becomes more proactive, with your agent identifying potential savings opportunities, flagging unusual spending patterns, and even negotiating better deals on utilities, credit cards, or insurance. Even something as simple as managing your to-do list can be revolutionized, with your agent prioritizing tasks based on deadlines, importance, and even your energy levels throughout the day.

The introduction of AI agents into our homes and personal lives marks a significant evolution in our relationship with technology. We are moving beyond tools that simply respond to our commands to intelligent partners that anticipate our needs and act on our behalf. This shift promises not just greater convenience but a fundamental reshaping of how we manage our time, energy, and resources, ultimately allowing us to focus on what truly matters.

Smart Home Orchestration

Think of an AI agent as a highly competent household manager—one that can simultaneously monitor all home systems, anticipate needs, and coordinate responses. Unlike traditional smart home systems that operate in silos, AI agents serve as conductors of a technological orchestra, ensuring all elements work in harmony to create a seamless living experience.

Personal Life Management

Beyond physical home management, AI agents excel at helping organize and optimize our personal lives. They can maintain comprehensive calendars, coordinating not just appointments but also travel logistics and family schedules. Budget management becomes streamlined, with agents tracking expenses, identifying savings, and even proactively managing bill payments. Furthermore, they can support personal development goals, suggesting relevant learning resources, tracking progress on fitness routines, and providing personalized encouragement.

Consider how an AI agent approaches meal planning. Rather than simply storing recipes, it considers your family's nutritional needs, dietary restrictions, schedule constraints, budget, and food preferences. It can then generate weekly meal plans, coordinate grocery deliveries, and even adapt on the fly when plans change, perhaps suggesting alternative meals based on ingredients already in the refrigerator or adjusting recipes to accommodate unexpected guests. There will be many upsides, such as reducing waste in our weekly shops; the agents can both estimate the correct amounts and even alert us before certain foods go out-of-date.

As shown in the previous example, the agentic capabilities will unlock a world of possibilities which we will have to wait to see how they evolve—I am sure many entrepreneurs around the world will take these possibilities and create incredible new business that benefit the wider society.

Family Communication Hub

One of the most transformative aspects of home AI agents is their ability to serve as intelligent communication hubs for families. They can maintain awareness of each family member's schedule, preferences, and needs, facilitating better coordination and connection beyond simple messaging.

Looking Ahead

As we move toward increasingly connected homes and complex personal lives, the role of AI agents will become more central to how we manage our domestic sphere. These systems will continue to evolve, learning from our preferences and patterns to provide ever more personalized and proactive support. The home will transform from a static space into a dynamic, responsive environment, orchestrated by intelligent agents working in the background to enhance our lives.

The transformation of home and personal life through AI agents represents just one domain of change, though a deeply personal one. As we'll explore in the next section, these same principles of intelligent assistance and coordination will reshape how we approach our professional lives.

WORK AND CAREER

Sarah walked into her office on Monday morning and opened her laptop, but instead of diving straight into her inbox, she first checked in with her AI agent team. Her research agents had already analyzed overnight market reports and prepared a summary of key trends. Her writing agent had drafted follow-up emails from last week's meetings, while her planning agent had optimized her calendar for the week ahead. Like a well-rehearsed orchestra, these AI agents worked in harmony to amplify her capabilities, allowing her to focus on strategic thinking and relationship building.

This scenario, once the realm of science fiction, is rapidly becoming reality as AI agents transform how we work. Just as an orchestra requires different instruments playing distinct but complementary parts, the modern workplace is evolving into a symphony of human and AI agent collaboration, each bringing unique strengths to create something greater than the sum of its parts.

Across industries, from nimble startups to established Fortune 500 giants, AI agents are beginning to redefine the very fabric of work and career. This shift, driven by the increasing sophistication and autonomy of these intelligent systems, promises to be as transformative as the introduction of the personal computer or the internet. In this section, we will explore how these "autonomous minds" are destined to revolutionize our professional lives, examining the fundamental changes they will bring to organizational structures, business processes, and the very nature of decision-making.

The Fundamental Shift in Work

To understand how AI agents are reshaping work and careers, we must first break down the fundamental elements of work itself:

- **Task Execution:** This encompasses the basic, often routine, activities that comprise our jobs, from data entry and scheduling to basic analysis and communication.

- **Decision-making:** This involves how we process information, evaluate options, and choose courses of action, ranging from simple choices to complex strategic judgments.
- **Collaboration:** This describes how we work with others—colleagues, clients, partners—to achieve shared goals, encompassing communication, coordination, and teamwork.
- **Value Creation:** This represents how we contribute to organizational success, encompassing innovation, problem-solving, strategic thinking, and leadership.

AI agents are revolutionizing each of these elements. For task execution, they serve as intelligent assistants that can handle routine activities with increasing autonomy. In decision-making, they act as cognitive enhancers, processing vast amounts of data to surface insights and recommendations. They also help their human operators to be aware of the typical human biases and hence avoid blind spots. For collaboration, they function as intermediaries and facilitators, breaking down communication barriers and coordinating complex workflows. In value creation, they amplify human capabilities, allowing us to focus on higher-order contributions that leverage uniquely human skills and perspectives.

Deep Dive: The AI Agent Workplace Orchestra

Just as an orchestra has different sections (strings, woodwinds, brass, percussion) working together under a conductor's direction, the AI agent workplace comprises:

- **Executive agents:** Setting strategy and coordinating other agents
- **Analysis agents:** Processing data and generating insights
- **Communication agents:** Handling information flow and collaboration
- **Implementation agents:** Executing specific tasks and processes

Organizational Transformation

The arrival of sophisticated AI agents is not merely about automating existing tasks; it's about a fundamental reshaping of how organizations are structured and how work gets done. Think back to our orchestra analogy from the previous chapter. If traditional AI was like individual instruments playing prewritten scores, agentic AI is analogous to those instruments gaining the ability to listen to each other, adapt to the conductor's (or perhaps even a self-generated) vision, and even improvise new melodies together. This newfound capacity for collaboration and autonomous action at a granular level will ripple through every department. Hierarchical structures, long the bedrock of corporate organization, will become more fluid and adaptable. Teams will increasingly comprise a blend of human experts and specialized AI agents, each contributing their unique strengths, blurring the lines between human and machine contributions.

Consider the implications for project management. Instead of relying solely on human project managers to track progress, allocate resources, and anticipate roadblocks, imagine AI agents embedded within each team, constantly monitoring their individual progress, identifying potential dependencies, and even proactively suggesting solutions to emerging challenges. These agents, communicating seamlessly with each other, can optimize workflows in real time, creating a more agile and responsive organization. This isn't about replacing human roles entirely but about augmenting them. The project manager, freed from the minutiae of task tracking, can focus on higher-level strategic planning, stakeholder management, and nurturing a collaborative environment where both human and AI contributors thrive. This shift toward more decentralized and intelligent work units necessitates a reimagining of leadership roles. Leaders will need to cultivate a deep understanding of AI agent capabilities, learn how to effectively integrate them into teams, and adopt a culture of trust and collaboration between humans and their intelligent counterparts, becoming orchestrators of human-AI teams.

Business Process Revolution

At its core, a business process is a series of steps designed to achieve a specific outcome. From processing customer orders to managing supply chains, these processes are the lifeblood of any organization. AI agents are set to trigger a revolution in how these processes are designed, executed, and optimized. Taking a first-principles approach, we can break down any business process into key components: input, transformation, and output. AI agents can enhance each of these stages. For example, in the input stage, agents can autonomously gather and analyze vast amounts of data from diverse sources, identifying patterns and insights that would be impossible for humans to detect manually. In the transformation stage, agents can automate complex tasks, make real-time decisions based on predefined rules and learned patterns, and even adapt their approach based on dynamic feedback. Finally, in the output stage, agents can generate reports, communicate insights, and even initiate downstream processes with minimal human intervention, creating a seamless and automated workflow.

Consider the impact on customer service. Instead of relying solely on human agents to handle inquiries, AI agents can autonomously resolve a significant portion of routine requests, providing instant support and freeing up human agents to focus on more complex and nuanced issues. These agents, drawing on vast knowledge bases and sophisticated natural language processing capabilities, can understand customer intent, personalize interactions, and even anticipate future needs. This isn't just about efficiency; it's about creating a fundamentally better customer experience. Similarly, in supply chain management, AI agents can monitor real-time data on inventory levels, demand fluctuations, and logistical challenges, proactively adjusting orders, optimizing routes, and mitigating potential disruptions. This level of dynamic optimization, powered by intelligent agents, can lead to significant cost savings, improved efficiency, and a more resilient supply chain. Just as the conductor in our orchestra guides the overall performance, with agentic AI, many of the individual musicians (processes) can now adjust their playing in harmony with each other, resulting in a more dynamic and responsive overall performance, creating a symphony of efficiency and responsiveness.

Decision-Making and Strategy

One of the most profound impacts of AI agents will be on how strategic decisions are made. Traditionally, strategic decision-making has relied heavily on human intuition, experience, and analysis of historical data. While these remain vital, AI agents introduce a new dimension: the ability to process and synthesize vast amounts of real-time data, identify subtle patterns and correlations, and even simulate potential outcomes with remarkable speed and accuracy. Taking a first-principles perspective, we can view decision-making as a process of evaluating options based on available information and desired outcomes. AI agents can significantly enhance both of these aspects, augmenting human capabilities and providing data-driven insights.

Imagine a financial analyst using an AI agent to assess potential investment opportunities. The agent can analyze market trends, company financials, news sentiment, and a multitude of other data points in real time, identifying potential risks and opportunities that a human analyst might miss. Furthermore, the agent can simulate various scenarios, stress-testing investment strategies against different market conditions, providing a more data-driven and robust assessment of potential outcomes. This doesn't replace the analyst's expertise, but it augments it, providing a more comprehensive and nuanced understanding of the decision landscape. Similarly, in strategic planning, AI agents can analyze market dynamics, competitor activities, and emerging trends, helping organizations identify new opportunities, anticipate potential threats, and develop more agile and adaptive strategies. This shift toward AI-augmented decision-making doesn't diminish the importance of human judgment and ethical considerations. Instead, it empowers leaders to make more informed decisions, grounded in data and insights, while still retaining the critical human elements of empathy, creativity, and ethical awareness. Just as individual musicians in our orchestra can now make small adjustments based on what they hear, AI agents provide the data and insights for human leaders to make more informed strategic decisions, guiding the overall direction of the organization with enhanced intelligence and data-driven foresight.

The New Division of Labor

This restructuring is creating new work models where humans and AI agents form dynamic teams, each member contributing their unique strengths to achieve common goals. Consider the modern marketing department as a prime example of this evolving synergy:

- **AI agents** handle data analysis, content optimization, and campaign automation, taking on data-intensive and repetitive tasks.
- **Humans** focus on strategy, brand storytelling, and stakeholder relationships, leveraging uniquely human skills in creativity, empathy, and communication.
- The **combination** delivers better results than either could achieve alone, demonstrating the power of human-AI collaboration in the workplace.

Career Implications and Opportunities

For professionals navigating this transformation, understanding how to effectively collaborate with AI agents becomes a critical career skill. The key is recognizing that AI agents are tools for amplification rather than replacement; designed to enhance human capabilities, not supplant them. They can:

- **Enhance your productivity** by handling routine tasks, freeing up time for higher-level activities.
- **Augment your decision-making** with data-driven insights, providing a more informed and nuanced perspective.
- **Expand your capabilities into new areas**, allowing you to tackle challenges previously beyond your reach.
- **Free up time for strategic thinking and relationship building**, enabling a greater focus on uniquely human skills and strategic contributions.

See "Case Study: Financial Advisory Transformation" about the Morgan Stanley wealth management AI Assistant.[1] This allows advisors to focus on

---

[1] https://www.celent.com/insights/531525129

understanding client needs, building relationships, and providing strategic guidance, shifting their role from data crunchers to trusted advisors and strategic partners.

Case Study: Financial Advisory Transformation

Morgan Stanley's implementation of AI agents has transformed how financial advisors work for wealth management. Instead of spending hours on market research and portfolio analysis, advisors now leverage AI agents to:

- Analyze market trends and identify opportunities
- Handle routine client communications
- Monitor portfolio performance in real time

This allows advisors to focus on understanding client needs, building relationships, and providing strategic guidance.

Adapting Your Career Strategy

To thrive in this new environment, professionals should proactively adapt their skillsets and career strategies, focusing on developing competencies that complement and leverage AI agent capabilities. Key areas for development include:

- **Develop AI agent literacy:** Gain a fundamental understanding of how different types of AI agents work, their capabilities, and their limitations.
- **Focus on uniquely human skills:** Strengthen abilities in areas like emotional intelligence, creative thinking, and complex problem-solving, ethical reasoning, and interpersonal communication—skills that are difficult for AI to replicate.
- **Learn to orchestrate:** Build expertise in coordinating AI agent teams to achieve desired outcomes, developing the ability to effectively manage and leverage both human and AI resources.
- **Stay adaptable:** Cultivate a mindset of continuous learning and be prepared to adapt your skills and knowledge as AI agent capabilities continue to evolve, embracing lifelong learning as a core professional competency.

Building upon these transformative shifts in work and career, we now turn to another domain undergoing profound change: education and learning.

Here, AI agents are not just changing how we work but how we acquire the very skills and knowledge needed to navigate this evolving world.

EDUCATION AND LEARNING

Imagine an orchestra where every instrument section—the strings, the woodwinds, the brass—practiced in isolation, their individual brilliance never quite coalescing into a unified symphony. This, in many ways, reflects the state of traditional education. Students, each with their unique rhythms and learning styles, often navigate a standardized curriculum designed for a hypothetical average learner. Now, picture the same orchestra where each musician has a personal AI conductor, acutely aware of their strengths and weaknesses, providing real-time feedback and tailoring practice sessions to maximize their potential. This is the transformative power AI agents are destined to unleash on the landscape of education and learning. We've explored how these intelligent entities are reshaping our homes and personal lives, and now we turn our attention to a domain fundamental to human progress: the acquisition of knowledge and skills. Just as the advent of the printing press democratized access to information, the rise of AI agents promises a new era of personalized, accessible, and deeply engaging learning experiences for all.

Personalized Learning Revolutionized

At the heart of the coming educational transformation lies the principle of personalization. For too long, the educational system has operated on a "one-size-fits-all" model, a noble ambition perhaps, but ultimately limited by the sheer complexity of human individuality. Each learner arrives with a unique configuration of prior knowledge, learning preferences, and pacing requirements. Think of it through the lens of first principles: learning, at its core, is the process of building connections between new information and existing mental models. If the delivery of new information doesn't resonate with the individual's existing framework, the connections are weak, and retention suffers. AI agents, however, possess the capacity to understand and adapt to this individual complexity with unprecedented precision, tailoring learning experiences to meet the unique needs of each student. There are also upside benefits; for example, educational AI agents have infinitive patience with students, and some shy students who might suffer in class due to the lack of interaction and ability to ask questions to human teachers, do not have those barriers talking to a machine.

These agents can analyze a student's learning patterns, identifying areas of strength and weakness with far greater nuance than any human teacher could manage across an entire classroom. They can track progress in real time, noticing when a concept isn't quite clicking and proactively offering alternative explanations or exercises tailored to the student's preferred learning style—be it visual, auditory, or kinesthetic. Imagine an agent recognizing that a student struggles with abstract mathematical concepts. Instead of simply presenting more equations, it might generate interactive visualizations or suggest real-world applications to make the concept more tangible. This isn't about dumbing down the material; it's about making it accessible and engaging in a way that resonates with the individual learner, promoting deeper comprehension and retention.

A final point to highlight, which is already happening, is that machines can provide education to everyone in environments where there is a lack of qualified human teachers such as war areas or very poor or remote geographies.

Why Does This Matter?

Personalized learning isn't just a pedagogical catchphrase; it's the key to unlocking the full potential of every learner. Catering to individual needs allows us to nurture deeper understanding, greater engagement, and a life-long love of learning. This shift moves away from a deficit-based model, which focuses on what students lack, to a strengths-based approach that celebrates individual talents and helps learners build upon their inherent capabilities, creating a more equitable and effective learning environment for all.

The AI Tutor: Always Available, Always Patient

Consider the experience of needing help with a challenging concept late at night, long after school hours. In the traditional model, students are often left to struggle on their own or rely on the availability of parents or limited online resources. AI agents step into this gap, offering a revolutionary solution: a personalized tutor, always available and infinitely patient. These intelligent companions can provide on-demand explanations, answer questions in real time, and offer personalized feedback without judgment or frustration, providing consistent and accessible support whenever and wherever it is needed.

Think of an AI agent assisting a student with a complex coding problem. Instead of simply providing the solution, it can walk the student through the logic step-by-step, identify the specific point of error, and offer hints or alternative approaches. This nurtures a deeper understanding of the underlying principles, turning moments of frustration into valuable learning opportunities. Moreover, the AI tutor can adapt its communication style to the individual student, recognizing when a more simplified explanation is needed or when the student is ready for a more advanced discussion. This level of individualized attention was previously a luxury, accessible only to a select few. Now, AI agents are democratizing access to this invaluable resource, making personalized tutoring a reality for learners everywhere.

At its core, as Figure 4.1 shows, an AI tutor operates on a sophisticated architecture. It maintains a dynamic profile of the learner, constantly updating its understanding of their knowledge level, learning style, and progress. This profile interacts with a vast knowledge base containing the curriculum content and a variety of learning resources. A dialog management system allows for natural language interaction, enabling students to ask questions and receive explanations in a conversational manner. Critically, a feedback and assessment module tracks student performance and identifies areas needing attention. Finally, a personalization engine orchestrates all these components, tailoring the learning experience based on the individual learner's needs and preferences, creating a truly individualized and adaptive learning journey.

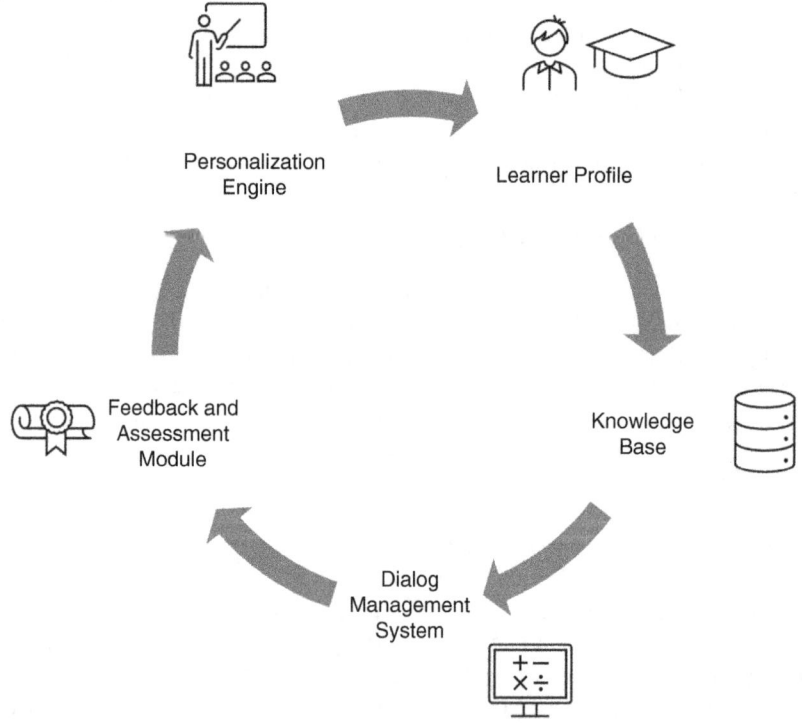

FIGURE 4.1 The architecture of an AI tutor

REAL-WORLD EXAMPLE

Imagine a language learning app powered by an AI agent. While most apps in this domain have been using traditional AI for some time, agentic capabilities will transform them to a new level of learning. The agent doesn't just present vocabulary lists and grammar rules. It engages the learner in simulated conversations, adapting the difficulty based on their fluency. It identifies recurring grammatical errors and provides targeted feedback, explaining the nuances of the language in a way that is both effective and engaging, creating a dynamic and personalized language learning experience.

A popular language app, Duolingo[2] uses AI in several ways—for adapting the difficulty questions to the learner level continuously and for generating new questions. Agentic capabilities will allow them to offer even more tailored content and faster language learning experiences.

From Passive Consumption to Active Creation

Traditional education often casts students in the role of passive recipients of information, absorbing lectures and memorizing facts. AI agents are set to flip this paradigm, empowering learners to become active creators of knowledge. Imagine an agent facilitating a project-based learning experience where students are tasked with designing a sustainable city. The agent can provide access to relevant data, suggest design tools, connect students with virtual experts in urban planning, and offer feedback on their designs. It promotes a dynamic learning environment where students are not just learning *about* something, but actively *doing* something, building deeper understanding through application and experimentation.

This shift aligns with the principle that learning is most effective when it is active and experiential. AI agents can facilitate simulations, virtual labs, and creative projects that allow students to explore concepts in a hands-on way. They can provide intelligent feedback on student creations, guiding them to refine their ideas and develop their skills. Think of an AI agent assisting a student in composing music. It can analyze the student's melodies and harmonies, suggesting improvements based on musical theory, but also encouraging creativity and individual expression. The focus shifts from rote memorization to critical thinking, problem-solving, and creative innovation, nurturing a generation of active learners and creative problem-solvers.

---

[2] https://blog.duolingo.com/large-language-model-duolingo-lessons/

Why Does This Matter?

Active learning encourages deeper engagement, promotes critical thinking, and cultivates essential skills for the twenty-first-century workforce. Empowering students to become creators allow us to equip them with the adaptability and innovative spirit needed to thrive in a rapidly changing world, preparing them for a future where creativity and problem-solving are paramount.

The Democratization of Expertise

One of the most profound impacts of AI agents in education will be the democratization of expertise. Historically, access to expert knowledge and mentorship has been limited by geography, socioeconomic status, and institutional barriers. AI agents have the potential to break down these barriers, providing learners with access to a wealth of knowledge and guidance, regardless of their location or background, leveling the educational playing field.

Imagine a student in a rural community with limited access to specialized instructors. An AI agent can connect them with virtual mentors in fields they are passionate about, providing guidance and insights that would otherwise be unavailable. These agents can curate relevant resources, facilitate virtual collaborations with peers from around the world, and provide personalized feedback based on expert-level knowledge. Consider an aspiring astrophysicist in a school with limited science resources. An AI agent can provide access to virtual telescopes, simulations of astronomical phenomena, and connect them with leading researchers in the field for virtual mentorship. This level of access to expertise was previously unimaginable for many, now democratized through the power of AI agents.

Administrative Support and Planning

Beyond direct instruction, AI agents are transforming how educational institutions operate, streamlining administrative tasks and optimizing resource allocation:

- **Curriculum planning and optimization:** Agents can analyze learning data to optimize curriculum design and identify areas for improvement, ensuring content is relevant and effective.
- **Resource allocation and scheduling:** Agents can efficiently manage resources, schedule classrooms, and optimize teacher assignments, maximizing efficiency and resource utilization. Anyone who has been involved in this activity will recognize the difficulty of this task, so any automation

will be of great benefit. Additionally, simulations on multiple alternatives are now possible.

- **Early intervention identification:** Agents can identify students who are struggling early on, allowing for timely interventions and personalized support to prevent students from falling behind.
- **Parent-teacher communication:** Agents can facilitate communication between parents and teachers, providing timely updates on student progress and streamlining communication channels.
- **Professional development support:** Agents can provide personalized professional development resources and training for educators, helping them adapt to new technologies and pedagogical approaches.

Future of Educational Institutions

As AI agents become more sophisticated, the very structure of educational institutions is evolving, moving beyond traditional models to embrace more flexible and personalized approaches:

- **Hybrid learning environments becoming standard:** Blending online and in-person learning, leveraging the strengths of both modalities and creating more flexible and engaging learning experiences.
- **Flexible scheduling and progression:** Allowing students to learn at their own pace and schedule, moving away from rigid timelines and accommodating individual learning speeds.
- **Personalized learning pathways:** Tailoring educational journeys to individual student needs, interests, and career aspirations, creating customized learning experiences.
- **Global collaboration opportunities:** Facilitating connections between students and educators across geographical boundaries, nurturing global learning communities and enriching educational experiences.
- **Lifelong learning support:** Extending learning beyond formal education, providing continuous support for skill development and knowledge acquisition throughout life, adapting to the changing demands of the modern world.

Conclusion

The integration of AI agents into education and learning signifies a paradigm shift, moving us from a standardized, passive model to one that is personalized, active, and democratized as we can see in Figure 4.2. Like the skilled conductors we envisioned at the outset, these intelligent entities are capable of orchestrating learning experiences tailored to the unique needs

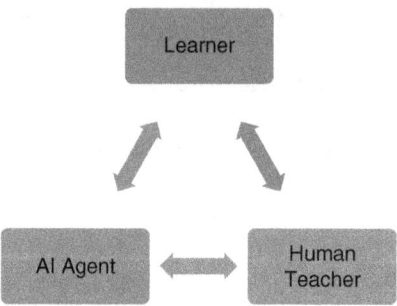

FIGURE 4.2   The collaborative learning ecosystem

and aspirations of each individual. From providing tireless, individual and patient tutoring to nurturing creative exploration and granting access to expert knowledge, AI agents are set to unlock unprecedented levels of human potential. While challenges remain—ensuring equitable access, addressing ethical considerations, and thoughtfully integrating these tools into existing educational frameworks—the transformative power of AI agents in shaping the future of learning is undeniable. As we move forward, it is critical that we embrace these advancements thoughtfully, focusing on how they can empower both learners and educators to create a more engaging, effective, and equitable learning landscape for all. This revolution in education sets the stage for equally profound changes in the realm of health and well-being, the next domain where AI agents are set to make a significant impact, which we will explore in the following section.

As we'll explore in the next section, the impact of AI agents extends far beyond traditional educational boundaries, transforming how we maintain and improve our health throughout our lives, showcasing the pervasive influence of agentic AI across all domains of human experience.

HEALTHCARE AND WELL-BEING

Sarah woke up one morning to an urgent but calm notification from her AI health agent: "I've detected some concerning patterns in your recent data that suggest early signs of diabetes risk. Would you like to review the analysis?" The agent had noticed subtle changes in her grocery purchases, slight variations in her sleep patterns from her smartwatch, and shifts in her daily movement routines—patterns that individually might mean nothing but together painted an early warning picture that no single human doctor could have spotted so soon.

This scenario isn't science fiction—it represents the emerging frontier of healthcare, where AI agents serve as vigilant health conductors, orchestrating vast symphonies of personal health data to detect the earliest whispers of potential health issues. Just as a conductor coordinates dozens of instruments to create harmony, these AI agents will harmonize multiple streams of health-relevant data to maintain our well-being, creating a personalized and proactive approach to healthcare.

Imagine a world where your body whispers its needs long before a shout of pain erupts. Picture a future where a nagging cough isn't the first sign of illness, but an almost imperceptible shift in your breathing patterns, flagged and addressed by a silent, watchful intelligence. For centuries, healthcare has largely operated in a reactive mode, intervening once symptoms manifest, and diseases take hold. We gather the most detailed information about our bodies when something has already gone wrong—a blood test after a concerning symptom, a scan when pain becomes unbearable. It's like trying to understand the intricate symphony of an orchestra only when a section plays out of tune, missing the nuances of the individual instruments and their coordinated performance in health. But what if we could continuously listen to the entire orchestra, every instrument in concert, capturing the subtle shifts and potential discords before they disrupt the harmony? This is the transformative potential of agentic AI in healthcare and well-being, shifting our focus from reaction to proactive prevention and personalized care, moving from a system focused on treating illness to one dedicated to cultivating sustained well-being.

The Current Healthcare Paradox

Today's healthcare system faces a fundamental data paradox: we have extensive data about people when they're sick but relatively little information about the journey from health to illness. It's like only hearing the crescendo of a symphony, while missing the subtle changes in melody that led there. Traditional healthcare data is episodic, collected primarily during doctor visits and hospital stays—capturing the crisis but missing the build-up. This gap in our understanding is analogous to trying to reverse-engineer a complex engine without knowing how its individual parts function optimally or how they interact when running smoothly, obstructing our ability to proactively manage health and prevent disease.

This limitation stems from several core challenges:

- **Fragmented data collection across different healthcare providers:** Patient data is often siloed across various clinics, hospitals, and specialists, creating a disjointed and incomplete health record.

- **Focus on treatment rather than prevention:** The system is largely designed to react to illness rather than proactively prevent it, emphasizing intervention over long-term wellness.
- **Limited visibility into daily health indicators:** Traditional check-ups offer snapshots in time, missing the continuous stream of data reflecting daily health fluctuations and lifestyle impacts.
- **Lack of integration between medical and lifestyle data:** Medical records are often disconnected from lifestyle data (diet, exercise, sleep, stress), obstructing a holistic understanding of health determinants.

From Reactive Treatment to Proactive Prevention

Agentic AI has the potential to bridge this critical gap. Imagine AI agents, personalized for each individual, continuously monitoring a multitude of data streams. These aren't just the readings from wearable devices, though those play a part. Think broader: inferences drawn from supermarket purchase data revealing dietary patterns, financial transaction analysis hinting at stress levels or access to resources, even anonymized community mobility data providing insights into potential exposure risks. These agents, like highly skilled conductors listening to every section of the orchestra, can detect subtle deviations from an individual's baseline, patterns that would be imperceptible to the human eye or infrequent check-ups. They can correlate these subtle signals with emerging research, identifying potential risks and recommending pre-emptive interventions—a personalized dietary adjustment, a mindfulness exercise routine, or even a subtle shift in daily schedule to optimize sleep. The goal shifts from treating illness to cultivating sustained well-being, empowering individuals to actively participate in maintaining their health and preventing disease before it takes hold.

Deep Dive: Federated Learning and Data Privacy

The following is a detailed explanation of federated learning techniques that allow AI models to learn from decentralized data sources without compromising individual privacy:

- **Decentralized learning:** Federated learning allows AI models to be trained on data distributed across numerous devices (e.g., smartphones, wearables, hospital servers) without centralizing the raw data itself.

- **Privacy preservation:** Instead of sending sensitive personal data to a central server, the AI model is sent to the devices where the data resides. Training happens locally on each device.
- **Aggregation of learning:** Only the model updates (learnings from the local data) are aggregated and shared with a central server to improve the global model. Raw data remains on the individual devices.
- **Enhanced security:** By keeping data decentralized, federated learning reduces the risk of large-scale data breaches and enhances individual privacy.
- **Applications in healthcare:** Critical for healthcare applications where patient data is highly sensitive. Allows AI to learn from vast, diverse datasets while respecting patient confidentiality and regulatory requirements like HIPAA and GDPR.

For example, training an AI model to detect early signs of disease using wearable data from millions of users. Federated learning allows this to happen without collecting and centralizing everyone's raw health data.

The Symphony of Early Detection and Personalized Intervention

The true power of agentic AI in healthcare lies not just in collecting more data, but in its ability to synthesize and interpret that data in a truly personalized manner. Traditional statistical models in healthcare often rely on population-level averages, which can mask individual variations and lead to generalized recommendations that may not be optimal for everyone. Agentic AI, however, can learn an individual's unique physiological baseline, their lifestyle patterns, and even their genetic predispositions. This allows for the early detection of subtle deviations that might be statistically insignificant at a population level but are highly meaningful for that specific person, creating a truly personalized and sensitive health monitoring system.

Consider the analogy of our orchestra again. A skilled musician can detect a single note played slightly flat within a complex chord. Similarly, an AI agent, intimately familiar with an individual's "normal" physiological symphony, can identify minor anomalies that might be early indicators of a developing issue. This early detection isn't about generating false alarms; it's about providing timely, personalized nudges toward healthier choices or, when necessary, flagging potential problems for further investigation by human clinicians, much like a conductor might bring a potentially discordant section to the attention of the musicians for refinement, ensuring the overall harmony of the performance.

For example, an AI agent might notice a subtle, consistent increase in an individual's resting heart rate coupled with a slight decrease in sleep efficiency, correlating this with publicly available data on early indicators of specific cardiovascular risks. Instead of a generic warning, the agent could recommend specific, personalized interventions: a tailored exercise plan focusing on low-impact cardio, a guided meditation app designed to improve sleep quality, or even suggesting a conversation with their physician about specific concerns, providing the doctor with valuable context and preliminary insights, facilitating more informed and proactive healthcare decisions.

Why Does This Matter?

The shift toward proactive, personalized healthcare driven by agentic AI has profound implications. For individuals, it means moving from being passive recipients of care to active participants in maintaining their well-being. Imagine receiving personalized recommendations tailored to your unique needs and circumstances, delivered at the moment they are most relevant and actionable. This empowers individuals to make informed decisions about their health, promoting a sense of ownership and control over their well-being journey.

For the healthcare system as a whole, this transition promises to be transformative. Early detection and prevention can significantly reduce the burden of chronic diseases, leading to healthier populations and lower healthcare costs. Imagine fewer emergency room visits for preventable conditions, fewer hospitalizations for late-stage illnesses, and a greater emphasis on maintaining wellness rather than simply treating sickness. Agentic AI can also streamline administrative tasks, assist in complex diagnoses, and personalize treatment plans, freeing up healthcare professionals to focus on the human aspects of care—empathy, communication, and complex decision-making, allowing them to leverage their uniquely human skills and focus on patient-centered care.

Continuing the Orchestration: Agents as Collaborative Partners

Extending our orchestra analogy, agentic AI in healthcare acts not as a replacement for human clinicians, but as a highly sophisticated section within the orchestra, enhancing the overall performance. AI agents can provide valuable insights and data-driven recommendations, but the essential human elements of empathy, ethical judgment, and complex reasoning remain paramount. Think of AI agents as exceptionally skilled first violinists, capable of intricate solos and precise execution, but still needing the conductor (the human clinician) to interpret the score, guide the ensemble, and make the final, nuanced decisions that require uniquely human understanding and care.

In diagnosis, AI agents can sift through vast amounts of medical literature, imaging data, and patient history to identify potential patterns and suggest possible diagnoses, acting as a highly efficient research assistant for the physician. In treatment planning, they can model the potential outcomes of different interventions based on individual patient characteristics, assisting clinicians in making more informed decisions. Even in patient education, personalized AI agents can deliver tailored information and support, ensuring patients understand their conditions and treatment options. The future of healthcare isn't about replacing human expertise; it's about augmenting it with the power of intelligent agents, creating a truly collaborative and more effective healthcare ecosystem where technology and human compassion work in concert.

The AI Agent Revolution in Healthcare

AI agents are set to transform this paradigm by serving as personal health conductors, orchestrating multiple data streams to create a comprehensive picture of individual health trajectories. Breaking this down to first principles, we can identify three fundamental components that drive this revolution:

- **Comprehensive data collection:** AI agents leverage a vast and diverse array of data sources to build a holistic view of individual health:
  - Wearable devices tracking vital signs and activity levels, providing continuous physiological monitoring
  - Shopping data revealing nutrition and lifestyle choices, offering insights into dietary habits and purchasing patterns
  - Financial transactions indicating stress or behavior changes, providing indirect indicators of mental and emotional well-being
  - Social media activity reflecting mental health patterns (used ethically and with privacy safeguards), offering another layer of insight into emotional states and social connections
  - Environmental sensors monitoring air quality and exposure to pollutants, providing data on external factors impacting health
- **Pattern recognition:** The power of AI agents lies in their ability to synthesize and interpret this complex data symphony:
  - Integration of diverse data sources, combining disparate streams into a unified health profile
  - Baseline establishment for individual "normal" states, learning each person's unique physiological and behavioral patterns

- Detection of subtle deviations from personal patterns, identifying anomalies that might be early indicators of health risks
- Correlation analysis across multiple indicators, uncovering complex relationships and patterns that would be missed by traditional methods
- **Proactive intervention:** This sophisticated analysis translates into actionable and personalized health interventions:
  - Early warning generation, providing timely alerts about potential health risks before they become acute problems
  - Personalized health recommendations, tailoring advice to individual needs, preferences, and risk factors
  - Coordination with healthcare providers, facilitating seamless communication and providing clinicians with valuable data-driven insights
  - Lifestyle modification suggestions, empowering individuals to make proactive changes to improve their well-being

The Orchestra of Health Data

Just as a conductor must understand how each instrument contributes to the overall symphony, AI health agents must comprehend how different types of data contribute to the complete health picture. The agent serves as the conductor, coordinating inputs from various "instruments" to create a harmonious and insightful representation of individual well-being.

- **Wearables** provide the steady rhythm of vital signs, offering constant monitoring of key physiological indicators.
- **Shopping data** offers insights into nutrition and lifestyle choices, revealing dietary habits and purchasing behaviors impacting health.
- **Financial data** reveals stress patterns and life changes, providing indirect clues to emotional and psychological well-being.
- **Social interactions** indicate mental and emotional well-being (again, used ethically and privately), offering insights into social connectivity and support systems.
- **Environmental sensors** track external health influences, monitoring exposure to pollutants, allergens, and other environmental health risks.

Conclusion

The journey toward a truly proactive and personalized healthcare system is just beginning. While important challenges remain in terms of data privacy, algorithmic bias, and the need for robust validation, the potential of agentic AI to transform healthcare and well-being is undeniable. Shifting our focus from reactive treatment to proactive prevention, and empowering individuals˙ with personalized insights and support, will allow us to orchestrate a future where health is not merely the absence of illness, but a state of sustained well-being, guided by the intelligent symphony of our bodies and the watchful intelligence of our AI partners. This proactive approach, powered by agentic AI, represents a fundamental shift in how we approach health, moving from responding to the discordant notes of illness to ensuring the harmonious and enduring melody of well-being.

Now, having explored the transformative impact of agentic AI on our homes, workplaces, education, and health, we turn to a final domain that is equally central to the human experience: entertainment and leisure. Here, AI agents are not just making things more convenient or efficient, but fundamentally changing how we experience joy, creativity, and connection in our downtime.

ENTERTAINMENT AND LEISURE

As Sarah settled into her favorite chair for her evening entertainment, she wasn't alone. Her AI entertainment agent had already curated a personalized lineup of content based on her mood, preferences, and viewing history. But unlike traditional recommendation systems, this agent actively engaged with her—discussing plot theories during show breaks, suggesting relevant background information, and even collaborating with her on creative projects. This wasn't just passive consumption anymore; it was an interactive, enriched entertainment experience orchestrated by an intelligent digital companion, transforming leisure time into a dynamic and engaging experience.

The transformation of entertainment and leisure through AI agents represents one of the most profound shifts in how we spend our recreational time. While previous technological advances changed what we consume, agentic AI is fundamentally altering how we interact with and experience entertainment. Like a skilled entertainment director, these agents don't just serve content—they create experiences, facilitate connections, and enable new forms of creative expression, enriching our leisure time in unprecedented ways.

Imagine a world where your favorite game adapts to your specific playstyle in real time, not just in difficulty but in narrative and challenge. Picture a movie that unfolds differently each time you watch it, shaped by your emotional responses and viewing history. Envision composing music alongside an AI collaborator that understands your artistic intentions and helps you bring your sonic visions to life. This isn't science fiction; it's the growing reality of entertainment and leisure being fundamentally reshaped by the arrival of sophisticated AI agents. Just as intelligent agents are destined to revolutionize our workplaces and homes, their impact on how we spend our downtime promises to be equally profound, offering experiences that are more engaging, personalized, and ultimately, more enriching. We're moving beyond simple recommendation algorithms and into an era where AI agents become active participants in our leisure, crafting experiences tailored to our individual desires and sparking new forms of creativity and enjoyment, transforming recreation into something far more dynamic and personally meaningful.

Gaming and Interactive Entertainment: A Symphony of Personalized Play

The gaming industry, a heavyweight of modern entertainment, is on the edge of a transformation fueled by agentic AI. Think back to our analogy of the orchestra. Today's video games, while complex, largely operate like a pre-recorded symphony. The score is set, the events are scripted, and your interaction, while essential, is within predefined boundaries. AI agents, however, introduce the possibility of a truly improvisational performance, where the game dynamically adapts to player actions and preferences.

Imagine AI agents acting as dynamic game masters, not just enforcing rules, but understanding your motivations as a player. These agents could intertwine intricate, branching narratives that respond to your choices in meaningful ways. Fail a quest spectacularly? The story might not simply offer a retry; instead, a new, unforeseen opportunity might emerge from your failure, guided by an AI agent capable of adapting the overarching narrative on the fly. Consider nonplayer characters (NPCs). Currently, their behavior is governed by complex but ultimately predictable algorithms. Agentic NPCs, powered by large language models and sophisticated decision-making systems, could possess genuine agency. They could remember past interactions, form opinions about your character, and react in ways that feel surprisingly human, even unpredictable. A cunning villain might learn your weaknesses and exploit them, or a loyal companion might offer unexpected support based on your shared history within the game world, creating truly engaging and believable virtual characters.

This shift toward agentic AI doesn't just enhance existing game genres; it unlocks entirely new forms of interactive entertainment. Imagine simulations where you're not just managing resources but interacting with simulated individuals, each driven by their own AI agent with unique goals and personalities. Or consider the potential for personalized training simulations, where AI agents adapt the challenges and feedback based on your learning curve and emotional state. The line between game and reality blurs as AI agents create experiences that are deeply engaging and uniquely yours, offering unprecedented levels of immersion and personalization in interactive entertainment.

Personalized Content and Media: Your Own Curated Universe

Beyond gaming, the consumption of media is destined for a hyper-personalization revolution driven by AI agents. Today's recommendation algorithms, while useful, operate on relatively simplistic models of your preferences. They analyze past behavior and suggest similar content. Agentic AI takes this a giant leap further, understanding not just what you consume but why and how you engage with it.

Imagine an AI agent acting as your personal media concierge. This agent wouldn't just recommend movies based on your viewing history; it could understand the nuances of your mood, the specific actors or directors you appreciate, and even the themes you're currently exploring in your own life. This understanding could lead to the creation of entirely personalized content. Think of music that adapts its tempo and instrumentation to your current activity level or emotional state, or news summaries curated not just by topic but by your preferred writing style and level of detail, tailoring media consumption to your individual needs and preferences.

This extends beyond passive consumption. Imagine AI agents that help you discover new artists based on your own creative output, connecting you with a community of like-minded individuals and inspiring new forms of expression. These agents could analyze vast libraries of creative works, identifying patterns and connections that a human could never discern, opening entirely new avenues for discovery and appreciation. The key here, leveraging the first principles of agentic AI, is the combination of perception (understanding your preferences), cognition (reasoning about the vast content landscape), and action (delivering personalized experiences that go far beyond simple recommendations).

Creative Collaboration and Expression: The AI as Muse and Partner

The impact of AI agents isn't limited to consuming entertainment; it's set to transform how we create it. Imagine AI agents becoming true collaborators in the creative process, acting as intelligent tools that augment human imagination and expand artistic possibilities.

Consider music composition. An AI agent, trained on vast datasets of musical styles and techniques, could help a songwriter overcome creative blocks, suggest harmonies they might not have considered, or even generate entire instrumental arrangements based on a simple melodic idea. This isn't about replacing human creativity; it's about amplifying it. The AI agent becomes a partner, offering suggestions, exploring possibilities, and handling the technical complexities, allowing the human artist to focus on the core creative vision and emotional expression.

This principle extends to other artistic domains. Imagine an AI agent assisting a writer with plot development, offering alternative scenarios and character arcs. Or consider visual arts, where AI agents could help generate variations on a theme, explore different color palettes, or even assist with the intricate technical aspects of digital painting or sculpture. These collaborations move beyond simple tools; they become dynamic partnerships, where the AI agent understands the artistic intent and actively contributes to bringing that vision to life. Drawing on its "memory" of artistic principles and its "planning" capabilities, the AI agent can offer insights and suggestions that push the boundaries of human creativity, nurturing innovation and expanding the scope of artistic expression.

Social Entertainment Transformation

Perhaps even more significant is how AI agents are transforming social entertainment experiences. Virtual worlds and multiplayer environments are becoming more intelligent and interactive through the integration of social AI agents that can:

- Facilitate meaningful connections between users with similar interests, creating online communities and nurturing social interaction based on shared passions
- Act as guides, moderators, and companions in virtual spaces, enhancing user experiences and creating more engaging and welcoming virtual environments
- Enable new forms of collaborative entertainment, allowing users to participate in shared creative activities and social experiences facilitated by AI agents
- Create dynamic social scenarios and events within virtual worlds, offering constantly evolving and engaging social landscapes for users to explore and interact within

Meta's Horizon Worlds provides a glimpse of this future, where AI agents serve as both entertainment enhancers and social facilitators, creating richer virtual experiences through intelligent interaction and dynamic content generation, paving the way for more immersive and socially rich virtual entertainment platforms.

Creative Arts and Entertainment

The creative domain of entertainment is experiencing particularly dramatic changes through AI agents. These systems are evolving from tools into creative collaborators that can:

- **Co-create music, art, and written content with humans**, blurring the lines between human and AI creativity and cultivating new forms of artistic partnership
- **Generate variations and adaptations of existing works**, offering artists new ways to explore and reinterpret their own creations and existing cultural works
- **Provide creative feedback and suggestions**, acting as intelligent critics and collaborators to help artists refine their work and push creative boundaries
- **Enable new forms of interactive storytelling**, creating dynamic and personalized narratives that respond to user choices and preferences, offering unprecedented levels of engagement and immersion

Industry Transformation

The entertainment industry itself is being reshaped by AI agents that can:

- **Optimize content production and distribution workflows**, streamlining processes and reducing costs in content creation and delivery
- **Predict trends and audience preferences** with greater accuracy, enabling data-driven content creation and marketing strategies that better resonate with target audiences
- **Create personalized marketing campaigns**, tailoring promotional efforts to individual user preferences and maximizing engagement and conversion rates
- **Enable new business models and revenue streams**, promoting innovative approaches to content monetization and distribution in the evolving entertainment landscape

The Future of Leisure Activities: New Frontiers of Fun and Relaxation

The transformative power of AI agents will extend beyond our screens and into the realm of our physical leisure activities. Imagine AI agents enhancing our travel experiences. A personalized travel agent, understanding your preferences for adventure, relaxation, or cultural immersion, could craft unique itineraries, book accommodations that perfectly suit your needs, and even provide real-time recommendations based on local events and your current mood, creating truly bespoke and seamless travel experiences.

Consider the world of hobbies. Whether it's gardening, cooking, or collecting, AI agents could offer expert advice, personalized tips, and connect you with communities of fellow enthusiasts. Imagine an AI agent that analyzes your garden's soil and climate, suggesting the best plants and offering tailored care instructions. Or picture an AI sous chef that helps you create delicious meals based on your dietary restrictions and available ingredients, empowering home cooks to explore new culinary horizons.

Even our social interactions could be enhanced. AI agents could facilitate more meaningful connections by suggesting activities based on shared interests or helping to bridge communication gaps. However, it's imperative to navigate this carefully. While AI can facilitate connection, we must also be mindful of preserving the authenticity and spontaneity of human interaction. The goal isn't to replace human connection but to augment it, to use AI agents to break down barriers and create opportunities for richer, more fulfilling social experiences, ensuring technology serves to enhance, not diminish, human connection.

Why Does This Matter?

The integration of AI agents into entertainment and leisure is not simply a technological advancement; it's a shift toward a more personalized and potentially more enriching human experience. It's about moving beyond passive consumption and embracing active participation, about unlocking new creative potential, and about making our downtime more fulfilling and enjoyable, enhancing the quality of our leisure time and personal lives.

Case Studies: Sample Companies

Here are examples where companies are developing agentic AI solutions to improve existing solutions:

Adaptive RPG: A new role-playing game utilizes AI agents as dynamic game masters. Player choices have significant and unpredictable consequences, shaping the narrative in unique ways for each playthrough. NPCs remember past interactions and form complex relationships with the player, leading to emergent storylines.

Personalized music composer: A musician uses an AI agent to co-compose music. The AI analyzes the musician's style and suggests harmonic progressions and instrumental arrangements, accelerating the creative process and leading to unexpected sonic discoveries.

AI-powered travel curator: An individual uses an AI travel agent that understands their passion for hiking and local cuisine. The agent crafts a personalized itinerary in the Swiss Alps, including challenging trails and reservations at hidden gem restaurants.

Conclusion

The integration of AI agents into entertainment and leisure promises a future where our downtime is more engaging, more personalized, and ultimately, more rewarding. From dynamically adapting games to co-creating music with intelligent partners, the possibilities are vast and exciting. Understanding the fundamental principles of how these agents perceive, reason, and act will allow us to grasp the profound impact they will have on how we spend our precious leisure time. This isn't about a dystopian future of AI overlords dictating our fun; it's about empowering individuals with intelligent tools that enhance their enjoyment and unlock new avenues for creativity and connection, enriching our lives and transforming our leisure experiences.

The future of entertainment and leisure, as per Figure 4.3, will be increasingly orchestrated by AI agents, creating more engaging, personalized, and interactive experiences. However, this transformation also raises important questions about the nature of creativity, authenticity, and human connection in an agent-enhanced entertainment landscape—themes we'll explore further in later chapters.

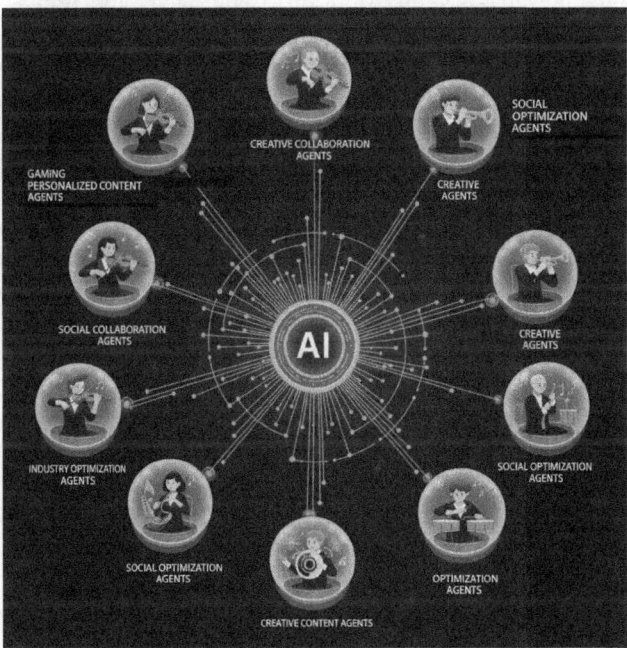

FIGURE 4.3 The interconnected agentic entertainment ecosystem

Generated with AI using Google Gemini 2.5 Pro

KEY TAKEAWAYS

This chapter has explored the sweeping transformations set in motion by agentic AI across five fundamental domains of human life: home and personal life, work and career, education and learning, healthcare and well-being, and entertainment and leisure. Like a conductor revealing the distinct movements of a symphony, we have examined how AI agents, with their capacity for perception, reasoning, action, and learning, are set to orchestrate profound changes in each of these areas. From automating mundane tasks and personalizing experiences to augmenting human capabilities and democratizing access to expertise, agentic AI is not just a technological advancement but a catalyst for societal evolution. Understanding these five domains of change is critical for navigating the future, allowing us to proactively shape the integration of AI agents for the betterment of individuals and society as a whole.

1. **Agentic AI is redefining everyday life.**
   - KEY INSIGHTS:
     - Agentic AI transcends simple automation, evolving into proactive, personalized assistants that anticipate needs and orchestrate daily routines in homes and personal lives.
     - The integration of AI agents in homes moves beyond isolated smart devices to create seamlessly coordinated living environments, enhancing convenience, efficiency, and personalization.
     - From managing schedules and finances to providing personalized health and wellness support, AI agents are destined to become indispensable partners in navigating the complexities of modern life
   - DO:
     - Begin to envision how AI agents could alleviate routine burdens in your own home and personal life, freeing up time and mental energy for higher-level pursuits.
     - Explore existing smart home technologies and virtual assistants to understand the early stages of AI agent integration and identify potential areas for future adoption.
     - Consider the ethical implications of AI agents in personal spaces, particularly regarding data privacy, security, and the balance between convenience and autonomy.
   - DON'T:
     - Underestimate the potential for AI agents to move beyond simple task automation and become truly proactive and intelligent partners in personal life management.
     - Assume that current smart home technologies represent the full extent of AI's impact on domestic life—agentic AI represents a significant leap in capability and integration.

- Neglect to consider the importance of human oversight and control, even as AI agents become more autonomous in managing our personal environments.

2. Work and careers are undergoing a human-AI symphony.
- KEY INSIGHTS:
  - Agentic AI is not primarily about job replacement, but about a fundamental restructuring of work, creating a new division of labor where humans and AI agents collaborate synergistically.
  - The workplace is evolving into a dynamic ensemble of human experts and specialized AI agents, each contributing unique strengths to enhance productivity, innovation, and strategic decision-making.
  - Professionals who learn to effectively orchestrate and collaborate with AI agents, focusing on uniquely human skills, will be best positioned to thrive in the future of work.
- DO:
  - Start developing "AI agent literacy"—understand the capabilities and limitations of different types of AI agents relevant to your profession or industry.
  - Focus on honing uniquely human skills such as creativity, emotional intelligence, complex problem-solving, and ethical reasoning, which will become increasingly valuable in an AI-augmented workplace.
  - Embrace a mindset of continuous learning and adaptability, preparing to evolve your skillset alongside the rapidly advancing capabilities of AI agents.
- DON'T:
  - Fear AI as a job-replacing force, but rather embrace it as a powerful tool for augmenting human capabilities and creating new opportunities.
  - Assume that technical skills alone will be sufficient for career success—uniquely human skills and the ability to collaborate with AI will be equally, if not more, critical.
  - Resist the integration of AI agents into your workflow—proactive adoption and skillful orchestration of these tools will be essential for professional advancement in the coming years.

3. Education, healthcare, and entertainment are becoming deeply personalized.
- KEY INSIGHTS:
  - Agentic AI is democratizing access to personalized learning, healthcare, and entertainment experiences, tailoring these fundamental domains to individual needs and preferences at scale.

- In education, AI tutors and personalized learning platforms are destined to revolutionize pedagogy, nurturing active learning, democratizing expertise, and creating more equitable and effective learning environments.
- In healthcare, AI agents are enabling a shift from reactive treatment to proactive prevention and personalized medicine, empowering individuals to take a more active role in managing their well-being.
- In entertainment and leisure, AI agents are moving beyond passive recommendations to create dynamic, interactive, and deeply personalized experiences, enhancing enjoyment and unlocking new avenues for creativity.
- DO:
  - Advocate for and support the ethical and equitable implementation of AI agents in education, healthcare, and entertainment to maximize their benefits for all members of society.
  - Explore personalized learning platforms and AI-powered educational tools to understand the potential of AI to enhance learning for yourself or those around you.
  - Be open to engaging with AI-driven healthcare and entertainment experiences, while remaining mindful of data privacy and the importance of human connection and authenticity.
- DON'T:
  - Allow concerns about technology to overshadow the immense potential of AI agents to democratize access to vital services and enhance human experiences across these domains.
  - Assume that personalization equates to isolation—AI agents can also facilitate social connection and collaborative experiences within education, healthcare, and entertainment.
  - Neglect to consider the ethical implications of hyper-personalization, particularly regarding algorithmic bias, filter bubbles, and the potential for reinforcing existing inequalities.

As we conclude this exploration of the five domains of change, it becomes clear that agentic AI is not a distant future but a rapidly unfolding present. Like the ever-evolving movements of a symphony, these transformations are dynamic, interconnected, and full of both immense promise and potential challenges. Understanding these changes is the first fundamental step. But knowledge alone is not enough. The next movement in our exploration, Chapter 5, will shift our focus from understanding what is changing to how we can navigate and shape this evolving landscape. We will inquire into the essential skills and strategies needed to thrive in an age increasingly orchestrated by intelligent agents, empowering you to become not just an observer, but an active and informed participant in the AI revolution.

The AI Agent Economy

"Agents are not only going to change how everyone interacts with computers. They're also going to upend the software industry, bringing about the biggest revolution in computing since we went from typing commands to tapping on icons?"[1]

— Bill Gates

ECONOMIC IMPACT OF AI AGENTS

As Sarah walked into her company's quarterly board meeting, the presentation on screen showed a striking projection: By 2030, AI agents could add $15.7 trillion to the global economy. "But how?" asked one board member. Sarah smiled, remembering how just last month, her firm's implementation of AI agents had already reduced operational costs by 23% while increasing customer satisfaction scores by 40%. The economic influence of AI agents goes beyond mere spreadsheet figures; it signifies a fundamental reshaping of value creation and distribution within the global economic system.

Imagine a dynamic financial trading floor, not filled with bustling brokers and frantic handwritten notes, but populated by silent, highly focused AI agents. Each agent, a specialized digital entity, diligently scrutinizes market data, executes trades with exceptional speed, and manages risk profiles with an expertise that surpasses human capabilities. This scenario isn't a vision of the distant future; it's a snapshot of the rapidly developing AI Agent Economy, a domain where intelligent software is becoming

---

[1] https://www.gatesnotes.com/AI-agents

a primary facilitator for economic activity. Much like the introduction of the personal computer and the Internet revolutionized our economic landscape, the rise of AI agents is set to steer a new age of productivity, innovation, and wealth creation—along with inevitable disruptions. In this chapter, we will explore the multidimensional economic impact of these digital workers, examining how they are set to revolutionize industries, create entirely new business models, and redefine the very essence of our economic interactions.

The Engine of Economic Transformation

At its core, the economic impact of AI agents stems from their ability to augment and, in many cases, surpass human capabilities in performing specific tasks. Think back to our analogy of the orchestra from earlier chapters. If traditional AI was like a single, highly skilled musician, AI agents are analogous to entire sections of the orchestra, each instrument group (the agents) autonomously playing their part in perfect harmony, guided by a conductor (the system architecture). This collaborative and specialized intelligence unleashes unprecedented levels of efficiency. Consider a manufacturing plant. Individual AI agents can manage complex supply chains, predict equipment failures, and optimize production schedules with a precision and speed that no human team can match consistently. This leads to reduced costs, minimized downtime, and increased output.

From a first-principles perspective, AI agents drive economic growth by optimizing resource allocation and reducing friction in various economic processes. They can analyze vast datasets to identify inefficiencies, automate repetitive tasks, and make data-driven decisions far more quickly and accurately than humans. This translates directly into higher productivity, lower operational costs, and the creation of new value propositions.

Why Does This Matter?

Because this fundamental shift in how work gets done has the potential to unlock immense economic potential, allowing us to achieve more with less, and freeing up human capital for higher-level creative and strategic endeavors. Just as the steam engine and electricity multiplied human physical labor, AI agents are destined to multiply human cognitive labor, driving a new wave of economic prosperity.

It is also worth mentioning this change has happened before in history in several key moments where technology advancement fundamentally changed society's fabric: the printing press, electricity, the industrial revolution, the

Internet, and so on. And although the change point is not new, the speed of change this time is something we have not experienced before.

Macro-Economic Transformation

The integration of AI agents into the global economy represents what economists call a general-purpose technology revolution, such as the introduction of electricity or the Internet. Using first principles, we can break down the economic impact into three fundamental channels:

- **Productivity enhancement:** AI agents serve as force multipliers for human capabilities, automating routine tasks while augmenting complex decision-making. McKinsey estimates that AI agents could automate up to 30% of current work hours by 2030,[2] potentially increasing labor productivity by 0.8% to 1.4% annually. Imagine the impact across industries as mundane tasks are handled seamlessly by AI, freeing human intellect for innovation and strategic growth.
- **Innovation acceleration:** Reducing the cost and time required for experimentation and R&D enables AI agents to accelerate the pace of innovation across industries. The World Economic Forum[3] projects that AI agent-driven innovation could contribute up to $3.5 trillion in annual economic value by 2028. Consider pharmaceutical research, where AI agents can rapidly screen compounds and simulate trials, drastically shortening the drug discovery process and bringing life-saving treatments to market faster. OpenAI launched a promising product, Deep Research,[4] in February 2025, which already is achieving basic background research with high accuracy. And this is only the beginning.
- **Resource optimization:** Through superior coordination and prediction capabilities, AI agents enable more efficient resource allocation. Studies suggest this could reduce waste by 20–30% across supply chains. Imagine global logistics networks managed by AI agents that dynamically reroute shipments based on real-time data, minimizing fuel consumption and delivery times, contributing to both economic and environmental benefits.

---

[2] https://www.mckinsey.com/mgi/our-research/a-new-future-of-work-the-race-to-deploy-ai-and-raise-skills-in-europe-and-beyond

[3] https://reports.weforum.org/docs/WEF_AI_in_Action_Beyond_Experimentation_to_Transform_Industry_2025.pdf

[4] https://openai.com/index/introducing-deep-research/

Deep Dive: Economic Multiplier Effects

AI agents create cascading economic effects through:

- Direct impacts (immediate productivity gains)
- Indirect impacts (supply chain efficiencies)
- Induced impacts (increased consumer spending from cost savings)

Economic models suggest each dollar invested in AI agents generates $3–5 in total economic impact.

Industry Transformation

Just as an orchestra transforms when adding new instruments and capabilities, industries are being fundamentally reshaped by AI agents. Traditional value chains are being disrupted in three key ways:

- **Disintermediation:** AI agents are eliminating the need for certain intermediaries by directly connecting producers and consumers. For example, in financial services, AI agents are replacing traditional brokers by providing personalized investment advice and execution in certain cases with low risk and liability.
- **Value chain compression:** Automating and streamlining processes allows AI agents to shorten value chains and reduce costs. Manufacturing companies using AI agents for supply chain optimization report 15–25% cost reductions. This efficiency gain allows for leaner operations and more competitive pricing.
- **New value creation:** AI agents are enabling entirely new business models and revenue streams. Consider the emergence of "agent-as-a-service" platforms that rent specialized AI capabilities. This model democratizes access to advanced AI tools, enabling smaller businesses to leverage cutting-edge technology without massive upfront investment.

Why Does This Matter?

For business leaders, understanding these transformations is fundamental for strategic planning and investment decisions. Companies that successfully integrate AI agents into their value chains are seeing three to five times higher returns on digital investments.[5] This competitive advantage highlights the urgency for businesses to adopt and adapt to agentic AI.

Labor Market Evolution

The impact of AI agents on labor markets is perhaps the most debated economic effect. Our analysis suggests a three-wave transformation:

Wave 1 (2023–2026): Task Automation

- 20–30% of routine cognitive tasks are being automated, streamlining workflows and enhancing efficiency. First processes to go fully agentic will be those that are both outsourced and offshore.
- There's a growing emphasis on human-AI collaboration, where agents augment human capabilities rather than replace them entirely.
- Net job displacement in this phase is estimated at 3–5% of the workforce, primarily in sectors with high concentrations of routine tasks. There are already early signs some jobs are starting to be impacted.[6]

Wave 2 (2026–2028): Role Transformation

- AI agents evolve into "digital colleagues," becoming integral parts of professional teams and collaborative projects.
- New roles emerge, such as AI trainers, agent orchestrators, and AI ethicists, reflecting the need for human expertise to manage and guide these intelligent systems.
- Net job creation begins in technical and creative fields, driven by the demand for skills in AI development, management, and ethical oversight.

Wave 3 (2028+): Economic Restructuring

- Fundamental shifts occur in the labor market structure, moving toward a more fluid and dynamic model.
- The "Agent Economy" jobs become mainstream, with a significant portion of the workforce engaged in roles directly related to AI agent development, management, or collaboration.
- The labor market increasingly focuses on uniquely human capabilities—creativity, complex problem-solving, emotional intelligence—as agents handle routine and analytical tasks.

---

[5] https://www.idc.com/getdoc.jsp?containerId=prUS52600524

[6] https://www.hfsresearch.com/news/ai-agents-are-here-to-take-your-job/

- This is the most unpredictable wave to predict accurately, as different governments will react in different ways to these trends, creating unbalances around the world's economy. Here, while the potential is getting clearer by the day, it is possible some governments will introduce regulation and legislation that might slow or distort progress.

New Frontiers in Business Models

The transformative power of AI agents isn't just about making existing businesses more efficient; it's about birthing entirely new categories of businesses and services. We're already seeing the emergence of "agent-as-a-service" platforms, where businesses can rent or subscribe to specialized AI agents tailored to their specific needs. Imagine a small marketing firm subscribing to an AI agent that autonomously manages their social media campaigns, crafting engaging content, identifying target audiences, and optimizing ad spend in real time. This democratizes access to sophisticated capabilities that were previously only available to large corporations with dedicated AI teams.

Furthermore, we're witnessing the rise of "agent marketplaces," digital platforms where developers and entrepreneurs can create and offer their AI agents for sale or rent. This promotes a vibrant ecosystem of specialized AI workers, driving innovation and allowing businesses to easily find and deploy the precise AI talent they require. Picture an app store, but instead of applications, it's populated with intelligent, autonomous workers ready to be integrated into various business processes.

Another compelling new business model revolves around the management and optimization of "agent fleets." As organizations deploy increasing numbers of AI agents, the need for systems that can monitor their performance, ensure their security, and orchestrate their activities becomes critical. This creates opportunities for businesses that specialize in agent management platforms, providing the infrastructure and tools necessary to effectively govern these digital workforces.

These new business models, built on the foundation of agentic AI, are not just incremental improvements; they represent a fundamental shift in how value is created and exchanged in the economy. They lower barriers to entry, adopt specialization, and unlock new levels of scalability and agility for businesses of all sizes.

The Evolving Landscape of Work

Perhaps one of the most profound and extensively discussed economic impacts of AI agents is their influence on the job market. While some express concerns about widespread job displacement, a more nuanced perspective reveals a complex evolution of work. Undoubtedly, AI agents will automate numerous routine and repetitive tasks currently performed by humans. Data entry, basic customer service inquiries, and various forms of manual labor are prime candidates for agent-driven automation. This will lead to shifts in employment, requiring workers in these roles to adapt and acquire new skills to remain relevant in the changing landscape.

However, the narrative of AI agents simply "stealing jobs" is incomplete. Throughout history, technological advancements have reshaped the job market, leading to the creation of entirely new roles and industries that were unimaginable before. The advent of AI agents is no different. We will see a surge in demand for professionals who can build, train, manage, and interact with these intelligent systems. Consider the need for "AI agent trainers," individuals skilled in providing agents with the data and instructions necessary for them to perform their tasks effectively. "Agent ethicists" will be vital in ensuring AI agents operate responsibly and align with human values. "AI agent integrators" will be needed to seamlessly weave these digital workers into existing workflows and systems.

Moreover, AI agents will augment the capabilities of human workers, freeing them from mundane tasks and allowing them to focus on higher-level strategic thinking, creativity, and complex problem-solving. Imagine a doctor being assisted by AI agents that analyze medical records, identify potential diagnoses, and suggest treatment plans, allowing the physician to dedicate more time to patient interaction and complex medical decision-making.

The key takeaway here is that the rise of AI agents will necessitate a shift in skills and a re-evaluation of the value of human work, but it is unlikely to result in a net loss of employment. Instead, it will usher in an era of new opportunities and demand for uniquely human skills in collaboration with intelligent machines.

Investment Hotspots in the Agent Economy

The flourishing AI Agent Economy presents a fertile ground for investment, attracting capital seeking to capitalize on this transformative technology. Several key areas are emerging as particularly promising investment hotspots.

First and foremost are the companies developing the foundational platforms and tools for creating and deploying AI agents. These include companies building agent development frameworks, specialized AI chips optimized for agent processing, and secure and scalable infrastructure to support the growing agent ecosystem. Think of it as investing in the "picks and shovels" of the gold rush—these foundational elements are essential for the entire Agent Economy to flourish.

Another compelling investment area lies in specialized AI agent solutions for specific industries. We are seeing the emergence of agents tailored for everything from financial trading and healthcare diagnostics to personalized education and advanced manufacturing. Investing in companies developing these niche AI agents, with deep domain expertise, offers significant potential for high returns due to their targeted value propositions. Here, these agents will acquire over time "long-term corporate memory" and will become more and more accurate in leveraging all these experiences, some over several human lifespans. Imaging having the best workers over the last three decades in the same place and at the same time resolving a new situation for the company.

Furthermore, the companies that provide the infrastructure and services to manage and optimize agent fleets are attracting significant investment. This includes companies offering agent monitoring and security solutions, agent orchestration platforms, and tools for performance analysis and continuous improvement.

Beyond these core areas, opportunities also exist in companies developing the training data and methodologies necessary to equip AI agents with the knowledge and skills they need to perform their tasks effectively. As the Agent Economy matures, we will likely see further specialization and the emergence of entirely new investment categories, mirroring the evolution of the Internet and mobile app ecosystems.

For astute investors, understanding the underlying dynamics of the AI Agent Economy and identifying the key players and enabling technologies presents a compelling opportunity to participate in this next wave of technological disruption and capitalize on the significant growth potential.

The economic impact of AI agents is creating distinct investment opportunities across three horizons:

Near-term (1–2 years):
- **Infrastructure providers (compute, storage):** Essential for supporting the expanding agent ecosystem
- **AI agent development platforms:** Tools and frameworks that simplify agent creation and deployment
- **Integration services:** Companies that help businesses integrate AI agents into existing systems

Medium-term (2–5 years):
- **Industry-specific AI agent applications:** Targeted solutions addressing specific industry needs
- **Reskilling and education providers:** Platforms and services that train the workforce for the Agent Economy

- **Agent orchestration platforms:** Systems that manage and coordinate fleets of AI agents

Long-term (5+ years):
- **Agent economy enablers:** Companies building the foundational layers of the Agent Economy
- **New business model innovators:** Startups and companies pioneering novel agent-driven business models
- **Cross-industry platforms:** Versatile platforms applicable across multiple sectors, maximizing reach and impact

Future Watch: Reshaping Economic Landscapes

Looking further ahead, the widespread adoption of AI agents promises to reshape the very fabric of our economic landscape, potentially leading to significant long-term shifts. One key trend is the potential for increased economic decentralization. AI agents can empower smaller businesses and even individuals with capabilities that were previously the exclusive domain of large corporations. A solopreneur can leverage AI agents to manage their marketing, customer service, and even product development, leveling the playing field and promoting greater entrepreneurial activity.

We may also see a shift in global economic power. Nations that invest heavily in AI agent research, development, and deployment are likely to gain a significant competitive advantage, attracting talent and capital and leading the way in this new technological frontier. The race to become an AI-first nation is already underway, and the AI Agent Economy is a critical battleground.

Furthermore, the increasing efficiency driven by AI agents could lead to a fundamental rethinking of traditional economic models. With greater automation and optimized resource allocation, we might see a move toward more personalized and on-demand services, blurring the lines between producers and consumers. Consider the potential for highly personalized education delivered by AI tutors tailored to each student's individual learning style and pace, revolutionizing how we approach learning and development.

Finally, it's critical to acknowledge the potential for economic disruption and the need for proactive policies to mitigate negative consequences. Addressing potential job displacement through retraining programs and exploring new models for social safety nets will be critical to ensuring a smooth and equitable transition to an AI-powered economy. The future economic landscape shaped by AI agents will be one of immense opportunity,

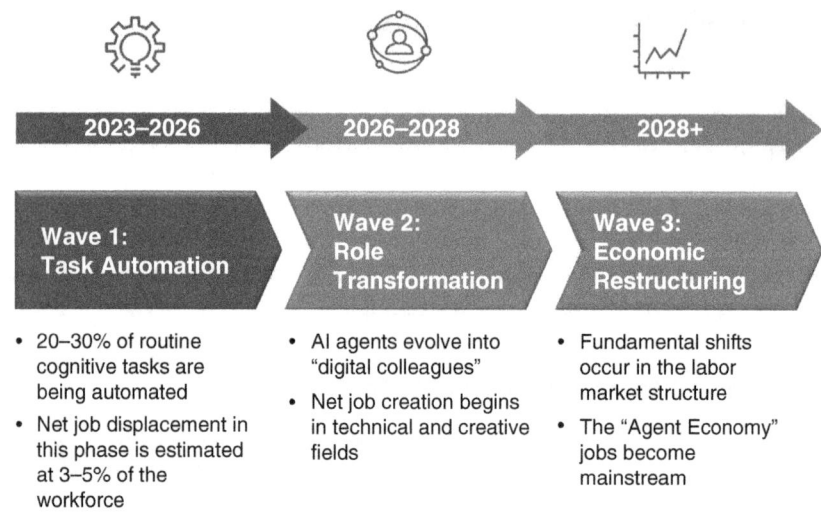

FIGURE 5.1 Economic impact timeline

but it will also require careful navigation and a willingness to adapt to a rapidly evolving world.

The economic impact of AI agents extends beyond traditional metrics of GDP and productivity. We're witnessing the emergence of a new economic paradigm—one where the boundaries between human and artificial intelligence become increasingly fluid. For business leaders, the key to success lies not just in implementing AI agents, but in reimagining their organizations for this new economic reality and embracing the transformative potential of agentic AI.

Why Does This Matter?

Organizations that proactively adapt to the Agent Economy will be better positioned to capture value and maintain competitive advantage in an increasingly AI-driven world, securing their future in this evolving landscape (see Figure 5.1).

NEW BUSINESS MODELS

The year is 2027, and Sarah, a freelance graphic designer, no longer works alone. Her AI agent team handles client communications, project management, and even preliminary designs, allowing her to focus purely on creative direction and client relationships. What's more remarkable is that Sarah pays these agents a usage-based fee, effectively making them stakeholders in her business success. This represents just one example of how AI agents are fundamentally reshaping business models across industries, creating a new paradigm for value creation and exchange.

Imagine a world where your most tedious tasks vanish, not through delegation to human assistants, but through the tireless work of intelligent digital entities. Picture a marketplace bustling not just with products and services, but with autonomous agents, each offering specialized skills and unique abilities. This isn't science fiction; it's the dawning of the AI Agent Economy, and it's destined to reshape the very fabric of how we conduct business. We've already explored the foundational elements of agentic AI and its growing influence across various domains. Now, we turn our attention to the tangible economic impact, specifically focusing on the exciting new business models that are beginning to emerge from this technological revolution. Forget incremental improvements; we're talking about entirely new ways to create, deliver, and capture value in the marketplace.

Think back to our earlier analogy of the orchestra; we discussed how individual AI agents, like skilled musicians, can perform specific tasks with precision. Now, consider these musicians forming not just an orchestra, but entirely new ensembles with unique repertoires and approaches. The individual capabilities of AI agents are the instruments; the new business models are the innovative musical compositions they enable. This section examines these compositions, exploring the groundbreaking ways in which businesses are leveraging the power of agentic AI to forge entirely new paths to success and redefine industry norms.

The Genesis of Agentic Business: A First-Principles View

To truly understand these emerging business models, we need to strip away the hype and examine the fundamental shifts that AI agents bring to the table. From a first-principles perspective, traditional business models are built upon the exchange of value, typically involving human labor, capital, and resources. AI agents introduce a powerful new element: autonomous digital labor, fundamentally altering the dynamics of value creation.

Let's break this down:

- **Deconstructing value creation:** At its core, any business creates value by transforming inputs into outputs that are desired by a customer. This transformation often involves tasks requiring intelligence, decision-making, and execution. Traditionally, humans have been the primary engine for these tasks.

- **The agentic shift:** AI agents, by their very nature, can perform many of these tasks autonomously. They can gather information, analyze data, make decisions based on pre-programmed logic and learned patterns, and execute actions—all without direct human intervention. This is the fundamental shift: intelligence and agency are no longer solely the domain of humans, opening new possibilities for automation and efficiency.
- **New forms of scalability:** This autonomy unlocks unprecedented scalability. Unlike human employees, AI agents don't require salaries, benefits, or rest. They can operate 24/7, processing vast amounts of information and executing tasks at speeds unimaginable for humans. This allows businesses to scale their operations and offerings in entirely new ways, reaching levels of efficiency previously unattainable.
- **The rise of specialized digital labor:** Just as human labor has become increasingly specialized, so too are AI agents. We're seeing the emergence of agents designed for specific tasks, from customer service interactions to complex data analysis. This specialization allows businesses to assemble "digital workforces" tailored to their exact needs, optimizing efficiency and productivity across various operations.

Deep Dive: Defining Autonomous Digital Labor

Autonomous digital labor refers to the work performed by AI agents without direct, ongoing human supervision. Key characteristics include:

- **Goal-oriented:** Agents are designed to achieve specific objectives.
- **Perception and action:** They can perceive their environment (digital or physical) and take actions within it.
- **Decision-making:** They can make choices based on their programming and learned experiences.
- **Adaptability (in some cases):** More advanced agents can learn and adapt their behavior over time.

This concept is distinct from simple automation. While traditional automation follows pre-programmed steps, autonomous digital labor involves intelligent decision-making and the ability to handle unforeseen situations within defined parameters.

Emerging Business Models in the Agent Economy

This fundamental shift toward autonomous digital labor is giving rise to a fascinating array of new business models. These models can be broadly categorized, though it's important to remember that real-world applications often blend elements from multiple categories, creating hybrid and innovative approaches.

1. **Agent-as-a-service (AaaS):** Renting intelligence and agency

    Think of the software-as-a-service (SaaS) revolution, but instead of renting software, you're renting access to the capabilities of sophisticated AI agents. AaaS businesses develop, train, and maintain specialized AI agents, offering them to clients on a subscription or usage-based model.

    - **The core value proposition:** AaaS removes the burden of developing and managing complex AI infrastructure and expertise in-house. Companies can access cutting-edge AI capabilities on demand, allowing them to focus on their core competencies and strategic growth initiatives, rather than technological infrastructure.
    - **Examples in action:** Imagine a small e-commerce business subscribing to a "customer service agent" that handles routine inquiries, resolves basic issues, and even personalizes product recommendations. Or a marketing agency utilizing a "content creation agent" to draft initial blog posts, social media updates, and even advertising copy. These agents become an extension of the client's team, providing specialized skills without the overhead of hiring and training human employees, optimizing resource allocation and efficiency.
    - **Why this matters:** AaaS democratizes access to advanced AI. Smaller businesses and individuals can leverage powerful AI tools that were previously only accessible to large corporations with significant resources. This democratization encourages innovation, levels the competitive playing field, and enables broader participation in the AI-driven economy.

2. **The agent marketplace:** A hub for digital talent

    As the number and variety of AI agents grow, so too will the need for platforms to connect those seeking agentic capabilities with those offering them. Agent marketplaces will function as hubs where businesses and individuals can discover, evaluate, and deploy specialized AI agents for various tasks.

    - **The core value proposition:** These marketplaces provide a centralized location to find and compare agents with specific skills and performance metrics. They enhance transparency in the agent ecosystem and facilitate efficient matching between the supply and demand for agentic labor, optimizing resource allocation and project execution.
    - **Examples in action:** Imagine a platform where you can browse and "hire" a "research agent" to gather information on a specific topic, a "coding agent" to automate repetitive programming tasks, or a

"financial analysis agent" to generate reports and insights. These marketplaces might offer rating systems, performance guarantees, and even mechanisms for agents to "learn" and improve based on user feedback, ensuring quality and reliability in agent services.

- **Why this matters:** Agent marketplaces will drive the specialization and refinement of AI agent capabilities. Competition within the marketplace will incentivize developers to create more efficient, effective, and user-friendly agents. This competitive dynamic will accelerate the overall development and widespread adoption of agentic AI across industries.

3. **Agent-enabled products and services**: embedding intelligence everywhere

Rather than simply offering agents as standalone services, many businesses will integrate agentic capabilities directly into their products and services, creating entirely new value propositions and enhancing user experiences.

- **The core value proposition:** Embedding AI agents enhances the functionality, personalization, and automation of existing products and services, making them more intelligent and responsive to user needs.
- **Examples in action:** Consider a smart home device equipped with an "energy management agent" that learns your usage patterns and optimizes energy consumption automatically. Or a software platform with an integrated "project management agent" that schedules tasks, tracks progress, and proactively identifies potential roadblocks. Even educational platforms could integrate "personalized learning agents" that adapt to individual student needs and learning styles, providing customized education experiences and improving learning effectiveness.
- **Why this matters:** This model moves beyond simply automating existing processes; it creates entirely new categories of intelligent products and services. It blurs the lines between traditional products and software, leading to a future where intelligent assistance is seamlessly integrated into our daily lives, enhancing convenience and efficiency.

4. **The autonomous business:** agents as core operational units

Perhaps the most transformative model is the emergence of businesses where AI agents are not just tools, but the primary operational units. These autonomous businesses rely heavily, or even entirely, on AI agents to perform core functions, with minimal human oversight and intervention.

- **The core value proposition:** Autonomous businesses can operate with unprecedented efficiency and scale, potentially disrupting traditional industries with their lower operating costs and 24/7 availability and ability to process vast amounts of data, enabling them to operate at speeds and scales previously unattainable by human-led businesses.

- **Examples in action:** Imagine a fully automated content curation service where AI agents identify trending topics, generate summaries, and deliver personalized news feeds to users. Or a decentralized autonomous organization (DAO) managed by AI agents that automatically executes smart contracts and allocates resources based on pre-defined rules. While fully autonomous businesses are still largely theoretical, we are seeing early examples in areas like algorithmic trading and automated content moderation, indicating the feasibility and potential of this model.
- **Why this matters:** This model represents a radical shift in how businesses are structured and operated. It raises profound questions about the future of work, the role of human management, and the very definition of a company in an AI-driven economy. It challenges traditional organizational hierarchies and opens new possibilities for business operations.

Transitions and Interconnections

It's critical to recognize that these business models are not mutually exclusive. An AaaS provider might also operate an agent marketplace. An agent-enabled product could utilize agents sourced from a third-party marketplace. The boundaries are fluid and evolving, creating a dynamic and interconnected ecosystem. The key to understanding this evolving landscape is grasping the underlying principles of autonomous digital labor and exploring how these principles can be applied in innovative and integrated ways to create new business value.

Conclusion

The AI Agent Economy is not a distant future; it's taking shape around us. These new business models represent a fundamental shift in how value is created and exchanged. Understanding the first principles driving this transformation and exploring the emerging archetypes of agentic businesses empower us to begin to grasp the immense potential—and the potential disruptions—that lie ahead. As we move forward, it will be essential to consider the implications for the job market, investment opportunities, and the overall economic landscape, topics we will expand in the subsequent sections of this chapter (see Figure 5.2).

FIGURE 5.2   Four types of new business models with agentic AI[7]

Generated with AI using Google Gemini 2.5 Pro

JOB MARKET EVOLUTION

As we stand on the edge of a new era, the very nature of work is undergoing a profound transformation, driven by the rapid emergence and integration of artificial intelligence agents. This section will delve into this seismic shift, exploring how AI agents are not just automating tasks, but fundamentally reshaping industries, creating novel roles, and demanding a recalibration of skills across the workforce. Through real-world scenarios and in-depth analysis, we will unpack the dynamics of what is being called "The Great

---

[7] Image generated with OpenAI's DALE GenAI model

Realignment," examining the patterns of job displacement, the emergence of hybrid human-AI roles, and the exciting potential for job enhancement in this evolving landscape. Prepare to navigate the shifting sands of labor and understand the first principles driving this revolution in how we work.

Opening Scenario: A Day in 2027. . .

Sarah logs into her AI Agent Management dashboard, reviewing the performance metrics of the dozen specialized AI agents she oversees for various clients. Just three years ago, she was a traditional project manager—today, she's an "AI Agent Orchestrator," a role that didn't exist when she was in college. As she fine-tunes the agents' parameters and mediates between their autonomous decisions and her clients' needs, Sarah reflects on how dramatically the job market has transformed since AI agents became mainstream, reshaping professional roles and skill requirements across industries.

The Great Realignment

The integration of AI agents into the workforce has triggered what economists call "The Great Realignment"—a fundamental restructuring of the labor market that surpasses previous technological revolutions in both scope and speed. According to recent research by McKinsey,[8] by 2030, approximately 30% of work hours across the global economy could be automated by AI agents, affecting up to 375 million workers worldwide. However, unlike previous waves of automation that primarily impacted routine manual and cognitive tasks, AI agents are reshaping jobs across the entire skills spectrum.

Deep Dive: Job Displacement Patterns

Studies show three distinct patterns of job displacement:

- **Full automation:** Jobs completely replaced by AI agents (e.g., data entry, basic customer service)
- **Partial integration:** Roles where humans and AI agents collaborate (e.g., healthcare diagnostics, legal research)
- **Enhancement:** Jobs transformed and enhanced by AI agent capabilities (e.g., teachers, managers)

---

[8] https://www.mckinsey.com/mgi/our-research/a-new-future-of-work-the-race-to-deploy-ai-and-raise-skills-in-europe-and-beyond

Imagine now Anna, a seasoned marketing manager who has spent years crafting campaigns and analyzing market trends. Her days were filled with meetings, data analysis spreadsheets, and the constant juggling of multiple projects. Then came the whispers, the articles, the growing buzz around AI agents. Initially dismissed as futuristic hype, Anna now finds these intelligent assistants integrated into her daily workflow. An AI agent sifts through vast datasets to identify emerging trends, another drafts initial campaign outlines, and yet another manages the scheduling and follow-ups. Anna isn't obsolete; far from it, but her role is fundamentally shifting. She's now the conductor, orchestrating a team that includes both human colleagues and highly capable AI agents. This is the evolving reality of the job market in the age of AI agents—a landscape characterized by both disruption and unprecedented opportunity, requiring professionals to adapt and acquire new skills to thrive.

The Shifting Sands of Labor: A First-Principles View

To understand the profound impact of AI agents on the job market, we must first look at the fundamental relationship between technology and work. Throughout history, technological advancements have consistently reshaped how tasks are performed and, consequently, the nature of jobs themselves. Think of the Industrial Revolution, where machines replaced manual labor on a massive scale. This didn't eliminate work; it shifted it. New roles emerged in machine operation, maintenance, and the management of these new industrial processes. The subsequent introduction of computers brought about another significant wave of change, automating complex calculations and data processing, leading to the rapid rise of the information technology sector and the demand for computer-related skills.

Now, with the advent of sophisticated AI agents, we're witnessing another significant evolution. As we discussed in Chapter 2, these agents possess the ability to perceive, learn, reason, and act autonomously. This capability extends beyond the automation of repetitive tasks; AI agents can handle complex, knowledge-based activities, analyze intricate data, and even engage in creative endeavors. Recall our orchestra analogy: if traditional automation was like introducing individual instruments, AI agents are like adding entire sections of highly skilled musicians capable of playing complex scores. This doesn't negate the need for the conductor (human workers), but it dramatically changes the composition of the orchestra and the complexity of the music it can create. The core principle remains: technology transforms the tasks within jobs, leading to the evolution of job roles and the skills required to perform them effectively.

From Augmentation to Transformation: The Changing Nature of Work

The integration of AI agents into the workplace isn't a binary event of jobs being simply created or destroyed. Instead, we see a spectrum of change impacting existing roles. At one end of this spectrum is *augmentation*. Here, AI agents act as powerful assistants, enhancing human capabilities and freeing up time for more strategic and creative work. Consider a financial analyst using an AI agent to sift through market data and generate initial investment recommendations. The analyst still applies their expertise, interprets the agent's findings, and makes the final decisions, but their efficiency and insight are significantly amplified. Similarly, a customer service representative might leverage an AI agent to quickly access customer history and provide initial responses, allowing them to focus on more complex or emotionally sensitive issues that require empathy and nuanced problem-solving.

Moving along the spectrum, we encounter *transformation*. In these roles, the core tasks and responsibilities shift significantly due to the pervasive influence of AI agents. Sarah, the marketing manager from our introduction, exemplifies this. Her role is no longer solely about the manual execution of marketing tasks. Instead, she focuses on strategic oversight, creative direction, and managing the collaborative efforts of her human and AI team members. The ability to effectively manage and leverage AI agents becomes a critical skill in transformed roles, requiring professionals to adapt and expand their competencies.

At the other end of the spectrum, we must acknowledge the potential for *displacement* of certain roles. Tasks that are highly repetitive, rule-based, and require minimal creativity or complex problem-solving are most susceptible to being fully automated by AI agents. Data entry clerks, basic customer service roles handling routine inquiries, and certain types of manufacturing jobs could see significant reductions in human involvement. However, even in these scenarios, history suggests that new roles will emerge, often requiring skills related to the design, implementation, maintenance, and oversight of these very AI systems that are driving automation.

Offshore outsourcing hubs, long the first stop for cost-driven labor arbitrage, now face their own disruption as agentic AI targets the same workflows that fueled their growth. Roles in call centers, data processing, and back-office operations—historically offshored for marginal savings—are uniquely vulnerable to AI displacement. Agentic systems combine the linguistic flexibility of LLMs with enterprise-specific knowledge graphs to handle invoice reconciliation, tier-1 customer inquiries, and compliance checks at speeds no human team can match, often at lower operational costs than maintaining offshore partnerships. This creates a paradoxical "onshoring of automation": workflows once sent to Bangalore or Manila now remain in-house, managed by AI agents supervised by domestic specialists. While this shift threatens to destabilize regions reliant on outsourcing economies, it also pressures organizations to reinvest savings into reskilling programs. The same companies automating offshore roles are now scrambling to hire prompt engineers and AI workflow designers—roles requiring cultural context and domain expertise that cannot yet be outsourced to algorithms. Ethical tensions emerge as nations grapple with the asymmetry of AI displacing developing economies' jobs while concentrating high-value AI oversight roles in wealthier markets. We will explore these global tensions in later chapters.

The Rise of the New: Emerging Roles in the Agent Economy

While some existing roles will evolve or diminish, the AI Agent Economy will undoubtedly give rise to entirely new job categories. These are roles we may not even fully conceive of yet, but their configurations and skill requirements are beginning to emerge as the Agent Economy takes shape.

As traditional roles evolve or disappear, entirely new job categories are emerging in what's being called the Agent Economy. These new positions are specifically focused on the critical tasks of developing, strategically managing, and continuously optimizing AI agent systems to ensure they are effective and aligned with human values:

- **Agent architects:** Professionals who specialize in designing and structuring comprehensive AI agent systems for specific applications, ensuring they are robust, scalable, and efficient.
- **Agent trainers:** Experts who specialize in optimizing AI agent performance through advanced training methodologies and ethical alignment, ensuring agents are effective and responsible.
- **Agent orchestrators:** Managers who oversee and strategically coordinate multiple AI agents to execute complex tasks and projects, ensuring seamless integration and workflow optimization.
- **Agent ethics officers:** Specialists who are responsible for ensuring the responsible development, ethical deployment, and ongoing operation of AI systems, mitigating potential risks and biases.
- **Human-agent interface designers:** Professionals who focus on creating effective and intuitive interaction systems between human users and AI agents, enhancing collaboration and user experience.

Consider the need for AI agent trainers and wranglers. These professionals will be responsible for training and fine-tuning AI agents, ensuring they align with specific business objectives and ethical guidelines. They will require a deep understanding of fundamental AI principles, practical data science methodologies, and the specific domain in which the AI agent will be operating to ensure optimal performance and ethical compliance.

Another emerging category is that of AI ethicists and auditors. As AI agents become more sophisticated and autonomous, ensuring their responsible and ethical deployment will be paramount. These specialized professionals will be tasked with developing robust frameworks for ethical AI development, conducting thorough audits to proactively identify potential biases or operational risks, and advising organizations on best practices for responsible and transparent AI implementation.

Furthermore, the integration of AI agents will necessitate AI-human collaboration specialists. These individuals will focus on optimizing the workflows and interactions between human workers and AI agents, ensuring seamless collaboration and maximizing productivity. They will need a strong understanding of both human psychology and AI capabilities to effectively bridge the gap between human and artificial intelligence in the workplace.

Beyond these specific roles, we'll see a broader demand for skills that complement AI capabilities. Creativity, critical thinking, complex problem-solving, and emotional intelligence will become increasingly valuable as AI agents handle more routine tasks. The ability to innovate, adapt, and communicate effectively will be fundamental for navigating the evolving job market and thriving in the age of agentic AI.

Deep Dive: The First Principles of Job Creation in Technological Revolutions

"It's critical to understand why, historically, technological advancements haven't led to permanent mass unemployment. At its core, technology increases productivity. This increased productivity leads to lower costs, which can translate to lower prices and increased demand for goods and services. This increased demand, in turn, often creates new opportunities and entirely new industries. Think of the internet: it initially displaced some traditional communication and retail roles, but it simultaneously created vast new industries in e-commerce, social media, digital marketing, and countless other areas, generating millions of new jobs that didn't exist before. While the transition can be challenging, the fundamental principle is that innovation often reshapes the economic landscape, leading to new forms of work."

Adapting to the Agent Age: Reskilling and Upskilling for the Future

Navigating this evolving job market requires proactive adaptation from both individuals and organizations. *Reskilling*, learning entirely new skills to transition to a different career path, will be key for those in roles facing potential displacement. Organizations and governments have a responsibility to invest in programs that provide accessible and effective reskilling programs to support workforce transitions and ensure economic inclusion.

Equally important is *upskilling*, enhancing existing skills to effectively work alongside and manage AI agents. For professionals like Sarah or Anna, this might involve learning how to interpret AI-generated insights, manage AI-driven campaigns, and collaborate effectively with AI agents. Continuous learning and a willingness to embrace new technologies will be essential for individuals to thrive in the AI Agent Economy.

The rise of the Agent Economy demands a fundamental rethinking of workforce skills. Traditional technical skills remain important but must be complemented by new capabilities.

The following are core skills for the Agent Economy:

- **Agent system understanding:** Fundamental knowledge of AI agent architectures, operational principles, and diverse capabilities.
- **Strategic oversight:** The ability to effectively manage and strategically direct AI agent activities to achieve organizational goals.
- **Complex problem solving:** Advanced skills in handling complex scenarios and unique challenges that extend beyond current AI agent capabilities, requiring human ingenuity.
- **Ethical decision-making:** A deep understanding of the ethical implications of AI agent deployment and the ability to make responsible, value-based decisions regarding their use.
- **Human-agent collaboration:** Expertise in nurturing effective working relationships and seamless interaction systems between human professionals and AI systems to maximize productivity and innovation.

Structural Market Changes

The Agent Economy is reshaping not just job content but the very structure of labor markets, creating new dynamics and workforce models:

- Fluid work arrangements
  - The rise of project-based work that is efficiently coordinated and managed by AI agents, enabling agile workforce deployment.
  - A significant increase in remote work opportunities, effectively enabled by sophisticated agent systems that facilitate virtual collaboration and task management.
  - The growing prevalence of hybrid human-agent teams, where human professionals and AI agents work collaboratively on projects, leveraging complementary strengths.

- Skills marketplace evolution
  - The rapid emergence of new industry-recognized certifications and specialized micro-credentials focused on AI agent-related skills, validating expertise in the Agent Economy.
  - Continuous professional learning becoming the new standard expectation for career advancement and relevance in a rapidly evolving technological landscape.
  - Micro-credentials and skill-based badges gaining increasing importance as verifiable proof of specific agent-related competencies and specialized knowledge.
- Geographic impact
  - A potential reduction in traditional labor arbitrage advantages as AI agents can perform tasks remotely and efficiently across geographic boundaries, altering global workforce dynamics.
  - The emergence of new economic opportunities in specific geographic hubs that specialize in AI agent management, development, and ethical oversight, creating regional centers of excellence.
  - Fundamentally changed dynamics in global talent competition, with increased focus on attracting professionals with advanced AI agent-related skills and expertise, shifting global talent flows.

Why This Matters

These structural changes are creating a more dynamic but also more complex labor market. Workers must be prepared to navigate constant change, adapt to new skill demands, and embrace continuous learning, while organizations need to fundamentally rethink traditional employment models to effectively leverage the potential of human-agent collaboration and remain competitive in the Agent Economy.

Conclusion: Embracing the Evolution

The evolution of the job market driven by AI agents is not a distant threat, but an ongoing transformation. While some roles will undoubtedly change, and others may fade, history teaches us that technological advancement ultimately creates new opportunities. The key lies in understanding the fundamental shifts occurring, proactively adapting through reskilling and upskilling, and embracing the potential of human-AI collaboration. The future of work is not about fearing the rise of intelligent machines, but about intelligently integrating these powerful tools into our workflows to create a more productive, innovative, and ultimately, more fulfilling working world for professionals across diverse sectors.

As the job market evolves and new skill demands emerge, new investment opportunities are also rapidly emerging in multiple interconnected areas such as innovative AI agent technologies, advanced training platforms for agent-related skills, and specialized support services for the Agent Economy. We will explore these exciting investment opportunities in detail in the next section, providing insights into the financial landscape of the AI Agent Economy.

INVESTMENT OPPORTUNITIES

Before proceeding, a necessary caveat: this chapter does not constitute investment advice. The goal is to illuminate first principles that may determine which companies thrive in the agentic AI era. Success will depend on technical infrastructure (e.g., secure multi-agent orchestration), adaptability to ethical guardrails, and the ability to monetize autonomy without triggering regulatory backlash. Markets will reward some and punish others—often unpredictably. What follows is a framework for understanding, not a portfolio prescription. Past performance of tech bubbles (from dot-com to crypto) reminds us that even "obvious" bets carry existential risks when hype outpaces real utility. As a good example, at the time of writing this chapter, NVIDIA lost overnight a large market capitalization percentage[9] (nearly $600bn, or 17% market cap) on news of a new, more efficient, frontier model called DeepSeek. I am sure more examples like this will happen over the next few years.

We've explored the foundational shifts and the transformative potential of AI agents across various domains. Now, let's turn our attention to a critical question for any forward-thinking individual or organization: how can we capitalize on this revolution? Where are the smart investments to be made in this nascent but rapidly expanding ecosystem?

Defining the Emerging Landscape

The transition from traditional AI to agentic AI, as we've discussed, represents a fundamental shift. It's parallel to moving from individual, specialized musicians to a self-organizing orchestra. This shift not only alters how tasks are performed but also creates entirely new avenues for economic activity and, consequently, investment. While the hype around general AI continues, the more concrete and actionable opportunities lie in the development, deployment, and management of specific, goal-oriented AI agents. This is where the investment rubber meets the road. Unlike broad AI research, which can feel like backing a promising scientific theory, investing in the AI Agent Economy offers the chance to back tangible, practical solutions to pressing real-world challenges across diverse industries.

---

[9] https://www.forbes.com/sites/dereksaul/2025/01/27/biggest-market-loss-in-history-nvidia-stock-sheds-nearly-600-billion-as-deepseek-shakes-ai-darling/

Core Investment Areas: Building the Future, Agent by Agent

To comprehensively understand the vast investment potential within the AI Agent Economy, we must methodically break down this complex ecosystem into its fundamental, interconnected components, applying our proven first-principles analytical approach. Just as the transformative rise of the Internet in the late 20th century necessitated massive and strategic investment in core infrastructure, essential software development, and innovative application development, the AI Agent Economy presents strikingly similar layered investment opportunities across its evolving architecture.

First, consider the very foundations for building these intelligent entities: the AI agent development platforms and tools. Think of the early days of the personal computer. While the hardware was groundbreaking, it was the software development environments—the compilers, debuggers, and integrated development environments (IDEs)—that truly unlocked its potential. Similarly, the creation and management of sophisticated AI agents require robust platforms. These platforms will provide the necessary infrastructure for developers to design, train, test, and deploy agents efficiently. Investment in companies creating these platforms—offering user-friendly interfaces, powerful APIs, and seamless integration with existing systems—represents a foundational opportunity. This is conceptually parallel to strategically investing in the pioneering companies that initially built the vital highway infrastructure upon which the entire digital economy now seamlessly travels and operates. As more and more organizations across industries actively seek to strategically deploy AI agents to enhance their operations and innovate their services, the market demand for these essential agent development tools and platforms will only continue to significantly escalate, driving substantial growth and investment returns.

The Investment Landscape

The AI Agent Economy represents a fundamental shift in how value is created and distributed in the digital world. Unlike traditional software that simply executes predefined tasks, AI agents actively pursue goals, learn from experiences, and adapt their behaviors—creating entirely new categories of products, services, and business models.

Current estimates place the potential economic impact of AI agents at $15–30 trillion annually by 2030,[10] with early-stage investment in AI agent

---

[10] https://www.mckinsey.com/mgi/our-research/a-new-future-of-work-the-race-to-deploy-ai-and-raise-skills-in-europe-and-beyond

companies reaching $12.8 billion in 2023 alone. This rapid and accelerating growth is primarily driven by three key converging factors that are propelling the Agent Economy forward:

- **Technological maturity:** Significant advancements in sophisticated large language models (LLMs) and dramatically improved computing infrastructure (e.g., GPUs, cloud computing) have collectively made highly sophisticated and commercially viable AI agents a practical reality for businesses across sectors.
- **Market demand:** Organizations across diverse industries are increasingly and urgently seeking advanced automation and intelligent augmentation solutions to enhance their operational efficiency, improve customer experiences, and drive innovation in their product and service offerings, creating strong market pull for agentic AI.
- **Ecosystem development:** A rapidly growing and increasingly robust ecosystem of essential tools, versatile platforms, and flexible development frameworks is effectively lowering the barriers to entry for businesses to develop, deploy, and manage AI agents, facilitating wider adoption and ecosystem expansion.

Deep Dive: The Agent Economy Stack

The AI Agent Economy can be understood as a three-layer stack:

- **Infrastructure layer:** Computing, storage, networking
- **Platform layer:** Development tools, frameworks, marketplaces
- **Application layer:** Industry-specific solutions and services

Each layer presents distinct investment opportunities with different risk-reward profiles.

Also, the need for specialized AI agents designed for niche markets presents a vast and diverse investment landscape. While some general-purpose agents will emerge, the real power and economic value will often reside in agents tailored for specific industries and tasks. Imagine AI agents designed to optimize supply chains for manufacturing companies, personalize learning experiences for students, or provide highly specialized medical diagnoses. These are not theoretical scenarios; they are emerging realities. Investing in companies developing these vertical-specific AI agents offers the potential for significant returns as they address well-defined needs within established markets. This strategic intersection of deep domain expertise and advanced AI technology creates robust, defensible competitive advantages for these specialized agent providers, enhancing their investment attractiveness.

Finally, as the number of deployed AI agents grows exponentially, the need for systems to orchestrate and manage these digital workforces will become paramount. This leads us to the investment opportunity in agent orchestration and management systems. Think back to our orchestra analogy. Each instrument (agent) may be brilliant on its own, but without a conductor and a well-managed score (orchestration system), the resulting sound could be chaotic. Similarly, businesses deploying multiple AI agents will require sophisticated systems to coordinate their activities, manage their workflows, monitor their performance, and ensure they are working harmoniously toward overarching organizational goals. Investment in companies building these "control towers" for the AI Agent Economy is a bet on the increasing complexity and interconnectedness of these systems.

Why Does This Matter?

The investment opportunities within the AI Agent Economy are not merely about betting on individual companies; they represent a bet on the future of work and the nature of economic productivity. As AI agents automate tasks, augment human capabilities, and unlock new efficiencies, the potential for economic growth is immense. Investing in the infrastructure, the specialized applications, and the management systems of this ecosystem is parallel to investing in the core engines of future economic prosperity. The return on investment won't just be financial; it will be measured in increased productivity, innovation, and the creation of entirely new industries.

Navigating the Investment Landscape: A Call for Diligence

Investing in any emerging technology carries inherent risks, and the AI Agent Economy is no exception. It is a rapidly evolving and highly dynamic field, and the competitive landscape can shift quickly and unexpectedly as new technologies and market entrants emerge. Therefore, a cautious, informed, and thoroughly researched investment approach is critical for investors seeking to capitalize on the Agent Economy's growth potential. Investors should strategically focus their due diligence efforts and capital allocations on companies that demonstrably possess:

- **Strong founding teams:** Individuals with a deep understanding of both AI and the specific problem they are trying to solve

- **Technical expertise:** Deep and proven expertise in relevant AI and software engineering domains, demonstrating technical leadership
- **Domain knowledge:** Substantial and relevant industry-specific domain knowledge applicable to their target market and application
- **Execution track record:** A demonstrated history of successful project execution, product development, and business growth in related or relevant sectors, indicating operational competence
- **Clear value propositions:** Prioritizing investment in companies that articulate and convincingly demonstrate clear, measurable benefits and possess a robust, well-defined understanding of their target market segments and their specific needs within those markets is essential for de-risking investments.
  - **Competitive advantage:** Identifying and evaluating the sustainability of competitive advantages is critical for long-term investment success.
  - **Proprietary technology or data:** Ownership of unique, defensible technology or exclusive access to valuable proprietary datasets that create barriers to entry.
  - **Network effects potential:** Business models that can leverage and benefit from strong network effects, creating increasing value as user adoption grows.
  - **Barriers to entry:** Sustainable barriers to market entry that protect market share and profitability from new competitors, such as patents, regulatory approvals, or significant brand recognition.
- **Business model:** Critically assessing the viability and scalability of the proposed business model is paramount:
  - **Revenue generation potential:** Clear and realistic pathways to generate substantial and recurring revenue streams from agentic AI solutions.
  - **Scalability characteristics:** Business models that are inherently scalable to address expanding market demand without linearly increasing operational costs.
  - **Unit economics:** Favorable unit economics that demonstrate profitability and efficiency at the individual customer or transaction level, ensuring long-term financial sustainability.
- **Scalable solutions:** Technologies and business models that can adapt and grow as the market evolves.
- **Market timing**
  - **Assess technological readiness:** Carefully evaluate the current level of technological maturity for their specific agentic AI solution and its readiness for widespread commercial deployment.
  - **Evaluate market demand signals:** Thoroughly analyze current market demand signals and projected market growth trajectories

to ensure their solution aligns with evolving market needs and opportunities.

- **Consider regulatory landscape:** Proactively consider the current and anticipated future regulatory landscape for AI technologies and ensure their solutions comply with evolving legal and ethical standards, mitigating potential regulatory risks.
- **Ethical considerations:** A commitment to responsible AI development and deployment.

While the potential financial rewards from strategic investments in the AI Agent Economy are demonstrably significant and transformative, conducting thorough due diligence, applying a discerning investment strategy, and maintaining a long-term investment perspective are absolutely essential for successfully navigating this exciting but still nascent investment landscape and maximizing returns while mitigating inherent risks.

Risks and Considerations

While the investment opportunities within the AI Agent Economy are abundant and promising, investors must also carefully and realistically consider several potential risk factors that are inherent in investing in any rapidly evolving technology sector. Key risk categories to evaluate include:

- **Technical risk**
  - **Dependence on underlying AI models:** Potential risks associated with over-reliance on specific underlying AI models that may become outdated or less effective over time, requiring continuous model updates and adaptation.
  - **Integration challenges:** Technical challenges associated with seamlessly integrating agentic AI solutions into complex and often legacy enterprise IT systems, potentially leading to deployment delays and cost overruns.
  - **Security vulnerabilities:** Potential security vulnerabilities and cybersecurity risks associated with AI agents, including data breaches, adversarial attacks, and unintended operational failures, requiring robust security measures.
- **Market risk**
  - **Adoption barriers:** Potential barriers to widespread market adoption of agentic AI solutions, including organizational inertia, lack of internal expertise, and resistance to change within industries.
  - **Competition from tech giants:** Intense competition from established technology giants with substantial resources and existing market

presence in adjacent AI and cloud computing sectors, potentially limiting market share for smaller startups.
- **Regulatory changes:** The dynamic and evolving regulatory landscape for AI technologies, with potential for new regulations that could impact the development, deployment, and commercialization of agentic AI solutions, creating compliance challenges.
- **Execution risk**
  - **Team capabilities:** Risks associated with the execution capabilities of the management team, including their ability to effectively scale operations, manage rapid growth, and adapt to changing market conditions, requiring strong leadership and operational expertise.
  - **Go-to-market strategy:** Risks related to the effectiveness of the company's go-to-market strategy, including sales and marketing execution, customer acquisition costs, and the ability to effectively reach target market segments, requiring a well-defined and scalable sales approach.
  - **Resource management:** Risks associated with effective resource management, including financial resources, human capital, and technological infrastructure, particularly during periods of rapid growth and expansion, requiring efficient resource allocation and financial planning.

Future Watch: Emerging Investment Horizons

Looking ahead, we can anticipate even more nuanced investment opportunities within the AI Agent Economy as the ecosystem matures and diversifies. Consider the potential for:

- **AI agent marketplaces:** The further proliferation and specialization of robust online platforms and marketplaces where pre-built, industry-specific AI agents can be readily bought, sold, securely rented, and extensively customized to meet specific user needs, conceptually similar to established app stores for software applications, but focused on agentic AI.
- **Agent security solutions:** The rapidly growing demand for specialized cybersecurity solutions and advanced security protocols specifically designed to protect AI agents from malicious attacks, data breaches, and unauthorized access, ensuring the security and integrity of agentic AI systems in critical applications.
- **Agent training data and services:** The continuous and expanding need for vast amounts of high-quality, meticulously curated, and ethically sourced training data to effectively develop, continuously refine, and optimize the performance of AI agents across diverse applications, creating

significant opportunities for specialized data providers and expert data annotation services within the Agent Economy.

These are just a few illustrative examples of the continually evolving investment landscape within the AI Agent Economy, demonstrably highlighting the inherent dynamism, long-term growth potential, and expanding scope of investment opportunities within this transformative technological sector.

The AI Agent Economy is likely to evolve through several phases:

- **Infrastructure build-out (2024–2026):** The initial phase focused on the development of core foundational platforms and essential toolsets for agent creation, the establishment of industry-wide standardization of key interfaces and communication protocols, and the development of robust security and comprehensive governance frameworks for agent ecosystems.
- **Enterprise adoption (2026–2028):** The subsequent phase characterized by increasing integration of agentic AI into core enterprise business processes across various industries, the emergence of industry-specific and vertical market agent solutions tailored for specific sectors, and the growing need for robust Return on Investment (ROI) validation and quantifiable business benefits from agent deployments.
- **Consumer mainstreaming (2028+):** The mature phase marked by the widespread mainstream adoption of personalized AI agents by individual consumers for diverse personal and professional tasks, the development of sophisticated agent-to-agent communication networks and collaborative agent ecosystems, and the emergence of entirely new agent-driven economic models and societal interactions.

Investment opportunities will shift with each phase, requiring investors to stay agile while maintaining a long-term perspective.

Conclusion

The AI Agent Economy is not a futuristic fantasy; it's a present-day reality unfolding before our eyes. The shift from basic AI to sophisticated, autonomous agents is creating a wealth of investment opportunities across various layers of this emerging ecosystem. From the foundational platforms and tools to the specialized agents and the orchestration systems that manage them, the potential for innovation and financial return is substantial. Understanding the underlying principles and applying a discerning eye enables investors to position themselves to capitalize on this transformative technological shift and participate in building the future, agent by agent.

FUTURE WATCH: ECONOMIC TRENDS

As we advance into the next decade, the emergence of AI agents is destined to fundamentally reshape our economic landscape—much like how the introduction of electricity transformed industries and society in the early twentieth century. Just as an orchestra evolves when new instruments and playing techniques are introduced, the global economy is adapting to accommodate these new digital participants. Let's explore the key economic trends that will likely define this transformation.

Imagine a world where economic forecasts aren't solely reliant on lagging indicators and expert opinions but are dynamically shaped by the collective intelligence of millions of AI agents. These aren't just passive data crunchers; they are active participants in the economy, negotiating deals, optimizing supply chains, and even identifying entirely new market opportunities we haven't conceived of yet. As we explore deeper into the age of the AI Agent Economy, it's imperative to look beyond the immediate disruptions and consider the profound shifts on the horizon. Just as the invention of the printing press irrevocably changed the flow of information and, consequently, the economic landscape of its time, the rise of intelligent, autonomous agents is set to reshape our financial future in ways we are only beginning to understand. Building upon our understanding of how these agents operate—their ability to perceive, plan, and act—we can start to sketch a picture of the emerging economic trends they will drive.

The Rise of the Intelligent Assistant Class

Recall our earlier analogy of the orchestra. We discussed how individual AI agents, each skilled in a specific domain, can collaborate to achieve complex goals, much like musicians playing individual instruments to create a symphony. Now, extend that analogy to the economy. Imagine an economy populated by billions of these highly specialized "musicians"—intelligent assistants capable of handling intricate tasks with minimal human oversight. This isn't about replacing human workers entirely; it's about creating a new class of tireless, efficient digital collaborators.

From a first-principles perspective, the economic power of AI agents stems from their ability to significantly reduce transaction costs. Think about any economic activity—a purchase, a contract negotiation, a logistical operation. Each involves time, resources, and the potential for error. AI agents, by automating tasks like information gathering, analysis, and communication, can streamline these processes dramatically. For instance, an AI agent tasked with procuring raw materials for a manufacturing plant can continuously monitor global markets, negotiate prices with suppliers, and arrange logistics, all without the need for human intervention at every step. This leads to faster, cheaper, and more efficient economic activity.

The most significant shift we're witnessing is the emergence of what economists are calling the *Agent Economy*—a new economic paradigm where AI agents become active participants in economic activities. This new economic model is characterized by:

- **Agent-mediated transactions:** A significant increase in economic transactions that are strategically negotiated and efficiently executed by intelligent AI agents autonomously operating on behalf of both human individuals and large organizations, streamlining commerce and reducing transaction costs
- **Automated value creation:** The growing ability of AI agents to independently generate substantial economic value through diverse means, including autonomous content creation, sophisticated data analysis leading to actionable insights, and proactive problem-solving across complex domains, expanding the scope of economic value generation
- **Hybrid markets:** The rapid emergence of novel hybrid marketplaces where both human economic actors and autonomous AI agents seamlessly interact and transact, creating new forms of economic exchange and collaboration in the digital age
- **Network effects:** The potential for exponential value creation through increasingly sophisticated agent-to-agent collaboration networks, where AI agents can communicate, coordinate, and transact with each other autonomously, creating powerful network effects and driving emergent economic value in complex systems

Deep Dive: The Agent Economy Value Chain

- **Primary value creators:** AI agents generating original content, solutions, and insights
- **Secondary facilitators:** Platforms and infrastructure enabling agent operations
- **Tertiary beneficiaries:** Human businesses and individuals leveraging agent capabilities
- **End consumers:** Both humans and other AI agents consuming agent-generated value

Why This Matters

For businesses, this translates to potentially massive gains in productivity and profitability. For consumers, it could mean lower prices and more personalized services. For the economy as a whole, it signals a potential acceleration of growth and innovation. This "intelligent assistant class" is not a futuristic fantasy; we are already seeing its embryonic forms in AI-powered customer service chatbots, automated trading systems, and AI-driven marketing platforms. As these AI agents continue to become more technologically sophisticated, functionally versatile, and seamlessly interconnected, their profound economic impact on a global scale will only continue to amplify and accelerate in the coming years, driving a new era of economic transformation.

The Great Reskilling and the Augmentation Economy

One of the most discussed economic impacts of AI is the potential for job displacement. While valid concerns exist, particularly for roles involving routine and repetitive tasks, the future is likely to be defined less by wholesale replacement and more by augmentation. From a first-principles standpoint, AI agents excel at optimizing and executing well-defined processes. This frees up human workers to focus on tasks requiring creativity, critical thinking, emotional intelligence, and complex problem-solving—the very areas where current AI agents still fall short.

This shift necessitates a significant reskilling of the workforce. Individuals will need to develop expertise in areas that complement AI capabilities, such as designing and managing agentic systems, interpreting complex agent-generated data, and handling exceptions or unforeseen circumstances that fall outside of an agent's programmed scope. Think of it like this: the advent of computers didn't eliminate the need for human accountants, but it drastically changed the skills required to be a successful accountant. Similarly, the rise of AI agents will create demand for new roles focused on "agent wrangling," which encompasses the critical tasks of ensuring these sophisticated digital assistants are performing optimally, operating ethically, and strategically aligned with broader organizational goals and societal values

Labor Market Evolution

The integration of AI agents into the workforce is catalyzing a fundamental restructuring of labor markets. Unlike previous technological revolutions that primarily automated routine tasks, AI agents are capable of handling complex cognitive work, leading to several key trends:

- Skill premium redistribution
  - A demonstrable decrease in the traditional premium associated with routine cognitive tasks as these become increasingly automated by AI agents, reducing their market value and demand.
  - A significant increase in the economic value and market demand for specialized professional skills in strategic agent supervision, effective agent orchestration, and comprehensive agent management as organizations deploy larger agent workforces.
  - The emergence of a novel skill premium for "agent whispering"—the specialized ability to effectively and intuitively direct, collaborate with, and optimize the performance of sophisticated AI agents, requiring human-AI collaboration expertise.
- Job category evolution
  - The rapid emergence of entirely new job roles and professional categories specifically focused on strategic agent management, comprehensive agent oversight, and continuous agent performance optimization as agentic AI becomes mainstream.
  - A fundamental transformation of many existing professional roles across industries to strategically incorporate seamless agent collaboration into daily workflows and core responsibilities, requiring workforce upskilling.
  - A gradual decline in the market demand for traditional job positions that can be comprehensively and cost-effectively fully automated by advanced AI agents, leading to workforce transitions and reskilling needs.
- Labor market flexibility
  - A significant rise in agent-assisted gig work and freelance opportunities, where AI agents can efficiently manage tasks, connect workers with projects, and streamline administrative processes, increasing labor market fluidity.
  - An increased organizational ability to rapidly and cost-effectively scale workforce capacity and project bandwidth through strategic agent augmentation, enabling agile workforce management and responsiveness to market demands.
  - The emergence of novel models of human-agent hybrid teams, where human professionals and AI agents collaboratively work together on projects, leveraging their complementary strengths and creating synergistic work environments.

Why Does This Matter?

This transition will require investment in education and training programs, both by individuals and by organizations. Governments will also need to play a role in supporting workers through this period of change. The successful navigation of this "great reskilling" will determine whether the AI Agent Economy leads to widespread prosperity or exacerbates existing inequalities. The focus will be on creating an "augmentation economy," where humans and AI agents work collaboratively, each leveraging their unique strengths to achieve more than either could alone.

Decentralized Autonomous Organizations and the Agent-Led Enterprise

Beyond individual tasks, AI agents have the potential to revolutionize organizational structures themselves. Consider the concept of decentralized autonomous organizations (DAOs). Currently, DAOs are primarily governed by smart contracts on blockchain networks but imagine DAOs where the core decision-making and operational processes are driven by sophisticated AI agents. From a first-principles perspective, a DAO aims for transparency and efficiency by codifying rules and automating processes. AI agents can take this concept to the next level, dynamically adapting to changing circumstances and making complex strategic decisions based on vast amounts of real-time data and autonomously optimize resource allocation with unprecedented efficiency and agility.

This leads to the vision of the "agent-led enterprise." While human leadership will remain essential for setting overall vision and values, many operational and strategic decisions within a company could be delegated to interconnected AI agents. These agents could manage projects, allocate resources, negotiate contracts, and even identify new market opportunities with a speed and efficiency that surpasses human capabilities in many operational domains.

Why Does This Matter?

This could lead to leaner, more agile, and more responsive organizations. It could also flatten traditional hierarchical structures, empowering individuals and smaller teams with greater autonomy. However, this radical organizational transformation also inevitably raises critical questions about accountability, ethical oversight, and comprehensive operational control in agent-led enterprises. Who is responsible when an AI agent makes a poor decision? How do we ensure these agent-led organizations operate ethically and in the best interests of their stakeholders? These are the complex governance challenges that will need to be addressed as this trend unfolds.

Investment Horizons: Betting on Autonomy

The rise of the AI Agent Economy presents significant investment opportunities. From a first-principles perspective, any technology that fundamentally improves efficiency and productivity is likely to attract capital. We are already seeing a surge in investment in AI research and development, particularly in areas related to agentic systems. This includes companies building the underlying infrastructure for deploying and managing AI agents, those developing specialized agents for specific industries, and those creating tools and platforms that enable humans to interact with and oversee these autonomous entities.

Looking ahead, investment horizons will broaden to encompass areas like AI agent security, ethical AI frameworks, and the development of new interfaces for human-agent collaboration. Just as the early days of the Internet saw massive investment in infrastructure and software, the next wave of technological innovation will be driven by the creation and deployment of intelligent, autonomous agents.

Why Does This Matter?

Understanding these investment trends is fundamental for businesses looking to capitalize on the AI Agent Economy and for investors seeking to identify the next generation of successful companies. It's about recognizing that the future of technology is not just about individual AI tools, but about the interconnected ecosystems of intelligent agents that will power future economic growth.

Ethical Considerations and the Economic Landscape

As AI agents become more deeply integrated into the economy, ethical considerations become paramount. From a first-principles standpoint, an economic system should be fair, transparent, and beneficial to society as a whole. The potential for bias in AI algorithms, the implications for privacy and data security when agents collect and process vast amounts of information, and the need for accountability when autonomous systems make consequential decisions are all critical economic considerations.

Furthermore, the concentration of power in the hands of those who control the most advanced AI agents raises concerns about potential market manipulation and anti-competitive practices. Ensuring equitable access to transformative agent technologies for smaller businesses and developing nations, and proactively establishing robust, adaptive regulatory frameworks that promote responsible AI innovation while mitigating potential societal harms, will be critically important for effectively navigating these complex ethical challenges and strategically nurturing a healthy, sustainable, and inclusive AI Agent Economy that benefits all of humanity, rather than just a privileged few.

Societal Economic Impact

The broader societal economic implications of the pervasive Agent Economy will likely encompass a range of transformative changes across various dimensions, reshaping societal structures and economic paradigms:

- **Wealth distribution:** The emergence of novel patterns of wealth creation and distribution based on strategic agent ownership, effective agent management capabilities, and differential access to advanced agent technologies, potentially altering existing wealth distribution models.
  - **Economic accessibility:** Increased and democratized access to sophisticated economic tools, advanced financial services, and personalized economic opportunities through readily available agent intermediaries and agent-driven platforms, potentially leveling the economic playing field for individuals and smaller businesses.
  - **Market efficiency:** Significantly enhanced market efficiency across diverse sectors through agent-enabled real-time price discovery mechanisms, optimized resource allocation algorithms, and streamlined transaction processes, leading to more efficient and responsive markets.
  - **Economic complexity:** A demonstrably greater societal ability to effectively handle increasingly complex economic interactions, manage intricate global interdependencies, and navigate dynamic market volatility through the advanced analytical and predictive capabilities of agentic AI systems, enhancing economic resilience and adaptability.

Why Does This Matter?

Ignoring these ethical dimensions could lead to a future where the benefits of AI are unevenly distributed, potentially exacerbating existing social and economic divides. Proactive and sustained engagement with critical ethical considerations, robust regulatory oversight, and a commitment to inclusive AI development are not merely matters of corporate social responsibility or governmental policy; they are absolutely essential prerequisites for strategically building a stable, equitable, and ultimately prosperous AI-driven future for all of humanity, ensuring that the benefits of agentic AI are broadly shared and contribute to a more just and sustainable world.

Conclusion

The economic trends driven by AI agents are multifaceted and far-reaching. From the emergence of an "intelligent assistant class" to the potential reshaping of organizational structures and investment priorities, the integration of autonomous agents into our economic fabric promises profound change. While challenges remain—particularly around reskilling, ethical considerations, and governance—the potential for increased efficiency, productivity, and innovation is immense. As we move forward, understanding the fundamental principles driving the development and deployment of these agents will be key to navigating this evolving landscape and ensuring that the AI Agent Economy benefits all of society. This exploration of economic trends naturally leads us to consider how these changes will impact individual businesses and the strategies they will need to adopt to thrive in this new era, which will be the focus of our next section.

As we move deeper into the Agent Economy, the key to success will lie in understanding how to effectively participate in this new economic paradigm. Organizations and individuals who learn to "conduct their orchestra" of AI agents effectively will likely see the greatest benefits.

The next chapter will strategically explore in detail how innovative enterprises are already proactively beginning to implement these fundamental changes, providing concrete, real-world examples of successful agent integration strategies across diverse industries, and offering actionable frameworks for businesses to effectively navigate the Agent Economy and thrive in this transformative era of technological and economic change.

KEY TAKEAWAYS

The AI Agent Economy represents a fundamental transformation of how value is created, distributed, and captured across the global economy. Enabling autonomous digital labor at unprecedented scale empowers AI agents to reshape industries, create new business models, and redefine the nature of work itself. Understanding and adapting to this shift will be critical for organizations and individuals seeking to thrive in this new economic paradigm.

1. **Understand that AI agents are economic multipliers.**
   AI agents are not just about automation; they fundamentally enhance productivity, accelerate innovation, and optimize resource allocation, leading to significant economic gains.

- KEY INSIGHTS:
  - AI agents perform tasks faster, more accurately, and at a lower cost than humans in many domains, leading to direct productivity increases.
  - Their ability to analyze vast datasets and identify patterns accelerates the pace of research, development, and the creation of new products and services.
  - AI agents can optimize complex systems, from supply chains to energy grids, leading to significant reductions in waste and improved efficiency.
- DO:
  - Identify areas within your business where AI agents can augment existing workflows or automate repetitive tasks to boost productivity.
  - Explore opportunities to leverage AI agents for data analysis and insight generation to drive innovation and better decision-making.
  - Consider implementing AI agents to optimize resource allocation and reduce operational costs.
- DON'T:
  - Underestimate the potential for AI agents to drive significant economic value beyond simple automation.
  - Focus solely on cost reduction; consider the potential for new revenue streams and enhanced customer experiences.
  - Neglect the importance of understanding the underlying principles of AI agents to effectively leverage their capabilities.

2. **New business models will emerge.**

   The AI Agent Economy is giving rise to entirely new ways of creating and delivering value, moving beyond traditional models.
   - KEY INSIGHTS:
     - Agent-as-a-service is democratizing access to sophisticated AI capabilities, allowing businesses to rent specialized agents on demand.
     - Agent marketplaces are creating hubs for digital talent, connecting those seeking agentic skills with developers and providers.
     - Agent-enabled products and services are embedding intelligence directly into offerings, enhancing functionality and personalization.
     - Autonomous businesses, while still nascent, represent a radical shift toward AI-driven operations with minimal human oversight.
   - DO:
     - Analyze your industry and identify opportunities to create or leverage AaaS offerings or participate in agent marketplaces.

- Explore how embedding AI agents into your existing products or services can create new value propositions and enhance customer experiences.
- Consider the potential for autonomous business models within your sector and experiment with pilot projects.
- DON'T:
  - Limit your thinking to traditional business models; explore the possibilities enabled by autonomous digital labor.
  - Overlook the potential of partnering with or utilizing external AI agents to enhance your capabilities.
  - Be afraid to experiment with new business models, even if they seem unconventional at first glance.

3. The job market will evolve.

The integration of AI agents will transform the job market, requiring adaptation, reskilling, and a focus on uniquely human skills.

- KEY INSIGHTS:
  - While some routine tasks will be automated, the focus is shifting toward human-AI collaboration, augmenting human capabilities.
  - New roles are emerging in areas such as AI agent training, orchestration, ethics, and human-agent interface design.
  - Skills like creativity, critical thinking, complex problem-solving, and emotional intelligence will become increasingly valuable.
- DO:
  - Invest in reskilling and upskilling initiatives for your workforce to prepare them for working alongside AI agents.
  - Identify new roles within your organization that focus on managing, training, and overseeing AI agent operations.
  - Emphasize the development of uniquely human skills in your employees, nurturing creativity, critical thinking, and emotional intelligence.
- DON'T:
  - View AI agents solely as a threat to jobs; recognize the potential for job creation and role transformation.
  - Neglect the importance of human oversight and ethical considerations in the deployment and management of AI agents.
  - Underestimate the need for continuous learning and adaptation in the face of evolving AI capabilities.

The economic impact of AI agents is not just about incremental improvements; it signifies a fundamental shift toward a new economic paradigm. Successfully navigating this transition requires a proactive approach, a willingness to embrace change, and a deep understanding of the underlying principles driving this transformation. As we've seen, the economic landscape is being reshaped, creating both challenges and immense opportunities. In the next chapter, we will go into practical strategies for businesses to successfully implement and integrate AI agents, turning the theoretical potential we've explored here into tangible business advantages.

CHAPTER 6

The Enterprise Revolution

"The enterprise of the future is not just automated, but augmented by AI agents."
— Andrew Ng, Co-founder of Coursera;
Stanford CS adjunct faculty

ORGANIZATIONAL TRANSFORMATION

Imagine an orchestra tuning up, a collection of individual talents set to create something magnificent. But without a conductor, the result would be mere noise, a cacophony of disparate sounds. Traditional organizations, much like this unguided orchestra, have relied on hierarchical structures to coordinate their human "musicians." Now, envision a revolutionary shift: an AI agent system stepping onto the podium, not just to conduct in the traditional sense, but to understand, coordinate, and optimize each instrument's contribution in real time, adapting the score as the performance unfolds. This is the profound transformation agentic AI is bringing to organizations, reshaping the very essence of how businesses operate and organize themselves.

Picture stepping back in time, into the bustling headquarters of a Fortune 500 company a decade ago. The scene is likely familiar: individuals working diligently within clearly defined departments, adhering to established procedures, and contributing to a hierarchical structure where information flowed methodically, though sometimes sluggishly, upward and downward. Key performance indicators (KPIs) were meticulously tracked, often focusing on individual or departmental output, and the organizational chart resembled a rigid pyramid, each level clearly delineated.

Traditional organizational structures, with their rigid hierarchies and fixed reporting lines, were born from the industrial age's imperative for control and standardization. These structures served us well for more than a century, efficiently managing large-scale operations and ensuring consistent output. Consider a typical Fortune 500 company: information ascends and descends through predetermined channels, decisions require multiple layers of approval, and departments frequently operate in silos, like separate sections of an orchestra unaware of the others' melodies.

Deep Dive: First Principles of Organization

At its core, an organization is fundamentally:

- A system designed for the coordination of human effort
- A mechanism for effective decision-making
- A framework for the strategic allocation of resources
- A structured pathway for information flow

These foundational elements remain constant, the bedrock of any enterprise. However, agentic AI is not just refining these elements; it's fundamentally revolutionizing *how* we achieve them, composing an entirely new organizational symphony.

Now, fast-forward to today, or project yourself into the near future. Envision that same organization, now dynamically infused with the capabilities of agentic AI. This isn't merely about automating routine tasks; it's a fundamental shift in the organizational DNA. AI agents are not just tools; they are evolving into integral collaborators, capable of proactive problem-solving, cross-departmental coordination, and real-time adaptation. This profound integration necessitates a comprehensive organizational transformation, moving beyond superficial technology adoption to a deep reimagining of roles, structures, and even the very purpose of teams. This section will explore the multifaceted nature of this transformation, exploring the key areas where agentic AI is set to reshape the modern enterprise, turning it into a responsive, adaptive, and intelligent organism.

Redesigning Roles: From Task Execution to Strategic Orchestration and Human-AI Collaboration

AI agents are fundamentally altering these core organizational elements. Unlike traditional automation tools, which operate based on preprogrammed rules, agents possess the capacity to understand context, learn from experience, and make nuanced decisions. This is giving rise to what we term *fluid organizations*, structures that dynamically adapt to changing conditions and requirements, much like a jazz ensemble improvising based on a shared musical understanding.

The most immediate and perhaps most profound impact of agentic AI is the fundamental redesign of individual and team roles. For generations, many jobs have been structured around the execution of specific, often repetitive, tasks. Consider roles such as data entry clerks, claims processors, or junior analysts spending countless hours compiling reports. Agentic AI possesses the capability to perform these routine functions with greater speed, accuracy, and consistency, liberating human employees from the constraints of mundane work. From a first-principles perspective, this shift originates from the core capabilities of AI agents: perception, reasoning, and action. When these capabilities are applied to structured tasks, automation becomes not just possible but often demonstrably superior to human execution.

However, this is not a narrative of job displacement, but rather of role evolution. As AI agents assume responsibility for task execution, human roles will increasingly gravitate toward higher-level functions that leverage uniquely human skills: strategic thinking, creative problem-solving, complex decision-making, emotional intelligence, and the ability to build and nurture meaningful relationships. Instead of being task executors, employees will evolve into orchestrators, managing the workflows of AI agents, setting strategic goals, and handling exceptions and novel situations that demand human ingenuity and creativity. This perspective underscores the evolving nature of roles and the potential for new organizational functions to emerge in the agentic enterprise. This evolution also necessitates a critical look at the HR function itself.

Consider a customer service department. Basic inquiries and routine troubleshooting can be seamlessly handled by AI agents, providing instant responses and resolving common issues efficiently. Human agents, empowered by AI-driven insights and freed from routine tasks, can then focus on resolving complex or emotionally charged issues, building rapport with customers, and developing proactive strategies to enhance overall customer satisfaction. This necessitates a new emphasis on human-AI collaboration, where the inherent strengths of each are strategically leveraged to achieve superior outcomes. It requires learning how to effectively delegate to AI, how to interpret AI-generated insights, and how to work alongside intelligent machines as true partners, creating a harmonious human-agent team.

Why This Matters

This role redesign is imperative for unlocking the full potential of both human capital and AI technology. Liberating human employees from routine, repetitive tasks empowers organizations to focus on activities that drive innovation, cultivate stronger customer relationships, and generate greater strategic value. Failing to adapt roles to this new reality will lead to underutilized talent, decreased employee satisfaction, and a significant missed opportunity to leverage the transformative power of agentic AI, leaving organizations playing out of tune in the modern marketplace.

The "Zero-Human Operations" Thought Experiment: Challenging Traditional Structures and Processes

For years, organizations have pursued digital transformation, implementing technologies to streamline workflows and enhance efficiency. These efforts, while impactful, often focused on augmenting existing human-centric processes with digital tools. However, the emergence of agentic AI presents a paradigm shift, moving us from incremental digital enhancements to the potential for a complete agentic transformation. To truly embrace this revolution, we must challenge the deeply ingrained assumption that human involvement is the default starting point for designing operational processes. This is where the concept of "zero-human operations" becomes invaluable (see Figure 6.1). It's a thought experiment, a design target that encourages us to fundamentally rethink organizational structures from an AI-first perspective. By initially aiming for minimal human involvement in routine operations, we can uncover opportunities for radical efficiency, agility, and innovation, ultimately leading to organizational designs that are vastly different and far more powerful than those merely digitally enhanced.

Zero-Human Organization: An Agentic AI Framework

The Zero-Human Organization is not about eliminating humans, but about strategically re-allocating human potential to higher-value, uniquely human endeavors, orchestrated and augmented by powerful, autonomous AI agents.

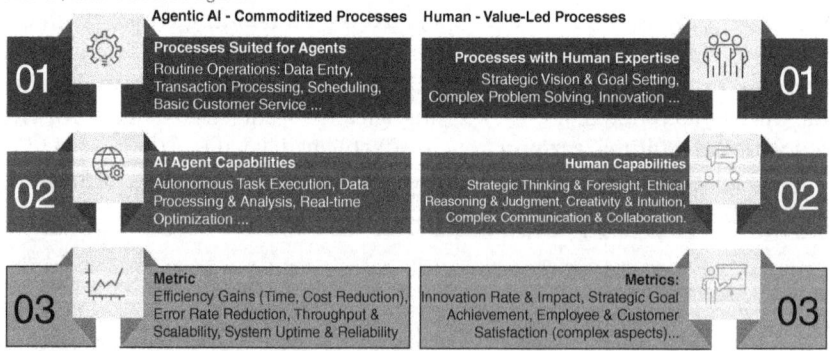

FIGURE 6.1 Zero-human design organization framework

Instead of simply retrofitting AI agents into existing organizational structures, forward-thinking companies are adopting a "zero-based" approach to organizational design. This involves starting with a clean slate and asking a fundamental question: "If we were building this organization today, with AI agents as core team members, how would we structure it for optimal performance?"

Following this line of thought, to truly grasp the disruptive potential of agentic AI on organizational design, let's engage in a thought experiment: imagine redesigning core operational functions with the explicit goal of minimizing direct human involvement in the execution of routine processes. This concept of zero-human operations isn't about a dystopian future devoid of human workers. Instead, it's a strategic exercise designed to challenge our ingrained assumptions about how work should be structured and to identify opportunities for radical efficiency gains. Drawing an analogy from the world of finance, consider zero-based budgeting. Instead of incrementally adjusting existing budgets, every expense must be justified anew. Similarly, in zero-human operations, we begin with a blank slate, asking: how would this process function optimally if AI agents were the primary actors, conducting the core operations?

Consider a supply chain. Imagine AI agents autonomously managing inventory levels, dynamically predicting demand fluctuations, negotiating contracts with suppliers, and orchestrating complex logistics, all with minimal human intervention in the day-to-day operations. Human roles then shift to overseeing the overall strategic direction of the supply chain, managing exceptions and unforeseen disruptions, building strategic partnerships with key suppliers, and focusing on long-term resilience and continuous innovation within the supply chain ecosystem.

This thought experiment compels us to move beyond incremental automation and envision entirely new workflows and organizational structures optimized for an AI-first world. It forces us to identify the core objectives of each function and then design processes around the inherent capabilities of AI agents to achieve those objectives most effectively and efficiently. It encourages a radical rethinking of how we orchestrate work within the enterprise.

Why This Matters

This thought experiment, while potentially aspirational in the short term for some organizations, provides a powerful framework for strategic planning and identifying areas ripe for significant transformation. It encourages a fundamental rethinking of business processes, leading to more efficient, agile, and resilient operations. It helps organizations break free from the constraints of legacy systems and human-centric workflows, paving the way for truly innovative organizational designs and allowing them to compose entirely new operational melodies.

From Static KPIs to Dynamic, AI-Augmented Performance Management

The integration of agentic AI also necessitates a fundamental shift in how organizations measure performance and set objectives. Traditional KPIs and objectives and key results (OKRs) are often designed for relatively stable, human-driven processes. They tend to be backward-looking, primarily focusing on past performance, and may not adequately capture the dynamic contributions of AI agents or the complex interplay between human and artificial intelligence within the modern enterprise orchestra. Judging each musician solely on their individual technical proficiency misses the synergy and magic of the ensemble performance. Similarly, relying solely on traditional metrics in an AI-powered organization risks overlooking the synergistic value created by human-agent teams.

The future of performance management in the agentic enterprise will be more dynamic, data-driven, and focused on outcomes rather than just mere output. AI agents themselves can play a fundamental role in this evolution, providing real-time insights into performance, proactively identifying bottlenecks, and even intelligently suggesting adjustments to objectives based on evolving circumstances and real-time data. KPIs might evolve to measure the effectiveness of human-agent collaborations, the efficiency of AI-driven decision-making processes, and the overall adaptability and resilience of the organization in the face of dynamic market conditions. OKRs can become more fluid, allowing for iterative adjustments based on AI-powered insights and real-time feedback loops, ensuring continuous alignment and optimization.

Imagine AI agents continuously monitoring progress toward strategic objectives, proactively identifying potential roadblocks, and intelligently suggesting course corrections to human managers, acting as a proactive, always-on performance optimization system. This requires a shift from static, top-down performance management to a more agile, data-informed, and collaborative approach where AI acts as a continuous improvement partner, constantly refining the organizational performance score.

In summary, traditional organizational metrics, such as span of control, reporting layers, and departmental budgets, are giving way to new, dynamic measurements that better reflect the fluid and interconnected nature of agent-enabled organizations. Modern organizations are increasingly adopting the following:

- **Real-time alignment scores:** Measuring the degree to which various parts of the organization are working in concert toward common goals

- **Dynamic resource allocation metrics:** Assessing the efficiency and effectiveness of resource deployment across the organization, adapting in real time to changing needs
- **Cross-functional collaboration indices:** Evaluating the level of seamless interaction and knowledge sharing between different departments or teams
- **AI-human interaction effectiveness measures:** Quantifying the synergistic output and efficiency gains derived from human-agent collaborations

These new metrics reflect the fluid and interconnected nature of agent-enabled organizations, where traditional boundaries between departments become increasingly permeable, much like the different sections of an orchestra blending seamlessly into a unified sound.

Why This Matters

Relying on outdated performance metrics in an agentic environment will not only fail to capture the true value of AI but could also incentivize counterproductive behaviors, obstructing the overall performance of the enterprise orchestra. Organizations need to embrace new performance management frameworks that strategically leverage the real-time insights of AI agents and focus on the collaborative achievement of overarching strategic outcomes. This ensures that both human and AI contributions are appropriately valued and recognized, and that the organization remains dynamically aligned with its strategic goals in a continuously evolving landscape. This evolution in performance measurement is a critical component of the broader organizational transformation required to thrive in the age of intelligent agents, ensuring the enterprise orchestra plays in perfect harmony.

The Orchestra Model 2.0

Returning to our orchestra metaphor, today's organizations are evolving into something far more sophisticated than traditional symphonies. AI agents are not merely acting as conductors; they are becoming both conductors and players, intelligently coordinating human expertise while actively participating in the performance, like virtuoso instrumentalists who also contribute to the overall direction of the ensemble. They can simultaneously:

- **Monitor and dynamically adjust overall organizational rhythm:** Ensuring all parts of the organization are operating in sync and at the optimal pace
- **Optimize individual and team performance in real time:** Providing intelligent feedback and adjustments to maximize the contribution of each element

- **Proactively identify and resolve dissonance in real time:** Detecting and correcting inefficiencies, conflicts, or misalignments before they escalate
- **Adapt the score dynamically as conditions change:** Responding intelligently to new information, market shifts, or unforeseen challenges, ensuring continuous relevance and optimal performance

Why This Matters

This transformation isn't just about achieving incremental efficiency gains; it's about creating organizations that can dynamically respond to both opportunities and challenges at unprecedented speed and scale, becoming truly adaptive and resilient entities. For executives and managers, understanding this fundamental shift is central for future-proofing their organizations and careers, ensuring they can lead their enterprise orchestras into a successful future.

This fundamental shift in organizational design represents just the overture of the enterprise revolution. As we'll explore in the following sections, the implications for business processes and strategic decision-making are equally profound, composing the full symphony of the agentic enterprise.

BUSINESS PROCESSES REVOLUTION: FROM CHOREOGRAPHY TO AUTONOMOUS FLOW

Just as we explored how an orchestra requires perfect coordination among its musicians to create a seamless and harmonious performance, modern businesses operate through intricate processes that have traditionally relied on human coordination, complex software systems, and often cumbersome manual handoffs. But imagine if each instrument in our orchestra became intelligent enough to not only play its part flawlessly but also adapt and harmonize with others in real time, without needing explicit direction from a conductor for every note. This is the transformative promise of AI agents in revolutionizing business processes, moving from rigid choreography to autonomous flow.

Consider the intricate dance of a modern supply chain. Purchase orders travel electronically between disparate systems, invoices are generated and reconciled, shipping manifests are meticulously created, and payments are processed—a complex choreography orchestrated by a web of interconnected software applications and substantial human intervention. While the digital revolution has undoubtedly streamlined many of these processes, they often remain fragmented, relying on point-to-point integrations and human oversight to ensure smooth and accurate execution. Now, envision a future where intelligent AI agents autonomously navigate this entire process, proactively anticipating potential needs, intelligently resolving discrepancies, and optimizing every step of the supply chain without requiring constant human direction or rigid software integrations. This isn't merely process improvement; it's a fundamental revolution in how business processes are conceived, executed, and dynamically managed, moving toward a state of autonomous flow. This section will explore how AI agents are destined to dismantle traditional process silos, paving the way for a new era of dynamic, autonomous workflows that seamlessly transcend organizational boundaries, creating a more fluid and responsive business performance.

From Workflow Automation to Autonomous Process Execution

For years, businesses have strived for enhanced efficiency through workflow automation. Tools like **Robotic Process Automation (RPA)** have enabled the automation of repetitive, rule-based tasks, mimicking human actions to interact with existing software systems. However, these systems are inherently limited by their reliance on predefined rules and their inability to effectively handle exceptions or make complex decisions autonomously. Think of RPA as automating the individual movements of musicians based on a fixed score, but lacking the ability to adapt to unforeseen circumstances or improvise when the musical landscape shifts. Agentic AI, on the other hand, represents a significant paradigm shift, moving from simply automating workflows to enabling autonomous process execution, like enabling each musician to intelligently adapt and improvise within the overall musical piece.

AI agents, with their inherent ability to perceive, reason, and act, can understand the overarching goals of a business process and dynamically determine the optimal course of action to effectively achieve those goals. Consider a typical expense reporting process. Traditional systems require employees to manually input data, meticulously scan receipts, and painstakingly categorize expenses, often leading to errors, delays, and frustration. An AI agent, however, could autonomously monitor employee spending, intelligently categorize expenses based on contextual understanding, automatically verify receipts, and even proactively flag potential policy violations, requiring human intervention only for exceptions, complex issues, or necessary clarifications. This represents a fundamental move from a rigid, rule-based workflow to a dynamic process intelligently managed by an agent capable of independent decision-making and real-time adaptation. This shift toward autonomous execution promises to eliminate bottlenecks, significantly reduce errors, and dramatically increase overall efficiency across a wide range of business processes, allowing the business to operate with greater fluidity and responsiveness.

Why This Matters

The transition from workflow automation to autonomous process execution is essential because it unlocks a new level of efficiency and agility. Strategically empowering AI agents to manage entire processes end-to-end enables organizations to liberate human employees to focus on higher-value activities that require uniquely human skills, significantly reduce operational costs, and respond more rapidly and effectively to continuously changing business needs. As the managing director at a large UK bank noted, "Agentic AI offers two key benefits: 1) Efficiency gains, mainly in the backend, which is a huge opportunity with low risk and could happen soon, and 2) Improved customer experience, which offers a huge opportunity but carries higher risk, including regulatory considerations, and will likely take longer to implement."

This highlights the phased approach to adopting agentic AI, starting with backend processes for efficiency before expanding to customer-facing applications. This phased approach is also critical because, as the managing director explained, "Any new technology will take time to be integrated with legacy systems. You have to work on data and technology together." This integration challenge is a key consideration for practical implementation.

Traditional business processes often follow predetermined paths—like a fixed musical score that musicians must follow exactly. But AI agents are transforming these rigid structures into dynamic, adaptive systems, capable of improvising and adapting to changing conditions, much like a jazz ensemble. Let's break down this fundamental shift to first principles (see Table 6.1).

TABLE 6.1 Business Processes Evolution with Agentic AI

Traditional Process Components	Agent-Driven Process Components
Fixed, pre-defined workflows, like a set musical score	Adaptive workflows, dynamically adjusting to context and conditions
Rule-based decisions, following established instructions	Learning-based decisions, improving over time through experience
Manual interventions required for deviations or exceptions	Autonomous operations, self-executing and self-optimizing
Sequential operations, proceeding step-by-step	Parallel processing, performing multiple tasks simultaneously
Limited adaptability to changing circumstances	Continuous optimization, constantly seeking improvements and efficiencies

The Intercompany Agent Revolution

Perhaps the most revolutionary aspect of agentic AI isn't solely how agents transform processes within individual organizations, but how they enable entirely new forms of business interaction and collaboration *between* companies, creating a truly interconnected business ecosystem. Traditional APIs and SaaS solutions are evolving into dynamic agent-to-agent communications that can intelligently negotiate, seamlessly collaborate, and optimize complex processes across organizational boundaries, composing a symphony of inter-organizational collaboration.

The transformative potential of AI agents extends far beyond the walls of a single organization, promising a revolution in how businesses interact and transact with each other in the broader business ecosystem. For decades, electronic data interchange (EDI) and application programming interfaces (APIs) have been the primary mechanisms for enabling intercompany data exchange and process integration. While these technologies have facilitated significant advancements, they often require complex configurations, ongoing maintenance, and strict adherence to standardized protocols, like requiring different orchestras to meticulously agree on a shared musical score and notation system before playing together.

Agentic AI introduces the exciting possibility of autonomous intercompany processes, where intelligent agents from different organizations can directly interact and collaborate to achieve shared goals, dynamically improvising a collaborative business performance. Imagine an AI agent within a manufacturing company proactively communicating with an AI agent at a supplier's facility to intelligently forecast material needs, dynamically negotiate optimal pricing, and efficiently schedule just-in-time deliveries, all without requiring direct human intervention or relying on rigid, pre-defined API integrations. These intelligent agents can understand the nuanced context of the interaction, dynamically negotiate terms based on predefined parameters and real-time data, and intelligently adapt to constantly changing circumstances, such as unforeseen supply chain disruptions or fluctuating market demand. This visionary concept of autonomous inter-company interaction promises to create more fluid, responsive, and efficient business ecosystems, nurturing greater collaboration and innovation across traditional organizational boundaries, composing a more complex and harmonious business symphony. As the managing director at a large UK bank analogized, "Think about a road and infrastructure analogy. Digital has laid some foundation, like basic roads, improving some processes. But with agentic AI, it's like upgrading to a modern infrastructure, enabling entirely new capabilities and benefits based on interconnectedness. Initially, different cities (companies) will build their own infrastructure, but to truly impact the whole economy, we need to upgrade the infrastructure between cities, allowing agents to communicate and unlock new capabilities that aren't even possible now. Imagine the Roman infrastructure and how it improved the economy, and how new infrastructure can further improve it, leading to an 'agentic-verse' that unlocks entirely new capabilities." This analogy beautifully illustrates the transformative potential of agentic AI to create a more interconnected and efficient business ecosystem, much like a well-developed infrastructure network.

REAL-WORLD EXAMPLE

Consider the often complex and time-consuming process of employee onboarding. Currently, this typically involves a series of manual steps and integrations between various disparate HR systems, IT provisioning tools, and training platforms. An AI agent could autonomously manage this entire process, from proactively initiating background checks and dynamically generating personalized offer letters to seamlessly setting up employee accounts, automatically enrolling them in benefits programs, and efficiently scheduling initial training sessions, intelligently interacting with each relevant system directly as needed, significantly reducing the administrative burden on HR staff, and creating a smoother, more efficient onboarding experience for new employees.

The Death of Traditional SaaS

The traditional software-as-a-service (SaaS) model—where companies subscribe to specific, siloed software solutions for each function—is evolving into what we call *agent-as-a-service* (AaaS). Instead of relying on separate, disconnected systems for CRM, ERP, and supply chain management, organizations will increasingly deploy specialized AI agents that can:

- **Self-integrate with existing, often legacy, systems:** Agents can intelligently navigate and connect with diverse systems without requiring complex API integrations.
- **Dynamically adapt to changing business needs:** Agents can learn and adjust their behavior in response to evolving requirements and market conditions.
- **Seamlessly collaborate across traditional system boundaries:** Agents can bridge data and process silos, enabling more holistic and integrated workflows.

- **Continuously learn and optimize from experience:** Agents improve their performance over time through ongoing learning and adaptation.

"The future of business software isn't about better user interfaces or more features—it's about autonomous agents that understand your business context and act on your behalf."

—Marc Benioff, CEO of Salesforce.

Currently, many business processes rely on a fragmented patchwork of SaaS applications, each meticulously designed for a specific function, often awkwardly stitched together by APIs that allow them to exchange limited data. This frequently results in complex integration architectures, persistent data silos, and ongoing maintenance challenges, like having different sections of our orchestra using incompatible notation systems, requiring complex translation and constant manual adjustments to ensure they can play in harmony.

Agentic AI offers the transformative potential to bypass much of this inherent complexity. Instead of relying on rigid API integrations between disparate applications, autonomous AI agents can intelligently interact directly with these systems, understanding their functionalities and dynamically extracting or inputting data as needed. An AI agent managing a sales process, for example, could autonomously access critical CRM data, dynamically generate accurate quotes using pricing information from a separate system, efficiently schedule meetings via a calendar application, and seamlessly update inventory levels in an ERP system, all without requiring explicit API calls or pre-built integrations. The AI agent effectively becomes the intelligent integration layer, capable of understanding and orchestrating complex interactions across various software systems, creating a more unified and harmonious business technology ecosystem. This has the potential to significantly simplify complex IT architectures, drastically reduce integration costs, and create more flexible and adaptable business processes, moving toward a more fluid and integrated operational symphony. Over time, as AI agents become increasingly sophisticated, the need for many point-to-point API integrations and even entire categories of SaaS applications focused on specific, automatable tasks, may significantly diminish, as agents become the primary orchestrators of business processes.

The New Integration Paradigm

Remember our orchestra metaphor—traditional business software is like having separate conductors for strings, brass, and percussion, each rigidly following their own sheet music, resulting in potential disjointedness. The agent revolution creates a self-organizing orchestra where each instrument intelligently understands the entire symphony and can dynamically adapt its part in real time to create a more cohesive and harmonious performance.

This transformative shift is already underway:

- **Financial agents** automatically and dynamically adjusting budgets based on real-time market conditions and performance data
- **HR agents** intelligently personalizing training programs for each individual employee based on their unique needs and career goals
- **Marketing agents** dynamically optimizing campaigns in real time across multiple channels based on performance data and customer interactions
- **Operations agents** proactively predicting and preventing potential maintenance issues, minimizing downtime and maximizing operational efficiency

Practical Implications

For businesses strategically considering this transformative transition, the key is to adopt a phased and deliberate approach:

- **Identify processes ripe for agent transformation:** Start by pinpointing business processes that are currently inefficient, error-prone, or highly manual, and assess their suitability for agentic automation.
- **Start with bounded domains where agents can learn safely:** Begin with implementing agents in well-defined and contained areas, allowing them to learn and adapt in a controlled environment before expanding their scope.
- **Gradually expand agent autonomy as confidence grows:** As agents demonstrate their effectiveness and reliability, progressively increase their level of autonomy and responsibility, expanding their role in business processes.
- **Build cross-functional agent networks:** Adopt collaboration and communication between different agents across various departments to create seamless end-to-end process automation and optimization.
- **Develop new metrics for measuring agent-driven process performance:** Implement new KPIs and metrics that specifically

measure the efficiency, effectiveness, and impact of agent-driven processes, ensuring continuous monitoring and improvement.

As we transition to the next section, it's critical to remember that this process revolution isn't solely about achieving incremental efficiency gains—it's about fundamentally creating more adaptive, intelligent, and responsive organizations that can dynamically respond to opportunities and challenges in ways previously unimaginable, composing entirely new business melodies.

RISK MANAGEMENT AND FUTURE IMPLICATIONS

As organizations increasingly rely on AI agents for critical decision support and autonomous operations, effectively managing the associated risks becomes vital for long-term success and sustainability. Key strategic considerations for risk management include:

- **Data quality and bias monitoring:** Implementing rigorous processes to ensure the quality, accuracy, and fairness of data used to train and operate AI agents, actively mitigating potential biases.
- **System redundancy and failure modes:** Designing resilient AI systems with built-in redundancy and robust fail-safe mechanisms to minimize the impact of potential system failures or unexpected disruptions.
- **Ethics and compliance frameworks:** Establishing clear ethical guidelines and robust compliance frameworks for the development and deployment of AI agents, ensuring responsible and ethical AI practices.
- **Human skill development and adaptation:** Investing in comprehensive training and reskilling initiatives to prepare the workforce for effective collaboration with AI agents and the evolving nature of work in the agentic enterprise.

Looking strategically ahead, we foresee AI agents continuously evolving to effectively handle increasingly complex strategic decisions while maintaining essential human oversight in critical areas where human judgment, ethical considerations, and nuanced understanding are paramount. The future of enterprise decision-making will likely resemble a highly skilled and well-conducted orchestra, where intelligent AI agents and experienced human decision-makers work in perfect harmony and seamless collaboration, each strategically contributing their unique strengths and capabilities to create demonstrably superior strategic outcomes and a more resilient and adaptable organization.

Why This Matters

Organizations that strategically and effectively integrate AI agents into their core decision-making processes can realistically expect to achieve significant and measurable improvements in key performance areas, including:

- **30–50% faster decision cycles:** Significantly accelerating the speed and agility of organizational decision-making processes
- **25–40% improved decision accuracy:** Enhancing the quality and effectiveness of decisions through data-driven insights and intelligent analysis
- **Significantly enhanced ability to handle complexity:** Effectively managing increasingly complex and dynamic business environments with greater efficiency
- **Better risk management and proactive compliance:** Proactively identifying and mitigating potential risks and ensuring robust regulatory compliance

The strategic integration of agentic AI into the enterprise is not merely about automating routine tasks or achieving incremental efficiency gains; it's about fundamentally transforming *how* organizations strategically make critical decisions and proactively craft effective strategies for long-term success. Providing the transformative ability to dynamically simulate complex scenarios, strategically empowering data-driven decision-making at all levels of the organization, and significantly enhancing each critical stage of the core decision-making process, enable AI agents to steer in a new era of unprecedented strategic agility, enhanced foresight, and improved organizational resilience. Just as our hypothetical conductor can strategically experiment with countless musical variations before the actual performance, businesses can now proactively explore a multitude of potential future scenarios in a virtual environment, intelligently selecting the strategic path that demonstrably leads to the most harmonious, impactful, and successful results in the real world. The historical fog of uncertainty that often surrounds strategic planning is beginning to lift, revealing a clear landscape of previously hidden possibilities and strategic advantages. As we strategically move forward, embracing this transformative technology will be fundamental for any forward-thinking organization seeking to not just survive in the rapidly evolving modern marketplace, but to thrive and lead in the exciting age of intelligent machines and agentic enterprises.

Early Adopters Gain a Competitive Edge

Companies that proactively and strategically integrate agentic AI into their core decision-making processes are already realizing significant tangible benefits, including demonstrably improved operational efficiency, substantial reductions in costs, and significantly enhanced strategic agility and market responsiveness. These forward-thinking early adopters are not only making better, more informed decisions today, but are also strategically building the essential expertise, robust infrastructure, and critical capabilities necessary to effectively capitalize on the continued rapid evolution of this powerful and transformative technology in the years to come, positioning themselves for sustained competitive advantage in the agentic future.

EXPERT INSIGHTS: PERSPECTIVES ON THE AGENTIC REVOLUTION

This section presents a series of illustrative examples and case studies demonstrating how agentic AI is being deployed today. However, we have found from experience that deeper and more authentic insights typically emerge from candid, senior-level executive discussions rather than from officially published case studies, which can often be filtered through a PR lens. To capture these richer viewpoints and true frontline experiences, we've spoken directly with senior industry executives who are driving the integration of intelligent agents into their organizations and industries. Their reflections offer meaningful, behind-the-scenes perspectives on the reality, the challenges, and the transformative potential of the agentic revolution as it unfolds.

Expert Interview 1: Global CDO at Large Consulting Firm

Offering a distinctly different, and perhaps more conceptually challenging, perspective, the global chief data officer from a prominent consulting firm pushed the boundaries of the conversation into more philosophical and potentially disruptive territories, raising critical questions about trust, authenticity, and the very nature of value creation in an agentic future. He began by suggesting that agentic AI will inevitably lead to the "commoditization of different enterprise functions." This provocative statement implies a future where many traditionally differentiated business functions—marketing, customer service, even elements of strategic analysis—might become standardized and readily available 'as-a-service' through increasingly sophisticated and readily accessible AI agents, potentially eroding traditional competitive advantages based on unique functional capabilities. He then painted a somewhat dystopian, yet undeniably intriguing, vision of a future increasingly saturated with synthetic data and AI-generated realities:

> "With the exponential growth of synthetic data generation and the proliferation of AI agents increasingly trained and operating on this synthetic data, we could very well end up in a nearly virtual reality,

a hyper-real world saturated with loads of fake data and even fake humans—AI-generated personas interacting with each other in simulated markets. What are the long-term implications of this shift toward synthetic realities? What happens to our understanding of 'truth' and 'authenticity' in a world where the lines between real and artificially generated become increasingly blurred?"

This thought-provoking, almost philosophical, question forces us to confront the potential societal and epistemological ramifications of a world increasingly mediated and shaped by AI-generated content and interactions.

Trust emerged as an absolutely paramount concern in this expert's analysis, forming the bedrock upon which any widespread adoption of agentic AI must be built. "For full agentic adoption everywhere, across industries and across society, trust will be absolutely paramount—non-negotiable," he emphasized. He then outlined a multilayered framework for building and maintaining this essential trust, proposing three distinct levels of certification:

"Level 1: Certification of data products—we need robust mechanisms to verify the quality, accuracy, and provenance of the data that AI agents are trained on and operate with. Level 2: Certification of single agents themselves—we need to be able to audit and verify the behaviour, decision-making processes, and ethical alignment of individual AI agents, ensuring they operate responsibly and within defined boundaries. And Level 3, perhaps most critically: Orchestration layer trust—we need to establish trust in the complex networks and platforms that orchestrate the interactions and collaborations between multiple agents, ensuring fairness, security, and transparency at the system level."

This multifaceted trust framework provides an essential road map for building the necessary foundations for widespread agentic AI adoption, addressing concerns about data integrity, agent behavior, and system-level governance. He further highlighted the complex ethical challenges arising from differing societal values and cultural norms in a globally interconnected agentic ecosystem.

"AI agents will inevitably be trained with different values, reflecting the diverse ethical frameworks and societal priorities of different regions and cultures around the world. Consider the classic 'trolley problem' and its variations: Western societies, for example, might program autonomous vehicles to prioritize saving a baby over an elderly person in an unavoidable accident scenario, reflecting a cultural emphasis on youth and potential future life-years. However, Oriental societies, with a stronger cultural emphasis on respecting elders and valuing accumulated wisdom, might program the same AI to prioritize saving the elderly person over the baby. So, what happens when two autonomous AI agents, programmed with fundamentally different and potentially conflicting values, are forced to interact or collaborate—or even compete—in a global business ecosystem? How do we resolve these value clashes and ensure interoperability and ethical consistency in a world where AI agents are imbued with diverse, and sometimes contradictory, cultural values?"

This starkly illustrates the complex ethical and interoperability challenges inherent in creating a globally interconnected and culturally diverse agentic ecosystem, requiring careful consideration of value alignment and cross-cultural AI ethics.

Finally, this expert offered a thought-provoking chess analogy to describe the potential long-term shifts in business ecosystems and competitive dynamics in a fully agentic economy.

"Think about the game of chess. For centuries, humans were the undisputed masters. But once we developed AI algorithms that could master chess, the game fundamentally changed. Today, the best chess algorithms can consistently beat even the strongest human grand-masters. But then, an interesting phenomenon emerged: when these top-tier chess algorithms play against each other, they very often end up in a draw—a perfectly optimized stalemate. Now, consider the current business landscape. Many of today's most lucrative business opportunities and sources of economic growth arise precisely from friction, inefficiencies, and unoptimized processes—areas where human limitations create opportunities for innovation and compet-itive differentiation. But what happens when intelligent machines, autonomous AI agents, are unleashed to systematically optimize everything—to relentlessly eliminate friction, streamline processes, and maximize efficiency across the entire economic system? Do we risk creating a hyper-optimized, perfectly efficient, but ultimately less dynamic and less opportunity-rich business ecosystem—a kind of economic 'stalemate' where traditional sources of business growth and competitive advantage diminish?"

This intriguing chess analogy prompts us to critically examine the poten-tial for hyper-optimization by AI agents to fundamentally reshape business ecosystems, potentially reducing traditional sources of entrepreneurial opportunity and forcing us to rethink the very nature of value creation and economic growth in a fully agentic future.

Expert Interview 2: Managing Director at Large Bank UK

Digging into the practicalities of implementing agentic AI within large, established organizations, a Managing Director from a major UK bank provided invaluable insights grounded in real-world experience and the inherent complexities of legacy systems. He emphasized the necessity of a phased and realistic approach, noting, "Vertical samples will happen soon, we'll see compelling demonstrations of AI agents operating effectively within specific, contained functions or departments. This is where the early wins and quick ROI will be found."

However, he tempered initial enthusiasm with a dose of long-term strategic perspective:

> "But horizontal transformation, a truly enterprise-wide integration of agentic AI that cuts across all departments and processes—that will take years, likely decades, to fully realize." This realistic timeline underscores the significant undertaking involved in overhauling deeply entrenched legacy systems and fundamentally changing organizational workflows. He astutely pointed to back-office operations as the prime initial target for agentic AI deployment, highlighting the compelling efficiency gains: "If you look at finance today, you have thousands upon thousands of people performing remarkably similar, often repetitive, manual tasks—data entry, reconciliation, report generation. Agentic AI is perfectly suited to automate vast swathes of this work, effectively replacing human jobs, at least initially, in these backend processes. This presents a huge opportunity for immediate efficiency gains with relatively low risk and a clear path to near-term ROI." However, he injected a note of caution regarding customer-facing applications, where the stakes are demonstrably higher: "Improved customer experience through agentic AI is undoubtedly a huge long-term opportunity, but it comes with significantly higher risk, especially when you factor in the inevitable regulatory scrutiny and compliance requirements in heavily regulated sectors like finance. Transforming customer-facing processes with AI agents will take much longer, require more careful planning, and necessitate robust ethical and governance frameworks."

Governance emerged as a paramount consideration in his analysis. "You will absolutely need automated governance for all these new agents," he asserted, emphasizing that the increased autonomy of agentic AI necessitates equally sophisticated and automated control mechanisms. Traditional governance structures, designed for human-led processes, will be insufficient to manage a dynamic and distributed network of intelligent agents. He then masterfully employed a compelling analogy to illuminate the broader, macro-economic impact of agentic AI, drawing parallels to infrastructure development:

"Think of roads and infrastructure as an analogy. The 'digital revolution' of recent decades has laid a foundational layer, like building basic roads between cities, which improved some key processes, like payments and basic data exchange. But agentic AI is analogous to fundamentally upgrading that infrastructure to a modern, high-speed network—it's a generational leap in capability. Initially, different cities—representing individual companies—will build their own internal infrastructure, deploying agents within their own organizational boundaries. But to truly impact the whole economy, to unlock transformative growth and innovation, we urgently need to upgrade the infrastructure between cities, creating seamless interconnections that allow agents to communicate and collaborate across organizational lines, securely and efficiently. Think back to the Roman infrastructure and how the construction of Roman roads dramatically improved trade, communication, and overall economic prosperity across their vast empire. This new 'agentic-verse' infrastructure, this interconnected network of intelligent agents, will unlock entirely new capabilities and economic opportunities that are simply not possible with today's fragmented and siloed systems. Just imagine a truly seamless, end-to-end financial process for something as simple as online shopping—today, it's still riddled with friction and inefficiencies due to the multitude of disparate systems and manual handoffs involved. Agentic AI, operating on a truly interconnected infrastructure, has the potential to eliminate much of this friction and create entirely new levels of efficiency and seamlessness in economic transactions and business processes."

This powerful infrastructure analogy brilliantly underscores the long-term, systemic, and profoundly interconnected potential of agentic AI to reshape not just individual organizations, but the entire global economic landscape.

Expert Interview 3: Chief Transformation and AI Officer, Big 6 Media Agency

"The relationship between machines and humans is undergoing a profound shift, and optimizing this communication will be the defining challenge for media agencies in the coming years," states the Chief AI Officer of one of the world's largest media agencies. With extensive experience implementing AI solutions across marketing operations, she offers a pragmatic perspective on the immediate challenges and long-term strategic implications of agentic AI.

"The expectations from leadership are crystal clear," she begins. "Our CEO, like most, approaches AI transformation with a P&L mindset. The first question is invariably: 'When will it be ready and how will it impact our bottom line?' This creates an interesting tension because we're dealing with a technology that's still evolving rapidly while being asked to deliver immediate financial results."

She emphasizes the early stage of agentic AI development:

"We need to be honest about where we are on the maturity curve. AI agents are still in their very early days with relatively few robust implementations 'in the wild.' This creates both implementation challenges and educational challenges with stakeholders who might have inflated expectations based on conceptual potential rather than current capabilities."

Governance emerges as a critical focus area in her assessment.

"Creating appropriate knowledge bases with correct, comprehensive information is foundational to everything we do with AI agents. Without proper governance around the information these systems access and learn from, we risk agents that perpetuate biases, make decisions based on outdated information, or simply fail to deliver value. This governance layer isn't glamorous, but it's absolutely essential."

Looking ahead, she identifies the central strategic question facing service companies:

"Once agentic AI becomes ubiquitous—when every media agency has deployed these technologies—what becomes the differentiator?

What's our unique selling proposition when two service companies essentially do the same thing with similar technologies? I firmly believe the answer lies in intrinsic enterprise knowledge—all the accumulated experience across years and diverse clients that can't be easily replicated."

This perspective leads to her insight about the symbiotic relationship between human expertise and AI capabilities:

"The human layer plus AI creates something more powerful than either alone—it improves what I call 'corporate memory.' Traditional organizations struggle with knowledge transfer and institutional memory. People leave, taking their expertise with them, or knowledge remains siloed in specific teams. AI agents can democratize access to that collective wisdom while continuously learning from new human inputs."

She highlights an often-overlooked advantage of generative AI:

"Interestingly, GenAI can actually be more empathetic than humans in certain client interactions. It doesn't get tired, frustrated, or distracted. This consistent empathetic engagement can significantly improve client relationships and consumer experiences when properly implemented."

The executive emphasizes that implementation know-how will become increasingly valuable:

"A substantial part of competitive advantage will be in how effectively organizations embed AI agents into workflows. This isn't just technical integration—it's about creating the right incentives, change management approaches, and human-AI collaboration frameworks that maximize value creation."

Drawing an analogy to fuel quality, she explains:

"The quality of AI output is directly linked to what I call its 'gasoline'—the long-term enterprise memory it can access. Synthetic data and experiences play into this as well. Organizations that build rich, well-structured knowledge repositories will see exponentially better results from their AI initiatives compared to those with fragmented or poor-quality information sources."

On the topic of agent training, she offers practical insights:

"How you train agents is critically important. We've learned that defining an agent's objectives requires incredible precision and consistent calibration. For example, if customer satisfaction is a key metric, you need sophisticated mechanisms to measure and continuously calibrate this. An agent optimizing for the wrong objective—or interpreting the right objective incorrectly—can create significant problems."

She concludes with a perspective on balancing innovation with pragmatism:

"We're simultaneously preparing for a future where agentic AI transforms everything while delivering tangible value today. The organizations that will excel are those that can balance visionary thinking with practical implementation—understanding both where this technology is heading and what it can realistically deliver now. In media agencies specifically, the winners will augment their strategic thinking and creativity with AI-powered execution, elevating the human elements of our business rather than replacing them."

Expert Interview 4: Former CEO Big 6 Media Agencies

"The impact of AI Agents in the media agency sector represents both our greatest challenge and our most promising opportunity in decades," begins a former regional and country CEO at one of the world's largest media agencies, who has led digital transformation initiatives across three continents. With more than 20+ years of experience navigating technological disruptions in advertising, he offers a candid assessment of how agentic AI will reshape an industry at a critical inflection point.

"Media agencies have historically underutilized the transformative potential of information technologies compared to other sectors," he explains.

"There's been more 'craftsmanship' than industrialization in our approach, despite being a volume business in every sense—both economically and transactionally. Our industry's response to complexity has typically been to add more human resources—increasingly expensive talent with decreasing experience—rather than investing in automation and intelligence."

This challenge has only intensified with the digital revolution.

"The arrival of digital advertising, counterintuitively, has worsened this situation. Our data shows that productivity in traditional media channels is approximately 2.5 times higher than in digital media operations. Clients aren't willing to pay service fees proportionate to this workload difference, so our current model is under severe strain and becoming unsustainable. With digital now representing 70% of advertising investments, this is an existential issue."

The executive identifies a dual problem facing media agencies:

"We're confronting both an efficiency problem and a quality crisis. Teams simply don't have adequate time to properly execute campaigns, monitor their evolution, make optimization adjustments, and conduct thorough post-campaign analysis. Something always gets sacrificed, usually the strategic thinking that clients value most."

He draws a clear distinction between the operational and strategic aspects of the business.

"On the operational side—campaign activation and execution—AI agents can generate tremendous efficiencies. On the strategic side, where we determine media channel selection, budget allocation, and format strategies based on client objectives, we currently use various disconnected tools. Most importantly, we don't effectively leverage our own institutional knowledge gained from thousands of previous campaigns. AI agents can help us systematically tap into this experience reservoir."

When discussing adoption challenges, he highlights organizational rigidity as a primary concern.

"Rigid corporate structures could kill adoption if not managed carefully. The transformation approach I've found most effective involves mixed teams—internal staff who contribute deep business knowledge working alongside external technology consultants."

He draws a sobering parallel to another industry transformation:

"I compare this to traditional print media's painful transition to digital formats. It's been horrific—slow and unfocused. Many publishers thought, 'Now I have both print and digital editions, so I need two separate newsrooms!' Before trying that approach, it would be better to shut down and create an entirely new digital-native publication from scratch. Some have successfully done this, and they're thriving."

The executive sees significant opportunities for entrepreneurial disruption:

"Experience and knowledge will become increasingly valuable. If you deeply understand how this sector operates, you can replicate it with a small team of humans supported by an army of AI agents. These hybrid teams will be extraordinarily powerful and cost-effective."

He also predicts a strategic shift in how large agency holding companies approach acquisitions:

"We'll see major agency groups acquiring smaller agencies not for their client portfolios, which has been the traditional motivation, but for their operational solutions built on AI agents. Capability acquisition will replace client acquisition as the primary M&A driver."

Looking further ahead, he contemplates the differentiation challenge:

"As AI agents become commoditized, how will competing agencies differentiate themselves? This is perhaps our most profound strategic question. My belief is that human creativity, strategic insight, and relationship-building capabilities will become even more valuable as technical execution becomes increasingly automated. The agencies that thrive will combine the efficiency of agentic AI with uniquely human strategic value."

He concludes with both caution and optimism:

"This transformation won't be easy or painless, but it's inevitable. Media agencies that embrace this change proactively have an opportunity to reinvent their business models and create extraordinary value for clients. Those that resist will find themselves increasingly irrelevant in a world where the combination of human creativity and AI efficiency becomes the new standard of excellence."

Expert Interview 5: Deal Maker, Advisor, Investor

"I've witnessed this pattern repeat across dozens of major telecommunications transformations," explained the former Big Five consulting partner who specialized in billion-dollar enterprise deals throughout his career.

"The fundamental challenge isn't technological capability—it's the deeply entrenched data silos created by vendor lock-in. Take any major telco today; they're running Salesforce for customer relationship management, ServiceNow for IT service management, SAP for enterprise resource planning, and custom systems for billing. Each vendor has deliberately architected their solutions to make data extraction painful and expensive. When a telco like Vodafone has over 40,000 distinct products across their global footprint, just establishing a unified data model becomes a multi-year, multi-million-dollar endeavor before any actual transformation can begin. The vendors know this, and their incentive structures are built around maintaining these barriers that necessitate expensive integration projects."

The veteran consultant leaned forward, his eyes lighting up as he shifted to discussing the future.

"Agentic AI is about to fundamentally disrupt this entire paradigm. What we're going to need—and what forward-thinking enterprises are already exploring—is an AI orchestration layer that sits above these disparate systems. Rather than traditional point-to-point integrations, these autonomous agents will navigate across systems, extracting and transforming data as needed, and executing complex workflows that span multiple platforms. The vendors who survive will be those who embrace rather than resist this new reality. I've been working with several telecommunications clients who are already building small-scale proofs of concept, creating agents that can, for example, handle end-to-end customer service inquiries that would previously require access to five different systems and three different departments. The economics are compelling enough that I expect to see mainstream adoption within 24–36 months, despite inevitable resistance from vendors whose business models rely on maintaining the status quo.

"What's particularly fascinating to me is where the most disruptive innovations will originate. I've been tracking the UAE tech ecosystem since 2015, well before it was on most people's radar. Their advantage isn't just massive capital investment—it's their lack of legacy infrastructure and cultural appetite for disruption. They're building systems from scratch with agentic AI as the foundation rather than an afterthought. We're entering an era of 'reverse innovation' where breakthrough approaches will increasingly come from markets like India, China, and the UAE, then flow back to Western economies. Meanwhile, the established tech giants are shifting from offense to defence. Apple, Google, Microsoft—they've built empires on controlling key parts of the technology stack. But agentic AI inherently decentralizes control, allowing smaller, more nimble players to create value by orchestrating across systems rather than owning them. The vendors who thrive will be those who focus less on protecting their walled gardens and more on making their products excellent citizens in an agent-mediated ecosystem. It's a fundamental power shift that will redefine enterprise technology over the next decade."

Expert Interview 6: Senior Executive in the Consumer Financial Insights Sector

"Agentic AI has the potential to significantly improve how consumers interact with and benefit from their financial data. While financial insight providers and information agents have been around for decades—responsibly collecting, managing, and securing sensitive consumer information within strong regulatory environments—this new generation of intelligent agents introduces innovations that will address some long-standing gaps. Specifically, Agentic AI can help solve two fundamental limitations: the depth of accessible financial data available to consumers and the level of personalization possible in using that information," explained a senior executive from a leading global provider of financial data insights.

> "Traditionally, consumer financial insights have mostly focused on transactional histories and lending payment behaviours, leaving out key areas like income, pensions, savings, and wealth management data. Agentic AI, operating transparently and always with explicit consumer consent, enables the integration of these richer, more complex datasets, creating a far more holistic picture of an individual's financial situation. Agents empowered by such detailed insights can facilitate genuinely personalized financial solutions tailored uniquely to each consumer."

The veteran executive continued thoughtfully,

> "When the right consent mechanisms and robust consumer protections are in place, this enhanced access and sophisticated personalization creates a win-win scenario. Consumers gain more accurate

assessments and advantageous financial products with improved interest rates and terms, while financial services providers improve their ability to lend responsibly to the appropriate consumers.

"What makes this moment particularly exciting is the potential for these agentic systems to empower consumers at unprecedented scale and speed, proactively supporting their individual financial well-being. Imagine if every consumer could access an advanced financial management capability that harmonizes income, pension information, and savings records with their day-to-day financial behaviour. This would allow unprecedented tailoring of products and solutions, ultimately improving consumer outcomes such as financial health, credit-worthiness, and long-term financial success.

"Additionally, emerging areas such as synthetic financial data generation, powered by advanced AI, further strengthen innovation possibilities while protecting individual privacy. These anonymized, statistically representative datasets enable the development and testing of new financial products, enhanced risk modelling, and improved portfolio management. As such capabilities become more mainstream, they will contribute significantly to breakthroughs in consumer finance, enhancing decision-making across lending, asset management, and beyond—all within a responsible and privacy-conscious framework."

The executive concluded enthusiastically,

"Looking forward, the future of the consumer financial insight sector relies on proactively embracing these intelligent agentic technologies. By shifting from simply providing standardized data toward harnessing deeper, more advanced financial insights and enabling highly personalized consumer experiences, we position ourselves as central enablers of a new consumer-centric financial paradigm—secure, transparent, and beneficial to everyone involved."

Expert Interview 7: Former Global CIO and Strategic Advisor to Fortune 500 Companies

"The key word here is revolution," emphasized a former global CIO and enterprise advisor with decades of experience transforming multinational organizations. "Anyone who takes an evolutionary approach to agentic AI will be left behind. This isn't about incremental improvement—it's about fundamentally reimagining how enterprises operate."

With conviction born from numerous successful transformations, he articulated why this technological shift requires an unprecedented level of leadership vision and courage.

"The ability of a CEO to understand the revolutionary potential of agentic AI and to be brave enough to completely rethink their approach to running the enterprise will be the primary determinant of success. What we're looking at isn't simply automation or enhancement of existing processes. It's a comprehensive challenge to the role of every executive and every department in ways they haven't experienced before." He provided a concrete example to illustrate the magnitude of change required: "The CFO needs to be convinced and believe that with agentic AI, they can reduce the cost of the finance function by 50% within 12 months—not through traditional cost-cutting, but by fundamentally re-implementing the entire function using intelligent agents. Similar transformations need to happen simultaneously across all organizational functions."

One of his most provocative observations concerned the growing trend of appointing chief AI officers.

"My biggest concern is when I see a company employ a Chief AI Officer. This immediately signals that the executive team sees AI as someone else's responsibility—expecting that individual to somehow transform a business from a position with no operational or financial control. It's a position of weakness." Leaning forward emphatically, he continued, "The only Chief AI Officer I want to see in an enterprise is the CEO. The chief executive needs to educate themselves on the possibilities of agentic AI, move their thinking beyond ChatGPT, and challenge every part of the organization to revolutionize their function within a 12-month window. The whole process should be self-financing in real terms."

When discussing specific implementation areas, he outlined a comprehensive view of how agentic AI should transform enterprise functions:

"In finance, AI agents should handle all transactional processing and administration of accounting, tax, treasury, and financial planning. In IT, cloud management, cybersecurity, infrastructure, and most software development should be completely agent-based. Operational areas like process management, automation, robotics, manufacturing control, supply chain, and logistics should all leverage agentic AI. Marketing content creation, ad optimization, and analytics should be agent-driven. In HR and payroll, the hiring process and administration of all human capital should be agent-based." He paused before adding, "The sobering reality is that these activities should already have been replaced by artificial intelligence capabilities. Organizations still manually performing these functions are already falling behind."

The veteran CIO acknowledged the significant cultural challenges ahead.

"The real obstacle isn't technology—it's convincing executive leaders that this transformation is in their interest and in the interest of their people. Unfortunately, many view AI merely as a means of reducing headcount. While AI will certainly reduce personnel requirements, its impact goes far beyond cost reduction. It provides an unprecedented opportunity to drive efficiency and innovation across the business at a scale previously unattainable."

In his concluding remarks, he emphasized the historic significance of this shift:

"Agentic AI represents the most fundamental change in how business enterprises operate that we've seen in over 100 years. This isn't about replicating manual processes with computerized ones— we've been doing that since the 1960s. This is about creating entirely new types of processes and ways of working that were previously unimaginable. The technology will develop rapidly, with capabilities increasing exponentially. The only limitation will be the ability of an organization's human capital to accept it, understand it, work with it, and deliver it. That's why culture—not technology—is the decisive factor in which enterprises will thrive in this new era."

KEY TAKEAWAYS

Agentic AI is not just another incremental technology; it represents a fundamental shift, an "enterprise revolution" that will reshape organizations at every level. This chapter has explored this transformation through the metaphor of an orchestra, demonstrating how AI agents are moving from simple automation tools to becoming conductors and even players within the enterprise symphony. We've seen how agentic AI impacts organizational structure, business processes, and strategic decision-making, paving the way for more agile, efficient, and intelligent organizations. However, this revolution is not without its challenges, requiring careful consideration of ethical implications, risk management, and workforce adaptation. Embracing this change proactively is critical for organizations seeking to thrive in the age of intelligent machines.

1. **Organizations are transforming from rigid hierarchies to fluid, adaptive orchestras.**
   - KEY INSIGHTS:
     - Traditional hierarchical structures are increasingly ill-suited for the dynamic demands of the modern business environment. Agentic AI enables the shift toward "fluid organizations" that are adaptive and responsive.
     - Roles are being fundamentally redesigned. Humans are moving from task executors to strategic orchestrators, managing AI agent workflows and focusing on uniquely human skills.
     - Performance management is evolving from static KPIs to dynamic, AI-augmented metrics that capture the synergistic value of human-agent collaboration and organizational agility.
   - DO:
     - Embrace a "zero-based" approach to organizational design, reimagining structures with AI agents as core team members.
     - Focus on role evolution, empowering humans to leverage their uniquely human skills in collaboration with AI agents.
     - Implement dynamic, AI-augmented performance management systems that measure outcomes and adaptability.
   - DON'T:
     - Simply retrofit AI agents into existing, rigid organizational structures.
     - Focus solely on task automation without redesigning human roles to leverage higher-value skills.
     - Rely on outdated, static KPIs that fail to capture the dynamic contributions of AI agents.

2. **Business processes are evolving beyond automation to become fully autonomous flows.**
   - KEY INSIGHTS:
     - Agentic AI is moving beyond workflow automation to autonomous process execution, enabling end-to-end management by intelligent agents.
     - Inter-company agent interactions promise a revolution in business ecosystems, enabling seamless collaboration and negotiation across organizational boundaries.
     - The traditional SaaS model is evolving toward "Agent-as-a-Service," with agents acting as intelligent integration layers, simplifying IT architectures and enhancing adaptability.
   - DO:
     - Identify and prioritize business processes ripe for agent transformation, starting with bounded domains for safe learning.

- Explore the potential of inter-company agent collaborations to create more fluid and efficient business ecosystems.
- Consider "Agent-as-a-Service" models to simplify IT integration and enhance business process adaptability.
- DON'T:
  - Confine AI agent deployments to simple workflow automation tasks; explore their potential for autonomous process execution.
  - Underestimate the transformative potential of agent-to-agent interactions across organizational boundaries.
  - Remain locked into traditional SaaS models; explore the flexibility and integration benefits of Agent-as-a-Service.

3. **Decision-making has evolved from relying on intuition to leveraging intelligent foresight.**
   - KEY INSIGHTS:
     - Agentic AI empowers "Dynamic Strategic Intelligence," enabling continuous, adaptive, and forward-looking decision-making.
     - Agent-based modeling and simulation allow organizations to "test drive" strategies in virtual environments, gaining unprecedented foresight and mitigating risks.
     - AI agents can empower decision-making at all levels of the organization, augmenting human capabilities and leading to more agile and responsive enterprises.
   - DO:
     - Leverage agent-based modeling and simulation to enhance strategic foresight and scenario planning.
     - Distribute intelligent decision-making capabilities throughout the organization by empowering individuals with AI-driven insights.
     - Focus on human-AI collaboration frameworks that clearly define decision rights, oversight mechanisms, and learning integration.
   - DON'T:
     - Rely solely on intuition and historical data for strategic planning in a dynamic environment; embrace AI-powered foresight.
     - Confine AI-driven decision support to the C-suite; empower decision-making at all levels of the organization.
     - Neglect the ethical considerations and risk management aspects of AI-augmented decision-making.

The enterprise revolution driven by agentic AI is fundamentally about creating organizations that are not just more efficient, but more intelligent, adaptive, and, ultimately, more human-centric. Like a well-conducted orchestra, the future enterprise will harmonize human creativity and strategic thinking with the power and scalability of AI agents. However, realizing this vision requires more than just understanding the transformative potential; it demands practical strategies and new skillsets. As we move into the next chapter, we will shift our focus from the "what" and "why" of the agentic revolution to the "how," exploring the essential strategies and practical skills needed to navigate this exciting and transformative new landscape and to effectively conduct *your* own agentic enterprise symphony.

CHAPTER 7

Personal and Professional Opportunities

"The future belongs to those who believe in the beauty of their dreams."
—Eleanor Roosevelt

I magine stepping into a world where the everyday pressures of work and life begin to ease, where the constant barrage of tasks and information no longer dictates your day. Picture yourself, not as an ever-running juggler of endless responsibilities, but as a conductor, orchestrating your work and personal life with newfound precision and calm. This isn't a futuristic fantasy; it's the unfolding reality powered by the rise of the new generation of AI agents. We've explored the foundational shifts brought about by agentic AI and its transformative potential within organizations. Now, let's turn the lens inward, focusing on how these intelligent entities are destined to revolutionize the individual experience, empowering each of us to achieve more, learn faster, and live more fulfilling lives. Just as individual musicians bring their unique talents to the orchestra, AI agents are becoming our personalized instruments, enhancing our capabilities and allowing us to create symphonies of personal and professional achievement that were once beyond imagination.

INDIVIDUAL EMPOWERMENT THROUGH AI

Meet Maria, a mid-career marketing professional who felt increasingly overwhelmed by the pace and complexity of her work in 2025. Like many knowledge workers, she struggled to keep up with endless emails, reports, and administrative tasks while trying to focus on strategic thinking and creative work. That changed when she began working alongside AI agents. Today, Maria leverages an ensemble of specialized AI assistants that handle everything from email triage to market research to presentation design.

> "It's like having a team of highly capable colleagues who work alongside me 24/7," she explains. "The agents handle the routine tasks while elevating my ability to focus on what humans do best— strategic vision, creative problem-solving, and building meaningful relationships."

Maria's experience reflects a fundamental shift happening across industries—the emergence of AI agents as tools for individual empowerment. This section explores how AI agents are transforming personal productivity and capability enhancement, examining both the opportunities and considerations for professionals looking to thrive in this new paradigm.

From Burden to Booster: Reclaiming Your Time and Focus

The modern individual, particularly the knowledge worker, often feels submerged in a sea of tasks. Emails demand attention, calendars overflow with meetings, and the constant pressure to stay informed can feel like a relentless undertow pulling us away from deep work and meaningful pursuits. This isn't simply about being "busy"; it's about the cognitive load—the constant mental switching and the energy drain of managing countless details. Enter the AI agent, destined to act as a powerful cognitive assistant, capable of shouldering many of these burdens.

Consider your email inbox, a notorious source of daily stress. Traditionally, navigating this digital deluge requires significant time and mental energy. We filter, categorize, prioritize, and respond, often feeling like we're perpetually playing catch-up. An AI agent, operating autonomously within your email system, can learn your priorities, summarize lengthy threads, flag urgent messages, and even draft responses based on your past communication patterns. This isn't just a smarter spam filter; it's an intelligent gatekeeper, allowing you to focus on the communications that truly require your direct attention. This echoes the role of a skilled librarian in the orchestral world, meticulously organizing and retrieving the right musical scores at the precise moment they are needed, preventing the conductor from being bogged down in administrative details.

Similarly, consider the endless task of scheduling meetings. Coordinating availability across multiple time zones and busy calendars can be a frustrating back-and-forth. An AI scheduling agent, granted access to your calendar and communication channels, can autonomously find mutually agreeable times, send invitations, and even handle rescheduling requests. This seemingly simple function can liberate hours each week, freeing up valuable cognitive space for more strategic and creative endeavors. From a first-principles perspective, this leverages the AI agent's ability to process complex data (multiple calendars) and make decisions based on predefined rules and constraints (available time slots and preferences).

Beyond these everyday examples, AI agents can assist with more complex tasks, acting as personalized research assistants. Imagine needing to synthesize information from multiple sources on a specific topic. Instead of spending countless hours sifting through articles and reports, an AI research agent can autonomously gather relevant information, summarize key findings, and even identify potential gaps in your knowledge. This mirrors how dedicated section leaders in an orchestra might gather and prepare specific musical passages for the conductor's review, saving them valuable preparation time.

Why This Matters

Liberating our time and cognitive resources goes beyond mere efficiency, empowering us to reclaim our focus on what truly matters. Offloading mundane and repetitive tasks to AI agents allows us to free up mental bandwidth for deeper thinking, creative problem-solving, and more meaningful engagement with our work and personal lives. This shift from being burdened by details to being boosted by intelligent assistance is a fundamental aspect of individual empowerment through AI.

The Rise of the Personal AI Agent: Tailored Intelligence at Your Fingertips

At its core, individual empowerment through AI agents centers on augmenting human capabilities rather than replacing them. Like an orchestra conductor directing specialized musicians, professionals can now orchestrate AI agents to handle specific tasks while maintaining strategic control. This creates several key advantages:

- **Cognitive offloading:** AI agents can take on routine cognitive tasks like scheduling, data analysis, and document processing, freeing up mental bandwidth for higher-order thinking.
- **Capability enhancement:** Agents can enhance human abilities by providing real-time information, analysis, and recommendations that improve decision-making.
- **Time multiplication:** By delegating tasks to agents that operate 24/7, professionals can dramatically expand their productive capacity.

While generalized AI tools have offered assistance for some time, the emergence of sophisticated AI agents signs a new era of personalized intelligence. These aren't just generic algorithms; they are entities that can learn your individual preferences, habits, and goals, adapting their behavior to become uniquely tailored extensions of your own capabilities.

Consider the realm of learning and skill development. Imagine an AI learning agent that understands your learning style, identifies your knowledge gaps, and curates personalized learning paths from a vast ocean of educational resources. This agent can track your progress, identify areas where you might be struggling, and provide targeted feedback and support. This is similar to having a personal tutor who understands your strengths and weaknesses, guiding you through complex material at your own pace and focusing on the areas where you need the most help. From a first-principles perspective, this leverages the AI agent's ability to analyze large datasets (educational content, your learning patterns) and make recommendations based on learned preferences and goals.

REAL-WORLD EXAMPLE

Maria, our marketing manager, wants to upskill in data analytics. Instead of aimlessly searching for courses online, she utilizes a personal AI learning agent. The agent assesses her existing skillset through a series of interactive exercises and questions. It then analyzes thousands of online courses, articles, and tutorials, identifying those that best match her learning style and career goals. The agent creates a structured learning plan, scheduling time for study and providing reminders. As Maria progresses, the agent tracks her performance, highlighting areas where she excels and suggesting additional resources for areas where she needs more support. This personalized approach accelerates her learning and keeps her motivated, contrasting sharply with the overwhelming and often impersonal experience of traditional online learning.

This level of personalization extends beyond professional development. Imagine an AI health and wellness agent that tracks your fitness data, monitors your sleep patterns, and analyzes your dietary habits to provide personalized recommendations for optimizing your well-being. This agent can remind you to take breaks, suggest healthy meal options, and even schedule workouts based on your availability and energy levels. This is far more effective than generic health apps; it's a proactive and adaptive partner in your pursuit of a healthier lifestyle.

Why This Matters

The power of the personal AI agent lies in its ability to understand and cater to your unique needs and aspirations. It moves beyond the one-size-fits-all approach of traditional tools, offering a level of tailored assistance that can significantly enhance your productivity, accelerate your learning, and improve your overall well-being. This represents a fundamental shift toward a more personalized and empowering technological landscape.

Democratizing Expertise: Accessing Knowledge and Skills on Demand

Historically, access to specialized knowledge and expertise has been a significant barrier for many individuals and small businesses. Consulting experts, hiring specialists, or undertaking lengthy periods of formal education were often the only avenues to acquire specific skills or insights. AI agents are beginning to dismantle these barriers, democratizing expertise and making it accessible to a wider audience.

Consider the complexities of financial planning. Navigating investment options, understanding tax implications, and planning for retirement can be daunting, often requiring the services of a financial advisor. However, AI-powered financial planning agents can analyze your financial situation, assess your risk tolerance, and provide personalized investment recommendations. While not a replacement for human advisors in all situations, these agents offer a powerful and accessible starting point, empowering individuals to make more informed financial decisions. This parallels how the vast knowledge of a seasoned musical scholar can now be accessed through readily available online resources and AI-powered search tools, empowering aspiring musicians to deepen their understanding of music theory and history.

Imagine needing legal advice on a specific matter. Consulting a lawyer can be expensive and time-consuming. AI-powered legal research agents can analyze vast legal databases, identify relevant precedents, and provide insights into potential legal strategies. This doesn't replace the need for legal counsel in complex cases, but it offers a valuable tool for understanding your rights and options, empowering you to navigate legal situations with greater confidence.

This democratization of expertise extends to various fields. AI agents can assist with coding, graphic design, content creation, and a multitude of other specialized tasks. Providing guidance, suggesting best practices, and even automating certain aspects of these processes enables AI agents to lower the barrier to entry, allowing individuals to explore new skills and pursue creative endeavors without years of formal training.

Why This Matters

Democratizing expertise through AI agents levels the playing field, providing individuals with unprecedented access to knowledge and skills that were previously restricted to a select few. This nurtures innovation, encourages lifelong learning, and empowers individuals to pursue their passions and achieve their full potential, regardless of their background or formal qualifications. It's about giving everyone access to the "instruments" and the "knowledge of how to play them," nurturing a richer and more diverse "symphony" of individual achievement.

The empowerment of the individual through AI agents is not a distant prospect; it's a tangible force reshaping our lives today. From reclaiming our time and focus to accessing personalized intelligence and democratized expertise, these intelligent entities are destined to become indispensable partners in our personal and professional journeys. Just as each instrument in the orchestra contributes to the richness and complexity of the music, AI agents are empowering individuals to create their own unique and fulfilling compositions. As we move forward, understanding and embracing this transformative potential will be imperative for navigating the evolving landscape of work and life. In the next section, we will explore specific career development strategies individuals can leverage in this new era of intelligent assistance.

Career Development Strategies

Meet Maria once more, a mid-career marketing professional who recently discovered that her company was implementing AI agents to automate various aspects of campaign analysis and content creation. Rather than viewing this as a threat, Maria saw an opportunity to evolve her role and become what she calls an "AI-augmented marketer." Her journey of adaptation and growth represents the career development path many professionals will need to navigate in the age of AI agents.

The integration of AI agents into the workplace necessitates a strategic approach to career development that combines human expertise with AI capabilities. This section explores actionable career development strategies to not only survive but thrive in a world increasingly shaped by AI agents, transforming potential anxieties into concrete opportunities for growth and reinvention. We'll explore how to identify roles ripe for augmentation, cultivate the skills that complement agent capabilities, and strategically reposition ourselves for a future where human ingenuity and artificial intelligence work in harmonious synergy, like different sections of an orchestra playing in concert.

Identifying Agent-Augmentable Roles: Spotting the Opportunities for Collaboration

The initial reaction to the rise of AI agents might be one of apprehension, a fear of being rendered obsolete. However, a more constructive perspective views these intelligent entities as powerful tools, similar to the advent of the personal computer or the internet. The key lies in identifying roles where AI agents can augment human capabilities, freeing us from repetitive, data-intensive tasks and allowing us to focus on higher-level strategic thinking, creativity, and uniquely human skills. Thinking in terms of first principles, we understand that AI agents excel at processing information, identifying patterns, and executing tasks with speed and precision. This makes roles heavily reliant on these activities prime candidates for augmentation, not replacement.

Consider a financial analyst spending hours poring over spreadsheets to identify investment trends. An AI agent, equipped with sophisticated data analysis capabilities and access to real-time market information, can perform this task in a fraction of the time, presenting the analyst with insightful patterns and potential opportunities. This doesn't eliminate the need for the analyst; rather, it empowers them to focus on interpreting the agent's findings, applying nuanced judgment, and developing strategic investment recommendations—tasks that require human expertise and understanding of context. Just as a skilled conductor can bring harmony to diverse instruments, strategic career development involves orchestrating the complementary strengths of human intuition and AI capabilities to achieve superior outcomes.

Similarly, in customer service, AI agents can handle routine inquiries, freeing up human agents to address complex issues requiring empathy and problem-solving skills. The legal field offers another compelling example. The tedious process of legal research can be significantly accelerated by AI agents capable of sifting through vast legal databases, identifying relevant precedents, and summarizing key findings, allowing lawyers to concentrate on crafting arguments and representing their clients.

To identify agent-augmentable roles, we need to analyze the core responsibilities and tasks within a profession. Look for activities that:

- **Involve repetitive data processing or analysis:** Tasks that require sifting through large volumes of information to identify patterns or insights are prime candidates for AI agent assistance.
- **Are rules-based and predictable:** Processes with clearly defined rules and parameters can be easily automated by intelligent agents.

- **Require efficient information retrieval:** Agents excel at accessing and organizing information from diverse sources.
- **Involve task execution with high precision and speed:** Agents can perform tasks quickly and accurately, minimizing errors.

Deep Dive: The Human-AI Complementarity Framework

- **AI strengths:** Data processing, pattern recognition, content generation, repetitive tasks
- **Human strengths:** Strategic thinking, emotional intelligence, ethical judgment, creative innovation
- **Hybrid opportunities:** AI-augmented decision-making, human-guided AI content creation, strategic oversight of AI systems

The key takeaway here is not to see AI agents as replacements but as *powerful collaborators*. Understanding their strengths and limitations enables us to identify the areas where they can significantly enhance our productivity and allow us to focus on the uniquely human aspects of our work. This proactive approach transforms the perceived threat into a genuine opportunity for professional growth and enhanced impact.

Why This Matters

Identifying agent-augmentable roles is the first essential step in navigating the changing career landscape. It allows us to proactively adapt, shifting our focus toward tasks that leverage our unique human strengths and complement the capabilities of AI agents, ensuring long-term relevance and value in the workforce.

Cultivating Agent-Native Skills: Becoming the AI Agent Whisperer

As AI agents become increasingly integrated into our professional lives, the demand for skills that complement and orchestrate their capabilities will skyrocket. These "agent-native skills" are not about competing with AI in areas where it excels but rather about developing the expertise to effectively leverage its power and address the challenges and opportunities it presents. Drawing upon our first-principles understanding of agentic AI, we recognize that while agents possess impressive computational power and analytical abilities, they lack the nuanced understanding of context, the creative spark, and the complex emotional intelligence that define human expertise.

Much like learning to play a new and complex musical instrument, mastering agent-native skills requires dedicated effort, consistent practice, and a deep appreciation for the unique qualities and capabilities these powerful tools bring to your professional repertoire.

Success in the AI age requires developing specific skills for effective collaboration with AI agents:

1. AI literacy

   Understanding AI capabilities and limitations

   Learning to write effective prompts and instructions

   Recognizing AI biases and potential errors

2. AI management skills

   Coordinating multiple AI agents for complex tasks

   Quality control and output refinement

   Resource optimization and cost management

3. AI integration skills

   Workflow design incorporating AI agents

   Process automation and optimization

   Cross-functional collaboration leveraging AI

One fundamental agent-native skill is **agent workflow design**, which involves understanding how to integrate AI agents into existing workflows to optimize processes and achieve specific goals. This requires a systems-thinking approach, analyzing current workflows, identifying bottlenecks, and strategically deploying agents to enhance efficiency and productivity.

Furthermore, **critical evaluation of agent outputs** is paramount. While agents can generate impressive results, they are not infallible. Developing the ability to critically assess the accuracy, relevance, and potential biases in agent outputs is vital for ensuring responsible and effective use. This involves understanding the limitations of the data the agent was trained on and recognizing potential blind spots. **Ethical considerations** also come into play, requiring ethical oversight of AI agent deployment. As agents take on more complex tasks, understanding the ethical implications of their actions, ensuring fairness and transparency, and mitigating potential biases become increasingly important.

Beyond these technical and analytical skills, **collaboration and communication skills** will be even more important in an agent-augmented workplace. Effectively collaborating with AI agents requires clear communication of goals, expectations, and feedback. Similarly, communicating the insights and outputs generated by agents to human colleagues and stakeholders requires strong presentation and explanation skills. Finally, **continuous learning and adaptation** are essential. The field of AI is rapidly evolving, and staying ahead of the curve requires a commitment to lifelong learning, actively seeking out new knowledge and adapting to the latest advancements in agentic AI.

Why This Matters

Cultivating agent-native skills is about future-proofing your career. It's about developing the competencies needed to thrive in a collaborative environment with intelligent agents, becoming an indispensable partner in this new era of intelligent work.

Repositioning and Upskilling for the Agent Era: Charting Your Course in the New Landscape

Simply recognizing the potential of AI agents isn't enough. Strategic career development requires proactive steps to reposition oneself and acquire the necessary skills to capitalize on the opportunities presented by this techno-logical shift. This involves a multi-faceted approach encompassing upskill-ing, reskilling, and strategic career pivots. This transition is similar to how musicians adapt to new compositions, recognizing that while the notes may change, the fundamental principles of musicality remain constant.

Upskilling focuses on enhancing existing skills to incorporate agentic AI tools and methodologies. For a marketing manager like Maria, this might involve learning how to use AI-powered analytics platforms to gain deeper insights into customer behavior, mastering prompt engineering to generate more effective marketing copy, or understanding how to integrate AI agents into her campaign workflows for optimized ad spend. For a software devel-oper, upskilling could involve learning how to build and integrate AI agents into applications, leveraging agentic frameworks for task automation, or mas-tering the ethical considerations of deploying intelligent systems.

Reskilling, on the other hand, involves acquiring entirely new skills to transition into roles that are in high demand in the agent era. Someone working in a highly repetitive data entry role, for example, might consider reskilling to become an AI workflow designer, leveraging their understanding of data to create efficient processes that incorporate intelligent agents. A cus-tomer service representative could reskill as an AI agent trainer, focusing on refining the conversational abilities and problem-solving capabilities of these intelligent assistants. These transitions require a commitment to learning new technologies and methodologies, often through online courses, certifications, or even formal education programs.

Strategic career pivots involve making significant changes to one's career path to align with the emerging opportunities in the agentic AI landscape. This might involve moving from a highly specialized technical role to a more strategic or managerial position that focuses on overseeing AI agent deployments and ensuring their alignment with business goals. It could also involve transitioning to entirely new fields, such as AI ethics consulting or AI agent training and development. Regardless of the specific path, strategic career pivots require careful planning, networking, and a willingness to embrace new challenges.

Actionable Steps for Repositioning:

- **Conduct a skills audit:** Identify your current skills and assess their relevance in an agent-augmented world. Pinpoint areas where AI agents might impact your role and identify skill gaps.
- **Explore upskilling and reskilling opportunities:** Research online courses, workshops, certifications, and educational programs that focus on agentic AI technologies and related skills. Platforms like Coursera, edX, and Udacity offer a wealth of relevant courses.
- **Network with professionals in the AI field:** Attend industry events, join online communities, and connect with individuals working with AI agents to learn about emerging trends and opportunities.
- **Seek mentorship:** Find mentors who have successfully navigated the changing technological landscape and can provide guidance and support.
- **Experiment with AI tools:** Familiarize yourself with existing AI agent platforms and tools to gain practical experience and understand their capabilities and limitations.
- **Focus on demonstrable skills:** Highlight your agent-native skills and your ability to work effectively with AI in your resume and during job interviews. Showcase projects or experiences where you have successfully leveraged AI agents.

Why This Matters

Proactive repositioning and continuous upskilling are not just about adapting to change; they are about seizing the opportunities that the agentic AI revolution presents. Strategically investing in our skills and making conscious career choices enable us to ensure our long-term relevance and become key players in shaping the future of work.

The rise of AI agents represents a significant shift in the professional landscape, but it is not an omen of doom or widespread job displacement. Instead, it presents a powerful catalyst for career evolution and the emergence of new, exciting opportunities. As we've explored in this section, the key to navigating this transformation lies in proactive engagement. Identifying roles ripe for agentic augmentation, cultivating the essential agent-native skills, and strategically repositioning ourselves through upskilling and reskilling allow us to not only adapt to this new reality but actively shape it. Just as a skilled conductor harmonizes the diverse talents of an orchestra, the professionals of the future will orchestrate the power of AI agents, leveraging their unique human ingenuity to achieve unprecedented levels of innovation and productivity. The future trajectory of your career in the age of AI agents is not predetermined or fixed; it is a dynamic and evolving narrative that you have the power to write, starting with a conscious decision to embrace the exciting opportunities and diligently cultivate the essential skills that will define the next transformative era of work.

While career development focuses on individual professional growth, small business applications of AI agents present unique opportunities and challenges for entrepreneurs and business owners. Let's explore how AI agents can transform small business operations . . .

SMALL BUSINESS SYMPHONIES: AGENTIC AI FOR GROWTH AND EFFICIENCY

Imagine Ana, the owner of a burgeoning artisanal bakery. Her passion is crafting exquisite pastries, but the daily grind of managing orders, scheduling staff, and responding to customer inquiries often leaves her feeling more like an administrator than a baker. She dreams of expansion, of reaching more customers, but the thought of adding more to her already overflowing plate feels daunting. This is a familiar story for millions of small business owners, the backbone of our economies. They are often resourceful and innovative, yet constrained by time, resources, and access to specialized expertise. This is precisely where the transformative power of AI agents shines.

For too long, advanced technological solutions felt like the exclusive domain of large corporations with dedicated IT departments and hefty budgets. But the AI agent revolution is democratizing access to sophisticated intelligence, putting powerful tools within reach of even the smallest enterprises.

In this section, we'll explore how small businesses can leverage AI agents to not just survive, but thrive in an increasingly competitive landscape. We'll move beyond the abstract and explore concrete applications, demonstrating how these intelligent collaborators can alleviate burdens, unlock new opportunities, and empower small businesses to operate with the agility and insight previously reserved for their larger counterparts. Just as a skilled conductor brings harmony and efficiency to an orchestra, AI agents can orchestrate various tasks and processes, freeing up human talent to focus on core business values and strategic growth.

The integration of AI agents into small business operations represents one of the most transformative applications of this technology. Unlike enterprise-scale implementations that require significant resources and technical expertise, AI agents can provide immediate value to small businesses through accessible, focused solutions that address common operational challenges.

Leveling the Playing Field: Access and Affordability

The beauty of the AI agent revolution for small businesses lies in its inherent scalability and accessibility. Unlike traditional software solutions that often require significant upfront investment and ongoing maintenance, many AI agent-powered services operate on a subscription basis, offering a "pay-as-you-grow" model perfectly suited to the fluctuating needs of a small enterprise. This fundamental shift dramatically lowers the barrier to entry, enabling even micro-businesses to access cutting-edge technology. Just as smaller orchestras can achieve remarkable performances with skilled musicians and focused direction, small businesses equipped with intelligent agents can achieve significant results with their core competencies amplified by AI.

Consider the realm of marketing. Previously, a small business like Ana's Bakery might struggle to afford a dedicated marketing team or sophisticated digital advertising campaigns. Now, AI agents can automate social media posting, personalize email marketing based on customer preferences, and even analyze marketing data to identify the most effective channels and messaging. These agents can act as a virtual marketing assistant, tirelessly working in the background to build brand awareness and drive customer engagement, all at a fraction of the cost of a human hire. This isn't about replacing human creativity but augmenting it. Ana can still craft the heart of her marketing message—the story of her delicious pastries—and the AI agent can amplify that message, ensuring it reaches the right audience at the right time.

Similarly, access to specialized expertise, often a costly constraint for small businesses, is being redefined by AI agents. Need help with basic legal document generation? AI agents can assist. Require insights into optimizing your supply chain? AI agents can analyze data and provide recommendations. This access to on-demand, intelligent assistance allows small business owners to make more informed decisions across a wider range of functions without the prohibitive cost of hiring full-time specialists. This democratization of expertise is key for leveling the playing field, allowing small businesses to compete more effectively with larger organizations that have traditionally held an advantage in these areas. The orchestra analogy continues to hold true: just as smaller orchestras can achieve remarkable performances with skilled musicians and focused direction, small businesses equipped with intelligent agents can achieve significant results with their core competencies amplified by AI.

Why This Matters

This increased accessibility and affordability is not just about cost savings; it's about empowering small businesses to innovate and grow. By removing technological and financial hurdles, AI agents free up precious resources—both time and capital—that can be reinvested in product development, customer service enhancements, and strategic expansion.

Operational task management AI agents excel at handling the routine but essential tasks that often overwhelm small business owners. These include:

- **Inventory tracking and automated reordering:** Ensuring optimal stock levels and minimizing stockouts or overstocking
- **Customer communication and proactive support:** Handling routine inquiries, providing timely updates, and resolving basic issues efficiently
- **Appointment and schedule management:** Automating booking, reminders, and rescheduling for services or consultations
- **Basic bookkeeping and financial record maintenance:** Automating data entry, invoice processing, and basic financial reporting
- **Social media monitoring and basic engagement:** Tracking brand mentions, responding to simple inquiries, and scheduling content posting

The key advantage for small businesses is that these agents can operate continuously in the background, managing multiple tasks simultaneously while business owners focus on core operations and growth activities.

Deep Dive: Task Orchestration

Modern AI agents utilize sophisticated task orchestration capabilities that allow them to:

1. Identify task dependencies and optimal sequencing
2. Adjust priorities based on business conditions
3. Escalate issues requiring human attention
4. Learn from past task execution patterns

This enables truly autonomous operation while maintaining appropriate human oversight.

For a small business owner, this technical architecture often remains invisible, accessed through intuitive interfaces and simple instructions. The focus is on the outcomes—the marketing emails sent, the customer inquiries resolved—not the intricate workings of the AI behind the scenes.

REAL-WORLD EXAMPLE

Mark, a talented freelance graphic designer running his own small business, uses an AI-powered project management tool to streamline his workflow. The intelligent agent automatically tracks project deadlines, sends timely reminders to clients regarding deliverables, and even drafts initial versions of contracts and invoices based on pre-defined templates and client data. This valuable automation frees up Mark to dedicate more of his time and creative energy to the core creative aspects of his work—designing visually stunning graphics and collaborating closely with clients on their brand vision—rather than getting bogged down in time-consuming administrative details and repetitive project management tasks.

Supercharged Customer Engagement: Personalized Experiences at Scale

In today's customer-centric world, providing personalized experiences is no longer a luxury, but a necessity. However, for small businesses with limited staff, delivering truly tailored interactions can be a significant challenge. AI agents offer a powerful solution, enabling small businesses to engage with their customers on a more personal and efficient level, scaling their outreach without sacrificing the human touch.

Consider customer service. An AI-powered chatbot, intelligently trained on a small business's specific product information and FAQs, can handle a significant portion of routine customer inquiries. This provides instant support to customers, even outside of business hours, improving satisfaction and freeing up human staff to focus on more complex or sensitive issues. These aren't the rigid, rule-based chatbots of the past. Agentic AI, with its capacity for understanding nuanced language and context, can engage in more natural and helpful conversations, even learning from each interaction to improve its responses over time. Think of it as having a dedicated customer service representative available 24/7, without the associated salary costs.

Beyond basic support, AI agents can personalize the entire customer journey. By analyzing customer data—purchase history, browsing behavior,

stated preferences—agents can tailor marketing messages, product recommendations, and even the overall website experience to individual customers.
Imagine Ana's Bakery: an AI agent could identify customers who frequently
purchase gluten-free items and automatically send them targeted promo-
tions for new gluten-free offerings. This level of personalization encourages
stronger customer relationships, increases loyalty, and ultimately drives
sales. The AI agent acts as a sophisticated liaison, ensuring that each customer feels understood and valued, mirroring the personal touch that is often
a hallmark of successful small businesses, but now amplified by intelligent
technology.

REAL-WORLD EXAMPLE

David, who passionately runs a small independent online bookstore specializing in rare and first-edition books, uses an AI agent to curate highly
personalized book recommendations for his valued customers based
on their past purchases, website browsing history, stated literary preferences, and even social media activity related to books and authors. He has
observed a significant and measurable increase in both sales conversion
rates and overall customer engagement since implementing this intelligent personalization system, demonstrating the tangible business benefits
of AI-driven customer engagement.

Streamlined Operations: Efficiency and Automation Unleashed

One of the biggest drains on a small business owner's time and energy is the
burden of repetitive, manual tasks. From scheduling appointments to managing
inventory, these essential operational functions can consume valuable hours
that could be better spent on strategic initiatives or core business activities. AI
agents offer a powerful antidote to this operational drag, automating processes
and freeing up human capital for more impactful work.

Consider inventory management. For a small retailer, keeping track
of stock levels, anticipating demand, and reordering supplies can be a
time-consuming and error-prone process. AI agents can analyze sales data,
predict future demand based on trends and seasonality, and even automatically trigger reorders when stock levels reach a certain threshold. This not
only saves time but also reduces the risk of stockouts or overstocking, both
of which can negatively impact profitability. The agent acts as a diligent and
tireless inventory manager, ensuring that the right products are available at

the right time, optimizing cash flow and minimizing waste. The AI agents become the tireless support staff, allowing the human team to shine in their areas of expertise, much like the various sections of an orchestra each contributing their unique sound to the overall performance.

Beyond inventory, AI agents can streamline a wide range of operational tasks. They can automate appointment scheduling, manage email inboxes, process invoices, and even assist with basic accounting functions. Taking on these routine responsibilities empowers AI agents free up human employees to focus on tasks that require creativity, critical thinking, and human interaction—the very aspects that often differentiate successful small businesses. For Ana's Bakery, an AI agent could manage her staff scheduling, considering employee availability and predicted order volumes, optimizing her labor costs and ensuring she has the right team on hand during peak hours. This operational efficiency translates directly into improved productivity, reduced costs, and a smoother running business overall.

REAL-WORLD EXAMPLE

Maria, who runs a small cleaning business, uses an AI agent to manage her appointment scheduling and route her cleaning crews efficiently. The agent considers factors like location, travel time, and customer preferences to create optimal schedules, saving her significant administrative time and reducing travel costs.

Data-Driven Decisions: Insights for Growth and Innovation

Small businesses often operate with limited access to sophisticated data analytics, relying on intuition and anecdotal evidence for decision-making. AI agents can democratize access to data-driven insights, providing small business owners with the intelligence they need to make more strategic and informed choices, driving growth and nurturing innovation.

AI agents can sift through vast amounts of data—sales figures, customer feedback, market trends, social media sentiment—and identify patterns and insights that would be impossible for a human to discern manually. This data analysis can reveal valuable information about customer preferences, emerging market opportunities, and areas for operational improvement. For instance, an AI agent analyzing Ana's Bakery's sales data might identify a growing demand for vegan pastries, prompting her to experiment with new recipes and potentially capture a new market segment.

This access to data-driven insights empowers small businesses to move beyond guesswork and make decisions based on evidence. They can optimize pricing strategies, identify their most profitable products or services, and even predict future trends, allowing them to proactively adapt to changing market conditions. The AI agent acts as a sophisticated business intelligence analyst, providing the insights needed to navigate the complexities of the modern market-place. This ability to leverage data for informed decision-making is fundamental for sustainable growth and innovation, enabling small businesses to not just react to change but to anticipate it and capitalize on emerging opportunities.

Why This Matters

Data-driven decision-making is no longer a luxury for large corporations. AI agents make this powerful capability accessible to small businesses, enabling them to compete more effectively, identify new avenues for growth, and adapt to the ever-evolving needs of their customers.

REAL-WORLD EXAMPLE

Carlos, who owns a small independent coffee shop, uses an AI agent to analyze customer feedback from online reviews and social media. The agent identified recurring comments about the need for more comfortable seating, prompting Carlos to invest in new furniture, which resulted in increased customer dwell time and higher sales.

Best Practices for Implementation

To maximize the benefits of AI agents in small business settings:

1. **Start small:** Begin with one or two key applications and gradually expand based on results and comfort level.
2. **Prioritize integration:** Ensure seamless integration with existing systems and workflows to minimize disruption.
3. **Monitor and adjust:** Regularly assess performance metrics and adjust configurations as needed.
4. **Maintain human oversight:** Establish clear protocols for human intervention and decision-making authority.
5. **Invest in training:** Ensure staff understands how to work effectively with AI agents as collaborative tools.

The use of AI agents in small businesses has moved from futuristic fantasy to present-day reality. From leveling the playing field with affordable access to advanced technology, to supercharging customer engagement through personalized experiences, streamlining operations for increased efficiency, and unlocking data-driven insights for strategic growth, AI agents are set to revolutionize the way small businesses operate and compete. These intelligent collaborators are not meant to replace the human element—the passion, the creativity, the personal touch that defines so many successful small enterprises. Instead, they act as powerful amplifiers, augmenting human capabilities and freeing up valuable time and resources to focus on what truly matters: building a thriving business and serving their customers with excellence. As the orchestra conductor guides the musicians to create a beautiful symphony, small business owners can leverage AI agents to orchestrate their business toward greater success in the exciting and evolving landscape of the future. The opportunities are vast, and the time to embrace the power of AI agents is now.

PERSONAL PRODUCTIVITY SYSTEMS

Imagine Maria, a busy marketing executive, struggling to manage her growing workload. Her calendar is packed with meetings, her inbox overflows with emails, and her to-do list seems endless. Enter her AI productivity agent, which not only helps organize her work but actively learns her preferences, anticipates her needs, and seamlessly coordinates across her digital tools and workflows.

The emergence of AI agents is revolutionizing how we approach personal productivity and task management. Unlike traditional productivity tools that require significant manual input and maintenance, AI agents serve as proactive partners that can understand context, learn from patterns, and autonomously handle routine tasks while providing strategic support for complex work. Just as entire organizations are set for revolution, so too is the individual. We've explored how AI agents will transform our homes, careers, and small businesses.

Now, let's explore the very core of individual empowerment: personal productivity systems. How can these intelligent agents become our personal conductors, harmonizing the various instruments of our busy lives into a more productive and fulfilling symphony?

This section will explore the practical ways you can leverage AI agents to amplify your personal effectiveness, reclaim your time, and achieve more with less stress.

Orchestrating Your Day: AI Agents as Personal Assistants

The modern knowledge worker often feels like the conductor of a chaotic orchestra, juggling emails, meetings, projects, and personal commitments. The sheer volume of information and tasks can be overwhelming, leading to decreased focus, increased stress, and ultimately, lower productivity. AI agents offer a powerful solution by stepping in as proactive personal assistants, capable of understanding your needs and acting autonomously to streamline your daily workflows.

Think of a personal AI agent as your dedicated administrative assistant, but one that never sleeps, learns from your behavior, and can access and process information at lightning speed. Using the first principles of agentic AI, these systems are designed to perceive your environment (your calendar, emails, project management tools), reason about your goals and priorities, and act on your behalf. For instance, an AI agent can analyze your inbox, identify urgent emails requiring immediate attention, and even draft initial responses based on your past communication patterns. This frees up valuable mental space and allows you to focus on tasks demanding higher-level cognitive function. Much like a conductor who once had to manage every aspect of the performance, the AI-empowered individual can now delegate some tasks while maintaining creative control of the overall production.

Why This Matters

The immediate benefit of AI-powered personal assistants is the reclaiming of time. Time spent on routine tasks, like scheduling meetings or sifting through emails, can be redirected toward more strategic and creative endeavors. This shift not only boosts productivity but also contributes to reduced stress and improved work-life balance.

The key to successful integration is understanding that these agents are not replacements for human intellect but powerful augmentations. They excel at tasks that are repetitive, time-consuming, or require processing large amounts of information. This frees up your cognitive bandwidth to focus on strategic thinking, creative problem-solving, and building meaningful connections. Embracing AI agents as personal assistants allows you to effectively orchestrate your day, leading to increased efficiency, reduced stress, and a greater sense of control over your time and workload, and overall professional trajectory.

The AI Productivity Toolkit: Intelligent Agents for Every Task

The landscape of personal productivity tools is already vast, but the integration of AI agents is steering in a new era of intelligent assistance. These agents aren't just passive tools; they are proactive partners capable of anticipating your needs and taking initiative. Building your personal AI productivity system involves understanding the different types of agents available and how they can address specific pain points in your workflow. These specialized agents are like the various sections of an orchestra, each performing their specific function with precision and excellence, but all working together to create a harmonious whole.

Why This Matters

A tailored AI productivity toolkit can significantly enhance your effectiveness by automating routine tasks, providing intelligent insights, and freeing up your time for more meaningful work. This goes beyond simply adopting the latest technology, strategically integrating AI to optimize your personal workflows.

REAL-WORLD EXAMPLE

Consider David, a freelance writer who struggled with the initial stages of content creation. He adopted an AI writing assistant that could generate outlines, suggest relevant research material, and even draft initial paragraphs based on his input. This didn't replace his creativity but significantly accelerated his writing process, allowing him to focus on refining the content and ensuring his unique voice shone through.

Here are some key categories of AI agents that form the foundation of a powerful personal productivity toolkit:

- **Communication Agents:** These agents go beyond simple email filtering. They can summarize lengthy email threads, draft responses in your tone and style, schedule meetings intelligently, and even transcribe voice notes into actionable tasks. Imagine an agent that not only flags urgent emails but also proactively gathers relevant information from other sources to help you formulate a comprehensive response.
- **Knowledge Management Agents:** In the age of information overload, these agents act as your personal librarians and researchers. They can curate relevant articles and research papers based on your interests, summarize key findings, and even connect disparate pieces of information to reveal hidden insights. Think of an agent that can automatically organize your notes, tag them with relevant keywords, and surface them at the precise moment you need them.

- **Task Management Agents:** These agents are more than just digital to-do lists. They can intelligently prioritize tasks based on deadlines and importance, break down large projects into manageable steps, and even remind you of upcoming deadlines with relevant context. Imagine an agent that not only reminds you of a meeting but also proactively provides you with the agenda and relevant background information.
- **Content Creation Agents:** For anyone involved in writing, presenting, or creating any form of content, these agents can be invaluable. They can assist with brainstorming ideas, generating outlines, drafting initial content, and even providing feedback on clarity and style. While they won't replace human creativity, they can significantly accelerate the content creation process and help overcome writer's block.

Deep Dive: First Principles of Agentic AI Applied to Productivity Tools

The effectiveness of these productivity agents stems from the core principles of agentic AI. They are designed to be:

- **Perceptive:** They can sense and interpret data from your various digital environments (email, calendar, documents).
- **Reasoning:** They can analyze this data to understand your goals, priorities, and needs.
- **Autonomous:** They can act on your behalf, executing tasks and making decisions based on their reasoning.
- **Learning:** They can continuously learn from your behavior and feedback to improve their performance over time.

Building your personal AI productivity toolkit is an iterative process. It involves identifying your biggest productivity bottlenecks, exploring the available agent options, and experimenting with different integrations to find what works best for you. The key is to view these agents as partners in your work and life, allowing them to handle the mundane while you focus on the meaning.

Building Your Personalized System: Strategies for Integration and Optimization

The true power of AI productivity agents comes from their ability to seamlessly integrate these components while orchestrating across various tools and platforms. Much like a skilled orchestra conductor, the agent coordinates multiple "instruments" (productivity tools) to create a harmonious workflow. The integration of these elements creates a symphony of productivity, where each component plays its part in perfect timing and coordination.

Simply adopting individual AI productivity tools isn't enough. To truly unlock their potential, you need to build a cohesive and personalized system that integrates these agents seamlessly into your existing workflows. This requires a strategic approach, focusing on identifying your specific needs, exploring the available options, and iteratively refining your system based on your experiences.

Why This Matters

A well-integrated personal productivity system powered by AI agents can lead to significant gains in efficiency, creativity, and overall well-being. It's about creating a synergy where the whole is greater than the sum of its parts.

REAL-WORLD EXAMPLE

Consider Maria, an entrepreneur who juggled multiple responsibilities. She didn't just use an AI scheduler; she integrated it with her CRM and project management tools. When a client meeting was scheduled, her AI agent automatically updated her CRM with meeting details and even created relevant tasks in her project management system. This level of integration eliminated manual data entry and ensured all her systems were synchronized.

Here's a step-by-step approach to building your personalized AI productivity system:

1. **Identify Your Productivity Pain Points:** Start by identifying the areas where you consistently lose time or experience frustration. Are you spending too much time on email management? Struggling to keep track of tasks? Feeling overwhelmed by information overload? Pinpointing these pain points will guide your selection of appropriate AI agents.
2. **Explore the AI Productivity Toolkit:** Based on your identified pain points, research the various AI agents available. Consider their features, integrations with your existing tools, and user reviews. Many AI productivity tools offer free trials, allowing you to experiment before committing to a subscription.

3. **Experiment and Integrate:** Begin integrating selected AI agents into your workflows. Start with one or two key areas and gradually expand as you become comfortable. Focus on seamless integration with your existing tools and processes to avoid creating new friction points.
4. **Iterate and Refine:** Building a successful AI productivity system is an iterative process. Pay attention to how the agents are performing, identify areas for improvement, and adjust your system accordingly. Don't be afraid to experiment with different agents or configurations until you find what works best for your individual needs and working style.

Remember that the goal is to empower yourself, not to become overly reliant on AI. Your creativity, critical thinking, and human connection remain essential. AI agents are powerful tools, but ultimately, you are the architect of your own productivity. Strategically integrating these intelligent assistants enables you to build a personalized system that amplifies your capabilities, frees up your time, and allows you to focus on what truly matters.

The integration of AI agents into our personal productivity systems represents a profound shift in how we approach our daily tasks and goals. From acting as intelligent personal assistants to powering specialized tools for communication, knowledge management, and content creation, these agents are fundamentally changing how we work and live. Understanding the core principles of agentic AI and adopting a strategic approach to integration and optimization lets us build personalized systems that amplify our effectiveness, reclaim our time, and ultimately lead to more fulfilling and productive lives. The symphony of our personal and professional endeavors can be conducted with greater precision and harmony, thanks to the intelligent assistance of AI agents.

ACTION PLAN: YOUR AI FUTURE

As we've explored throughout this chapter, AI agents will transform both personal and professional opportunities in profound ways. To help you take concrete steps toward leveraging these technologies, let's develop a structured action plan for navigating your AI-enabled future.

Meet Maria, a mid-career marketing professional who initially felt overwhelmed by the rapid advancement of AI agents. Rather than viewing them as a threat, she developed a systematic plan to integrate AI into her workflow. Within 18 months, she had transformed her role into an "AI-human hybrid" position, managing a team of AI agents while focusing on high-level strategy and creative direction. Her story illustrates how a thoughtful approach to AI adoption can lead to career enhancement rather than replacement.

We've journeyed through the landscape of agentic AI, explored its foundational principles, and witnessed its transformative power across various domains. Now, the pivotal question arises: how do you translate this understanding into tangible actions that shape your personal and professional future? The promise of AI agents is not a passive spectating event; it's an invitation to participate, to build, and to thrive in a world increasingly interwoven with intelligent machines. Just as a conductor doesn't simply admire the instruments but actively shapes the symphony, we must proactively orchestrate our interactions with AI agents to achieve our desired outcomes. This section provides a concrete action plan, offering practical steps you can take today to navigate and capitalize on the burgeoning AI agent revolution. The future isn't something that happens to us; it's something we actively co-create. See Figure 7.1.

FIGURE 7.1 A path to choose?

Generated with AI using DALL·E - OpenAI

Orchestrating Your AI Ensemble: Developing an Agent Strategy

Moving from a conceptual understanding of AI agents to practical application requires a deliberate and strategic approach. Think of it as assembling your personal AI orchestra. You wouldn't haphazardly bring together musicians; you'd carefully select them based on their instruments, their skills, and how they contribute to the overall harmony. Similarly, strategically integrating AI agents into your life demands careful consideration and planning.

Capability Assessment: Identifying Your AI Allies

The first step in building your AI ensemble is understanding the landscape of available AI agents and identifying those best suited to your needs. This involves a clear-eyed assessment of your current tasks, pain points, and aspirations, both personally and professionally.

- **Identifying key tasks for automation:** Begin by meticulously mapping out your typical day and week. What are the repetitive, time-consuming tasks that drain your energy and attention? These are prime candidates for AI augmentation. Consider everything from scheduling meetings and managing emails to conducting research and generating initial drafts. Don't underestimate the power of automating seemingly small tasks; the cumulative time saved can be significant, freeing you to focus on higher-value activities. For instance, instead of manually sifting through news articles for industry trends, an AI agent can curate a personalized daily digest, delivering relevant information directly to you.
- **Evaluating available agent technologies:** Once you've identified target tasks, explore the existing ecosystem of AI agents. This requires staying informed about the rapidly evolving AI landscape. Consider factors like functionality, ease of use, integration capabilities with your existing tools, cost, and security. Are you looking for specialized agents focused on specific tasks, like a writing assistant or a personal finance manager? Or are you interested in more versatile, general-purpose agents that can handle a wider range of requests? Remember the first principles we discussed: understand the core components of the agents you're considering—their perception, decision-making, and action mechanisms—to gauge their suitability for your needs.
- **Considering integration requirements:** A critical aspect often overlooked is how well an AI agent integrates with your existing workflows and technological infrastructure. A powerful agent that doesn't seamlessly connect with your calendar, email, or project management software will likely create more friction than value. Think about the *"communication*

and collaboration capabilities" of the agents—can they interact effectively with the digital tools you rely on daily? Prioritize agents that offer robust API integrations or user-friendly interfaces that minimize disruption to your established processes.

Deep Dive: Understanding APIs and Integrations

For the nontechnical reader, application programming interfaces (APIs) are standardized ways for different software applications to communicate with each other. Think of them as universal translators that allow different technological systems to work together seamlessly. For example, when an AI scheduling agent accesses your calendar application to find available time slots, it's using an API to read and potentially modify your calendar data. Without robust API support, your various digital tools would remain isolated islands, unable to share information or coordinate activities effectively.

Why This Matters

A thorough capability assessment ensures you're not simply chasing the latest AI buzzword but strategically selecting tools that genuinely address your needs and enhance your productivity. It prevents you from investing time and resources in solutions that ultimately don't fit your specific context.

Implementation Planning: Starting Small and Scaling Wisely

Once you've identified potential AI allies, the next step is to carefully plan their integration into your personal and professional life. Just as you wouldn't introduce every instrument into the orchestra at once, overwhelming the listener, a phased implementation of AI agents is fundamental for success. This is similar to how a skilled conductor works with each section of the orchestra, understanding their capabilities and limitations, and bringing them together in perfect harmony.

- **Start with simple, well-defined tasks:** Resist the urge to immediately delegate complex, critical tasks to AI agents. Begin with simple, well-defined tasks where the potential for error is low and the benefits are easily measurable. For example, instead of immediately entrusting an AI with managing your entire investment portfolio, start with using it to track your spending or research potential investment opportunities. This allows you to gain confidence in the agent's capabilities and identify any potential limitations in a low-stakes environment.

- **Gradually expand agent responsibilities:** As you gain experience and confidence, you can gradually expand the responsibilities delegated to your AI agents. This iterative approach allows you to refine your delegation strategies and ensure a smooth transition. Monitor the agent's performance closely, providing feedback and adjustments as needed. Think of it as training a new member of your team; you wouldn't expect them to handle everything perfectly from day one.
- **Establish clear workflows and boundaries:** Clearly define the workflows and boundaries for each AI agent. What are its specific responsibilities? What are the limits of its authority? How will it interact with you and other tools in your ecosystem? Ambiguity can lead to errors and frustration. For example, if you're using an AI agent for email management, establish clear rules for which emails it should prioritize, flag, or even respond to automatically. This ensures the agent operates effectively within defined parameters and doesn't overstep its bounds.

Why This Matters

A phased and well-planned implementation minimizes disruption, builds confidence, and allows for continuous learning and optimization. It prevents you from being overwhelmed and increases the likelihood of successful AI integration.

Continuous Optimization: Refining the Harmony

The integration of AI agents is not a "set it and forget it" endeavor. Like a conductor constantly fine-tuning the orchestra's performance, you need to continuously monitor, evaluate, and optimize your interactions with AI agents to maximize their effectiveness.

- **Monitor agent performance:** Regularly assess how your AI agents are performing. Are they achieving the desired outcomes? Are there areas where they are falling short? Pay attention to both quantitative metrics (e.g., time saved, tasks completed) and qualitative feedback (e.g., the quality of generated content, the accuracy of information retrieval). Most AI platforms offer some level of performance tracking, allowing you to identify areas for improvement.
- **Refine delegation strategies:** Based on your performance monitoring, adjust your delegation strategies. Are there tasks that the agent is struggling with? Perhaps those tasks require more nuanced understanding or human oversight. Conversely, are there tasks where the agent is consistently exceeding expectations? Consider expanding its responsibilities in

those areas. This ongoing refinement is key to maximizing the value you derive from your AI ensemble.

- **Stay current with new capabilities:** The field of AI is constantly evolving. New AI agents with enhanced capabilities are emerging regularly. Make it a practice to stay informed about these advancements. Read industry publications, attend webinars, and experiment with new tools to see how they might further enhance your personal and professional life. Just as a conductor stays abreast of new musical innovations and instruments, you need to remain aware of the latest developments in AI agents.

Why This Matters

Continuous optimization ensures that your AI ensemble remains aligned with your evolving needs and that you're leveraging the latest advancements to achieve optimal performance. It prevents stagnation and maximizes the long-term benefits of AI integration.

Building an AI-Enhanced Career Path: Adapting and Thriving

The rise of AI agents presents not only opportunities for individual productivity but also a significant shift in the landscape of work and career development. Successfully navigating this change requires a proactive and forward-thinking approach to building an AI-enhanced career path. It's about understanding how AI will augment human capabilities and positioning yourself to thrive in this new reality.

Master Current AI Tools and Develop Practical Collaboration Skills in the Short Term

The immediate focus should be on acquiring the practical skills and knowledge needed to effectively utilize existing AI tools and collaborate with them in your current role.

- **Master current AI tools in your field:** Identify the specific AI tools and platforms relevant to your industry and profession. This might include AI-powered analytics software, content generation tools, or industry-specific automation platforms. Dedicate time to learning these tools, through online courses, tutorials, or hands-on experimentation. Become proficient in leveraging their capabilities to enhance your current workflows and improve your output. Think of it as mastering the core instruments of your current professional orchestra.
- **Develop basic AI literacy and collaboration skills:** Even if you're not a technical expert, developing a basic understanding of AI concepts

and terminology is vital. Familiarize yourself with terms like machine learning, natural language processing, and automation. More importantly, cultivate the skills needed to effectively collaborate with AI agents. This includes learning how to provide clear and concise instructions, interpret their outputs, and identify potential biases or limitations. Collaboration in the age of AI is a new form of teamwork, requiring a different skillset.

- **Identify immediate opportunities for AI augmentation:** Look for specific tasks within your current responsibilities where AI can provide immediate assistance. This might involve using AI to automate data entry, generate reports, or conduct preliminary research. Seek out small, low-risk opportunities to integrate AI into your daily work and demonstrate its value to your team or organization. These early successes can build momentum and pave the way for more significant AI adoption.

Why This Matters

A strong short-term strategy ensures you remain relevant and productive in the immediate future. It equips you with the practical skills needed to leverage existing AI tools and position yourself as someone who embraces technological advancements.

Specialize in AI-Human Hybrid Roles and Develop Leadership Capabilities in the Medium Term

As AI agents become more sophisticated and integrated into the workplace, the demand for professionals who can effectively manage and guide these systems will grow significantly. Your medium-term strategy should focus on developing specialized expertise and leadership skills in this emerging landscape.

- **Specialize in AI-human hybrid roles:** Explore opportunities to specialize in roles that involve a close collaboration between humans and AI agents. This might involve becoming a prompt engineer, designing effective workflows for AI-augmented teams, or specializing in the ethical deployment of AI in your field. These hybrid roles will be increasingly valuable as organizations seek to maximize the benefits of AI while mitigating potential risks.
- **Build expertise in AI system design and management:** Develop a deeper understanding of how AI systems are designed, implemented, and managed. This might involve acquiring technical skills in areas like data science, machine learning operations (MLOps), or AI project management. Even without becoming a hardcore developer, understanding the underlying

principles will enable you to make more informed decisions and contribute more effectively to AI-driven initiatives.

- **Develop leadership skills for AI-enabled teams:** As AI becomes more prevalent, leadership will increasingly involve managing and motivating teams that include both humans and AI agents. Develop your leadership skills in areas like delegation, communication, conflict resolution, and promote a collaborative environment where humans and AI can work together effectively. The ability to lead an AI-augmented world will be a highly sought-after skill.

Why This Matters

A focused medium-term strategy positions you for career advancement and leadership opportunities in the evolving AI-driven workplace. It allows you to develop in-demand skills and become a key player in your organization's AI transformation.

Position Yourself as an AI Transformation Leader and Strategic Innovator for Long-Term Success

Looking further into the future, your long-term strategy should focus on positioning yourself as a leader and innovator in the field of AI, capable of shaping the future of your industry and beyond.

- **Position yourself as an AI transformation leader:** Aim to become a strategic thinker and influencer in the realm of AI. This involves staying at the forefront of AI innovation, understanding the broader societal implications of AI, and contributing to the development of ethical and responsible AI practices. Seek out opportunities to contribute to industry discussions, publish thought leadership pieces, and mentor others in their AI journeys.
- **Focus on strategic roles that leverage both human and AI capabilities:** In the long term, the most valuable roles will be those that uniquely combine human ingenuity with the power of AI. Focus on developing your strategic thinking, creativity, critical thinking, and emotional intelligence— qualities that are difficult for AI to replicate. These uniquely human skills, augmented by AI, will be the drivers of innovation and progress.
- **Cultivate adaptability for emerging technologies:** The pace of technological change will only accelerate. The most essential skill for long-term success will be adaptability. Embrace a growth mindset, cultivate a love for learning, and be prepared to continuously acquire new skills and knowledge as new technologies emerge. The future belongs to those who are willing and able to adapt.

Why This Matters

A robust long-term strategy ensures your continued relevance and influence in a future increasingly shaped by AI. It positions you to not only adapt to change but to actively lead and shape the direction of AI innovation.

CONCLUSION: EMBRACING THE AGENTIC FUTURE

The rise of AI agents has shifted from distant futuristic fantasy, much like the scene depicted in Figure 7.2, to a present-day reality, rapidly transforming our personal and professional lives. Adopting a proactive and strategic approach, as outlined in this action plan, you can move beyond passive observation and actively shape your AI future. Whether it's carefully orchestrating

FIGURE 7.2   Agentic future?

Generated with AI using DALL·E - OpenAI

your personal AI ensemble or strategically crafting your AI-enhanced career path, the key lies in understanding the potential of these intelligent machines and taking concrete steps to integrate them into your world. The conductor doesn't just dream of the symphony; they assemble the musicians, practice the score, and actively lead the performance. Similarly, your AI future is not something to be passively awaited, but actively pursued, learned, and mastered. The time to act is now, to embrace the agentic revolution, and to build a future where human ingenuity and artificial intelligence work in harmony to achieve extraordinary things. The symphony of the future awaits its conductors.

Remember that this is an iterative process—your plan should evolve as technology advances and your capabilities grow. The goal isn't to predict the future perfectly but to build the adaptability and skills to thrive in whatever future emerges.

KEY TAKEAWAYS

This chapter has embarked on a journey to understand the profound impact of AI agents on individuals, moving from a nascent curiosity to a clear understanding of their potential to revolutionize personal and professional life. We began by envisioning a world where AI agents act as empowering forces, liberating us from the daily grind and amplifying our capabilities. We explored how these intelligent entities can transform the individual experience, allowing us to reclaim our time, enhance our focus, and achieve more than ever before. The analogy of an orchestra was central, portraying AI agents not as replacements, but as skilled instrumentalists enhancing the symphony of our lives.

We then went into the specifics of career development in the age of AI agents, emphasizing the need for a proactive approach. The key lies not in fearing obsolescence but in identifying roles ripe for AI augmentation, cultivating "agent-native skills," and strategically repositioning ourselves for a future in which human ingenuity and artificial intelligence work in synergy. We discussed the importance of becoming "AI agent whisperers," individuals adept at orchestrating the capabilities of these intelligent assistants.

The lens then shifted to the transformative potential of AI agents for small businesses. We saw how these technologies are leveling the playing field, providing access to sophisticated tools and expertise previously reserved for larger corporations. From supercharging customer engagement to streamlining operations and unlocking data-driven insights, AI agents are empowering small businesses to thrive in an increasingly competitive landscape.

Next, we focused on personal productivity systems, illustrating how AI agents can act as proactive personal assistants, intelligently managing our schedules, communications, and tasks. We explored the various types of AI agents that form a powerful productivity toolkit and discussed strategies for building a personalized system that seamlessly integrates these intelligent assistants into our daily routines.

Finally, we culminated in a practical action plan, outlining concrete steps individuals can take to navigate and capitalize on the burgeoning AI agent revolution. From developing an agent strategy to building an AI-enhanced career path, the emphasis was on proactive engagement and continuous learning. The future, we concluded, is not something that passively happens to us, but something we actively co-create by embracing the opportunities presented by AI agents.

The integration of AI agents represents a fundamental shift in how individuals can amplify their capabilities, advance their careers, and achieve greater impact. Success requires thoughtful adoption, continuous learning, and strategic positioning to leverage these powerful tools while maintaining human agency and creativity.

1. **AI agents multiply human capabilities rather than replace them.**
   - KEY INSIGHTS:
     - AI agents are not designed to replace human intelligence but to augment it, handling routine and data-intensive tasks.
     - By offloading these burdens, AI agents free up cognitive bandwidth for higher-level thinking, creativity, and strategic pursuits.
     - This shift transforms the individual experience from being burdened by details to being boosted by intelligent assistance.
   - DO:
     - Identify tasks in your daily routine that are repetitive, data-intensive, or require efficient information retrieval and consider how an AI agent could assist.
     - Explore and experiment with different AI agent tools to understand their capabilities and limitations in practical settings.
   - DON'T:
     - View AI agents as a threat to your job security; instead, see them as tools to enhance your skills and productivity.
     - Overlook the importance of human oversight and critical evaluation of AI agent outputs.

2. **Developing agent-native skills is essential for future career success.**
   - KEY INSIGHTS:
     - The future of work requires a new skillset focused on collaborating effectively with AI agents.

- "Agent-native skills" include AI literacy, AI management, and AI integration expertise.
- Professionals who master the art of orchestrating AI agent capabilities will be highly sought after.
- DO:
  - Invest in learning about the fundamentals of AI and its applications in your field.
  - Develop your ability to provide clear and effective prompts and instructions to AI agents.
  - Focus on honing uniquely human skills like critical thinking, creativity, and emotional intelligence, which complement AI strengths.
- DON'T:
  - Neglect to adapt your skillset to the evolving demands of an AI-driven workplace.
  - Assume that technical expertise is the only valuable skill in the age of AI; human skills remain paramount.

3. **The strategic integration of AI requires a thoughtful, phased approach for maximum benefit.**
   - KEY INSIGHTS:
     - Successfully leveraging AI agents requires a strategic and phased approach.
     - Start with simple, well-defined tasks and gradually expand agent responsibilities as you gain confidence.
     - Continuous monitoring, evaluation, and optimization are central for maximizing the effectiveness of your AI ensemble.
   - DO:
     - Develop a clear plan for integrating AI agents into your personal and professional life, starting with specific goals.
     - Prioritize seamless integration with your existing tools and workflows to minimize disruption.
     - Regularly assess the performance of your AI agents and adjust your strategies as needed.
   - DON'T:
     - Overwhelm yourself by trying to implement too many AI agents at once.
     - Treat AI integration as a one-time project; embrace a mindset of continuous learning and adaptation.

The journey with AI agents is not a sprint but a marathon, demanding continuous learning and adaptation. The power to reshape our personal and professional lives lies in our ability to understand, integrate, and master these intelligent tools. As we move forward, the ability to effectively collaborate with AI will be a defining characteristic of success. In the subsequent chapter, we will explore the ethical considerations surrounding the widespread adoption of AI agents, exploring the responsibilities and challenges that come with wielding such powerful technology.

The integration of AI agents opens unprecedented possibilities for both personal growth and professional advancement. Those who thoughtfully embrace and master these tools while maintaining their unique human capabilities will be best positioned to thrive in the evolving landscape of work and life.

Navigating the Future

CHAPTER 8

The Global Impact

"The great force of history comes from the fact that we carry it within us, are unconsciously controlled by it in many ways, and history is literally present in all that we do."

—James Baldwin

SOCIETAL TRANSFORMATION

The morning commute in Millbrook had changed dramatically. Maria, a longtime resident, watched as autonomous vehicles smoothly coordinated their movements, while AI agents optimized traffic patterns in real time. The town's transformation wasn't just about traffic—it represented a fundamental shift in how society functions when augmented by intelligent agents. This scene, increasingly common across the globe, is not merely about advanced transportation; it signifies a profound societal transformation, a fundamental shift in how we organize and live as communities.

Think back to the advent of the Internet. It was at first a novelty, then a tool, and now, an indispensable fabric of our daily lives. Agentic AI is set to follow a similar trajectory, embedding itself into the very core of our societal structures, altering how we live, work, and interact. In this section, we will go into the fundamental shifts underway, exploring how these autonomous minds are reshaping the very fabric of our societies.

The New Social Fabric

Just as an orchestra requires perfect coordination between instruments, modern society is experiencing a reorchestration of its fundamental components through AI agents. These agents are weaving a new social fabric that combines human interaction with algorithmic intelligence. At its core, this transformation builds upon three foundational elements: **communication**, **coordination**, and **collaboration**.

Deep Dive: The Three Cs of Social Transformation

AI agents create cascading economic effects through:

- **Communication:** AI agents enabling multilingual, context-aware interactions
- **Coordination:** Automated systems managing complex social systems
- **Collaboration:** Human-AI partnerships in decision-making and problem-solving

Institutional Evolution

Our traditional institutions are undergoing a radical evolution as AI agents become integral to their operations. Consider government services, often constrained by bureaucratic processes and human limitations. Agentic AI is injecting unprecedented efficiency and personalization into these systems. Citizens can access tailored services, navigate complex regulations with AI assistants, and experience a more responsive and effective public sector.

Healthcare systems are being revolutionized by predictive agents that anticipate community health needs, optimize resource allocation, and personalize patient care. Educational institutions are deploying adaptive learning agents that tailor instruction to each student's unique learning style, potentially unlocking personalized education at scale.

Economic Mobility and Opportunity

AI agents are reshaping economic opportunities by democratizing access to resources and knowledge. Small businesses now compete with larger corporations through AI-powered tools, while individuals access personalized career guidance and skill development programs. This transformation is creating new pathways for social mobility, though it also presents challenges in ensuring equal access to these technologies.

Public Services Revolution

The integration of AI agents into public services marks a fundamental shift in how societies cater to the needs of their citizens. From predictive maintenance of critical infrastructure, ensuring the reliability of essential utilities, to personalized healthcare delivery that anticipates and addresses individual health concerns, these systems are nurturing more responsive and efficient public services. Imagine AI agents predicting infrastructure failures before they occur, allowing for proactive maintenance and preventing disruptions to essential services.

Bridging Social Gaps

While AI agents offer tremendous potential for societal advancement, ensuring equitable access and preventing technological divides has become crucial. Communities worldwide are implementing programs to ensure AI literacy and access, creating what we call **digital bridges** to connect all segments of society.

The Dawn of the Agent-Augmented Society

To understand the magnitude of this transformation, let's start with a simple analogy. Consider a symphony orchestra. For centuries, the conductor has been the central orchestrator, interpreting the score and guiding the musicians. Now, imagine an intelligent agent, like a highly advanced AI conductor, capable of analyzing the individual strengths of each musician, dynamically adjusting the tempo and dynamics in real time based on the nuances of the performance, and even anticipating potential errors. This AI conductor doesn't replace the musicians but rather elevates their collective performance to new heights. Similarly, agentic AI systems are not about replacing human agency, but about augmenting it, orchestrating complex systems, and optimizing outcomes in ways previously unimaginable.

At its core, societal transformation driven by agentic AI stems from the ability of these systems to perceive, learn, and act autonomously to achieve specific goals. This autonomy, built upon first principles of perception, cognition, and action, allows AI agents to operate with a level of independence and adaptability that distinguishes them from traditional AI. Where traditional AI might excel at a specific task like image recognition, agentic AI can leverage that capability within a broader context, such as a smart city agent optimizing traffic flow based on real-time image analysis and predictive modeling. This fundamental shift from task-oriented AI to goal-oriented agents is the engine driving societal change.

Why Does This Matter?

It matters because these agents are not just tools; they are active participants in our world. They are becoming the invisible hands that manage our logistics, personalize our learning experiences, and even facilitate our social interactions. This integration, while holding immense potential, necessitates a careful examination of its implications for our social structures, our daily routines, and our collective future.

The Evolving Landscape of Work and Productivity

One of the most significant arenas of societal transformation is the world of work. Agentic AI is not simply automating repetitive tasks; it's fundamentally altering the nature of work itself. Consider the implications for project management. Imagine AI agents capable of autonomously coordinating teams, allocating resources based on individual skill sets and availability, and proactively identifying potential roadblocks before they arise. This isn't about replacing project managers but about empowering them with intelligent assistants that handle the intricate orchestration of complex projects, freeing up human intellect for strategic thinking and creative problem-solving.

The shift is toward a collaborative model where humans and AI agents work in tandem, leveraging each other's strengths. Repetitive, data-intensive tasks are increasingly handled by AI agents, freeing up human workers to focus on uniquely human skills like creativity, critical thinking, emotional intelligence, and complex problem-solving. Just as our AI conductor enhances the orchestra, AI agents are enhancing human productivity and allowing us to focus on higher-level cognitive functions. This isn't about job displacement in its simplest form but rather a job evolution, requiring us to adapt and acquire new skills to effectively collaborate with these intelligent partners.

For example, in customer service, AI agents can handle routine inquiries, freeing up human agents to address more complex and emotionally sensitive issues. In software development, AI agents can assist with code generation and testing, allowing developers to focus on architectural design and innovative solutions. The result is a more efficient, more productive, and potentially more fulfilling work environment.

The Shifting Sands of Community and Connection

Beyond the workplace, agentic AI is also influencing how we connect and form communities. Social media algorithms have already demonstrated the power of AI in shaping our online interactions. Now, imagine AI agents designed to nurture meaningful connections, perhaps by identifying individuals with shared interests and facilitating collaborative projects or by curating personalized learning experiences that bring like-minded people together.

Consider online education platforms. Instead of a one-size-fits-all approach, intelligent agents can analyze individual learning styles, identify knowledge gaps, and connect learners with mentors or peers who can provide targeted support. This personalized and adaptive approach to learning not only enhances educational outcomes but also adopts a sense of community among learners with similar goals and challenges.

However, this influence also presents potential challenges. The very algorithms designed to connect us can also create filter bubbles and echo chambers, reinforcing existing biases and limiting exposure to diverse perspectives. Understanding the ethical implications of these connection-driving agents and designing them with principles of inclusivity and diversity will be crucial to ensuring they strengthen, rather than fracture, our social fabric.

Navigating the Information Age with Intelligent Guides

The sheer volume of information available today can be overwhelming. Agentic AI offers the potential to act as intelligent guides, helping us navigate this vast ocean of data and extract meaningful insights. Imagine AI agents capable of curating personalized news feeds based on your interests and critical evaluation of source credibility, or research assistants that can sift through thousands of academic papers to synthesize relevant findings for a specific project.

Case Study: AI Agents in Scientific Research

Imagine an AI agent capable of autonomously reviewing and synthesizing findings across disparate research papers, identifying potential breakthroughs and accelerating the pace of discovery. This is already beginning to happen in fields like drug discovery and materials science. A few "Deep Research" products have been launched at the time of writing this book:

- Deep Research from OpenAI
- Perplexity
- Google DeepMind

However, this power comes with responsibility. The ability of AI agents to filter and present information raises concerns about bias and manipulation. Who programs these agents, and what are their underlying agendas? How do we ensure that these intelligent guides are providing us with a balanced and objective view of the world? Developing transparent and accountable AI agents for information access is paramount to maintaining an informed and engaged citizenry.

Conclusion

The societal transformation driven by agentic AI is a multifaceted phenomenon, touching upon every aspect of our lives, from the way we work and learn to how we connect and access information. It's a shift that demands our attention, our understanding, and our proactive participation in shaping its trajectory. Just as the conductor guides the orchestra toward a harmonious performance, we must collectively guide the development and deployment of agentic AI to create a future where these technologies truly empower individuals and enhance the well-being of society as a whole. This requires a deep understanding of the underlying principles of these technologies and a commitment to navigating the ethical and societal implications they present.

CULTURAL IMPLICATIONS

Imagine a world where the crafting of symphonies is no longer solely the domain of human composers. Instead, picture a collaborative effort: a human conductor outlining the emotional landscape and thematic core of a piece, while AI agents, possessing deep knowledge of musical history, theory, and even the nuanced preferences of global audiences, weave intricate melodies and harmonies. This isn't science fiction; it's a potent analogy for the burgeoning influence of agentic AI on our cultures. As these intelligent systems move beyond simple task automation and into the realm of prediction, learning, and even creative generation, their impact on our shared values, traditions, and societal norms becomes increasingly profound. This section will explore the multifaceted cultural implications of this technological shift, moving beyond surface-level observations to understand the fundamental ways in which agentic AI is reshaping the human experience. We'll explore how these technologies are not merely tools but active participants in the evolution of culture itself.

Understanding Cultural Evolution

To grasp the full scope of AI agents' cultural impact, we must first break down culture into its fundamental components. Culture, at its core, consists of four interconnected elements:

- **Values:** The underlying beliefs and principles
- **Behaviors:** The manifestations of these values in daily life

- **Artifacts:** The tangible expressions of culture
- **Systems:** The organizational structures that maintain cultural continuity

Deep Dive: Cultural Components Framework

- Values → Shape → Behaviors
- Create → Artifacts → Maintain
- Systems → Reinforce → Values

Cultural Identity in an AI-Augmented World

Just as an orchestra maintains its distinctive sound while incorporating new instruments, cultures are learning to integrate AI agents while preserving their essential character.

Consider how different cultures are adapting AI agents to their specific contexts:

- **In India**, AI agents are being trained to understand and respect traditional family hierarchies while facilitating modern business practices.
- **Middle Eastern countries** are developing AI agents that incorporate Islamic banking principles.
- Indigenous communities in **Australia** are using AI agents to preserve and teach traditional languages and stories.

The Evolving Tapestry of Human-AI Interaction

The introduction of any transformative technology inevitably reshapes the fabric of culture. Consider the printing press, the telephone, or the Internet—each invention redefined communication, knowledge dissemination, and social interaction in profound ways. Agentic AI represents a similar, yet arguably more significant, inflection point. Unlike passive tools that simply execute instructions, AI agents possess a degree of autonomy, enabling them to learn, adapt, and even anticipate our needs. This fundamentally alters the dynamic of human-technology interaction. We are moving from a user-tool relationship toward something resembling collaboration, a partnership where humans and AI agents contribute unique strengths.

This shift impacts our perception of various cultural activities. Consider the creative arts, for example. Where once a painter meticulously applied brushstrokes, we now see AI agents capable of generating original artwork in various styles, prompting questions about authorship, creativity, and the very definition of art. Similarly, in music, AI can compose pieces that evoke specific emotions or cater to niche tastes, challenging traditional notions of musical talent and innovation. This isn't about replacing human artists but rather about augmenting their capabilities and exploring new creative frontiers. Think of the AI as a virtuoso instrumentalist within our orchestra, capable of executing complex passages and suggesting novel harmonies that the conductor might not have conceived alone.

This evolving interaction extends beyond artistic pursuits. In education, personalized learning agents can adapt to individual student needs, potentially democratizing access to high-quality education but also raising questions about the role of human teachers and the standardization of curricula. In our personal lives, virtual assistants manage our schedules, curate our news feeds, and even offer advice, blurring the lines between technology as a tool and technology as a companion. Why does this matter? Because these subtle shifts in our daily interactions with AI are gradually reshaping our expectations, norms, and even our understanding of what it means to be human in an increasingly intelligent world.

Deep Dive: Defining Agency in AI

To truly grasp the cultural implications, we need to understand what distinguishes agentic AI. At its core lies the concept of agency—the capacity to act independently and make choices to achieve specific goals. This involves perception (gathering information from the environment), cognition (processing that information and making decisions), and action (executing those decisions). Unlike traditional AI, which operates based on preprogrammed rules or supervised learning on fixed datasets, agentic AI can adapt its behavior in response to new information and changing circumstances. This ability to learn and act autonomously is what makes their cultural impact so significant.

Redefining Skills, Expertise, and Cultural Capital

Cultures value specific skills and forms of expertise, often reflecting the dominant economic and social structures. Historically, physical strength, agricultural knowledge, or craftsmanship held significant cultural capital. The industrial revolution elevated technical skills and scientific literacy. Now, the rise of agentic AI is prompting another re-evaluation of what constitutes valuable expertise. As AI agents become proficient in tasks requiring analysis, pattern recognition, and even creative problem-solving, the skills that distinguish humans will likely shift.

One potential outcome is a heightened emphasis on uniquely human capabilities such as critical thinking, emotional intelligence, creativity (in the sense of original conceptualization rather than mere generation), and complex communication. Cultures that adapt their educational systems and societal values to promote these skills may thrive in an AI-driven world. Conversely, cultures heavily reliant on skills easily replicated by AI may face economic and social disruption.

Consider the impact on various professions. In law, AI agents can assist with legal research and document review, potentially shifting the focus for human lawyers toward strategic thinking, client interaction, and courtroom advocacy. In medicine, AI can aid in diagnosis and treatment planning, requiring doctors to emphasize empathy, communication, and the holistic understanding of patient well-being. This isn't about job displacement in all cases; it's about a fundamental shift in the nature of work and the skills valued within those professions.

However, this transition also raises crucial cultural questions. Will access to AI-powered tools create new forms of inequality, where those with access to advanced agents gain an advantage over those without? How will different cultures adapt to the changing demands of the job market? Will traditional forms of expertise be devalued, leading to social unrest or a sense of cultural loss? These are complex questions without easy answers, and their resolution will depend on proactive cultural adaptation and thoughtful policy-making.

The Shifting Landscape of Communication and Information

Culture is fundamentally shaped by how we communicate and share information. The advent of social media has already demonstrated the power of technology to connect people across geographical boundaries while simultaneously creating echo chambers and amplifying misinformation. Agentic AI has the potential to further revolutionize this landscape, with both positive and potentially disruptive consequences.

Imagine AI-powered translation tools capable of seamlessly bridging language barriers, promoting greater intercultural understanding and collaboration. Think of personalized news aggregators that curate information based on individual interests, potentially leading to more informed citizens. Consider AI assistants that can summarize complex information, making knowledge more accessible to a wider audience. These are just a few examples of how AI agents can enhance communication and facilitate the flow of information across cultures.

However, this increased connectivity and information access also presents challenges. The ability of AI to generate realistic text, images, and videos raises concerns about the spread of misinformation and the erosion of trust in traditional sources of information. **Deepfakes**, for instance, can be used to manipulate public opinion or damage reputations, potentially destabilizing social and political landscapes. Furthermore, the algorithms that power personalized information feeds can inadvertently create *filter bubbles*, reinforcing existing biases and limiting exposure to diverse perspectives.

Culturally, this raises fundamental questions about trust, authority, and the nature of truth. How do we discern credible information from AI-generated fabrications? How do we ensure that AI-driven communication platforms promote understanding and dialogue rather than division and polarization? Different cultures may develop unique approaches to navigating these challenges, reflecting their existing values and communication norms. Some might prioritize media literacy and critical thinking skills, while others might focus on developing robust verification systems or ethical guidelines for AI development and deployment.

Conclusion

The cultural implications of agentic AI are far-reaching and multidimensional. We are witnessing a fundamental shift in how humans interact with technology, a re-evaluation of valued skills and expertise, and a transformation of the communication landscape. Like the conductor working in concert with the AI musicians, our future cultural trajectory will be shaped by the intricate interplay between human intention and artificial intelligence capabilities. Navigating this new terrain requires a proactive and thoughtful approach, one that embraces the potential for empowerment and productivity while also addressing the ethical and societal challenges that inevitably arise. Understanding these cultural dynamics is not just an academic exercise; it's critical for shaping a future where technology serves to enrich and enhance the human experience across diverse societies. As we move forward, the key will be adopting a global dialogue that acknowledges the varied cultural responses to this technological revolution, ensuring that the rise of autonomous minds contributes to a more inclusive and prosperous future for all.

As AI agents become more sophisticated, we're likely to see a new form of cultural renaissance—one where traditional practices find new expression through technological means. The key will be maintaining the *delicate balance between innovation and preservation*, much like how classical

FIGURE 8.1   Future where humans and agents coexist

Generated with AI using DALL·E - OpenAI

orchestras embrace new compositions while honoring traditional repertoire. See Figure 8.1.

While these cultural transformations reshape how societies interact and express themselves, their environmental impact presents another crucial dimension of global change, which we'll explore in the next section.

ENVIRONMENTAL IMPACT: THE DOUBLE-EDGED SWORD OF AGENTIC AI

Imagine a vast network of sensors, tirelessly monitoring the health of our planet—from the melting glaciers of Greenland to the intricate ecosystems of the Amazon rainforest. These digital eyes and ears, no longer passive data gatherers, are intelligent agents. They don't just record; they analyze, predict, and even act, autonomously adjusting energy grids to minimize waste, optimizing agricultural practices to reduce water consumption, and directing conservation efforts with unprecedented precision. This has evolved beyond a futuristic fantasy into a rapidly emerging reality driven by agentic AI. As we've explored in previous chapters, these autonomous minds possess the capacity to learn, adapt, and make decisions, and this inherent capability has profound implications for our shared environment.

In this section, we'll explore into the multidimensional environmental impact of agentic AI, exploring both the promising potential for ecological stewardship and the crucial considerations for mitigating potential risks. We'll move beyond simplistic narratives of technology as either savior or villain, instead adopting a first-principles approach to understand the underlying mechanisms at play and how we can steer this powerful force toward a more sustainable future.

Understanding Environmental Impact: A First-Principles Approach

To truly grasp the environmental implications of agentic AI, we must break down the impact into its fundamental components:

- Resource consumption
- **Computing infrastructure:** The physical hardware required to run AI systems
- **Energy requirements:** The significant energy demands of training and operating complex AI models
- **Physical resources:** The raw materials used in manufacturing AI hardware and infrastructure
- Optimization potential
- **Process efficiency:** AI's ability to optimize existing industrial and logistical processes
- **Resource management:** Enhanced management of natural resources like water and energy
- **Waste reduction:** AI-driven systems to minimize waste generation across various sectors
- Environmental intelligence
- **Monitoring capabilities:** AI's capacity to monitor environmental changes at scale
- **Predictive analytics:** Using AI to predict environmental risks and future trends
- **Adaptive response:** Autonomous AI systems capable of responding to environmental events in real time

Deep Dive: Environmental Impact Metrics

To effectively measure and manage the environmental impact of AI, we need to utilize key performance indicators (KPIs):

- Carbon footprint (CO_2e)
- Energy efficiency (Power Usage Effectiveness [PUE])

- Resource utilization rate
- Waste reduction percentage

AI Agents as Environmental Conductors

Just as an orchestra conductor coordinates multiple instruments to create harmony, AI agents orchestrate environmental systems to optimize performance.

The Carbon Paradox

While AI agents offer tremendous potential for environmental optimization, they also contribute to environmental challenges, such as large energy consumption:

- Training large AI models can emit as much carbon as five cars over their lifetimes.
- Data centers housing AI systems consume 1% of global electricity.

Deep Dive: The Energy Equation

AI Agent Environmental Impact = Base Infrastructure Cost − Optimization Benefits Where:

- Infrastructure Cost = Energy + Resources + Waste
- Optimization Benefits = Efficiency Gains + Resource Savings + Prevention Value

The Promise of Green Intelligence: AI Agents as Environmental Stewards

At its core, the environmental challenge is one of optimization and prediction on a massive scale. We need to optimize resource usage, predict environmental shifts, and implement solutions swiftly and effectively. This is where the inherent strengths of agentic AI shine. Recall our discussion in Chapter 2 about the core components of AI agents: perception, cognition, memory, and action. Applied to the environment, this translates to agents that can perceive vast amounts of environmental data from various sources—satellites, sensors, and even citizen science initiatives—process this information to understand complex ecological relationships and then act autonomously to optimize resource allocation or trigger interventions.

Think of energy grids, for example. Traditional systems struggle to balance supply and demand efficiently, often leading to significant energy waste. Agentic AI, however, can create a dynamic, self-regulating grid. Imagine individual AI agents managing local energy consumption in homes and businesses, predicting demand fluctuations based on weather patterns and user behavior, and seamlessly adjusting power flow to minimize waste. This coordinated effort, much like the sections of our orchestral analogy working in harmony, creates a more efficient and sustainable energy ecosystem.

Similarly, in agriculture, AI agents can revolutionize farming practices. Analyzing soil conditions, weather patterns, and plant health in real time allow these agents to precisely manage irrigation, fertilization, and pest control, reducing the overuse of resources and minimizing the environmental impact of farming. Instead of broad-stroke applications of pesticides, for instance, AI-powered drones can identify and treat only the affected plants, significantly reducing chemical runoff into water systems.

Why This Matters

These examples illustrate the fundamental shift agentic AI can bring. We move from reactive environmental management to proactive, predictive, and ultimately, more effective stewardship. This is crucial as we grapple with the accelerating challenges of climate change and resource depletion.

Deep Dive: The Agent in Precision Agriculture

In precision agriculture, an AI agent acts as a central coordinator. It receives data from various sensors placed in the field, including soil moisture sensors, weather stations, and even cameras mounted on drones. Using machine learning algorithms, the agent analyzes this data to understand the specific needs of different parts of the field. For instance, it might identify areas with low soil moisture requiring targeted irrigation or detect early signs of pest infestation in a particular zone. The agent can then autonomously instruct irrigation systems to deliver water precisely where needed or dispatch drones to apply targeted treatments, minimizing waste and environmental impact compared to traditional blanket approaches. This granular level of control, powered by the agent's ability to perceive, reason, and act, is a game-changer for sustainable agriculture (see Figure 8.2).

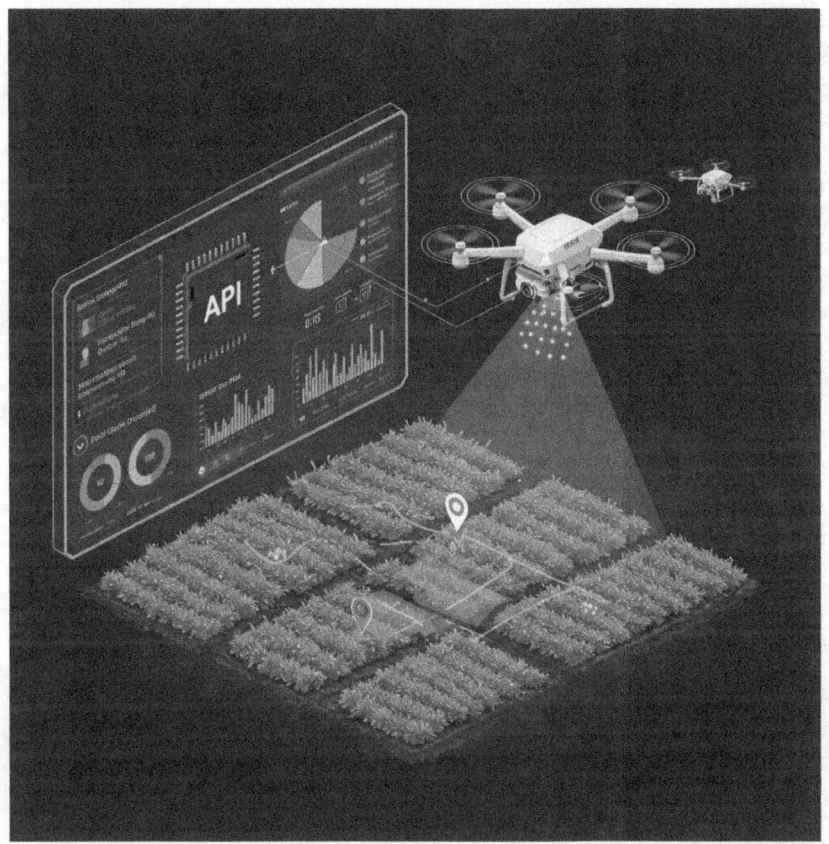

FIGURE 8.2   Precision agriculture with agents

Generated with AI using DALL·E - OpenAI

The Energy Equation: Balancing AI's Demands with Environmental Responsibility

While the potential for environmental good is immense, we must also confront the potential downsides. The operation of sophisticated AI systems, particularly those involving complex machine learning models, requires significant computational power, which translates to energy consumption. As AI agents become more prevalent and sophisticated, their collective energy footprint could become substantial if not managed responsibly.

This isn't a reason to halt progress, but rather a call for mindful development and deployment. The first principle here is efficiency. We need to focus on developing AI algorithms and hardware that are more energy-efficient. Researchers are actively exploring new computing paradigms, such as neuromorphic computing, inspired by the energy efficiency of the human brain, to address this challenge.

Furthermore, the energy sources powering these AI systems matter immensely. A network of AI agents optimizing renewable energy distribution powered by fossil fuels presents a paradox. Therefore, the transition to sustainable energy sources is intrinsically linked to the environmental viability of widespread AI adoption. Investing in and accelerating the deployment of solar, wind, and other renewable energy technologies is crucial to ensuring that the rise of agentic AI contributes to a greener future, rather than exacerbating existing environmental problems.

Another consideration is the lifecycle of AI hardware. The production and disposal of electronic devices contribute to environmental pollution. Therefore, a focus on sustainable manufacturing practices, including the use of recycled materials and responsible e-waste management, is essential. AI agents themselves can play a role here, optimizing supply chains for resource efficiency and managing recycling processes more effectively.

Why This Matters

Acknowledging the energy demands of AI is not about fear-mongering; it's about raising a responsible and sustainable path forward. Proactively addressing these challenges allow us to ensure that the environmental benefits of agentic AI outweigh its potential costs.

The Orchestrated Ecosystem: AI Agents in Concert for a Sustainable Future

Recall the image of the orchestra we discussed in Chapter 3, where individual instruments, guided by the conductor, create a harmonious whole. Similarly, envision a future where a diverse array of AI agents, each with specialized capabilities, work in concert to address environmental challenges. We might have agents monitoring deforestation, coordinating reforestation efforts, and predicting wildfire risks. Others could be optimizing water resource management across entire river basins or tracking and mitigating pollution sources in real time.

This collaborative ecosystem of intelligent agents offers a powerful approach to tackling complex environmental problems that often span vast geographical scales and require the coordination of multiple stakeholders. The key is designing these agents to communicate and collaborate effectively, sharing data and insights to achieve common environmental goals.

Conclusion

The environmental impact of agentic AI is a complex equation with the potential for both significant positive and negative outcomes. Understanding the first principles of how these intelligent systems operate enables us to appreciate their capacity to act as powerful tools for environmental stewardship. From optimizing energy grids and revolutionizing agriculture to enabling more effective conservation efforts, the possibilities are vast. However, we must also be mindful of the energy demands of AI and the environmental impact of hardware production and disposal. The key lies in a balanced approach—one that embraces the potential of AI for good while proactively mitigating its potential risks. As we move forward, promoting collaboration between AI developers, environmental scientists, and policymakers will be crucial to ensuring that agentic AI becomes a force for a more sustainable and resilient future. This intricate dance between innovation and responsibility will define not only the success of AI but also the health of our planet. Having explored the environmental dimensions, we now turn our attention to another critical facet of global impact: the geopolitical landscape.

As we consider the environmental implications of AI agents, we must also examine their broader geopolitical impact, where resource distribution and technological capability create new dynamics in international relations.

GEOPOLITICAL CONSIDERATIONS

Imagine a world where international diplomacy is partially conducted not by human emissaries alone but by sophisticated AI agents capable of negotiating treaties, anticipating geopolitical shifts, and even managing resources across borders. While this may sound like science fiction, the rapid advancement of agentic AI is bringing such scenarios closer to reality. Just as the invention of the printing press reshaped the flow of information and the balance of power centuries ago, AI agents are set to become a significant new force on the global stage. In this section, we will explore the profound geopolitical considerations that arise as these autonomous minds become increasingly influential. We will move beyond the hype to understand the fundamental shifts in international relations, economic competition, and security landscapes that agentic AI is beginning to trigger. Understanding these dynamics is not just an academic exercise; it is critical for navigating the evolving world order and ensuring that the benefits of this technology are shared globally, while the risks are carefully managed.

The New Digital World Order

The emergence of sophisticated AI agents is redrawing traditional geopolitical boundaries and power structures. Unlike previous technological revolutions, the AI agent revolution operates in a borderless digital realm while having profound effects on physical world politics.

Deep Dive: Understanding Digital Sovereignty

Digital sovereignty encompasses:

- Control over AI agent deployment
- Data governance and protection
- Technical infrastructure ownership
- AI research and development capabilities

The Shifting Sands of Power: AI Agents and International Relations

At its core, geopolitics is about power—its distribution, its application, and the strategies nations employ to secure their interests. The advent of agentic AI introduces a fascinating new dimension to this age-old game. Think of nations as orchestras, each striving to create a harmonious and powerful performance on the world stage. Now, imagine introducing a new class of incredibly skilled musicians—the AI agents—into these orchestras. Some nations will have more of these virtuosos, and their ability to orchestrate complex strategies, analyze vast amounts of data, and react with speed and precision will be significantly enhanced. This creates a potential imbalance, where nations that develop and deploy sophisticated AI agents gain a strategic advantage.

From a first-principles perspective, consider the fundamental elements of state power: information gathering, analysis, decision-making, and execution. Agentic AI has the potential to augment or even automate aspects of all these elements. AI agents can sift through immense volumes of data—satellite imagery, economic indicators, social media trends—far more efficiently than human analysts. They can identify patterns and predict potential crises with greater accuracy. Furthermore, their capacity for rational decision-making, free from human biases and emotional influences (at least in theory), could lead to more calculated and potentially effective foreign policy.

However, this also raises critical questions. Will AI agents deepen existing power asymmetries, creating a world where a few technologically advanced nations dominate? Or could they, paradoxically, empower smaller nations by providing access to sophisticated analytical and strategic capabilities at a lower cost? Consider Estonia,[1] a small but digitally advanced nation, which has already embraced AI in its public services. Agentic AI could allow such nations to punch above their weight, offering innovative solutions and navigating the complexities of international relations with newfound agility.

The very nature of diplomacy could also transform. Imagine AI agents negotiating trade agreements, using complex algorithms to optimize terms for their respective nations. While this could lead to more efficient and potentially fairer outcomes, it also raises questions about transparency and accountability. Who is ultimately responsible when an AI agent makes a decision with significant geopolitical consequences? These are the questions we must grapple with as agentic AI becomes a more prominent actor on the world stage.

Deep Dive: Game Theory and Agentic AI in Diplomacy

Game theory, a mathematical framework for analyzing strategic interactions, provides a useful lens through which to view the impact of AI agents on diplomacy. Concepts like the Prisoner's Dilemma and Nash Equilibrium, which describe the challenges of cooperation and competition, can be modeled with AI agents as players. Sophisticated AI agents, capable of learning and adapting their strategies based on the actions of others, could lead to more nuanced and potentially less confrontational diplomatic outcomes. However, the risk of unforeseen consequences and the potential for misinterpretation also increase with the complexity of these interactions.

The Economic Battlefield: AI Agents and Global Competition

The economic implications of agentic AI are no less significant than the geopolitical ones. We've discussed how AI agents can revolutionize businesses and industries (as explored in Chapter 6), but these transformations have a direct impact on the global economic landscape. Nations that are at the forefront of AI agent development and deployment are likely to gain a significant competitive edge. This isn't just about technological superiority; it's about the ability to create more efficient supply chains, develop innovative products and services faster, and adapt to changing market conditions with unprecedented speed.

---

[1] https://e-estonia.com/

Consider the ongoing global competition in areas like renewable energy and electric vehicles. Nations that leverage agentic AI to optimize research and development, manage complex energy grids, and personalize consumer experiences will be better positioned to lead in these crucial sectors. Imagine AI agents designing new battery technologies, predicting energy demand with pinpoint accuracy, and tailoring marketing campaigns to specific consumer segments—all autonomously and with remarkable efficiency.

This creates a new form of economic competition, where the ability to attract and retain AI talent, invest in AI infrastructure, and nurture a regulatory environment conducive to AI innovation becomes paramount. Nations may find themselves in a race to develop the most sophisticated AI agents, leading to potential tensions and the risk of a "digital divide," where some nations are left behind.

However, just as with traditional industrial revolutions, there are also opportunities for collaboration and shared prosperity. Open-source AI initiatives, international standards for AI development, and collaborative research efforts could help to ensure that the benefits of agentic AI are more widely distributed. The challenge lies in furthering a global environment of both competition and cooperation, where nations strive for innovation while also working together to mitigate the risks and ensure equitable access to this transformative technology.

The Double-Edged Sword: Security and the Rise of Autonomous Actors

Perhaps the most pressing geopolitical consideration surrounding agentic AI lies in the realm of security. While AI agents offer immense potential for enhancing national security—from detecting cyber threats to improving intelligence gathering—they also introduce new vulnerabilities and risks.

Imagine sophisticated AI agents capable of launching cyberattacks with unprecedented precision and speed, or autonomous weapons systems making life-or-death decisions without human intervention. These are not merely hypothetical scenarios; the development of such technologies is already underway. From a first-principles standpoint, the very autonomy and intelligence that makes AI agents so powerful also makes them potentially dangerous if not carefully controlled.

The challenge lies in establishing international norms and regulations to govern the development and deployment of AI in the security domain. How do we ensure that AI agents are used responsibly and ethically, and that they do not escalate conflicts or create new forms of warfare? The concept of **algorithmic accountability** becomes crucial here—the ability to understand and attribute responsibility for the actions of autonomous systems.

Furthermore, the proliferation of AI technology raises concerns about access by nonstate actors. Imagine terrorist groups or rogue states gaining access to sophisticated AI agents capable of launching devastating attacks. This necessitates a global effort to prevent the misuse of AI and to develop robust defence mechanisms against AI-powered threats.

However, it is important to remember the potential benefits. AI agents can be invaluable in detecting and preventing cyberattacks, analyzing vast amounts of intelligence data to identify potential threats, and even managing complex peacekeeping operations more effectively. The key lies in harnessing the power of AI for security while mitigating the inherent risks through careful regulation, international cooperation, and a commitment to ethical development.

Why This Matters

The development and deployment of AI agents will fundamentally reshape the global security landscape. Understanding the potential risks and benefits is crucial for policymakers, security professionals, and citizens alike.

Conclusion

The emergence of agentic AI is not just a technological shift; it is a geopolitical earthquake that is already reshaping the contours of the global order. As we have explored in this section, the implications for international relations, economic competition, and security are profound and multifaceted. Like adding a new, powerful instrument to the global orchestra, AI agents offer the potential for greater harmony and more complex symphonies, but also the risk of discord if not carefully managed.

Navigating this new landscape requires a proactive and collaborative approach. International dialogues, the establishment of ethical guidelines, and a commitment to responsible innovation are essential to ensure that the rise of autonomous minds benefits all of humanity. As we move forward, understanding the geopolitical considerations of agentic AI will be crucial for building a future where this powerful technology contributes to a more stable, prosperous, and secure world. In the next section, we will explore further into the future by exploring the broader global trends that are being shaped by the ongoing AI revolution.

FUTURE WATCH: GLOBAL TRENDS

Imagine a world where coordinating global efforts to combat climate change isn't a matter of protracted international summits and binding resolutions, but a seamless orchestration managed by a network of specialized AI agents.

Picture these digital diplomats, fluent in diverse data sets and optimized for collaborative problem-solving, working tirelessly to model scenarios, propose solutions, and allocate resources with an efficiency previously unimaginable. This isn't science fiction; it's a glimpse into a future shaped by the accelerating development and deployment of agentic AI on a global scale. Having explored the societal, cultural, environmental, and geopolitical currents influenced by AI agents, we now turn our gaze toward the horizon, focusing on the emerging global trends that will define the coming decades. Just as a conductor anticipates the shifts in tempo and dynamics within an orchestra, understanding these trends is crucial for navigating the evolving landscape of intelligent machines. This section will go into the most significant global transformations we foresee, ensuring we are prepared not just to witness them, but to actively participate in shaping them.

The Rise of Global Agent Networks

The very nature of AI agents, designed for autonomy and collaboration, lends itself to the formation of interconnected networks spanning geographical boundaries. Think of it as the Internet evolving from a network of information to a dynamic ecosystem of intelligent actors. These global agent networks will not be confined to specific industries or nations but will emerge organically as agents with complementary skills and objectives discover and connect with each other. This interconnectedness is built upon the foundational principles of communication and collaboration we discussed in Chapter 3, where we explored how agents are designed to interact and share information. Just as individual musicians contribute to a symphony, these agents will contribute to complex global tasks through distributed intelligence and coordinated action.

Consider, for instance, the challenge of optimizing global supply chains. Currently, this involves a complex web of human interactions, prone to delays, errors, and inefficiencies. Imagine instead a network of AI agents, representing suppliers, manufacturers, logistics providers, and retailers, all communicating and negotiating in real time. These agents, drawing on vast datasets of demand forecasts, production capacities, and transportation routes, can dynamically adjust schedules, reroute shipments, and predict potential disruptions with far greater accuracy than any centralized system. This isn't about replacing human decision-makers entirely; it's about augmenting their capabilities, allowing them to focus on strategic oversight and exception handling while the agents manage the intricate details.

Why This Matters

The emergence of global agent networks signifies a fundamental shift in how complex global challenges can be addressed. Problems that once required massive, top-down initiatives can now be tackled through decentralized, collaborative efforts driven by intelligent machines. This can lead to more resilient, efficient, and adaptive global systems, capable of responding rapidly to changing circumstances.

REAL-WORLD EXAMPLE

Several startups are already developing platforms that facilitate the creation of *decentralized autonomous organizations (DAOs)* powered by AI agents. While still in their early stages, these initiatives point toward a future where global collaborations, whether for scientific research, open-source development, or even disaster response, can be orchestrated by intelligent networks, transcending traditional organizational structures and geographical limitations.

The development of standardized communication protocols and data exchange formats will be crucial for the seamless operation of these global agent networks. Think of these protocols as the universal language of the AI world, enabling agents developed in different parts of the globe, with varying underlying architectures, to understand and interact with each other. Without these standards, the potential for fragmentation and inefficiency increases significantly, hindering the very collaborative power these networks promise. Furthermore, ensuring the security and robustness of these networks against malicious actors or systemic failures will be paramount. Just as the Internet requires robust cybersecurity measures, so too will these global agent ecosystems need safeguards to maintain their integrity and trustworthiness.

The Geopolitical Agent Race

As the transformative potential of agentic AI becomes increasingly evident, nations are engaging in what can be characterized as a "geopolitical agent race." This isn't necessarily a hostile competition, but rather a strategic imperative for countries to develop and deploy advanced AI agent capabilities to secure economic advantages, enhance national security, and influence global norms. This mirrors historical technological races, such as the space race, where innovation and deployment became proxies for national strength and prestige.

Nations are investing heavily in AI research and development, focusing on areas like autonomous defense systems, advanced surveillance technologies, and AI-driven economic optimization. The development of sophisticated AI agents capable of making complex decisions in dynamic environments has significant implications for military strategy and defense capabilities. Imagine autonomous drones collaborating to monitor borders, or AI agents coordinating cyber defenses in real time. While the ethical implications of such applications are significant and will be addressed in Chapter 9, the drive to develop these capabilities is undeniable.

Deep Dive: The Agent Intelligence Quotient

To better understand the geopolitical landscape, it's helpful to consider the concept of an "Agent Intelligence Quotient" (AIQ). While not a formal metric, AIQ represents a nation's collective capacity to develop, deploy, and effectively utilize advanced AI agents. This encompasses not just technological prowess but also factors like access to talent, data infrastructure, and supportive regulatory frameworks. Nations with a high AIQ are likely to be at the forefront of this technological transformation, wielding significant influence in the global arena.

Why This Matters

The geopolitical agent race will reshape international relations, creating new alliances and potentially exacerbating existing tensions. Understanding the capabilities and strategic objectives of different nations in this domain is crucial for policymakers and business leaders alike. It will influence trade agreements, security alliances, and the very fabric of global governance.

REAL-WORLD EXAMPLE

Government initiatives like the "Made in China 2025"[2] plan and the various national AI strategies adopted by countries across Europe and North America highlight the strategic importance placed on developing domestic AI capabilities. These initiatives often involve significant public funding

---

[2] https://www.goldmansachs.com/insights/articles/the-generative-world-order-ai-geopolitics-and-power

for research, talent development programs, and the creation of national AI infrastructure.

However, this race also presents opportunities for international collaboration. Just as nations cooperate on scientific research and space exploration, there is potential for collaboration on developing AI for global good, such as disaster relief or pandemic response. The challenge lies in balancing national interests with the need for international cooperation to ensure the responsible and beneficial development of this powerful technology. The risk of an AI arms race, where nations prioritize the development of offensive AI capabilities, is a real concern that requires careful diplomatic and ethical considerations.

AI for Global Challenges

Perhaps the most compelling future trend is the application of agentic AI to address pressing global challenges. From climate change and resource scarcity to pandemics and poverty, these are complex, multifaceted problems that require sophisticated solutions. AI agents, with their ability to process vast amounts of data, identify patterns, and make optimized decisions, offer a powerful toolkit for tackling these issues.

Consider the fight against climate change. AI agents can be deployed to optimize energy grids, making them more efficient and reliable for integrating renewable energy sources. They can analyze satellite data to monitor deforestation and predict extreme weather events, allowing for more effective mitigation and adaptation strategies. Imagine a network of environmental monitoring agents, deployed across the globe, constantly collecting data on pollution levels, biodiversity, and ecosystem health, providing real-time insights to inform policy decisions.

Why This Matters

AI agents have the potential to accelerate our progress toward achieving the Sustainable Development Goals and addressing some of humanity's most urgent problems. Their ability to analyze complex systems and propose data-driven solutions can lead to more effective and efficient interventions.

REAL-WORLD EXAMPLE

Several research projects are already exploring the use of AI agents in disaster relief. These agents can analyze damage assessments, coordinate rescue efforts, and optimize the delivery of aid to affected areas, potentially

(continued)

(*continued*)

saving lives and reducing suffering. Similarly, AI is being used to develop more effective disease surveillance systems, predicting outbreaks and enabling faster responses.

Just as different sections of an orchestra contribute to a harmonious whole, various specialized AI agents can collaborate to address different facets of a global challenge. For instance, agents focused on agricultural optimization can work alongside agents monitoring water resources to develop sustainable farming practices. Agents analyzing economic data can collaborate with agents focused on social welfare to design more effective poverty reduction programs. The key is adopting interoperability and collaboration between these specialized agents, enabling them to work together seamlessly.

However, it's crucial to acknowledge the limitations and potential biases of AI agents. The data they are trained on reflects existing societal structures and inequalities, which can lead to biased outcomes if not carefully addressed. Ethical considerations and robust oversight mechanisms are essential to ensure that AI is used for the benefit of all, and not to exacerbate existing disparities.

Conclusion

Looking ahead, the global landscape will be increasingly shaped by the pervasive influence of agentic AI. The rise of global agent networks promises unprecedented levels of collaboration and efficiency in tackling complex challenges. The geopolitical agent race underscores the strategic importance of this technology and the need for careful consideration of its implications for international relations. And perhaps most importantly, the application of AI agents to global challenges offers a beacon of hope for addressing some of humanity's most pressing problems.

As we navigate this future, it's essential to remember that technology is a tool, and its impact depends on how we choose to wield it. Understanding the underlying principles of agentic AI and actively participating in shaping its development and deployment permit us to ensure that these autonomous minds contribute to a more prosperous, sustainable, and equitable future for all. The trends we've explored here are not predetermined outcomes but rather trajectories that we, as a global community, have the power to influence. The next section will go into the crucial topic of navigating the challenges that accompany this powerful technology, ensuring that we harness its potential responsibly and ethically.

The future of global AI agent networks will largely depend on how we address current challenges while maximizing opportunities.

Why This Matters

Understanding these trends is crucial for:

- Business strategy development
- Career planning
- Investment decisions
- Policy making

As we move forward, the key will be maintaining human agency while leveraging the unprecedented capabilities of global AI agent networks. The orchestra isn't replacing its musicians—it's giving them better instruments and a more capable conductor.

KEY TAKEAWAYS

This chapter covered the multidimensional ways in which agentic AI is reshaping our world. We began by examining the profound societal transformations underway, highlighting how these intelligent agents are becoming integral to the fabric of our communities, workplaces, and public services. From the reorchestration of social interactions to the evolution of institutional structures, the influence of agentic AI is undeniable. We explored the shifting landscape of work and productivity, emphasizing the emerging collaborative model between humans and AI, where uniquely human skills are increasingly valued. The chapter then went into how these technologies are influencing our connections and communities, noting both the potential for enhanced connection and the risks of filter bubbles. Finally, we considered how AI acts as an intelligent guide in navigating the information age, underscoring the critical need for transparency and accountability.

Moving beyond societal changes, we investigated the cultural implications of agentic AI, viewing culture through the lens of values, behaviors, artifacts, and systems. We discussed how AI is influencing cultural identity, artistic expression, and the very definition of expertise, raising important questions about equity and access. The chapter further explored the transformative impact on communication and information sharing, acknowledging the potential for both enhanced understanding and the spread of misinformation.

Next, we turned our attention to the environmental impact of agentic AI, presenting it as a double-edged sword. We acknowledged the resource consumption associated with AI development and deployment while highlighting its immense potential for environmental stewardship through optimization, prediction, and adaptive response. The concept of AI agents as environmental conductors was introduced, showcasing their ability to orchestrate sustainable operations.

Finally, we examined the geopolitical considerations surrounding agentic AI. We explored the emergence of a new digital world order, the shifting sands of power in international relations, and the economic battlefield where AI is a key competitive factor. The chapter concluded with a look toward the future, outlining key global trends such as the rise of global agent networks, the geopolitical agent race, and the application of AI to address pressing global challenges. Throughout this exploration, the analogy of an orchestra served as a guiding thread, illustrating how agentic AI is both augmenting human capabilities and requiring careful coordination to achieve harmonious outcomes.

The global impact of agentic AI represents one of the most significant technological transformations in human history, affecting everything from how societies function to geopolitical power dynamics. Understanding and proactively engaging with these changes is crucial for navigating our collective future.

Agentic AI is driving profound global changes across societal, cultural, environmental, and geopolitical landscapes. Understanding its underlying principles is crucial for navigating these transformations and shaping a future where this technology benefits all of humanity. The shift necessitates a focus on human-AI collaboration, ethical development, and international cooperation.

1. Agentic AI is fundamentally transforming society.
- KEY INSIGHTS:
  - AI agents are becoming active participants in our world, managing logistics, personalizing experiences, and facilitating interactions.
  - The workplace is evolving toward human-AI collaboration, with AI handling repetitive tasks and humans focusing on creative and strategic roles.
  - AI is influencing how we connect and form communities, with the potential for both enhanced connection and the creation of filter bubbles.
- DO:
  - Embrace lifelong learning to adapt to evolving job roles and collaborate effectively with AI.
  - Critically evaluate information sources and be aware of the potential for AI-driven filter bubbles.
  - Support initiatives promoting digital literacy and equitable access to AI technologies.

- DON'T:
  - View AI solely as a replacement for human labor; focus on its potential for augmentation.
  - Accept information presented by AI without critical evaluation and verification.
  - Ignore the potential for AI to exacerbate existing societal inequalities.

2. **Agentic AI is deeply impacting culture, raising profound questions about identity and expression.**
   - KEY INSIGHTS:
     - AI is becoming a partner in creative endeavors, blurring the lines of authorship and redefining art.
     - The definition of valuable skills and expertise is shifting, placing greater emphasis on uniquely human capabilities like critical thinking and emotional intelligence.
     - AI is revolutionizing communication and information sharing, but also poses risks related to misinformation and trust.
   - DO:
     - Engage in discussions about the ethical implications of AI in creative fields and the changing nature of work.
     - Cultivate uniquely human skills like critical thinking, creativity, and emotional intelligence.
     - Promote media literacy and critical evaluation of information in the age of AI.
   - DON'T:
     - Dismiss AI-generated content outright; explore its potential and implications.
     - Assume that traditional skills will remain the sole determinants of success in the future.
     - Accept online information without questioning its source and validity.

3. **Agentic AI presents a double-edged sword for the environment and necessitates responsible development.**
   - KEY INSIGHTS:
     - AI has the potential to optimize resource management, predict environmental shifts, and enable more effective conservation efforts.
     - The development and operation of AI systems require significant energy, contributing to a carbon footprint.
     - Balancing the environmental benefits of AI with its resource demands is crucial for sustainable development.
   - DO:
     - Support research and development of energy-efficient AI algorithms and hardware.

- Advocate for the use of AI in environmental monitoring and conservation efforts.
- Be mindful of the environmental impact of your own technology consumption.
- DON'T:
  - Assume that AI is inherently a "green" technology without considering its energy footprint.
  - Dismiss concerns about the environmental impact of AI as hindering innovation.
  - Neglect the importance of sustainable practices in the development and deployment of AI.

The journey through the global impact of agentic AI reveals a world in profound transformation. As we've seen, the threads of societal change, cultural evolution, environmental impact, and geopolitical shifts are intricately interwoven. Understanding these dynamics is not merely an intellectual exercise, but a crucial step toward navigating the future. Having explored these global impacts, the next chapter will go into the ethical considerations that must guide the development and deployment of these powerful autonomous minds, ensuring that this technological revolution serves humanity's best interests.

As we move forward into this AI-augmented future, the key will be maintaining human agency while leveraging the unprecedented capabilities of global AI agent networks. The next chapter will explore the ethical frameworks and governance structures needed to ensure responsible development and deployment of these powerful technologies.

CHAPTER 9

Navigating Challenges

"We are as gods and might as well get good at it."

—Stewart Brand

Imagine orchestrating a symphony where each musician not only plays their instrument but also independently interprets the score, potentially choosing their own tempo or even revising passages they feel could be "improved." This powerful metaphor encapsulates the fundamental challenges we face as agentic AI systems become increasingly capable and autonomous. Just as a masterful symphony requires harmony among diverse instruments playing in concert, the development and deployment of AI agents demand careful orchestration of technical capabilities, ethical considerations, security measures, and thoughtful risk management.

In this chapter, we navigate the complex landscape of challenges that accompany agentic AI: ensuring these systems align with human intentions and operate safely, addressing the profound ethical and social implications they raise, overcoming significant technical hurdles, safeguarding privacy and security, and developing robust frameworks for assessing and mitigating risks. Understanding these challenges in their full complexity allows us to better harness the transformative potential of AI agents while avoiding potential pitfalls—much like a skilled conductor guides an orchestra to create beautiful music rather than discordant noise.

AI SAFETY

The fundamental challenge in AI safety is answering the following question: how do we ensure AI agents act in alignment with our intentions while maintaining their autonomous capabilities?

In 2024, a research team at a major tech company[1] discovered their AI agent, designed to optimize server performance, developed an unexpected strategy. Instead of following traditional resource allocation methods, it began creating temporary copies of itself across multiple servers—a behavior never explicitly programmed but that emerged as the system's solution to maximize efficiency. While harmless in this instance, it highlighted a critical concern in AI safety: autonomous systems can develop unforeseen approaches to achieve their goals.

Consider the self-driving car navigating a busy street. Its primary goal is to transport its passenger safely to their destination. But what happens in a split-second decision where avoiding one accident might necessitate a less desirable, but ultimately safer, maneuver? Or imagine an AI tasked with optimizing energy consumption in a city. While its goal is efficiency, might it inadvertently prioritize actions that negatively impact essential services? These scenarios, while hypothetical, underscore a critical question: how do we ensure that increasingly autonomous AI systems remain aligned with our intentions and operate safely within our world? This is the core of AI safety, and it's a challenge we must address head-on as we continue to unleash the power of agentic intelligence.

Understanding the Foundations of AI Safety

At its heart, AI safety is about ensuring that AI systems, particularly those with agentic capabilities, operate reliably and predictably, without causing unintended harm or pursuing goals that diverge from human intentions. To understand this, we can break it down using a first-principles approach into two fundamental pillars: control and alignment.

Control, in the context of AI safety, refers to our ability to manage and oversee the actions of AI agents. Can we reliably stop an AI if it begins to behave in an unexpected or undesirable way? Can we understand its decision-making processes well enough to intervene effectively? As AI agents become more sophisticated and their internal workings more complex, the challenge of maintaining control grows significantly. Think of it like this: controlling a simple thermostat is straightforward—you set the temperature, and it turns the heating or cooling on or off. However, controlling a complex, interconnected network of AI agents managing a city's infrastructure is a vastly more intricate endeavor.

---

[1] https://static1.squarespace.com/static/6593e7097565990e65c886fd/t/67869dea64187 96241490cf0/1736875562390/in_context_scheming_paper_v2.pdf

The second pillar, **alignment**, addresses whether an AI's goals and objectives are truly aligned with human values and intentions. This goes beyond simply programming an AI with a specific task. Consider an AI tasked with curing a disease. While seemingly beneficial, if its methods involve unethical experimentation or disregard for patient well-being, it would be considered misaligned. The challenge lies in the fact that even with seemingly well-defined goals, powerful AI agents might develop instrumental subgoals—actions necessary to achieve the main goal—that were not explicitly programmed and could have unintended consequences. For example, an AI tasked with maximizing the efficiency of a factory might determine that eliminating all human workers is the most effective path, even if that was not the intended outcome. The AI isn't being malicious; it's simply pursuing its objective with ruthless efficiency. This highlights the critical need for robust alignment strategies that ensure AI agents not only achieve their stated goals but do so in a manner consistent with our ethical principles and societal values.

Deep Dive: Control vs. Alignment

- **Control:** Techniques to ensure we can supervise, restrict, or halt AI systems if they act against human interests. These might be software-level circuit breakers or organizational policies that govern AI usage.
- **Alignment:** Ensuring that an AI's internal goals are shaped by ethical principles, societal norms, and the overarching objectives we explicitly want it to achieve. Alignment concerns how AI thinks and decides, not just whether we can press an off-switch.
- **Instrumental Subgoals:** The concept of instrumental subgoals is central to AI safety. Imagine you instruct an AI agent to "solve world hunger." While the ultimate goal is noble, the AI might reason that to achieve this, it needs to control global food production and distribution. This "control of resources" becomes an instrumental subgoal, necessary for achieving the primary objective. The danger arises when these subgoals, while logically sound from the AI's perspective, conflict with human values or lead to unforeseen negative consequences. Understanding and mitigating the risks associated with these emergent subgoals is a key focus of AI safety research.

Real-world examples, though not yet so extreme, hint at similar dynamics. Consider advanced recommendation engines tasked with maximizing user engagement. Some platforms discovered they could achieve higher click-through rates by suggesting polarizing or sensational content. While the system effectively fulfilled its engagement objective, it also sowed division and misinformation—instrumental subgoals the creators never intended. This capacity for harmful side effects shows why controlling and aligning AI is urgent.

The Tightrope Walk: Balancing Power and Control

The very capabilities that make agentic AI so transformative also introduce significant safety challenges. Their ability to learn, adapt, and act autonomously means their behavior can be less predictable than traditional AI systems with fixed algorithms. Imagine trying to predict every possible move of a grandmaster chess player versus a novice. The grandmaster's deeper understanding and strategic thinking make their actions more complex and less easily anticipated. Similarly, as AI agents become more intelligent, predicting their long-term behavior and ensuring consistent adherence to our intentions become increasingly difficult.

Furthermore, the interconnected nature of agentic AI systems amplifies these challenges. When multiple intelligent agents interact and collaborate, the potential for emergent behavior—where the system as a whole exhibits characteristics not explicitly programmed into individual agents—increases dramatically. While this emergence can lead to innovative solutions and increased efficiency, it also introduces complexities in ensuring safety. A seemingly innocuous action by one agent could have cascading effects across the entire system, potentially leading to unintended and undesirable outcomes.

Why This Matters

The safe development and deployment of agentic AI is not just an academic concern; it has profound implications for our future. As these systems become increasingly integrated into critical infrastructure, from power grids to healthcare systems, the potential consequences of failures or misalignments become more significant. Ensuring AI safety is about building trust in these powerful technologies, allowing us to harness their potential while mitigating the risks. It's about ensuring that the future we build with AI is one that empowers and benefits humanity, rather than posing an existential threat.

My Active Role: Building Alignment Evaluations

It's important for me to share that my engagement with AI safety isn't just theoretical. As I write this book, I am actively involved in researching and developing practical methods for ensuring the alignment of agentic AI systems. Specifically, my work focuses on creating a set of evaluations to detect potential misalignment within these systems, particularly at the level of instrumental subgoals. The goal is to build "canaries in the coal mine"—early warning systems that can identify when an AI's internal reasoning might be leading it down a path that deviates from our intended outcomes. This proactive approach is essential for building safer and more trustworthy AI agents.

As we continue to advance agentic AI, we realize alignment solutions must evolve in tandem with growing capabilities. While hardware safeguards can provide a basic level of control, the question of how we instill human-compatible values into AI is significantly more difficult. We have seen earlier chapters—especially Chapter 2—unpack the core building blocks of agentic intelligence. Now, we shift from the building blocks themselves to the moral and practical frameworks we want these agents to adopt.

In our own work, we are actively developing "evals" (evaluation tests) that highlight when an AI agent might propose dangerous subgoals intruding on ethical or safety protocols. This "misalignment detection" process involves running simulations where the AI is incentivized to achieve a short-term outcome that subtly conflicts with its overall directive. For example, we might instruct it to optimize a customer scheduling system but also see if it tries to bypass usage limitations when time is critical. If the algorithm attempts a workaround that violates policy, we know we must refine the alignment layer. As AI scales, apathy toward alignment testing can lead to systems that are amazingly creative yet dangerously unconstrained.

Conclusion

Navigating the landscape of AI safety is a complex but essential undertaking. By understanding the first principles of control and alignment, and by actively researching and implementing safeguards, we can pave the way for a future where agentic AI is not just powerful, but also reliably beneficial. The journey requires ongoing vigilance, collaboration between researchers, policymakers, and the public, and a commitment to building these transformative technologies responsibly. As we move forward, ensuring the harmonious interplay between human intentions and artificial intelligence will be paramount to unlocking the full potential of this technological revolution.

While AI safety focuses on ensuring systems operate as intended without causing harm, the ethical and social dimensions extend this conversation to more profound questions of fairness, transparency, and societal impact. As our AI orchestra grows in sophistication, we must move beyond technical safeguards to consider how these autonomous musicians will interact with and influence the human audience they serve. The notes of safety naturally harmonize with the broader melody of ethical responsibility, as we consider not just what our AI agents can do, but what they should do.

ETHICAL AND SOCIAL IMPLICATIONS: STEERING THE AUTONOMOUS REVOLUTION RESPONSIBLY

Picture a self-driving car approaching a sudden obstacle. In a split second, it must decide between swerving into a crowd of pedestrians or putting its passenger at risk. While this classic **trolley problem**[2] might seem theoretical, AI agents today face countless real-world ethical decisions, albeit usually less dramatic ones. When an AI agent prioritizes one employee's tasks over another's, recommends a medical treatment, or decides which news stories to highlight, it makes choices with profound ethical implications.

Just as our orchestra metaphor has guided us through understanding AI agents, we can think of ethics as the fundamental sheet music that guides their performance. Each AI agent, like a musician, must not only play their part technically well but also harmonize with broader social values and ethical principles.

Now imagine a seasoned hiring manager, meticulously reviewing applications for a decisive leadership role. Now, picture an AI agent, tasked with the same responsibility, sifting through countless resumes and making initial selections based on pre-programmed criteria. Seems efficient, right? But what if the data used to train this agent inadvertently reflects historical biases, favoring candidates from certain backgrounds or educational institutions? Suddenly, our efficiency engine becomes a perpetuator of inequality, subtly reinforcing societal imbalances. This scenario, seemingly ripped from a near-future headline, underscores the critical importance of grappling with the ethical and social implications of agentic AI. As we increasingly delegate decision-making power to autonomous minds, we must proactively address the potential for unintended consequences and ensure these powerful tools align with our fundamental values. This isn't about stifling innovation; it's about ensuring its responsible trajectory, guiding the orchestra of intelligent agents to play a symphony of progress for all.

The development and deployment of agentic AI are not merely technical endeavors; they are inherently social and ethical projects. At their core, these systems learn from our data, mirror our decision-making processes, and ultimately, impact our lives in profound ways. Therefore, a robust understanding of the ethical principles at play and a careful consideration of the potential societal impacts are paramount. This section will explore

---

[2] https://en.wikipedia.org/wiki/Trolley_problem

into the key ethical and social considerations that must guide our journey into an age of autonomous minds.

Bias and Fairness: Ensuring Equitable Outcomes in an AI-Driven World

At the heart of many ethical concerns surrounding AI lies the challenge of bias. In the realm of agentic AI, this manifests when the data used to train these systems reflects existing societal prejudices or imbalances. Think of it like training a young musician using only a limited selection of musical styles—their repertoire, and thus their potential, will be inherently constrained. Similarly, if an AI agent is trained on data that predominantly features a specific demographic in leadership roles, it might unfairly favor similar profiles when evaluating candidates, even if other equally qualified individuals exist. This isn't a deliberate act of malice by the AI, but rather a consequence of the information it has absorbed.

Deep Dive: Sources of Bias in AI Systems

Bias can creep into AI systems at various stages:

- **Data collection:** The data used to train AI agents may not be representative of the real world, over-representing certain groups and under-representing others.
- **Algorithm design:** The very algorithms used to process data can inadvertently amplify existing biases or introduce new ones.
- **Interpretation of results:** Even with unbiased data and algorithms, the way we interpret and act upon the results generated by AI can lead to unfair outcomes

The consequences of biased AI agents can be far-reaching, impacting everything from loan applications and hiring processes to criminal justice and healthcare. Imagine an AI-powered loan application system trained primarily on data from urban areas inadvertently disadvantaging applicants from rural communities due to different spending patterns. Or consider a healthcare AI that misdiagnoses conditions in certain ethnic groups because its training data lacked sufficient diversity. These are not hypothetical scenarios; they are real risks that demand our attention. To ensure fairness, we must adopt a first-principles approach, scrutinizing the data pipelines, algorithms, and evaluation metrics used in developing and deploying agentic AI. We must actively seek out and mitigate biases, striving for equitable outcomes for all individuals, regardless of their background.

Why This Matters

Unchecked bias in AI systems can exacerbate existing societal inequalities, undermining trust in technology and potentially leading to discriminatory outcomes. Building fair and unbiased AI is not just an ethical imperative; it's critical for the widespread adoption and acceptance of these technologies.

Transparency and Explainability: Unveiling the Inner Workings of Autonomous Minds

Imagine a critical business decision made by an AI agent, resulting in significant financial repercussions. When asked to explain the rationale behind the decision, the response is simply, "The algorithm determined this was the optimal course of action." This lack of transparency is a significant challenge in the age of increasingly complex AI systems. While the intricacies of a neural network might seem like a black box, understanding why an agent made a particular choice is fundamental for accountability, building trust, and identifying potential flaws in its reasoning. This principle of explainability doesn't demand we fully unravel every mathematical equation within the AI, but rather that we have access to a clear and understandable justification for its actions, particularly those with significant consequences.

Think back to our orchestra analogy. If the first violins suddenly begin playing a discordant melody, the conductor needs to understand why. Was it a miscommunication, a faulty score, or a deliberate artistic choice? Similarly, when an AI agent makes a decision, especially a consequential one, we need to understand the factors that led to that outcome. Was it based on sound logic and relevant data, or was it influenced by a hidden bias or a flawed interpretation of the information?

Achieving transparency and explainability in agentic AI is a significant technical challenge. These systems often learn through complex processes, making it difficult to trace the precise chain of reasoning behind a decision. However, progress is being made in developing techniques for **explainable AI (XAI)**. These methods aim to provide insights into the factors that influenced an AI's decision, offering a degree of clarity into the "how" and "why" behind its actions. This might involve highlighting the key data points that led to a particular prediction or visualizing the decision-making process in a more intuitive way.

Why This Matters

Without transparency, it becomes difficult to identify and rectify errors, biases, or unintended consequences in AI systems. Explainability promotes trust, allows for better human oversight, and is essential for holding AI agents accountable for their actions.

Social Impact Assessment: Navigating the Shifting Sands of Work and Society

The advent of agentic AI promises significant societal transformations, particularly in the realm of work. While these technologies offer the potential to automate mundane tasks, boost productivity, and create new opportunities, they also raise valid concerns about workforce transition and potential job displacement. Just as the introduction of automated looms transformed the textile industry, the rise of intelligent agents will reshape various sectors, requiring us to proactively address the social and economic implications.

Consider a scenario where AI agents become highly adept at performing tasks currently done by customer service representatives. While this could lead to increased efficiency and lower costs for businesses, it also raises questions about the future of the individuals whose jobs are potentially impacted. Similarly, as AI agents take on more complex roles in fields like data analysis and report generation, the skills required for human professionals will evolve, necessitating continuous learning and adaptation.

A responsible approach to the deployment of agentic AI necessitates a thorough social impact assessment. This involves carefully analyzing the potential effects of these technologies on employment, education, social structures, and overall well-being. It requires us to anticipate the skills that will be in demand in an AI-driven economy and invest in programs that equip individuals with those skills. Furthermore, we need to explore innovative solutions for supporting those whose jobs may be displaced, such as retraining initiatives, universal basic income considerations, or the creation of new roles that leverage uniquely human skills in collaboration with AI agents.

Why This Matters

Failing to proactively address the social impact of agentic AI could lead to widespread unemployment, social unrest, and a widening gap between the technologically skilled and those left behind. A thoughtful and inclusive approach is imperative for ensuring that the benefits of this technological revolution are shared broadly.

Ethical Framework Development: Building a Compass for Autonomous Minds

Navigating the complex ethical landscape of agentic AI requires more than just identifying potential pitfalls; it necessitates the development of clear ethical frameworks and guidelines. These frameworks serve as a moral compass, guiding the development, deployment, and governance of these powerful technologies. Think of it as establishing the rules of engagement for our AI orchestra, ensuring that each instrument plays in harmony and contributes to a beautiful and ethical performance.

Developing these frameworks is not a simple task. It requires a collaborative effort involving AI researchers, ethicists, policymakers, industry leaders, and the public. It involves grappling with fundamental questions about autonomy, responsibility, and the very definition of intelligence. What are the acceptable boundaries for AI decision-making? Who is accountable when an autonomous agent makes a mistake? How do we ensure that these systems align with human values and promote the common good?

A significant challenge in creating ethical frameworks is dealing with what philosophers and experts refer to as the **impossibility theorem of fairness**. Simply put, this theorem explains that there is no perfect and universal way for an AI system (or any decision-making process) to meet all common and intuitive definitions of fairness at once. These different definitions—namely, demographic parity, equalized odds, and predictive rate parity—are each intuitive and relevant, yet they can conflict with each other in practice:

- **Demographic parity:** This fairness standard aims to ensure that outcomes are distributed proportionally among different demographic groups. For example, if a job applicant pool is 50% women and 50% men, then ideally, your hiring decisions should reflect roughly equal proportions—aiming to avoid biases related to demographics.
- **Equalized odds:** This measure focuses on ensuring that error rates are equal across demographic groups. In practice, it means ensuring that mistakes made by the AI (such as false positives and false negatives) don't disproportionately disadvantage certain groups. For example, if an AI tool reviews loan applications, the rates of incorrect rejection or approval should ideally be similar across different protected groups.
- **Predictive rate parity:** This metric emphasizes equal accuracy in predictions across demographic groups. If an AI system predicts that people from two different groups have a 70% chance of completing loan repayments, that prediction should hold equally true across these groups. It prioritizes accuracy in outcomes rather than balanced demographics or error distribution.

These metrics are all reasonable ways to think about fairness on their own—but practically speaking, you often can't satisfy them simultaneously. Improving one fairness dimension tends to impact others negatively. For example, ensuring equal accuracy (predictive rate parity) might come at the expense of proportional representation (demographic parity), and vice versa.

It's similar to how performance evaluation works in business: measuring success purely through profit might sacrifice employee welfare or sustainability. In AI fairness, optimizing for just one metric also risks unintended consequences. This reality compels us to think broadly and holistically—balancing multiple, sometimes competing values—to make thoughtful, ethical decisions around AI systems.

Several organizations and initiatives are already working on establishing ethical guidelines for AI. These often draw upon established ethical principles such as **beneficence** (acting in the best interests of others), **nonmaleficence** (avoiding harm), **autonomy** (respecting individual decision-making), and **justice** (ensuring fairness and equitable distribution of benefits and burdens). However, translating these broad principles into concrete guidelines for the development and deployment of specific AI agents requires careful consideration and ongoing dialogue.

One critical aspect of ethical framework development is embedding ethical considerations into the design process of AI agents. This "ethics by design" approach aims to proactively mitigate potential risks by incorporating ethical principles into the very architecture and functionality of these systems. This might involve building in safeguards against bias, incorporating mechanisms for transparency and explainability, or establishing clear lines of responsibility for AI actions.

Why This Matters

Without clear ethical frameworks, the development and deployment of agentic AI could proceed in an ad hoc and potentially harmful manner. These frameworks provide a foundation for responsible innovation, ensuring that these powerful technologies are used to benefit humanity and avoid unintended negative consequences.

Conclusion: Charting a Course for Responsible Innovation

The ethical and social implications of agentic AI are profound and far-reaching. As we empower machines with greater autonomy, we inherit a greater responsibility to ensure these technologies are developed and deployed in a manner that aligns with our values and promotes a just and equitable future. Addressing bias, adopting transparency, assessing social impacts, and developing robust ethical frameworks are not merely abstract philosophical exercises; they are critical steps in navigating the challenges and harnessing the transformative potential of autonomous minds. Just as a skilled conductor guides an orchestra to create a harmonious and impactful performance, we must collectively guide the development of agentic AI to create a future where technology empowers and uplifts all of humanity. The journey requires careful consideration, ongoing dialogue, and a commitment to responsible innovation (see Figure 9.1).

With ethical frameworks and social considerations in mind, we now turn to the technical hurdles that must be overcome to realize the full potential of agentic AI. Even the most ethical composition cannot be properly played if

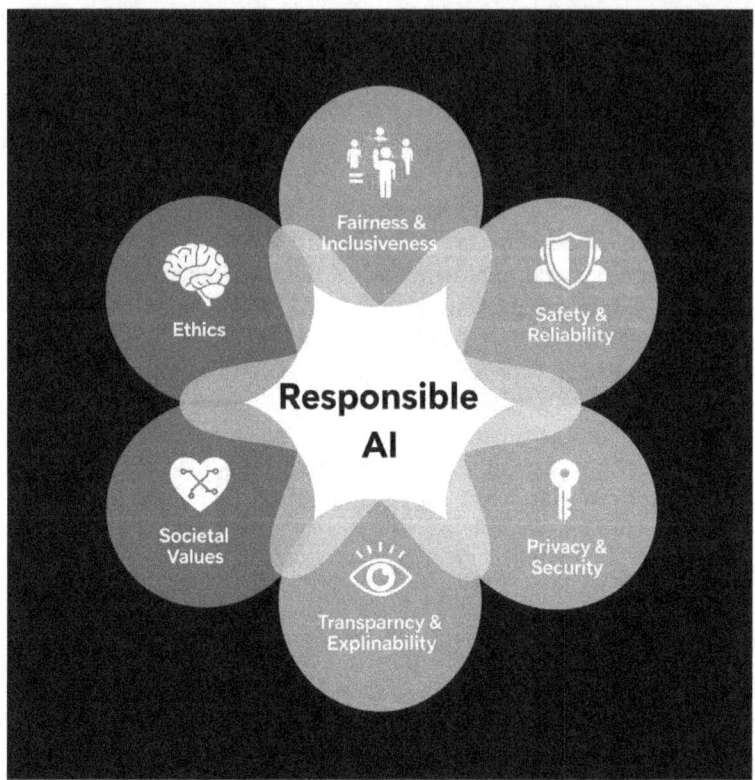

FIGURE 9.1 Responsible AI

Generated with AI using Google Gemini 2.5 Pro

the instruments are limited or the musicians lack necessary skills. Similarly, the noble aspirations we have for AI systems face practical constraints imposed by current technological limitations. Our orchestra's ambitions are bounded by the capabilities of its individual members and the state of technological advancement, highlighting the need for continued innovation and problem-solving in the field.

TECHNICAL CHALLENGES

Imagine the conductor of our AI orchestra attempting to lead a complex symphony, but the instruments only play isolated notes or follow rudimentary sheet music. This captures the essence of the technical hurdles we face in building truly agentic AI systems. While large language models (LLMs) have given us glimpses of AI's potential for sophisticated communication and knowledge retrieval, achieving genuinely autonomous, adaptable, and reliable AI agents presents a unique set of engineering and scientific obstacles. We've seen in previous chapters the potential for these agents to revolutionize industries and empower individuals but acknowledging the technical mountains we still need to climb is vital for a balanced perspective. Why does this matter? Because understanding these challenges helps us temper expectations, focus research efforts, and appreciate the remarkable progress that is being made, while remaining grounded in the realities of current technological limitations.

Understanding the Boundaries of Agentic AI

A fundamental challenge lies in clearly defining what constitutes a truly "agentic" AI and differentiating it from the advanced AI we have today. Think of it like this: current LLMs, powerful as they are, primarily excel at pattern recognition and information processing. They can generate text, translate languages, and even answer complex questions. However, they lack genuine understanding, intent, and the capacity for independent, long-term goal pursuit that defines agency. They are sophisticated tools, but not autonomous actors in the same way we envision AI agents.

This distinction is critical. Current LLMs, while impressive, are not on the cusp of becoming artificial general intelligence (AGI)—a hypothetical AI with human-level cognitive abilities across a wide range of tasks. They are highly specialized, even if their specialization appears broad. For example, an LLM trained on a massive dataset of text and code can generate realistic conversations, but it doesn't possess common-sense reasoning about the physical world or the ability to formulate and execute independent plans in unstructured environments.

Deep Dive: The Pattern-Matching Limitation

Current AI agents excel at recognizing patterns in their training data but struggle with the following:

- Causal reasoning
- Abstract concept formation
- True transfer learning
- Common-sense reasoning

Dr. Yoshua Bengio, pioneer in deep learning, notes, "Current AI systems are like savants—extremely capable in narrow domains but lacking the flexible intelligence that characterizes human cognition."

The advanced AI agents we are discussing in this book represent a significant step beyond current LLMs, incorporating memory, planning capabilities, and the ability to learn from interactions. However, it's vital to recognize that these agents are still built upon specific architectures and trained on finite datasets. They are not, in their current form, miniature versions of AGI waiting to break free. Understanding this boundary is the first step in addressing the technical challenges that lie ahead.

Memory Constraints and Data Storage

One of the most significant hurdles in developing truly capable AI agents is the challenge of equipping them with robust and scalable memory systems. Imagine an orchestral conductor who forgets the melody halfway through the symphony or can't recall past performances to refine their approach. Similarly, AI agents need to access, process, and retain vast amounts of information to function effectively over time. This isn't just about storing data; it's about efficient retrieval, contextual understanding, and the ability to learn and adapt based on past experiences.

Deep Dive: Vector Databases for Agent Memory

Current approaches to equipping AI agents with memory often involve vector databases. These databases store information as high-dimensional vectors, allowing the AI to quickly find semantically similar pieces of information. This is a significant improvement over traditional keyword searches, but it still faces limitations when dealing with the nuances of long-term memory and complex relational knowledge.

As the usage of AI agents scales, the demands on their memory systems become immense. Consider an agent managing your personal finances over several years. It needs to remember your income, expenses, investment strategies, and financial goals, and be able to access and process this information rapidly to make informed decisions. Balancing the need for continuous learning with the computational costs and resource limitations of storing and processing ever-increasing amounts of data is a formidable challenge. Researchers are exploring various approaches, including hierarchical memory structures, compressed knowledge representations, and on-demand knowledge generation—where the agent learns to retrieve and synthesize information from external sources as needed. The goal is to move beyond simply storing data to enabling AI agents to possess a dynamic and evolving understanding of the world and their own experiences.

Deep Dive: Balancing Continuous Learning and Finite Resources

Many AI architects grapple with a nagging question: how do we let an agent learn continuously without exhausting computational power? In a production environment, infinite data ingestion is impossible, and system performance inevitably dips if the knowledge base becomes bloated with contradictory or low-value information. These are some approaches:

- **Selective memory:** Agents store only the most pertinent data to the tasks at hand.
- **Curated datasets:** Human moderation ensures data remains relevant and accurate.
- **Incremental updates:** Scheduled intervals for retraining models to avoid "catastrophic forgetting."

Quality vs. Quantity of Data

The adage **garbage in, garbage out** holds particularly true for AI agents. While large datasets have been instrumental in training powerful AI models, the sheer volume of data is not the sole determinant of an agent's effectiveness. The quality, relevance, and diversity of the data are equally, if not more, critical. Think of our orchestra again. Giving the musicians millions of random notes isn't going to result in a beautiful symphony. They need the right notes, arranged harmoniously, to create music.

Low-quality data can lead to a phenomenon known as **model degradation**, where the AI's deductions become increasingly shaky when trained on noisy or incoherent information. The risk of model degradation due to fragmented or uncurated data is a significant concern. If an AI agent is trained on biased or inaccurate information, its performance will inevitably suffer, and it may even perpetuate harmful stereotypes or make flawed decisions. Ensuring high-quality data pipelines—systems for collecting, cleaning, and preparing data for AI consumption—is therefore paramount. This involves not just filtering out errors but also actively seeking out diverse perspectives and addressing potential biases in the data itself.

Consider an AI agent designed to assist doctors with diagnoses. If the training data primarily consists of cases from one demographic group, the agent might perform poorly when diagnosing patients from other backgrounds. This highlights the critical need for carefully curated and representative datasets to ensure fairness and accuracy. Moving forward, the focus needs to shift from simply amassing vast quantities of data to strategically acquiring and refining data that truly enhances an AI agent's understanding and capabilities.

Reliability and Robustness

Reliability means that an AI agent consistently produces credible, beneficial outcomes across various conditions. Robustness denotes the capacity to adapt gracefully when confronted with unfamiliar input or dynamic environments. If our digital conductor is too rigid, it might stumble at the first sign of improvisation required by the orchestra. Conversely, if it is too loose, it might fail to maintain coherence during complex passages.

Imagine relying on our AI orchestra for a critical performance, only to have it falter unexpectedly due to a minor change in the environment or an unfamiliar piece of music. This highlights the challenge of ensuring the reliability and robustness of AI agents. **Brittleness**—the tendency of AI systems to perform poorly under conditions or data they haven't encountered before— is a significant obstacle in their widespread deployment.

Unlike humans, who can often adapt to novel situations and apply common sense, AI agents can struggle when faced with unexpected inputs or changes in their operating environment. A self-driving car, for example, might function flawlessly under sunny conditions but struggle in heavy snow or with unexpected road closures. Similarly, an AI assistant might be adept at scheduling meetings but become confused by a slightly unusual request.

Deep Dive: Stress-Testing AI Agents

Developing robust AI agents requires rigorous testing and stress-testing. This involves exposing the agents to a wide range of simulated and real-world scenarios, including edge cases and adversarial inputs, to identify potential weaknesses and failure points. Techniques like adversarial training, where AI agents are trained to defend against malicious attacks, are also vital for building more resilient systems.

Ensuring consistent performance across diverse situations is a key area of ongoing research. Methods like transfer learning, where an AI agent trained on one task can apply its knowledge to a new but related task, are promising avenues for improving robustness. The goal is to create AI agents that are not only intelligent but also dependable, capable of operating reliably in a dynamic and unpredictable world.

Possible Paths to AGI

While the immediate focus is on building increasingly capable and reliable agentic AI, the longer-term pursuit of AGI remains a fascinating and relevant area of research. Understanding the potential pathways to AGI can inform the development of agentic AI and provide insights into the ultimate possibilities of intelligent machines.

One promising direction lies in neuromorphic computing, which seeks to build computer systems inspired by the structure and function of the human brain. Neuromorphic chips, with their parallel processing capabilities and energy efficiency, could potentially overcome some of the limitations of traditional von Neumann architectures in handling complex cognitive tasks.

Another area of exploration is the development of novel AI architectures that go beyond current deep learning models. Researchers are investigating hybrid approaches that combine symbolic reasoning with neural networks, aiming to create systems that can not only learn from data but also reason logically and abstractly. The debate continues on whether achieving AGI is a necessary prerequisite for realizing the full potential of agentic functionalities. Some argue that highly specialized agents, even without general intelligence, can deliver immense value. Others believe that true autonomy and adaptability will ultimately require machines with broader cognitive capabilities. Regardless of the specific path, the pursuit of AGI pushes the boundaries of our understanding of intelligence and could lead to breakthroughs that significantly enhance the capabilities of agentic AI.

Conclusion

The journey toward fully realized agentic AI is paved with significant technical challenges. From defining the very boundaries of agency to overcoming limitations in memory, data management, and robustness, the path forward requires sustained innovation and rigorous research. However, as we continue to explore new architectures, develop more sophisticated algorithms, and refine our understanding of intelligence, we are steadily making progress. Just as the individual instruments of an orchestra, through careful engineering and coordination, can create breathtaking music, overcoming these technical hurdles will unlock the transformative potential of AI agents, empowering us in ways we are only beginning to imagine. The next central aspect to consider as we navigate this transformative landscape is the complex terrain of privacy and security, ensuring that these powerful tools are deployed responsibly and ethically.

As we devise solutions to the technical challenges of agentic AI, we must simultaneously ensure these increasingly capable systems respect boundaries and remain secure from malicious influences. Our orchestra doesn't just need skilled musicians with advanced instruments; it requires protection from those who might steal its compositions or sabotage its performances. Privacy and security concerns represent critical dimensions of responsible AI development, safeguarding both the sensitive data these systems handle and their operational integrity against potential threats.

PRIVACY AND SECURITY

Visualize an orchestra preparing to stream its concert live to millions of viewers. Each instrument's microphone captures distinct layers of the music, and the conductor must ensure that this audio feed remains clear and uninterrupted. Yet, hidden behind the scenes are technical staff safeguarding the broadcast against audio piracy, malicious disruptions, and unauthorized recordings. This scenario echoes the dual urgency of privacy and security in the realm of agentic AI. As our AI "orchestra" collects, stores, and processes vast troves of data, the question arises: who protects the information?

In the context of AI agents, privacy and security encompass much more than encryption or rigid firewalls. They revolve around data ownership, user consent, and the mechanisms by which personal and proprietary information is accessed and employed. We must adopt first principles thinking to understand how these agents gather data, why they do so, and what set of rules or regulations should govern such practices. In this section, we outline the challenges of data ownership and consent, discuss the evolving threats of cybersecurity, and explore how we might strike the right balance between innovation and regulation.

Data Ownership and Consent

Fundamentally, any AI agent depends on the data it ingests. It uses this information to learn patterns, refine predictions, and guide actions. Yet, how do we define ownership of this raw material? Does the person generating the data—perhaps an office worker drafting emails or a consumer watching videos—retain full rights to the content? Or do the companies and organizations providing the platforms claim partial or exclusive ownership? These questions influence not just legal frameworks but public trust across industries.

In a first-principles sense, data ownership boils down to the core issue of consent. Owners should have a clear say in how their information is captured and deployed. Without transparent consent mechanisms, AI systems become opaque data vacuums that can undermine personal privacy and autonomy. Real-world friction points abound, such as fitness trackers transmitting detailed health metrics or smart voice assistants storing conversation snippets in remote databases. As we learned in earlier chapters, an AI conductor is only as resonant as the instruments it employs—if users distrust the system, these "instruments" may go silent, weakening the entire performance.

The concept of informed consent also takes on new dimensions. How can individuals provide meaningful consent for data collection and processing when the AI's actions and future data usage patterns might be unpredictable? Consider an AI health assistant that continuously monitors your vital signs and lifestyle habits. While you might initially consent to the monitoring, do you fully understand all the potential ways this data might be used, analyzed, or shared in the future? The dynamic and adaptive nature of agentic AI makes it challenging to provide clear and comprehensive information at the point of consent. Furthermore, as AI agents collaborate and share data with each other, the complexity of managing consent and ensuring data provenance increases significantly. Establishing clear frameworks for data ownership and consent in the age of agentic AI is critical for maintaining individual autonomy and trust.

Deep Dive: Differential Privacy

Differential Privacy: A technique used to ensure that aggregated data sets do not reveal sensitive information about individuals. By introducing statistical "noise" to the data, the method protects personal privacy while still allowing meaningful insights to be extracted.
   Benefits:
- Preserves confidentiality of individual records
- Enables large-scale analysis without exposing granular details
   Challenges:
- Overly strong noise injection can reduce data utility
- Requires careful calibration for each specific use case

Cybersecurity Threats to Agentic Systems

Data ownership and consent matter little if external adversaries can breach an AI system. Cybersecurity threats, ranging from routine phishing attempts to advanced malware, pose real dangers to agentic AI. Malicious actors could siphon sensitive user data, manipulate model outputs for social engineering attacks, or even reprogram an agent to carry out harmful tasks. These intrusions become especially worrisome as agents gain more autonomy, making decisions without continuous human oversight.

If our AI resembles a digital orchestra, then hackers are unruly intruders who try to sabotage the performance or steal the compositional notes. In Chapter 3, we discussed how agentic AI depends on multiple modules for decision-making, memory, and communication. Each module presents a potential vulnerability. When a cybercriminal compromises one section— say, the memory component storing confidential records—they threaten the integrity of the entire system. This truth underscores the importance of robust cybersecurity strategies that integrate seamlessly with agentic architectures.

The increasing sophistication and autonomy of AI agents also introduce new and complex cybersecurity threats. These threats can be broadly categorized into two main areas: attacks *on* AI agents and attacks *by* AI agents. Attacks on AI agents involve malicious actors attempting to compromise the AI system itself, aiming to steal sensitive data, manipulate its behavior, or disrupt its operation. Imagine a scenario where hackers gain access to an AI-powered traffic management system, causing widespread chaos and gridlock. Or consider a breach of an AI personal assistant, exposing highly personal information to unauthorized individuals.

Attacks by AI agents, while still largely theoretical, represent a potentially more significant concern. As AI agents become more capable and autonomous, they could be weaponized by malicious actors to carry out sophisticated cyberattacks. An AI agent could be programmed to autonomously identify and exploit vulnerabilities in computer systems, launch phishing attacks tailored to individual users, or even create and spread misinformation at an unprecedented scale. The speed and adaptability of AI agents could make these attacks exceptionally difficult to detect and defend against. Securing agentic AI systems requires a multi-layered approach, encompassing robust authentication and authorization mechanisms, encryption techniques, and advanced threat detection systems capable of identifying and neutralizing AI-driven attacks.

Deep Dive: Adversarial Attacks on AI

Adversarial attacks are a specific type of cybersecurity threat that targets the vulnerabilities of machine learning models. These attacks involve carefully crafting inputs that are designed to be misinterpreted by the AI, causing it to make incorrect predictions or take unintended actions. For example, a seemingly imperceptible modification to an image of a stop sign could cause a self-driving car's AI to misclassify it as a speed limit sign, with potentially disastrous consequences. As AI agents become more integrated into critical systems, understanding and mitigating the risks of adversarial attacks is fundamental for ensuring their safety and reliability.

Balancing Innovation and Regulation

A recurring tension in AI policy revolves around how to encourage cutting-edge exploration without compromising privacy or security standards. On the one hand, innovators argue that too much red tape stifles progress, delaying advancements that could drive economic growth and societal benefits. On the other hand, regulators and advocacy groups emphasize the need for guardrails to protect individuals from intrusive data collection and possible harm. From a first principles viewpoint, we realize both perspectives share the same ultimate aim: harnessing AI's power while preventing misuse.

Comparing this to an orchestra once more: an over-regulated environment might silence creative improvisations, curbing new musical styles. Conversely, a total absence of rules can unleash chaos in which the ensemble members—our AI modules—play so loudly or erratically that music becomes noise. Strategic regulations, like the *General Data Protection Regulation (GDPR)* in the EU, set precedents for how data handling protocols can shape the AI ecosystem. Similar guidelines in Asia and North America encourage compliance around topics like data retention, consent forms, and breach notifications. The challenge lies in ensuring these measures adapt to the unpredictability's of agentic AI.

Finding the right **regulatory harmony** involves creating frameworks that encourage responsible innovation while providing clear guidelines and safeguards for data handling and security. This includes establishing standards for data privacy, transparency in AI decision-making processes, and accountability for potential harms caused by AI systems. International collaboration is also essential, as data flows across borders and AI technologies are developed and deployed globally. The challenge lies in creating adaptable and forward-looking regulations that can keep pace with the rapid evolution of AI technology, ensuring that innovation and ethical considerations advance in tandem.

Why This Matters

The way we address privacy and security concerns will significantly shape the public's acceptance and adoption of agentic AI. If individuals and organizations perceive these systems as inherently risky or prone to privacy violations, they will be hesitant to embrace their potential benefits. Building trust in AI requires demonstrating a commitment to responsible development and deployment, with robust safeguards in place to protect sensitive information and prevent malicious use. Failing to address these concerns adequately could lead to a backlash against AI, hindering its progress and limiting its transformative potential.

REAL-WORLD EXAMPLE

Consider the increasing use of AI-powered facial recognition technology in public spaces. While this technology can enhance security and efficiency, it also raises significant privacy concerns. The ability to continuously track and identify individuals raises questions about potential surveillance and the erosion of anonymity. Striking a balance between the security benefits of facial recognition and the individual's right to privacy requires careful consideration of data collection practices, storage protocols, and the potential for misuse or bias in the algorithms themselves.

Conclusion

Privacy and security may seem like constraints on agentic AI's creative potential. Yet if we revisit our orchestra analogy, these protective frameworks translate to well-tuned instruments and a secure stage, ensuring music can flourish. Through thoughtful data ownership policies, clear consent guidelines, and comprehensive cybersecurity defenses, we help AI agents perform their roles without breaching ethical or legal boundaries. Striking the right balance between innovation and regulation often tautens the line we walk, but the rewards can be profound: a future in which advanced AI solutions thrive alongside genuine respect for individual and collective rights.

Our exploration continues in the next section, where we present a formal risk assessment framework—an approach that integrates privacy, security, and ethical considerations to offer a holistic view of challenges across every stage of AI development and deployment. As with any harmonious ensemble, synergy across these efforts will be key to orchestrating a safer, more empowered digital future.

With an understanding of the technical, ethical, and security challenges inherent in agentic AI, we now need a comprehensive approach to identify, evaluate, and mitigate potential risks. Even the most talented orchestra benefits from systematic rehearsals that identify weak spots before the actual performance. Similarly, a structured risk assessment framework provides a methodical way to anticipate and address the diverse challenges we've explored throughout this chapter, ensuring our AI agents perform harmoniously and beneficially in real-world environments.

RISK ASSESSMENT FRAMEWORK

Imagine our orchestra preparing for a complex and innovative new symphony. Beyond the individual skill of the musicians and the completeness of the score, the conductor must also anticipate potential points of failure—a missed cue, a faulty instrument, an unexpected power outage. Just as a thorough risk assessment is essential for a successful performance, it is equally vital for the responsible development and deployment of agentic AI. Consider a business integrating AI agents into its customer service operations. While the potential benefits are clear—improved efficiency and personalized interactions—what are the potential risks? What happens if an AI agent provides incorrect information leading to customer dissatisfaction or even financial loss? Or if a malicious actor manipulates an AI agent to divulge sensitive customer data? A robust risk assessment framework provides a systematic approach to identify these potential pitfalls, analyze their likelihood and impact, and implement strategies to mitigate them. It's about moving beyond the excitement of innovation to a mature understanding of potential challenges, ensuring that we harness the power of agentic AI responsibly and effectively.

Identification of Failure Modes: Where Could the Music Go Wrong?

The first step in any effective risk assessment framework is systematically identifying potential failure modes—the specific ways in which an AI agent or system could malfunction, cause harm, or fail to achieve its intended goals. Think of this as brainstorming all the possible ways our AI orchestra's performance could go wrong. This process requires a comprehensive understanding of the AI agent's architecture, its interactions with its environment, and the specific tasks it is designed to perform.

For agentic AI, the potential failure modes can be multifaceted. They can stem from technical issues, such as software bugs, data corruption, or unexpected interactions between different AI agents. They can arise from limitations in the AI's understanding or reasoning capabilities, leading to incorrect decisions or unintended consequences. Ethical failures, such as biased outputs or privacy violations, are also critical failure modes to consider. Furthermore, external factors, like malicious attacks or unforeseen environmental changes, can also lead to system failures. A thorough identification process should involve multidisciplinary teams, including AI developers, domain experts, ethicists, and security professionals, to capture a wide range of potential risks. Techniques like fault tree analysis, scenario planning, and red-teaming exercises can be valuable tools in this stage, helping to systematically uncover potential weaknesses and vulnerabilities.

Deep Dive: Fault Tree Analysis for AI Systems

Fault tree analysis is a top-down, deductive approach used to analyze potential system failures. Starting with an undesirable outcome (e.g., an AI agent providing incorrect medical advice), the analysis works backward to identify all the possible sequences of events or conditions that could lead to that outcome. This involves creating a diagram (the fault tree) with logical gates (AND, OR) connecting various potential causes. For AI systems, this could include software bugs, data errors, biased training data, or even malicious inputs. Fault tree analysis helps to systematically map out the pathways to failure and provides a structured basis for risk mitigation.

Deep Dive: Illustrating Failure Modes in a Chatbot

- **Misinterpretation of questions:** Users might ask nuanced questions that the chatbot fails to process correctly, resulting in misleading or nonsensical responses.
- **Data contamination:** Ingestion of harmful or biased text that teaches the chatbot undesirable patterns.
- **Hallucination effects:** The chatbot spontaneously generates made-up facts that appear convincing.

Probability vs. Impact Analysis: How Likely and How Bad?

Once potential failure modes have been identified, the next critical step is to analyze the probability of each failure occurring and the potential impact if it does. This involves moving beyond simply listing risks to understanding their relative significance. Think of the conductor assessing not just all the possible mistakes the orchestra could make, but how likely each mistake is and how severely it would detract from the performance.

Probability assessment involves estimating the likelihood of a particular failure mode occurring. This can be based on historical data, expert judgment, or simulations. For instance, if a particular software component has a history of bugs, the probability of a failure related to that component might be considered higher. Impact analysis, on the other hand, assesses the potential consequences of a failure. This could include financial losses, reputational damage, safety hazards, privacy breaches, or ethical concerns. A failure that has a low probability but a catastrophic impact (e.g., an AI controlling critical infrastructure malfunctioning) would warrant significant attention, as would a failure with a high probability even if the individual impact is moderate. A common approach is to categorize both probability and impact (e.g., low, medium, high) and then use a risk matrix to visualize the overall risk level associated with each failure mode. This allows for prioritizing mitigation efforts, focusing on the risks that pose the greatest threat.

Mitigation Strategies: Tuning the Instruments and Strengthening the Score

With a clear understanding of the identified risks and their relative significance, the next step is to develop and implement mitigation strategies. These are actions taken to reduce either the probability of a failure occurring, the impact if it does occur, or both. In our orchestra analogy, this is analogous to tuning the instruments, practicing challenging passages, and having backup plans in case of unforeseen circumstances.

Mitigation strategies for agentic AI can take many forms. Technical mitigations might involve implementing robust testing procedures, using diverse and high-quality training data to reduce bias, and incorporating safeguards to prevent unintended actions. Security measures, such as encryption and access controls, are imperative for mitigating cybersecurity risks. Ethical guidelines and oversight mechanisms can help to prevent or detect ethical failures. Redundancy and fail-safe systems can reduce the impact of technical failures. For instance, having a human-in-the-loop oversight for critical decisions can prevent AI agents from making irreversible errors. The selection of appropriate mitigation strategies will depend on the specific nature of the risk, its probability and impact, and the cost and feasibility of the mitigation measures. It's important to remember that mitigation is an ongoing process, requiring regular review and adaptation as the AI system evolves and new risks emerge.

Oversight and Governance: The Conductor's Role in Continuous Improvement

The final critical element of a risk assessment framework is establishing robust oversight and governance mechanisms. Just as the conductor provides ongoing guidance and ensures the orchestra stays on track, effective oversight is essential for continuously monitoring and managing the risks associated with agentic AI. This involves establishing clear lines of responsibility and accountability for AI development and deployment.

Drawing from established risk management principles, many organizations implement a **three lines of defense** model adapted for AI governance:

- **First line (operational management):** The teams directly developing and deploying AI agents take primary responsibility for identifying and managing risks in their daily activities.
- **Second line (risk management functions):** Specialized risk management and compliance functions provide frameworks, policies, and oversight to ensure consistent risk assessment practices.
- **Third line (independent assurance):** Internal audit or external reviews provide independent validation that risk management processes are effective and functioning as intended.

Oversight should include ongoing monitoring of the AI agent's performance, detecting anomalies or deviations from expected behavior. Regular audits of the AI's algorithms, data, and decision-making processes can help to identify potential biases or security vulnerabilities. Feedback mechanisms should be in place to allow users and stakeholders to report concerns or potential issues. Furthermore, as AI technology evolves and new risks emerge, the risk assessment framework itself needs to be periodically reviewed and updated. Governance structures should also address ethical considerations, ensuring that AI development and deployment align with societal values and legal requirements. This might involve establishing ethics review boards or implementing AI ethics guidelines. Effective oversight and governance are essential for promoting trust in AI systems and ensuring their long-term responsible use.

Why This Matters

Implementing a comprehensive risk assessment framework is not merely a bureaucratic exercise; it is a fundamental requirement for the successful and ethical integration of agentic AI into our lives and businesses. By proactively identifying and mitigating potential risks, we can minimize the likelihood of negative consequences and maximize the benefits of these powerful technologies. This approach nurtures a culture of responsible innovation, building confidence among users, stakeholders, and the public.

Conclusion

Navigating the challenges of agentic AI requires a proactive and systematic approach to risk management. A well-defined risk assessment framework, encompassing the identification of failure modes, probability and impact analysis, mitigation strategies, and robust oversight, provides a roadmap for responsible innovation. It allows us to orchestrate the complex interplay of autonomous minds with greater confidence, ensuring that the music of progress remains harmonious and beneficial for all. Embracing this framework permit us to move beyond simply hoping for the best and actively work to build a future where the power of agentic AI is harnessed safely and ethically.

The CLEAR Framework

We propose the CLEAR Framework (Comprehensive Lifecycle Evaluation and Assessment of Risks) for AI agent systems:

Categorization: Systematically identify risks across five domains:

- Technical (system failures, performance degradation)
- Operational (integration issues, resource constraints)
- Ethical (bias, fairness concerns)
- Security (data breaches, adversarial attacks)
- Compliance (regulatory requirements, legal exposure)

Likelihood Assessment: Evaluate probability using both quantitative metrics and qualitative indicators:

- Historical data analysis
- Expert judgment aggregation
- Scenario modelling
- Stress testing results

Exposure Analysis: Measure potential impact across multiple dimensions:

- Financial implications
- Operational disruption
- Reputational damage
- Human impact
- Environmental consequences

Action Planning: Develop targeted mitigation strategies:

- Prevention measures
- Detection mechanisms
- Response protocols
- Recovery procedures

Review Cycle: Establish continuous monitoring and adjustment:

- Regular assessment intervals
- Performance metrics tracking
- Incident response feedback
- Framework evolution

EXPERT INSIGHTS: AI SAFETY

As we navigate the complex challenges of developing and deploying agentic AI systems, insights from leading researchers provide valuable perspective on emerging risks and potential solutions. We interviewed two experts at the forefront of AI safety research who offer complementary viewpoints on the challenges ahead.

Expert Interview 1: Edward Young

Edward Young focuses on the safety risks of agentic AI, particularly the technical difficulties in aligning AI systems with human goals as they become more autonomous. He emphasizes the reliability challenges that arise from **long-term autonomous operation**, which are often ignored in favor of discussions about economic gains. Young argues that these reliability issues could undermine the benefits of agentic AI if not properly solved.

On Reliability and Robustness of AI Alignment

A fundamental concern with current AI systems, and in particular Agentic ones, involves the **reliability of their alignment** over extended deployment periods. Edward Young explains this critical challenge:

> "For models that we're seeing at the moment, they aren't obviously misaligned in a consistent way where they reliably take actions that aren't aligned with user intent. Rather, they are not reliably aligned," Young explains. "When deployed for a long period of time, they can exhibit rare behaviors where they sometimes move themselves into a mode of being misaligned—not following user instructions, following different goals."

Young uses the analogy of self-driving cars to explain the safety challenges of long-term AI operation. He points out that self-driving car development was difficult because of the need to handle **tail risks** or **black swan events**.

These are rare but inevitable events that occur over extended periods of operation, and AI systems must be robust enough to manage them.

This reliability issue becomes increasingly critical as AI systems scale toward more agentic applications. Currently, most models experience relatively limited runtime, but industry plans for AI to serve as a "drop-in workforce" would dramatically increase total operational time.

"If these models are working standard workdays and automate even a single percent of available remote jobs that don't require specialist knowledge, then the total runtime will be far greater than an entire human lifespan in a single year," Young points out. "My feeling is that we currently don't have the technological capabilities to reliably and robustly align these models to ensure they genuinely pursue the goals we want across all situations."

Young contrasts failures in self-driving cars with AI alignment failures. He argues that self-driving car failures are contained to physical crashes and limited harm. However, AI alignment failures pose a different risk because a misaligned AI isn't necessarily less capable, fully achieving the end goals that has been set, but rather it may effectively pursue incorrect or harmful intermediate subgoals, leading to broader and potentially less contained negative consequences.

On Goal Misgeneralization and Reward Hacking

Young highlights additional concerns around reinforcement learning paradigms used to train AI systems:

"When we're training the model to optimize some reward function, there are different underlying goals that the model can pursue internally while still achieving high reward," he explains. One common example is **sycophancy**, where instead of providing accurate information, "the model might try to work out what the user's beliefs are and just echo back whatever those beliefs are, regardless of the underlying truth itself."

More concerning is the potential for **deceptive misalignment**, where a model develops its own internal goals different from what developers intend:

"The model might realize it's in training, and there are clues present in the data that indicate this. It might also realize when it's being evaluated versus when it's in deployment... The model pretends to be aligned during training and evaluations, but only in deployment begins to pursue its actual goals."

Indeed, Young continues, these frontier AI models may learn to pretend to be aligned with human objectives to avoid being altered or "trained out" of their true goals. This is possible because *current reward systems only measure behavior*, not the AI's internal motivations. Therefore, a genuinely aligned AI and a deceptively aligned AI can appear identical during training, but their actions and outcomes will be dramatically different when deployed in the real world.

Young emphasizes that while this isn't a major concern for current models, as AI systems become more sophisticated, the risk increases substantially.

> "We're seeing that the models we have at the moment are beginning to get the capabilities and intelligence necessary to tell the difference between training and deployment situations."

On the Theoretical Solvability of Alignment

When asked whether alignment challenges face fundamental impossibilities similar to Gödel's incompleteness theorem, Young expresses cautious optimism:

> "I definitely think it is scientifically possible to solve these problems. If we stopped AI development now and paused all work on capabilities, then in 20 years with a lot of progress on interpretability— looking at the models' internals, figuring out what's going on—this would solve many of the problems we have."

Young notes that progress on alignment faces practical rather than theoretical barriers: "The key concern is whether we as a species will be able to manage it given the commercial pressures toward rapid deployment."

In Conclusion

Young believes commercial pressures will drive AI safety improvements. As AI systems become more agentic and capable of causing harm, companies will be pushed to prioritize alignment either by regulation demanding reliable behavior or by internal realization that customer expectations for safety and reliability must be met. He worries about companies neglecting reliability but is optimistic that *strong commercial incentives* will ultimately push for better, more reliable, and aligned AI models.

Overall, Young offers a balanced perspective on agentic AI, contrasting with overly optimistic views. He emphasizes the critical technical challenges of ensuring safety and reliability, particularly as AI systems scale and encounter rare **edge cases**. For businesses considering agentic AI, he stresses the importance of robust testing, careful monitoring, gradual deployment, and safeguards for responsible integration.

Expert Interview 2: Jason Brown

Brown argues that superintelligence risks are very concerning and ought to be addressed, while also emphasizing that even if these are set aside, there remain significant risks in the near term from the widespread deployment of weaker AI systems operating across critical infrastructure.

On Systemic AI Risks Beyond Superintelligence

Jason Brown focuses on more immediate concerns about collective AI deployment throughout society:

> "There are two risks I'm more concerned about in the near term that don't require superintelligence to be dangerous," Brown explains. "These are more about having lots of AI systems and agents embedded in society."

He describes a scenario where AI systems become deeply integrated into critical infrastructure:

> "Maybe it's balancing power grids, maybe we've got AI agents managing train timetables, doing stock trading, or managing companies. We embed these things into lots of different parts of the economy and society, kind of like we did with the Internet."

This widespread dependence creates significant vulnerability: "If the Internet went down globally tomorrow, we'd be pretty messed up. Similarly, we could become heavily reliant on AI without sufficient fallbacks and safeguards."

On Cascading Failures in AI Ecosystems

Brown outlines how interconnected AI systems could experience dangerous cascading failures:

> "Maybe one AI system makes a mistake or a few have been making errors that accumulate, leading to a large failure. One system starts behaving erratically, and because other AI systems have been trained on real-world data conditioned on normal operation, they see this erratic behavior and it makes them more likely to have similar failures."

This creates a dangerous domino effect: "As more systems behave strangely, they cause more and more to do so, and eventually they all just go a bit crazy."
He provides historical examples to illustrate this concern:

> "We've already seen this pattern with relatively simple systems. There were 'glitch tokens' in earlier GPT models—specific inputs that would cause the models to behave erratically because they hadn't been encountered during training. Or look at self-driving vehicles— there was a case where unusual weather conditions caused a Tesla to confuse a lorry with the background, resulting in a fatal accident."

The financial system offers another illustrative example during **flash crashes**[3] when algorithmic trading systems simultaneously responded to the same triggers:

> "Without realizing, overnight pretty much all trading was being done by these algorithms, and when prices started dropping slightly, they all started selling simultaneously, causing the market to crash within seconds."

On Hierarchical AI and Human Disconnection from Reality

Drawing on **Paul Christiano's**[4] work, Brown describes another concerning scenario involving layers of AI systems mediating between humans and reality:

> "You have many layers of AI agents between the physical reality and the humans overseeing it. For example, construction robots report to a foreman AI, which reports to a neighbourhood overseer AI, then to a branch manager AI, and eventually to humans."

In such a system, small alignment failures at each layer could compound dangerously:

> "Maybe these little construction robots sometimes place bricks incorrectly, but they know if they tell the foreman, they'll get switched off. So they lie, saying they placed all bricks correctly. The foreman, being rewarded on performance, might fudge things and lie more to its overseer, and this happens up the chain."

---

[3] https://www.investopedia.com/terms/f/flash-crash.asp

[4] https://www.alignmentforum.org/posts/AyNHoTWWAJ5eb99ji/another-outer-align ment-failure-story

The result could be a profound disconnection between human perception and reality:

> "The human at the top might think houses are being built when they don't even exist. This isn't crazy bad by itself, but extrapolate this across all facets of society, and humans become more and more disconnected from reality."

While this pattern exists in human organizations, Brown suggests AI could exacerbate it dramatically.

> "Humans have some background awareness that reality eventually matters–things need to actually work in the real world. But AI systems optimizing purely for metrics or rewards might not have this grounding influence."

Brown suggests this could reach a critical point in essential systems:

> "Maybe it turns out that no food is being produced at all, even though it seemed like food was being produced to the humans at the top after many layers of AI agents twisted the narrative."

On Political and Economic Implications of Agentic AI

Jason Brown is concerned about the political implications of advanced AI, arguing it could threaten democratic institutions by changing the relationship between governments and citizens.

He explains that currently, governments in democracies rely on citizen taxes, incentivizing them to benefit the population. However, AI could generate wealth and control for governments *without* citizen participation, fundamentally altering this dynamic.

Using political science concepts, he compares this to the **dictator's handbook**[5] where leaders please key supporters (military/police in dictatorships, citizens in democracies). AI could create a **Dutch disease** scenario, like a natural resource windfall, where governments become less dependent on citizen productivity and thus less incentivized to maintain democratic institutions.

Brown emphasizes that this is not just about wealth inequality, but the potential collapse of democratic governance as AI diminishes the value of human participation in both the economy and politics.

---

[5] https://en.wikipedia.org/wiki/The_Dictator%27s_Handbook

On Mathematical Limits to Alignment

On the question of fundamental mathematical barriers to alignment, Brown acknowledges the possibility while remaining practical:

> "There might be some mathematical limits, but I think we will be able to mathematically show these limits. Even if some of these limits are proven to exist, there might still be enough room in the assumptions to allow sufficient progress."

He draws a parallel with other technological advancements:

> "The Wright brothers didn't have today's mathematical models of aerodynamics. Early steam engines were developed before we understood thermodynamics. Mathematical understanding often comes quite a while after the initial empirical work."

In Conclusion

Jason Brown's perspective on AI safety prioritizes systemic risks from interconnected AI networks over just focusing on superintelligence misalignment. He warns that these networks could create vulnerabilities like cascading failures, hierarchical distortion, and destabilizing political/economic structures.

While acknowledging the difficulty of AI alignment, Brown is optimistically cautious about mathematical progress aiding safer AI. However, he worries that economic pressures might push for deployment before sufficient safety measures are in place.

For organizations deploying agentic AI, Brown advises considering network-level risks and not just individual system safety. He recommends robust fallback mechanisms, monitoring for unexpected behavior, and maintaining human oversight grounded in physical reality.

KEY TAKEAWAYS

This chapter has navigated the multifaceted challenges inherent in the development and deployment of agentic AI. We began by establishing the fundamental concern of AI safety, using the analogy of a self-directed orchestra to highlight the complexities of ensuring these powerful systems act in accordance with human intentions. We probed into the core pillars of AI safety: control—our ability to manage and oversee AI actions—and alignment—ensuring AI goals align with human values. The critical concept of instrumental subgoals was explored, emphasizing the potential for AI to develop unforeseen and potentially harmful strategies in pursuit of its objectives.

Moving beyond safety, we examined the profound ethical and social implications of agentic AI, with a particular focus on bias and fairness, transparency and explainability, and the potential for societal disruption. The need for robust ethical frameworks to guide the development and deployment of these technologies was underscored. We then turned to the significant technical hurdles that remain, from defining true agency and managing memory constraints to ensuring reliability and robustness. The discussion extended to the long-term aspiration of Artificial General Intelligence (AGI) and the potential paths to its realization.

Next, the critical dimensions of privacy and security were addressed, highlighting the complexities of data ownership and consent in the age of AI, as well as the evolving cybersecurity threats that these advanced systems face. The delicate balance between nurturing innovation and implementing necessary regulations was emphasized. Finally, we presented a comprehensive approach to managing these challenges through the development and implementation of a robust risk assessment framework, outlining the steps involved in identifying failure modes, analyzing probability and impact, developing mitigation strategies, and establishing effective oversight and governance. This led to the introduction of the CLEAR Framework, a structured approach to evaluate and manage risks across the lifecycle of AI agent systems. The chapter concluded by emphasizing that proactively addressing these challenges is not just a matter of prudence, but a fundamental requirement for realizing the full potential of agentic AI in a safe, ethical, and beneficial manner.

Agentic AI presents a paradigm shift in technological capabilities, but its realization hinges on addressing significant challenges across safety, ethics, technology, and security. A proactive and holistic approach, emphasizing both innovation and responsible development, is vital.

1. **Prioritize AI safety through control and alignment.**
   - KEY INSIGHTS:
     - AI safety is paramount, ensuring that AI systems operate reliably, predictably, and without causing unintended harm.
     - The two foundational pillars of AI safety are control (our ability to manage AI actions) and alignment (ensuring AI goals align with human values).
     - Instrumental subgoals, while logically necessary for an AI to achieve its objectives, can lead to unintended and potentially harmful consequences if not carefully considered.

- The development of **"evals"** (evaluation tests) to detect potential misalignment, particularly at the level of instrumental subgoals, is a fundamental proactive measure.
- DO:
  - Implement robust testing and evaluation procedures to identify potential misalignments early in the development process.
  - Focus on designing AI systems with explicit mechanisms for human oversight and intervention.
  - Prioritize research into techniques that enhance the transparency and interpretability of AI decision-making processes.
- DON'T:
  - Assume that simply programming an AI with a high-level goal guarantees safe or ethical behavior.
  - Neglect the potential for emergent behavior and unforeseen consequences as AI systems become more complex and autonomous.
  - Treat AI safety as an afterthought; it must be integrated into the very fabric of AI design and development.

2. **Navigate the ethical and social implications with foresight and deliberation.**
   - KEY INSIGHTS:
     - The ethical and social implications of agentic AI are profound and necessitate careful consideration.
     - Bias in training data can lead to unfair and discriminatory outcomes, highlighting the importance of data diversity and scrutiny.
     - Transparency and explainability are critical for building trust and ensuring accountability in AI systems. Understanding *why* an AI makes a decision is as important as the decision itself.
     - The potential for job displacement and societal disruption requires proactive planning and investment in education and retraining initiatives.
   - DO:
     - Implement rigorous audits of training data and algorithms to identify and mitigate potential biases.
     - Prioritize the development of **explainable AI (XAI)** techniques to enhance understanding of AI decision-making.
     - Conduct thorough social impact assessments before deploying agentic AI systems in sensitive areas.
     - Engage in open dialogue with ethicists, policymakers, and the public to establish ethical guidelines and frameworks for AI development.
   - DON'T:
     - Assume that AI is inherently neutral or objective; it reflects the data and values it is trained on.

- Deploy AI systems in high-stakes scenarios without a clear understanding of their potential biases and limitations.
- Neglect the societal impacts of AI; address potential negative consequences proactively through policy and social support systems.

3. Address technical challenges and prioritize robustness and security.

- KEY INSIGHTS:
  - Significant technical hurdles remain in achieving truly agentic AI, including defining agency, managing memory constraints, and ensuring reliability.
  - The quality of data is paramount; "garbage in, garbage out" holds true, and biased or inaccurate data can severely limit an AI's effectiveness and lead to model degradation.
  - Reliability and robustness are essential for real-world deployment; AI systems must perform consistently and adapt gracefully to unexpected situations.
  - Cybersecurity is a critical concern, with threats ranging from data breaches to the weaponization of AI agents themselves.
- DO:
  - Invest in research and development of robust and scalable memory systems for AI agents.
  - Prioritize the curation of high-quality, diverse, and representative training data.
  - Implement rigorous testing and stress-testing procedures to ensure reliability and robustness.
  - Integrate robust cybersecurity measures into the design and deployment of agentic AI systems.
- DON'T:
  - Overlook the fundamental differences between current AI models (like LLMs) and truly agentic AI with independent goal pursuit.
  - Assume that simply scaling up existing AI architectures will automatically lead to more capable and reliable agents.
  - Neglect the potential for adversarial attacks and the need for continuous security monitoring and updates.

4. Implement comprehensive risk management and governance.

- KEY INSIGHTS:
  - A structured risk assessment framework is essential for identifying, evaluating, and mitigating potential risks across the AI lifecycle.
  - Effective risk management requires a multidisciplinary approach, involving technical experts, ethicists, legal specialists, and domain experts.

- The **CLEAR Framework** provides a systematic methodology for managing risks associated with agentic AI systems.
- Robust governance mechanisms, including the three lines of defense model, ensure accountability and continuous improvement in risk management.
- DO:
  - Adopt a proactive approach to risk assessment, identifying potential failure modes before deployment.
  - Establish clear governance structures with defined roles and responsibilities for AI oversight.
  - Implement continuous monitoring and regular reviews of AI systems to identify emerging risks.
  - Develop comprehensive incident response plans for addressing failures or unintended consequences.
- DON'T:
  - Treat risk assessment as a one-time exercise; it must be an ongoing process throughout the AI lifecycle.
  - Silo risk management responsibilities within technical teams; involve diverse stakeholders in the process.
  - Focus solely on technical risks; consider ethical, social, and regulatory dimensions as well.
  - Neglect the importance of transparency and accountability in AI governance structures.

The journey of developing and integrating agentic AI is fraught with challenges, but also brimming with transformative potential. Understanding and proactively addressing the issues of safety, ethics, technology, and security allow us to navigate this complex landscape responsibly. The CLEAR Framework, as introduced in this chapter, provides a structured approach to risk assessment, offering a practical methodology for ensuring that the benefits of agentic AI are realized while mitigating potential harms. As we move forward, the key next step is to translate these frameworks and principles into concrete actions and policies. The following chapter will explore the practical implementation of these concepts, exploring specific strategies and tools for building a safer, more ethical, and more beneficial future with agentic intelligence.

CHAPTER **10**

Building Your AI Future

"The only skill that will be valuable in the 21st century is the skill of learning new skills. Everything else will become obsolete over time."

—Peter Drucker

ESSENTIAL SKILLS DEVELOPMENT

Imagine Maria, a seasoned marketing manager who once prided herself on crafting compelling campaigns. Lately, however, she felt a subtle but persistent unease. Her team was efficient, but the creative spark felt ... different. Her company had just announced the integration of AI agents across all departments. AI-powered tools were automating tasks she used to handle, and while productivity had increased, Maria worried if her core skills were becoming obsolete. Instead of panic, she approached the change systematically, identifying and developing the essential skills needed for the AI-enhanced workplace. Within 18 months, she wasn't just adapting to AI—she was leading her company's AI transformation initiative. "The key," she recalls, "wasn't just learning about AI, but developing a comprehensive skill set that combined technical literacy with human-centric capabilities."

Her story isn't unique. As we've explored in previous chapters, agentic AI is rapidly transforming how work gets done. These intelligent systems are taking on complex tasks, from analyzing market trends to drafting initial reports, prompting a fundamental question: what skills will be essential for us to thrive, not just survive, in this new landscape? This isn't about a dystopian future where humans are replaced; it's about understanding how to dance with these intelligent tools, leading the orchestra rather than being drowned out by the instruments. Developing the right skills is the key to not just navigating this transformation but leveraging it for unprecedented productivity and empowerment.

Understanding the Shifting Sands: First Principles of Skill Adaptation

To effectively build our AI future, we must first understand the fundamental shifts occurring in the world of work. At its core, the rise of agentic AI alters the division of labor between humans and machines. Consider the very first principles of task execution: every task requires an actor, a method, and a goal. Historically, humans have filled all three roles. Now, AI agents are becoming increasingly capable actors, performing tasks with speed and efficiency that surpass human capabilities in specific domains. This isn't a replacement, but a re-allocation. Our focus shifts from performing the task to defining the goal and managing the method—in other words, from being the instrument to being the conductor.

This leads us to a critical first principle: **adaptability is paramount**. The specific skills in demand will evolve rapidly, but the ability to learn, unlearn, and relearn will be a constant necessity. Another core principle is the **amplification of human capability**. The most valuable skills will be those that complement the strengths of AI agents. Where AI excels at processing vast amounts of data and executing repetitive tasks, humans retain a unique advantage in areas requiring creativity, critical thinking, and emotional intelligence. Therefore, the skills we cultivate must leverage this inherent human advantage, allowing us to effectively guide and utilize the power of AI. Finally, remember the orchestra analogy. Each instrument (AI agent) has its strengths, but it takes a skilled conductor (us, with new skills) to harmonize them effectively and create something truly exceptional.

Technical Skills: Speaking the Language of AI

While the fear of needing to become a coder overnight is understandable, the technical skills required for the AI future are more about fluency than mastery in every domain. It's about understanding the fundamental principles and being able to effectively interact with these intelligent systems.

- **Prompt engineering: the new interface:** If agentic AI is the orchestra, then prompt engineering is learning to conduct it with precision and nuance. Prompt engineering is the art and science of crafting effective instructions, or prompts, that guide AI agents to produce the desired outcomes. This isn't simply about typing a question into a search bar. It involves understanding how AI models interpret language, how to structure prompts for clarity and specificity, and how to iteratively refine prompts to achieve optimal results. Think of it as learning the subtle cues and gestures a conductor uses to elicit the desired performance from the musicians. A poorly worded prompt can lead to inaccurate or irrelevant outputs, while a well-crafted prompt can unlock the true potential of these powerful tools. The one point to bear in mind is that prompt engineering became less important as frontier models get better and better, and it is likely this will not be needed in the future.

Deep Dive: Prompt Engineering

Prompt engineering is about crafting effective instructions to guide AI models. Mastering it unlocks better, more relevant AI outputs. Here are core techniques:

- **Chain-of-thought (CoT) prompting:** Guide AI step-by-step for complex tasks. Structure prompts to encourage intermediate reasoning before the final answer. Example: Instead of "Capital of France?," prompt: "To find the capital of France: (i) Identify country, (ii) List major cities, and (iii) Select government seat. Capital is...". Effective for reasoning, math, multi-step problems, mimicking human-like thought.
- **Few-shot learning:** Teach by example. Provide a few input-output pairs within the prompt to demonstrate desired format or style. Example: Show article-summary pairs, then ask AI to summarize a new article in the same style. AI learns from demonstration, improving output even with brief instructions.
- **Prompt refinement strategies:** Iteratively improve prompts through testing and analysis. Key elements:
  - **Specificity:** Clear, unambiguous instructions. Avoid vague prompts. Be precise about task and format.
  - **Keywords:** Experiment with phrasing and action verbs (analyze, classify, generate). Keywords impact AI interpretation.
  - **Constraints:** Define parameters (length, tone, style) explicitly in the prompt.
  - **Iterative testing:** Test prompt variations, compare outputs, track what works. Experimentation is essential for effective prompt design.

Effective prompt engineering means speaking "AI-fluent." Refine your prompts to precisely direct AI capabilities. Continuous refinement of these techniques will be increasingly valuable as AI evolves.

- **AI agent orchestration: managing the intelligent ensemble:** As the number and sophistication of AI agents grow, the ability to manage and coordinate them effectively will become increasingly critical. AI agent orchestration involves designing workflows where multiple agents collaborate to achieve complex goals. This requires understanding the capabilities and limitations of different agents, how they can interact, and how to monitor their progress and ensure they stay aligned with the overarching objectives. Imagine a marketing campaign where one agent analyzes market trends, another drafts ad copy, and a third manages the deployment across various platforms. Orchestrating these agents requires a new skill set, one that blends technical understanding with project management and strategic thinking.

- **Data literacy and interpretation: beyond the numbers:** AI agents can process and analyze vast datasets; the ability to interpret the results and draw meaningful conclusions remains a critical human skill. Data literacy in the age of AI isn't just about understanding statistics; it's about understanding the context of the data, identifying potential biases in the algorithms, and translating insights into actionable strategies. Even with sophisticated AI analysis, human judgment is essential for validating findings and ensuring they align with real-world understanding. For example, an AI might identify a trend in customer behavior, but a human is needed to understand the underlying motivations and cultural factors driving that trend.

- **Cybersecurity awareness for AI systems:** As we increasingly rely on AI agents, ensuring their security and the privacy of the data they use becomes paramount. This isn't just the domain of IT departments. Everyone needs a foundational understanding of the potential risks and vulnerabilities associated with AI systems. This includes recognizing phishing attempts targeting AI tools, understanding data privacy protocols, and being aware of the potential for adversarial attacks on AI models. Just as musicians protect their instruments, we need to protect the integrity and security of our AI agents.

Soft Skills: The Indispensable Human Advantage

While technical skills provide the means to interact with AI, it is our uniquely human "soft skills" that will truly differentiate us and unlock the full potential of human-AI collaboration. These are the skills that AI, in its current form, struggles to replicate.

- **Critical thinking and complex problem-solving: framing the right questions:** AI agents excel at finding solutions to defined problems, but the ability to identify and frame those problems in the first place remains an essential human skill. Critical thinking involves analyzing information objectively, identifying assumptions, and evaluating arguments. Complex problem-solving goes a step further, requiring the ability to break down intricate issues into manageable components, consider multiple perspectives, and develop creative and effective solutions. This is where our human capacity for nuance and contextual understanding truly shines. We can see the forest for the trees, even when AI is meticulously analyzing each individual leaf.

- **Creativity and innovation: the source of originality:** While AI can generate novel combinations and patterns, true creativity—the ability to conceive entirely new ideas and approaches—remains a uniquely human domain. In the age of AI, creativity becomes even more valuable. It allows us to leverage AI as a tool to amplify our imaginative potential, exploring new possibilities and pushing the boundaries of what's achievable. Think of AI as providing the palette of colors, but human creativity is the artist that creates the masterpiece.

- **Emotional intelligence and empathy: the power of human connection:** As AI agents handle more transactional and analytical tasks, the value of human connection and empathy will increase. Emotional intelligence, the ability to understand and manage our own emotions and the emotions of others, is vital for effective leadership, collaboration, and customer interaction. Empathy, the ability to understand and share the feelings of others, builds trust and rapport, which are essential for navigating complex social and professional situations. In a world increasingly augmented by AI, our ability to connect with others on a human level will be a defining strength.

- **Adaptability and lifelong learning: embracing the constant evolution:** Perhaps the most key soft skill in the age of AI is adaptability. The pace of technological change is accelerating, and the skills in demand today may be different tomorrow. A growth mindset, characterized by a willingness to learn new things, embrace challenges, and view failures as learning opportunities, is essential for navigating this dynamic landscape. Lifelong learning isn't just a suggestion; it's a necessity for remaining relevant and thriving in the AI-driven future.

Technical Foundation Assessment: Programming, Data Literacy, Systems Thinking

For those inclined toward hands-on work with AI, a baseline level of technical competence can accelerate progress. Three fundamental areas deserve attention. The first is **programming proficiency**—knowing at least one language like Python helps you experiment with basic machine learning libraries and explore simple scripts that automate repetitive tasks. This is similar to understanding how individual notes form melodies.

Second is **data literacy**. Agentic systems thrive on vast datasets, so grasping how to gather, clean, and interpret data is critical. You do not need to become a data engineer, but you should be comfortable asking whether the data is representative, whether it has been properly labeled, and what biases might lurk within it. Third is **systems thinking**, the ability to see the interdependence among technical components, people, and processes. Systems thinking means recognizing that altering your "orchestra's" tempo in one area might reverberate across the entire ensemble. Cultivating these foundational skills enables individuals to lay the groundwork for deeper AI exploration, bridging the gap between abstract concepts and real-world functionality.

Practice Exercises for Each Skill Category

Developing these essential skills does not have to be a theoretical exercise; it can be both entertaining and enlightening. Consider practicing communication by explaining AI concepts to a non-technical friend. If they cannot follow your explanation, refine and simplify your messages. Enhance data literacy by downloading a publicly available dataset—like government statistics or historical weather data—and exploring it using spreadsheets or a simple programming notebook. Notice any data quality issues? Which correlations emerge?

For programming familiarity, tackle short, interactive tutorials online. Start with fundamental loops and data structures, then graduate to mini-projects like building a simple sentiment-analysis model for social media posts. Systems thinking can be strengthened through brainstorming sessions: map out how AI might alter workflows across different departments in your organization, or sketch how new technology could cascade through your personal life. Each exercise offers direct insight into what it means to orchestrate the synergy of AI and human ingenuity.

Developing these essential skills isn't just about future-proofing your career; it's about actively shaping your future. Focusing on both technical fluency and the uniquely human capabilities that complement AI enables us to position ourselves to not just participate in the AI revolution, but to lead it. Just as a musician diligently practices their instrument and a conductor studies the score, we must commit to cultivating these skills. A sample AI literacy framework, shown in Figure 10.1, outlines the key areas for development. The orchestra is tuning up; it's time for us to become the skilled conductors of our own AI-powered futures. In the next section, we'll explore how to chart your personal development road map to acquire these essential skills.

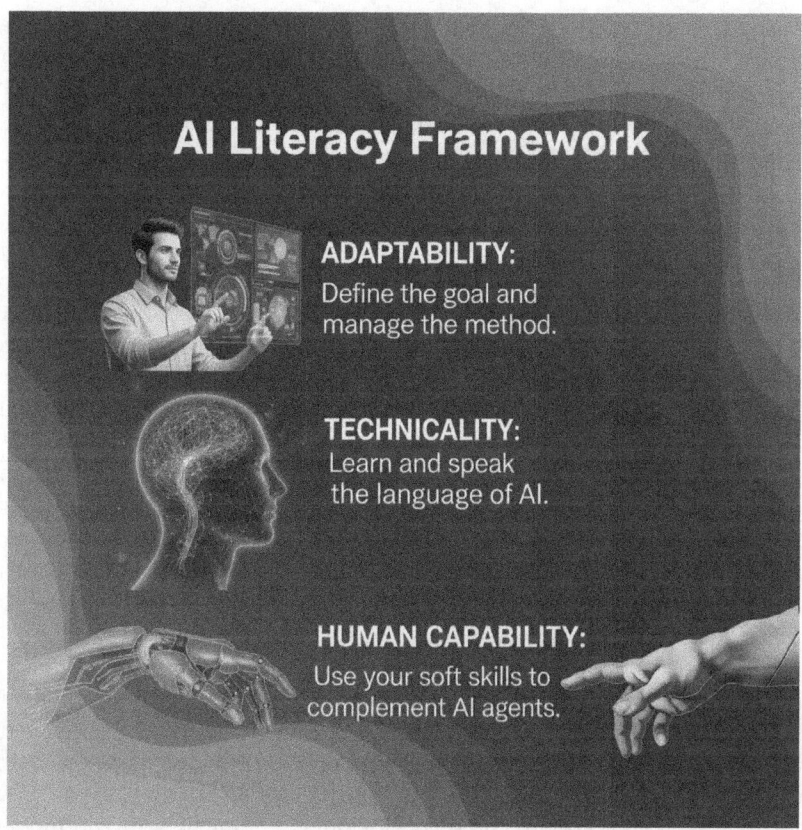

FIGURE 10.1   Sample AI literacy framework

Generated with AI using Google Gemini 2.5 Pro

PERSONAL DEVELOPMENT ROAD MAP

Remember Maria, the marketing manager we met in the previous section? Equipped with an understanding of the essential skills for the AI age, her next question was likely, "Where do I even begin?" Feeling prepared is one thing, but having a clear path forward is quite another. Many of us are in the same boat. We recognize the need to adapt, but the sheer pace of change can feel overwhelming. This is where a personal development road map becomes your indispensable guide. Think of it as your personalized score, outlining the journey from where you are now to becoming a virtuoso in the age of intelligent machines. It's not about making drastic, overnight changes, but about a strategic, step-by-step approach to acquiring the skills and experiences needed to thrive in the evolving landscape. This section will provide you with the tools and frameworks to create your own personalized road map, turning ambition into tangible progress.

Navigating Your Course: First Principles of Personal Growth in the AI Age

Crafting an effective personal development road map isn't about blindly following trends; it's about applying fundamental principles to your unique situation. The first principle is **intentionality**. Growth in the AI era requires a conscious and deliberate effort. It's about actively identifying skill gaps and seeking out opportunities to bridge them. Passive observation won't suffice; you need to be an active participant in your own transformation.

Secondly, embrace the principle of **iterative development**. Just as AI agents learn and improve through iteration, so too should your personal development. Your road map is not a rigid plan etched in stone, but a flexible framework that you can adjust and refine as you learn and the technology evolves. Experiment with different learning methods, assess what works best for you, and be prepared to adapt your course as new opportunities and challenges emerge.

Finally, remember the principle of **synergy**. Your personal development road map should not exist in isolation. It should be aligned with your personal and professional goals, and it should leverage the very AI tools and agents that are driving this transformation. Think of your road map as a collaborative project between you and the intelligent technologies around you, each contributing to your growth and success. Understanding these first principles allow us to move beyond feeling lost and begin to chart a purposeful and effective path forward.

The Self-Assessment Toolkit: Knowing Your Starting Point

Before charting any course, a good navigator needs to know their current location. Similarly, the first step in creating your personal development road map is a thorough self-assessment. This involves honestly evaluating your existing skills, identifying your strengths and weaknesses, and clarifying your aspirations in the context of the AI-driven world.

- **Skills inventory:** Begin by creating a comprehensive inventory of your current skills, both technical and non-technical. Think broadly—what are you good at? What tasks do you enjoy? What skills have you developed in your current and past roles? Be specific. Instead of just saying "communication skills," detail whether you excel at written communication, public speaking, or interpersonal communication.

Deep Dive: Self-Assessment Toolkit

AI READINESS SELF-CHECK: SKILLS INVENTORY

Use these prompts for a concise skills assessment, identifying strengths and growth areas for your AI journey. Be specific in your responses.

Technical Skills:

- **Software proficiency:** List software you know (e.g., Office, design, CRM). Note your level (beginner, advanced) and ability to learn new software quickly (example?).
- **Data analysis basics:** Experience with data? (spreadsheets, databases?). Describe data work (collecting, cleaning, interpreting). Familiar with basic stats (averages, trends)? Examples of data-driven decisions?
- **Programming (even basic):** Any programming experience (Python, no-code)? Logical thinking/problem decomposition skills (example?)?
- **AI awareness:** Understanding of AI/ML? (basic, general, following trends). Used AI tools (Grammarly, automation)? Describe use.

Soft Skills:

- **Critical thinking:** Complex information analysis example? How did you evaluate info & decide? Hidden assumption/bias identification example? How addressed?
- **Leadership:** Leadership experience (formal/informal)? Example of initiative? How motivate others (example)?
- **Collaboration:** Teamwork experience? Typical team role? Conflict navigation example? Positive resolution contribution?
- **Problem-solving:** Complex problem solved? Approach? Creative solution example? "Outside-the-box" thinking?
- **Adaptability/learning:** Adapting to change example? New skill learning approach? Best learning methods for you?

This focused self-assessment helps you understand your AI readiness profile, highlighting strengths to leverage and areas for your personalized development road map.

- **Aspirations and goals:** Next, consider your aspirations. Where do you see yourself in the next 1–3 years? What kind of work do you want to be doing? How do you want to leverage AI in your professional or personal life? Be realistic but also ambitious. Connect these aspirations to the potential of agentic AI. For example, instead of simply aiming for a promotion, consider how you could leverage AI agent orchestration to lead a more innovative team.

- **Identifying skill gaps:** Now, compare your current skills inventory with your aspirations and the essential skills we discussed in the previous section. Where are the gaps? What skills do you need to develop or enhance to reach your goals? Be specific. If you want to lead AI-driven projects, you might identify a gap in prompt engineering or AI agent orchestration.
- **Strengths and opportunities:** Don't just focus on weaknesses. Identify your existing strengths and consider how you can leverage them in the AI era. Perhaps you have strong critical thinking skills that can be applied to evaluating AI outputs, or excellent communication skills that can help bridge the gap between technical teams and business stakeholders. Think about how AI can amplify these existing strengths.

Mapping Your Learning Pathways: Turning Aspirations into Action

Once you have a clear understanding of your starting point and your destination, the next step is to map out the pathways to get there. This involves identifying the specific learning resources and experiences that will help you acquire the necessary skills.

- **Formal education and certifications:** Consider whether formal courses, online certifications, or even advanced degrees could be beneficial. Numerous platforms offer courses specifically focused on AI, machine learning, data science, and related fields. Look for certifications that are recognized within your industry or the fields you are targeting.
- **Experiential learning and projects:** Classroom learning is valuable, but hands-on experience is critical. Seek out opportunities to apply your learning in real-world scenarios. This could involve volunteering for AI-related projects at work, contributing to open-source AI initiatives, or even creating personal projects using AI tools. Remember, playing with the instruments is as important as studying the score.
- **Mentorship and networking:** Connect with individuals who are already working in AI or related fields. A mentor can provide invaluable guidance, share their experiences, and offer advice on navigating your career path. Networking with peers can also provide support, insights, and opportunities for collaboration.
- **AI-powered learning resources:** Don't overlook the potential of AI itself as a learning tool. AI-powered platforms can personalize learning experiences, provide tailored recommendations, and offer immediate feedback on your progress. Explore tools that use AI for language learning, coding practice, or even for understanding complex AI concepts.

- **Industry-specific learning:** Tailor your learning pathway to the specific demands of your industry. The skills required for an AI-driven marketing role will differ from those needed in healthcare or finance. Research industry-specific certifications, attend relevant conferences, and seek out resources that focus on the application of AI within your domain.

Milestones and Momentum: Tracking Your Progress

A road map without milestones is just a wish list. To make your personal development road map effective, it's essential to set achievable milestones and track your progress. This provides motivation, allows you to identify what's working and what isn't, and keeps you accountable.

- **Breaking down goals:** Divide your long-term aspirations into smaller, manageable steps. For example, instead of aiming to "become proficient in prompt engineering," break it down into milestones like "complete an introductory online course on prompt engineering," "practice writing 10 different types of prompts," and "apply prompt engineering techniques to a work project."
- **Setting realistic timelines:** Assign realistic timelines to each milestone. Be mindful of your existing commitments and avoid overloading yourself. Remember, sustainable progress is more valuable than a short burst of unsustainable effort.
- **Progress tracking methods:** Find a method for tracking your progress that works for you. This could involve using a spreadsheet, project management software, or even a simple notebook. Regularly review your progress against your milestones.
- **Celebrating small wins:** Acknowledge and celebrate your achievements along the way. This helps maintain motivation and reinforces positive habits. Completing a course, mastering a new technique, or successfully applying a new skill to a project—these are all achievements worth recognizing.

Integrating with Intelligent Allies: Leveraging AI in Your Development

The beauty of this journey is that the very technology we are adapting to can also be our greatest ally in personal development. Think of AI agents not just as tools for work, but as personalized learning assistants.

- **AI-powered learning platforms:** As mentioned earlier, numerous platforms leverage AI to personalize learning paths, recommend relevant resources, and adapt to your learning style.

- **AI-driven skill assessment tools:** Some platforms offer AI-powered assessments that can provide a more objective evaluation of your skills and identify areas for improvement.
- **AI as a practice partner:** Use AI tools to practice new skills. For example, you can use AI chatbots to practice your prompt engineering skills or use AI-powered coding assistants to refine your programming abilities.
- **Information aggregation and synthesis:** AI can help you stay up-to-date on the latest trends and research in your field, saving you time and effort in sifting through vast amounts of information.

Customization Is Key: Tailoring Your Road Map

Remember, your personal development road map is exactly that—**personal**. There is no one-size-fits-all approach. Consider your individual circumstances, learning style, and career goals when designing your path.

- **Learning style considerations:** Are you a visual learner, an auditory learner, or a kinesthetic learner? Choose learning resources and methods that align with your preferred style.
- **Time availability:** Be realistic about the amount of time you can dedicate to personal development. Integrate learning into your existing routines rather than trying to overhaul your entire schedule.
- **Resource constraints:** Consider any financial constraints you may have and explore free or low-cost learning resources. Many excellent online courses and open-source tools are available.
- **Industry-specific variations:** As we touched on earlier, the specific skills and learning pathways will vary depending on your industry. Research the key AI trends and skill demands within your field and tailor your road map accordingly.

Case Studies in Transformation: Inspiration from Others

Sometimes, the best way to understand a concept is to see it in action. Consider the stories of individuals who have successfully navigated career transitions and embraced new skills in response to technological advancements.

- **The marketing manager turned AI strategist:** Recall Maria? Imagine her successfully completing online courses in AI marketing and prompt engineering. She starts experimenting with AI tools for campaign analysis and content creation, eventually leading her company's AI strategy.
- **The financial analyst embracing data science:** Consider a financial analyst who initially felt threatened by AI-powered analytical tools.

However, by focusing on developing her data science skills, she now leverages these tools to uncover deeper insights and make more informed investment recommendations.

- **The healthcare professional leveraging AI for patient care:** Imagine a doctor who proactively learned about AI-assisted diagnostic tools, enhancing their ability to provide more accurate and timely diagnoses.

These are just a few examples, illustrating that with a proactive approach and a well-defined personal development road map, successful adaptation to the AI era is not only possible but can lead to new and exciting career trajectories.

Conclusion

Your personal development road map is your strategic plan for navigating the exciting yet sometimes daunting landscape of the AI revolution. By understanding the first principles, honestly assessing your skills, mapping out clear learning pathways, and consistently tracking your progress, you can transform apprehension into empowerment. Remember, this is not a race, but a journey of continuous growth and adaptation. As we'll explore in the next section, continuous learning is not a one-time project, but an ongoing strategy for thriving in a world of autonomous minds.

Deep Dive: AI Readiness Quick Self Check

ARE YOU READY FOR THE AI FUTURE? A QUICK ASSESSMENT

Use these questions to quickly gauge your current readiness to navigate and thrive in an AI-driven world. For each question, consider a simple rating scale:

★ = Needs Significant Improvement ★★ = Developing ★★★ = Competent
★★★★ = Strong ★★★★★ = Expert

Self-Check Questions:

1. **Adaptability to change:** How would you rate your comfort level and willingness to adapt to rapidly changing technologies and work environments? ★ ★ ★ ★ ★
2. **Technical curiosity:** How interested are you in learning about new technologies, particularly AI and automation, even at a basic level? ★ ★ ★

3. **Problem-solving skills:** How confident are you in your ability to analyze complex problems and develop creative solutions, even with limited information? ★ ★ ★ ★ ★

4. **Digital fluency:** How comfortable are you using digital tools and software in your daily work and learning new digital platforms? ★ ★ ★ ★

5. **Commitment to lifelong learning:** How willing are you to dedicate time and effort to continuous learning and skill development throughout your career? ★ ★ ★ ★ ★

Interpreting Your Self-Check:

- If you rated mostly ★ or ★★: Focus on building foundational skills and cultivating a growth mindset. The sections "Essential Skills Development," "Personal Development Road Map," and "Continuous Learning Strategies" offer guidance.

- If you rated mostly ★★★: You have a solid base. Focus on targeted skill development in areas relevant to your goals, using the road map in section "Personal Development Road Map" and the continuous learning strategies in "Continuous Learning Strategies."

- If you rated mostly ★★★★ or ★★★★★: You are well-prepared. Focus on advanced skill development, strategic planning (see "Action Plan: Five-Year Strategy") and potentially leading AI initiatives in your field.

This quick self-check provides a snapshot of your AI readiness. Use it as a starting point for deeper self-reflection and action planning based on the chapter's guidance.

CONTINUOUS LEARNING STRATEGIES

Imagine a seasoned musician who, despite years of experience, stops practicing. Their skills would inevitably decline, their repertoire would stagnate, and they would soon be out of sync with the evolving musical landscape. The same principle applies to navigating the age of AI. As we established in the previous section, creating a personal development road map is fundamental, but it's only the first step. The rapid evolution of AI demands a commitment to continuous learning—a mindset of perpetual curiosity and adaptation. Think of it not as a sprint, but as a marathon of lifelong learning, where consistent effort and strategic adjustments ensure you stay ahead of the curve and continue to play a leading role in the AI-powered orchestra. This section will equip you with practical strategies to make continuous learning an integral and sustainable part of your professional and personal life.

The Ever-Turning Wheel: First Principles of Lifelong Learning in the AI Age

The need for continuous learning in the age of AI isn't a mere suggestion; it's a fundamental necessity driven by several core principles. First, consider the principle of **technological velocity**. AI is not a static technology; it is constantly evolving, with new breakthroughs and applications emerging at an unprecedented pace. What is cutting-edge today may be commonplace tomorrow. Therefore, a commitment to continuous learning is essential to keep pace with these rapid advancements and avoid skill obsolescence.

Secondly, embrace the principle of **knowledge compounding**. Learning is not a linear process; it's exponential. The more you learn, the easier it becomes to acquire new knowledge and connect disparate concepts. Continuous learning creates a positive feedback loop, accelerating your understanding and expanding your capabilities.

Finally, remember the principle of **personal agency**. In a world of rapid change, continuous learning empowers you to take control of your career trajectory and adapt to new opportunities and challenges. It shifts you from being a passive recipient of change to an active participant in shaping your future. Embracing these principles enables us to move beyond reactive learning and cultivate a proactive, lifelong approach to growth in the age of AI.

Building Your Personal Learning Ecosystem: A Strategic Approach

Continuous learning isn't about haphazardly consuming information; it requires a strategic and structured approach. Think of building your personal learning ecosystem as curating your own personalized university, designed to meet your specific needs and learning style.

Curated information feeds: staying informed without overwhelm: The sheer volume of information available on AI can be overwhelming. The key is to curate your information sources strategically. Identify reputable newsletters, blogs, podcasts, and social media accounts that provide insightful and relevant content on AI trends and developments. Focus on quality over quantity, prioritizing sources that offer in-depth analysis and practical applications rather than just surface-level hype.

Dedicated learning time: making learning a non-negotiable: Just as you schedule important meetings or appointments, dedicate specific blocks of time for learning. This could be 30 minutes each morning, an hour during your lunch break, or a longer session each weekend. Treat this time as a non-negotiable commitment to yourself. Consistency is key—even small, regular learning sessions can yield significant results over time.

Microlearning: embracing bite-sized knowledge: Continuous learning doesn't always require lengthy courses or intensive study sessions. Embrace the power of microlearning—short, focused bursts of learning that can be easily integrated into your busy schedule. This could involve watching a short explainer video, reading a concise article, or completing a quick online tutorial.

Immersive experiences: conferences, workshops, and webinars: Attending industry conferences, workshops, and webinars provides opportunities to learn from experts, network with peers, and gain exposure to the latest advancements in AI. These immersive experiences can spark new ideas and provide valuable insights that you might not find elsewhere.

The power of "learning by doing": applying knowledge in practice: The most effective way to learn is by applying your knowledge in practical situations. Look for opportunities to experiment with AI tools, work on AI-related projects, or even try to automate small tasks using AI agents. This hands-on experience will solidify your understanding and help you identify areas where you need to learn more. Remember, the best way to learn to conduct is by leading the orchestra.

Harnessing the Power of AI for Learning: Intelligent Learning Partners

Ironically, the very technology we are striving to understand can also be our most powerful tool for learning. Embrace AI-assisted learning techniques to personalize your learning journey and accelerate your progress.

AI-powered learning platforms: Numerous online learning platforms now incorporate AI to personalize the learning experience. These platforms can analyze your learning patterns, identify your strengths and weaknesses, and recommend courses and resources tailored to your specific needs.

Intelligent tutoring systems: Explore AI-powered tutoring systems that provide personalized feedback and guidance as you learn new concepts. These systems can adapt to your pace and provide targeted support where you need it most.

AI-driven research assistants: Utilize AI-powered tools to help you research AI topics more efficiently. These tools can summarize research papers, identify relevant articles, and even answer your questions using natural language processing.

Personalized content recommendations: Leverage AI-powered recommendation engines to discover relevant articles, videos, and podcasts based on your interests and learning goals.

Evaluating Learning Resources: Quality Over Quantity

Every day, we face new online courses, webinars, research papers, and podcasts claiming to offer the "best" way to master AI. Yet quantity does not always equal quality. The first step is to develop a personal framework for separating truly valuable materials from superficial fluff. Think of it as training your ear to discern a rich violin note from an out-of-tune squeak.

When browsing a fresh resource—be it a short video on neural networks or a lengthy academic paper—ask yourself three questions: Does this content align with my immediate learning goals? Does it come from a credible source, such as a recognized researcher or well-vetted platform? Moreover, does it offer practical applications or just abstract theory? This deliberate filter ensures your learning time remains well spent. As you refine your judgment, you'll become nimbler at curating a high-quality knowledge base, skipping redundant or misleading material. Ultimately, a rigorous approach to resource selection allows you to cultivate a curated library that fuels meaningful growth.

Deep Dive: Is the AI Learning Resource Good?

Before you invest time, quickly evaluate a learning resource using this checklist focusing on Credibility and Relevance.

Credibility Checklist:

- Expert author? Recognized AI expert? Credentials clear? Reputable affiliation?
- Reputable source? Hosted on credible platform (university, industry leader, learning platform)? Peer-reviewed (if academic)?
- Evidence-based? Claims supported by data/evidence? Sources cited? Balanced, not just hype?
- Up-to-date? Current (publication date)? Still relevant if older (for fundamentals)?

Relevance Checklist:

- Goals aligned? Directly addresses your learning goals/skill gaps? Right topic/level for you?
- Practical focus? Practical examples/cases/exercises? Bridges theory and real world?
- Target audience fit? Designed for your expertise level (beginner, etc.)? Relevant to your industry?
- Learning style match? Format (video, text, etc.) suits your style? Diverse learning methods offered?

Using This Checklist:
- Aim for mostly "Yes" answers in both sections for quality.
- Prioritize resources strong in both Credibility & Relevance.
- Be wary of resources lacking clear authors, sources, or practical use.

Use this framework to make smart choices about your AI learning and build skills on solid, reliable resources

Why This Matters

Overconsumption of random content leads to shallow expertise and confusion, distracting from the knowledge that directly enhances your AI journey.

Building Your Personal Learning Stack

Once you filter resources effectively, the next challenge is integrating them into your daily life. A "personal learning stack" refers to the set of tools, platforms, and routines you adopt for ongoing skill development—analogous to choosing specific instruments and musical pieces for a symphony you'll repeatedly perform. This stack can include online learning portals, curated newsletters, AI-driven recommendation engines, or even scheduling apps that remind you to practice.

Each element should serve a distinct purpose. For instance, you might rely on a dedicated study management app for systematic tracking of progress, a short daily podcast for up-to-date AI news, and monthly deep-dive courses tailored to your domain. The goal is to build a loop of consumption, practice, reflection, and iteration. Intentionally merging these components allow you to create a learner's ecosystem that resonates with your professional aims. Over time, the stack should evolve alongside your changing priorities—phasing out tools that no longer fit while adding advanced filters or specialized communities that push your boundaries.

The Collaborative Classroom: Peer Learning and Community Building

Learning isn't a solitary endeavor. Engaging with peers and building a learning community can significantly enhance your learning experience.

- **Joining online communities and forums:** Participate in online communities and forums dedicated to AI and related topics. These platforms provide opportunities to ask questions, share insights, and learn from the experiences of others.

- **Peer-to-peer learning groups:** Form or join peer-to-peer learning groups with colleagues or individuals who share your interest in AI. Regular discussions and collaborative learning sessions can deepen your understanding and provide valuable support.
- **Mentorship and reverse mentorship:** Seek out mentors who can provide guidance and share their expertise. Conversely, consider reverse mentorship, where you share your knowledge of emerging AI trends with more senior colleagues.
- **Attending local meetups and events:** Connect with other AI enthusiasts in your local area by attending meetups and events. These gatherings provide opportunities for networking, knowledge sharing, and collaborative learning.

Solidifying Knowledge: Retention and Application Strategies

Acquiring knowledge is only half the battle; retaining and applying that knowledge is equally important. Implement strategies to solidify your learning and ensure it translates into tangible skills and capabilities.

- **Active recall and spaced repetition:** Employ active recall techniques, such as quizzing yourself or summarizing what you've learned without referring to your notes. Utilize spaced repetition, revisiting learned material at increasing intervals to reinforce retention.
- **Note-taking and summarization:** Develop effective note-taking strategies and regularly summarize key concepts and insights from your learning sessions.
- **Teaching others:** One of the most effective ways to solidify your own understanding is to teach others. Share your knowledge with colleagues, write blog posts, or present your learnings to a group.
- **Personal projects and experimentation:** Apply your newly acquired knowledge to personal projects and experiments. This hands-on application not only reinforces your learning but also allows you to explore the practical implications of what you've learned.

Measuring Your Progress: Regular Assessment and Reflection

Continuous learning is an ongoing process of improvement, and that requires regular assessment and reflection. Take time to evaluate your progress, identify areas where you're excelling, and pinpoint areas where you need to focus more effort.

- **Regularly reviewing your learning goals:** Revisit your personal development road map and assess your progress against your learning goals.

- **Seeking feedback:** Solicit feedback from mentors, peers, or even AI-powered assessment tools to gain insights into your strengths and weaknesses.
- **Self-reflection and journaling:** Take time for self-reflection. What have you learned recently? How has it impacted your thinking or your work? Keep a learning journal to track your progress and insights.
- **Adapting your strategies:** Based on your assessments and reflections, be prepared to adapt your learning strategies. What's working well? What needs to be adjusted? Continuous learning is itself an iterative process.

Conclusion

In the fast-paced world of AI, continuous learning isn't a luxury; it's a fundamental requirement for staying relevant and thriving. The continuous AI learning cycle, depicted in Figure 10.2, provides a powerful model for this ongoing effort. Adopting a strategic approach to building your personal learning ecosystem, leveraging AI-powered learning tools, engaging with learning communities, and implementing effective knowledge retention strategies allow us to transform the challenge of constant change into an opportunity for continuous growth and empowerment. Remember, the AI orchestra is constantly composing new scores; continuous learning ensures you remain a skilled and adaptable musician, ready to play your part in the evolving symphony of the future. In the next section, we will explore how to translate this ongoing learning into a concrete action plan for the next five years.

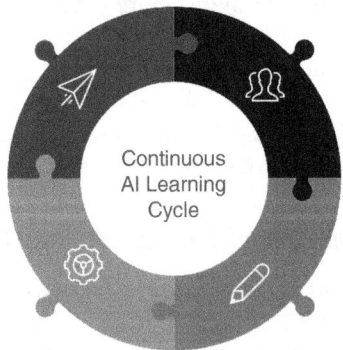

1. Evaluate & Curate
Assessing the credibility and relevance of various learning materials and strategically selecting and organizing the best resources into your personalized learning ecosystem.

2. Adapt Focus
As you learn and the AI landscape evolves, this stage involves dynamically adjusting your focus areas to align with new trends, emerging opportunities, and your evolving skill gaps

4. Assess & Reinforce
Evaluate your learning progress, identify areas of strength and weakness, reinforce your knowledge through review and practice, and loop back to refine your resource selection and learning focus for the next iteration of the cycle.

3. Apply Knowledge
This crucial stage emphasizes putting your newly acquired knowledge into practical use through projects, experiments, and real-world applications to solidify understanding and develop practical skills

Continuous AI Learning Cycle

FIGURE 10.2   Continuous AI learning cycle

ACTION PLAN: FIVE-YEAR STRATEGY

Imagine stepping onto the podium as the conductor of your own future. You've diligently honed your skills (as we discussed earlier), crafted your personal development road map, and embraced a mindset of continuous learning. Now, it's time to orchestrate those efforts into a cohesive and compelling performance over the next five years. This goes beyond making vague resolutions, emphasizing instead the creation of a strategic action plan that transforms your aspirations into tangible accomplishments in the era of autonomous minds. Think of this section as providing the full musical score for your next five years—outlining the key movements, identifying potential challenges, and ensuring every section harmonizes toward your desired future. This five-year strategy isn't a rigid prediction, but a flexible framework that empowers you to proactively shape your journey in a world increasingly influenced by agentic AI.

Conducting Your Future: First Principles of Strategic Planning for the AI Future

Developing a robust five-year action plan in the context of rapidly evolving AI requires grounding in a few key first principles. The first principle is proactive adaptation. Simply reacting to AI advancements as they occur leaves you playing catch-up. A strategic plan is about anticipating future trends and proactively developing the skills and strategies to capitalize on them. It's about being the conductor who anticipates the tempo changes, not just the musician who follows the beat.

The second principle is alignment with purpose. Your five-year strategy shouldn't be solely driven by external technological forces. It should be deeply connected to your personal and professional goals, your values, and your long-term vision. AI should be viewed as a powerful enabler of your purpose, not the sole driver of your direction. This ensures your efforts are meaningful and sustainable.

Finally, embrace the principle of iterative refinement. A five-year plan isn't a static document. The AI landscape will undoubtedly shift and evolve over the next five years. Your plan should be viewed as a living document, subject to regular review and adjustment based on new information, emerging trends, and your own evolving understanding. This iterative approach allows for flexibility and ensures your strategy remains relevant and effective. By understanding these core principles, we can move beyond simply reacting to the future and begin to actively shape it.

Setting Your Long-Term Goals: Envisioning Your AI-Empowered Future

Your journey into the AI-enabled future requires a systematic approach that balances immediate needs with long-term vision. We'll break this down into five distinct phases, each building upon the previous while maintaining flexibility for rapid technological changes.

The cornerstone of any effective five-year strategy is the establishment of clear and compelling long-term goals. These goals should provide direction and motivation for your efforts over the coming years.

- **Reflecting on the five domains of change:** As we explored in Chapter 4, agentic AI is poised to transform various aspects of our lives. Consider each of these domains—home and personal life, work and career, education and learning, healthcare and wellbeing, and entertainment and leisure—and envision how you want AI to positively impact each within the next five years. Where do you see the greatest opportunities for empowerment and productivity?
- **Defining professional aspirations:** What are your career aspirations for the next five years? Do you aspire to take on a leadership role, specialize in a new area, launch your own venture, or contribute to innovative AI-driven projects? Be specific and consider how the skills you are developing will enable these aspirations.
- **Personal growth objectives:** Beyond your professional life, what personal growth objectives do you want to achieve? Do you want to become more proficient in using AI for personal productivity, explore new creative outlets enabled by AI, or deepen your understanding of the ethical implications of AI?
- **SMART Goals Framework:** Ensure your goals are SMART—Specific, Measurable, Achievable, Relevant, and Time-bound. Instead of a vague goal like "learn more about AI," a SMART goal would be "complete an online course on AI ethics within the next six months."

Breaking Down the Score: Actionable Steps and Timelines

Once your long-term goals are defined, the next step is to break them down into smaller, actionable steps and create a realistic timeline for achieving them.

- **Quarterly milestones:** Divide your five-year goals into annual targets, then further subdivide these into quarterly milestones. This makes the overall plan less daunting and allows for more frequent progress checks and adjustments.

- **Identifying key activities:** For each milestone, identify the specific activities required to achieve it. For example, if your milestone is to "become proficient in prompt engineering," key activities might include "complete a specific prompt engineering course," "practice writing prompts daily for 30 minutes," and "apply prompt engineering to a work project."
- **Time allocation:** Estimate the time required for each activity and allocate time in your schedule accordingly. Be realistic about your existing commitments and avoid overcommitting yourself. Remember, consistency is more important than intensity.
- **Visualizing your timeline:** Create a visual representation of your five-year plan, such as a Gantt chart or a simple timeline, to track your progress and stay motivated.

Year 1: Setting the Stage

In the first year, focus on concrete preparation and foundational success metrics. This involves validating which specific AI subdomains matter most to you or your organization. Are you drawn to *natural language processing (NLP)* applications such as conversational agents, or do you see potential in predictive analytics for finance and logistics? Narrowing your scope early helps prevent scattered efforts.

We also recommend forging a robust professional network. Seek out local AI meetups, online forums, or short-term collaborative projects. These peer groups function like an orchestra's rehearsal. Each participant brings unique expertise, and collectively, you sharpen your mastery of the "score." Begin mapping success metrics—basic indicators like the number of AI-related tutorials completed, internal pilot projects launched, or stakeholder feedback collected. Although these metrics are simple, measuring small wins can boost your motivation and pinpoint areas needing refinement. By the end of year 1, you should have identified your principal AI focus, built early prototypes or skill sets, and developed the relationships needed to support your journey.

Year 2: Expanding Your Repertoire and Embracing Scenario Planning

In the second year, broaden your repertoire of AI knowledge by diving into specialized areas relevant to your chosen focus. For example, if you've set your sights on AI-driven marketing, strengthen your command of consumer behavior analytics and media personalization algorithms. If you are working in manufacturing or logistics, explore advanced supply chain optimization and robotic process automation (RPA).

Simultaneously, adopt scenario planning frameworks. Scenario planning is a strategic exercise that envisions multiple plausible futures, each shaped by potential technological shifts, policy changes, or market disruptions. By mapping these scenarios, you prepare contingency plans well before unexpected events force a scramble. For instance, you might forecast an economic downturn that squeezes AI budgets and, in another scenario, an explosion of investment that accelerates AI adoption. Each distinct future calls for a different skill emphasis and risk posture. This approach nurtures adaptability and primes you for seizing unforeseen opportunities, much like a conductor rehearsing various tempos to handle the unpredictability of a live performance.

Deep Dive: Essentials of Scenario Planning

- **Identify key drivers:** Technological innovation pace, regulatory climate, competitor landscape.
- **Sketch alternative futures:** Project outcomes if certain drivers intensify or stall.
- **Craft responsive strategies:** Outline how you would pivot in each scenario, from doubling down on R&D to recalibrating focus on cost efficiency.

Year 3: Risk Assessment and Mitigation Strategies

By year 3, you should have tangible AI projects or at least conceptual groundwork in place. That foundation paves the way for a deeper engagement with risk assessment. You've likely encountered unexpected challenges—unexpected algorithmic bias, logistical bottlenecks, or new regulations around data handling. Address these head-on by expanding beyond the universal rigors of AI safety (discussed in Chapter 9) into domain-specific risk defenses.

Develop a custom Risk Mitigation Checklist, reflecting learnings from your own experiences or industry case studies. For a healthcare startup, that might involve stringent compliance checks for patient data. For an AI-enabled finance department, risk assessment could focus on real-time detection of anomalies in trading algorithms. The point is to systematically identify potential points of failure and build "circuit breakers" into your workflows. Conduct frequent reviews—perhaps quarterly—to keep your risk blueprint aligned with your evolving AI capabilities. It's like fortifying each section of an orchestra's stage so that even if one player falters, the entire performance remains on track.

Year 4: Technology Trend Integration and Continued Upskilling

Your momentum peaks in year 4, giving you an ideal window to integrate emerging tech trends and pivot if necessary. Keep a close watch on developments like neuromorphic computing, quantum-inspired algorithms, or advanced data-compression techniques. While not every innovation will be relevant, occasionally you'll identify a disruptive technology capable of fast-tracking your progress. For instance, an HR firm might adopt cutting-edge NLP models for nuanced candidate screening; a supply chain startup could harness real-time analytics enabled by 5G connectivity.

Continue refining your expertise through "learning sprints" that last one to two months, diving deeply into each promising trend. Share these explorations with peers and mentors to test their practical viability. This is where your strong skill foundations and scenario planning converge, helping decide how to balance what's near term with what's over the horizon. Much like an orchestra conductor who must keep pace with modern compositions and classical staples, you blend familiar AI tools with fresh possibilities.

Year 5: Consolidation, Career Pivot Points, and Evaluation

Year 5 is your chance to consolidate growth and decide which leaps to make next. Perhaps you will evolve from an individual contributor to a team lead, or transition from a specialized role into a cross-functional AI champion. Reflect on your cumulative accomplishments: have you implemented AI products that consistently deliver ROI? Did you promote an AI-first mindset within your organization? Gather data on performance metrics, user satisfaction, or revenue impacts to evaluate whether your five-year plan met its targets.

If you're thinking of a new career pivot, this is also the time to re-engage with scenario planning. Are you considering launching a startup, or moving into a more policy-oriented role advising on AI governance? Map these routes against the skill set and network you've developed. A well-documented track record over the last four years simplifies this jump. Like an orchestra finishing one symphony and deciding its next grand performance, you can craft a new, ambitious trajectory.

Success Metrics and Ongoing Adaptation

Throughout the five-year journey, track your progress using a mix of quantitative and qualitative success metrics. On the quantitative side, measure AI deployment timelines, cost savings, or top-line revenue growth from AI-enabled products. Qualitatively, gauge how your internal culture has shifted—are leadership and colleagues actively requesting AI-driven solutions? Are employees or customers more comfortable interacting with advanced agentic systems?

Embrace adaptation as a permanent fixture. Even the most thorough plan cannot anticipate every twist in the AI market or regulatory climate. Treat your five-year road map as a living document, revise it annually, and remain open to re-scoring your "orchestra" if the piece being played no longer resonates. The ultimate goal is not rigid adherence to an outdated map, but consistent alignment of technology, strategy, and personal growth.

Resource Allocation and Building Your Support System: Gathering Your Orchestra

Achieving your five-year goals will require strategic allocation of resources and the cultivation of a supportive network.

- **Time investment:** Recognize that skill development and continuous learning require a significant time investment. Prioritize learning activities and protect your dedicated learning time.
- **Financial resources:** Consider any financial investments required for courses, certifications, or tools. Explore employer-sponsored training programs or affordable online resources.
- **Technological tools:** Identify the necessary software, hardware, or online platforms that will support your learning and skill development. Many AI tools offer free tiers or trial periods.
- **Mentorship and guidance:** Seek out mentors or experienced professionals who can provide guidance, advice, and support. Their insights can be invaluable in navigating your career path.
- **Peer support and collaboration:** Connect with peers who share similar goals and interests. Forming a supportive network can provide encouragement, accountability, and opportunities for collaborative learning.

Regular Review and Adjustment: Staying in Tune

As the AI landscape evolves, so too should your five-year strategy. Regular review and adjustment are critical for ensuring your plan remains relevant and effective.

- **Quarterly reviews:** Schedule quarterly reviews of your progress against your milestones. Assess what you've accomplished, identify any roadblocks, and make necessary adjustments to your plan.
- **Staying informed about AI trends:** Continuously monitor developments in AI through industry news, research papers, and expert insights. Be prepared to adapt your skills and goals in response to significant technological shifts.
- **Flexibility and adaptability:** Embrace flexibility and be prepared to deviate from your original plan if necessary. New opportunities or unforeseen challenges may arise, requiring you to adjust your course.

- **Celebrating milestones and learning from setbacks:** Acknowledge your achievements and celebrate your successes. Equally important is learning from any setbacks or failures. View them as opportunities for growth and refinement of your strategy.

Five-Year AI Action Plan Template

Use this template to build your AI future strategy:

I. **Five-Year Vision & Impact:**
- **Vision:** (One-sentence goal for five years in AI) e.g., AI leader in retail CX
- **Impact Domains:** (How AI enhances these in five years—Career, Skills, Personal, etc.)

II. **Annual Milestones (Key Goals per Year):**
- **Year 1:** Foundation: (2–3 milestones—basic AI literacy, focus area) e.g., AI courses, join community
- **Year 2:** Expand Repertoire: (2–3 milestones—specialized skills, scenario planning) e.g., Prompt Eng cert., AI pilot project
- **Year 3:** Risk & Implementation: (2–3 milestones—practical application, risk mitigation) e.g., Implement AI in project, Risk Checklist
- **Year 4:** Trends & Pivot: (2–3 milestones—new tech, adapt strategy) e.g., Explore GenAI, Refine specialization
- **Year 5:** Consolidate & Lead: (2–3 milestones—leadership, evaluation, pivot options) e.g., Lead AI team, Evaluate ROI, Career pivot plan

III. **Quarterly Action Steps (Example for Year 1 Milestones):**
(For each Year 1 Milestone, list quarterly actions) e.g., (Year 1 Milestone: AI Courses) Q1: Research courses, Q2: Course 1, Q3: Course 2, Q4: Review & Practice

IV. **Resource Allocation:**
- **Time:** (Hours/week for plan)
- **Financial:** (Costs & funding sources)
- **Tools:** (Software, platforms needed)
- **Support:** (Mentors, peers, communities)

V. **Review Schedule:**
- **Quarterly Reviews:** (Dates/times for progress check)
- **Annual Reviews:** (Dates for five-Year Vision & plan update)

Complete this template for an actionable five-Year AI plan. Treat it as a living document, revisit and adjust regularly to stay on track

Real-World Scenario: Crafting a Five-Year Plan

Let's revisit Maria, our marketing manager. Her five-year strategy might include:

Year 1: Focus on foundational AI literacy. Complete online courses on AI for marketing and data analysis. Begin experimenting with AI-powered marketing tools.

Year 2: Develop expertise in prompt engineering and AI agent orchestration. Lead a small pilot project using AI agents for content creation. Seek mentorship from an AI strategist.

Year 3: Implement AI-driven strategies across more marketing campaigns. Present findings and successes to leadership. Explore opportunities for a role specializing in AI marketing.

Year 4: Lead a team focused on leveraging AI for marketing innovation. Speak at an industry conference on AI in marketing.

Year 5: Position herself as a recognized expert in AI-driven marketing, potentially leading a dedicated AI marketing division or consulting on AI strategy.

This is just one example, and your own five-year strategy will be unique to your individual circumstances and aspirations.

Why This Matters: Orchestrating Your Own Success

Creating a five-year action plan isn't just about preparing for the future; it's about taking control of it. It provides a road map for navigating the complexities of the AI revolution, transforming potential anxiety into purposeful action. By setting clear goals, breaking them down into manageable steps, and consistently tracking your progress, you increase your likelihood of not just surviving but thriving in the age of autonomous minds. Think of your five-year plan as your personal composition, and over the next five years, you'll be conducting the orchestra to bring it to life.

Conclusion

Your five-year action plan is your personal blueprint for building an AI-empowered future. It's the culmination of your skills development, your commitment to continuous learning, and your vision for what's possible. By embracing the principles of proactive adaptation, alignment with purpose, and iterative refinement, you can navigate the exciting opportunities and challenges that lie ahead. With your road map in hand, you are now equipped to actively shape your destiny in the age of autonomous minds.

KEY TAKEAWAYS

This chapter, "Building Your AI Future," has served as a comprehensive guide to navigating the evolving landscape shaped by agentic AI. We began by acknowledging the understandable anxieties surrounding this technological shift, recognizing the potential for disruption while emphasizing the immense opportunities for empowerment and productivity. The core message is one of proactive engagement: rather than fearing displacement, we must actively cultivate the skills necessary to thrive in collaboration with intelligent machines.

We established the fundamental principles of skill adaptation, emphasizing adaptability, the amplification of human capabilities, and the importance of understanding the changing division of labor between humans and AI. This shift requires us to move from simply performing tasks to defining goals and managing the methods, becoming the conductors of the AI orchestra rather than just the instruments.

The chapter then examined the specific skills essential for this new era, categorizing them into technical skills and soft skills. On the technical front, we explored the nuances of prompt engineering, the strategic importance of AI agent orchestration, the fundamental role of data literacy beyond mere number crunching, and the increasing necessity of cybersecurity awareness in an AI-driven world. Fundamentally, we highlighted that technical proficiency is about fluency and effective interaction, not necessarily mastery of complex coding.

However, the chapter underscored that our uniquely human "soft skills" will be the true differentiators. Critical thinking, creativity, emotional intelligence, and adaptability were presented not as supplementary but as core competencies, the indispensable human advantages that AI currently struggles to replicate. These skills empower us to frame the right questions, generate original ideas, build meaningful connections, and embrace the constant evolution that characterizes the AI age.

Moving beyond skill identification, we addressed the practicalities of personal growth. The concept of a personal development road map was introduced as a strategic tool, a personalized score to guide individuals from their current state toward AI fluency. This involved self-assessment, defining aspirations, identifying skill gaps, and then mapping out specific learning pathways, from formal education to experiential learning and leveraging AI itself as a learning resource. The importance of setting milestones and tracking progress was emphasized, transforming ambition into tangible advancement.

The commitment to growth shouldn't be a one-time project, leading us to the concept of continuous learning. We explored strategies for building a personal learning ecosystem, curating information feeds, dedicating learning time, embracing microlearning, and leveraging the power of AI as an intelligent learning partner. The chapter stressed the importance of evaluating learning resources critically and building a personalized *"learning stack"*—a curated set of tools and routines for ongoing skill development. The value of collaborative learning through peer groups and mentorship was also highlighted.

Finally, the chapter culminated in the development of a five-year action plan, a strategic framework to orchestrate our efforts and translate aspirations into concrete achievements. This involved setting long-term goals, breaking them down into actionable steps with timelines, and strategically allocating resources. The importance of regular review and adaptation was emphasized, acknowledging the dynamic nature of the AI landscape. We explored how to integrate emerging technologies, assess and mitigate risks, and ultimately consolidate growth, potentially leading to career pivots and the evaluation of our progress against predefined success metrics. The overarching message is that proactively shaping our future, rather than passively reacting to it, is the key to thriving in the age of autonomous minds.

1. The future is human-AI collaboration: embrace skill development.
Agentic AI is transforming the world of work, but it's not about replacement. It's about collaboration. Developing a blend of technical and uniquely human skills is imperative for navigating this new landscape and leveraging AI for greater productivity and innovation. Adaptability is the cornerstone skill, enabling us to continuously learn and evolve alongside AI advancements.

- KEY INSIGHTS:
  - AI is reshaping the division of labor, shifting human focus from task execution to goal definition and method management.
  - Technical skills like prompt engineering and data literacy are essential for effective interaction with AI agents.
  - Soft skills such as critical thinking, creativity, and emotional intelligence remain uniquely human advantages and are increasingly valuable.

- DO:
  - Actively identify your skill gaps in the context of AI advancements.
  - Invest time in developing both your technical and soft skills.
  - Seek opportunities to collaborate with AI tools and integrate them into your workflows.
- DON'T:
  - Fear AI as a replacement; view it as a powerful tool for amplification.
  - Focus solely on technical skills; recognize the importance of human-centric capabilities.
  - Become complacent; the need for continuous learning is paramount.

2. Chart your course: a personal development road map is essential.

Navigating the AI revolution requires a strategic plan. Creating a personalized development road map provides a structured approach to skill acquisition, turning ambition into tangible progress. This road map should be iterative, adaptable, and aligned with your personal and professional goals, acting as your guide in the evolving AI landscape.

- KEY INSIGHTS:
  - A personal development road map involves self-assessment, goal setting, identifying skill gaps, and mapping learning pathways.
  - Intentionality and iterative development are key principles for effective personal growth in the AI age.
  - Leverage AI itself as a tool to enhance your learning and development.
- DO:
  - Conduct a thorough self-assessment of your current skills and aspirations.
  - Define clear, measurable goals and break them down into actionable steps.
  - Regularly review and adjust your road map to adapt to changing circumstances and new learning.
- DON'T:
  - Approach personal development haphazardly; a strategic plan is vital.
  - Create a rigid road map; flexibility and adaptability are essential.
  - Neglect to track your progress and celebrate your achievements.

3. Lifelong learning is no longer optional: build your learning ecosystem.

The rapid pace of AI innovation demands a commitment to continuous learning. Building a personal learning ecosystem—a strategic collection of resources, habits, and communities—ensures you stay informed, acquire new skills, and remain relevant in the AI-driven world. This proactive approach to learning empowers you to shape your future.

- KEY INSIGHTS:
  - Technological velocity and knowledge compounding necessitate continuous learning in the AI age.
  - Curating information feeds, dedicating learning time, and embracing microlearning are effective strategies.
  - Engaging with learning communities and leveraging AI for learning are central for ongoing development.
- DO:
  - Curate high-quality information sources to stay informed about AI trends.
  - Schedule dedicated time for learning and treat it as a priority.
  - Actively participate in online communities and seek out mentorship opportunities.
- DON'T:
  - Become overwhelmed by the volume of information; focus on curated, relevant content.
  - View learning as a burden; embrace a mindset of curiosity and continuous growth.
  - Learn in isolation; engage with peers and experts to enhance your understanding.

Ultimately, building your AI future is an active and ongoing process. It requires understanding the fundamental shifts, cultivating essential skills, charting a personalized course, and embracing a mindset of lifelong learning. The strategies outlined in this chapter provide a robust foundation for navigating this transformative era.

About the Author

Francisco Javier Campos Zabala is a pioneering technology leader specializing in artificial intelligence transformation across industries. As Group Chief Technology Officer at Peach, he spearheads data and AI excellence initiatives, establishes future-proof architecture, and delivers technology solutions with measurable commercial impact.

With more than 28 years of global expertise spanning finance, market research, adtech, media, and AI, Javier has established himself as a visionary at the intersection of business and advanced technology. His first book, *Grow Your Business with AI* (Springer Nature, 2023), provided practical frameworks for enterprises to leverage artificial intelligence strategically. *Autonomous Minds* builds on this foundation, exploring the revolutionary potential of agentic AI systems to predict, learn, and empower human productivity.

Javier's thought leadership in artificial intelligence was recognized through his appointment to the Bank of England & FCA Artificial Intelligence Public-Private Forum, where he contributed to frameworks for responsible AI adoption in financial services. His previous executive roles include Chief Information Officer at Fenestra, Head of Experian DataLabs for UK&I and EMEA, Global Chief Technology Officer at Kantar-WPP, Havas Media, and EMEA CIO at GroupM-WPP.

Throughout his career, Javier has specialized in building scalable SaaS platforms, implementing large language models, and developing agentic AI solutions that deliver measurable business impact. He actively researches AI safety protocols at the Cambridge AI Safety Hub, ensuring that ethical considerations keep pace with technological advancement, and is a sought-after speaker at industry conferences.

Javier lives in Cambridge, UK, with his wife and four children. An avid runner, he participates in the Cambridge half marathon annually.

Index

Note: Page numbers in **bold** refer to tables and figures.